# THE LOUISIANA TIGERS IN THE GETTYSBURG CAMPAIGN
## JUNE-JULY 1863

# THE
# LOUISIANA TIGERS
## IN THE
# GETTYSBURG
# CAMPAIGN
## JUNE–JULY 1863

SCOTT L. MINGUS, SR.

Foreword by BRENT NOSWORTHY

Louisiana State University Press ✻ Baton Rouge

Published by Louisiana State University Press
Copyright © 2009 by Louisiana State University Press
All rights reserved
Manufactured in the United States of America
Louisiana Paperback Edition, 2014

Designer: Tammi L. deGeneres
Typefaces: Arno Pro, Egyptienne
Typesetter: J. Jarrett Engineering, Inc.

Library of Congress Cataloging-in-Publication Data

Mingus, Scott L.
    The Louisiana Tigers in the Gettysburg campaign, June–July 1863 / Scott L. Mingus, Sr. ;
foreword by Brent Nosworthy.
        p. cm.
    Includes bibliographical references and index.
    ISBN 978-0-8071-3479-5 (cloth : alk. paper) — ISBN 978-0-8071-5913-2 (pbk. : alk. paper) —
ISBN 978-0-8071-3672-0 (pdf) — ISBN 978-0-8071-4655-2 (epub) — ISBN 978-0-8071-4656-9
(mobi)  1. Gettysburg Campaign, 1863.  2. Confederate States of America. Army. Louisiana
Brigade, 1st.  3. Hays, Harry T. (Harry Thompson), 1820–1876.  4. Louisiana—History—
Civil War, 1861–1865—Regimental histories.  5. United States—History—Civil War, 1861–
1865—Regimental histories.  I. Title.
    E475.51.M56 2009
    973.7'349—dc22

                                                                                2009010266

In all the operations in the neighborhood of Gettysburg, I am happy to state that both officers and men, while animated with a spirit of daring that disdained to concede any obstacle to their progress unsurmountable, were yet amenable to all the orders of their leaders, and accepted readily any position assigned them.

—BRIGADIER GENERAL HARRY T. HAYS,
FIRST LOUISIANA BRIGADE, CSA

# CONTENTS

# MAPS

# FOREWORD

A CONSCIENTIOUS HISTORIAN can be forgiven for focusing a large portion of any research effort upon various primary source materials written contemporaneously to or shortly after the period under study. Realistically, there is a definite limit to the number of works that can be digested during any project (probably somewhere in the three- to five-hundred range) and, confronted by the virtual cornucopia of Civil War literature and sources, one is forced to concentrate on what appears to be the most relevant and promising sources of information.

There are other reasons to not totally immerse oneself in later secondary sources. Modern writers frequently inject contemporary views, attitudes, and assumptions unwittingly into their treatment. Although usually subtle, when taken together these impose intellectual "filters" between the reader and the historical period and subject matter under study. Gradually, they impose a received wisdom that eventually is considered beyond question. Moreover, all too often, secondary sources have a one-dimensional quality about them. Too many times is the text merely a banal recitation of how far so-and-so's force marched each day and what supplies were moved to such and such location. Too frequently, modern works concentrate on one particular topic or strata. How often have you read a work dealing with a particular campaign during the Civil War and discovered that the author's treatment is almost exclusively limited to a description of the military events that took place during that campaign, with but token descriptions of some of the main personalities that were involved?

Real historical events involve real people, and thus, by necessity, are always multilayered. Politicians, for example, eat, sleep, have friendships, and in most cases read a range of different types of literature. No matter how much they are involved in politics and political events, their day-to-day life also involves many other types of activities and concerns. So, too, it is with military people. Even during the hardest fought campaign, the soldiers and officers invariably encountered a wide range of experiences, frequently nonmilitary in nature. True, much of the time in the Civil War was spent marching, encamping, and performing the miscellany of tasks that are an essential part of day-to-day campaigning. Pickets were sent out; depending upon circumstances, defense works erected; and, later in the war, trenches were often dug.

However, sooner or later, soldiers had to eat, sleep, and occasionally, bathe, wash their clothing, and clean their equipment and weapons. Numbers of men, especially those in the southern armies, had to spread out through the countryside and forage for much sought after food and drink. On such occasions, as well as when they passed through towns, almost invariably they encountered civilians, either friendly, espousing the same cause for which they were fighting, or openly hostile. The resulting interactions took on every conceivable form, from momentary friendships and fleeting positive encounters to outright hostilities, even violence and misdeeds. Looking at the events treated in the present study, one would expect the northern civilians to have been uniformly unfriendly to Lee's men as they entered Pennsylvania in the summer of 1863. As it turned out, there was greater variation in the interaction between the southerners and the Pennsylvanian citizenry than would have been expected.

Now, these nonmilitary events and phenomena might at first glance appear secondary, even irrelevant, to someone interested in the warfare during the great American conflagration or its various campaigns. Nevertheless, these events do, in fact, frequently provide valuable insights into how its combatants fought and their fighting capabilities, as well as how they experienced the rigors of day-to-day campaigning. One cannot completely separate a soldier's fighting capability from what motivates him in combat and from his prior experiences in life. Not only does a broader view place the events under study within a wider context, it also frequently provides clues that would otherwise be overlooked or ignored. It is not unreasonable, for example, to expect a man who has been highly motivated by the cause he is fighting for, or has formed a strong bond with his brothers-at-arms, to have at least slightly more staying power in the face of the horrors of combat than someone who went reluctantly to war. It is important, therefore, at least occasionally to see officers and their men as individual personalities, not merely as names on a unit's roster.

It is exactly Scott Mingus's ability to provide such a textured tale that makes *The Louisiana Tigers in the Gettysburg Campaign, June–July 1863* so compelling even to the most casual of readers, and of such value to the most knowledgeable of buffs. Of course, the author provides the mandatory detailed narrative of the military events that befell Brigadier General Harry T. Hays' First Louisiana Brigade from the moment it left the Fredericksburg area and headed northwest toward Culpeper Court House on June 3, 1863; the participation of Hays' Louisianans' during the Second Battle of Winchester; and the main course, so to speak, the Louisiana Tigers' attack against Union forces on East Cemetery Hill at the end of the second day of fighting at Gettysburg.

Over the last several decades, it has become commonplace for modern historians, when weaving together a regiment or brigade's experiences during battle or campaign, to shift their focus up and down the chain of command. Not only does this produce a more detailed and compelling picture, it more readily sheds light on the experience of battle. The present work not only demonstrates Scott Mingus to be an artful practitioner of this literary device, but that he has to some extent taken this approach to a new and exciting level. Not limiting his focus strictly to Hays' Louisianans, Mingus expands the treatment to frequently include those that were only proximate to this command, not only those others in nearby units, both friend and foe, but civilians who were not able to (or who chose not to) leave their homes and as a result witnessed the carnage surrounding them. Not just a quantitative dimension, weaving in additional sources, this produces a qualitative change in the narrative, producing a more dynamic shift from perspective to perspective, much like adoption of hand-held cameras in modern cinematography.

Several dozen wounded Union prisoners were temporarily housed in several large buildings on Gettysburg's southern periphery. Momentarily shifting the perspective to these POWs peering out the windows to glimpse the sniping between Union sharpshooters on Cemetery Hill and the Louisianans, for example, the author simultaneously broadens the framework while creating a more detailed picture of the unfolding events. Expanding the narrative to include the experiences of civilians such as Joseph and Sarah Broadhead, who periodically came up from a cellar to observe the fighting, has a similar effect and adds the perspective of noncombatants.

However, it is in the story of the campaigning leading up to Gettysburg where Mingus employs these techniques to the greatest effect. While marching into the Cumberland Valley on June 23, a Confederate approached a woman on a porch and asked for a much needed drink of water. The two began a cordial conversation and he eventually befriended her two boys, one of whom was taken along to a dance at the Louisiana brigade's camp that night. With his eye for detail and willingness to momentarily digress from the main military story, the author succeeds in creating a powerful "you are there" feeling—it's as though the reader is actually observing these events. The reading process, as a result, is very much a discovery process, where one is sometimes entertained and other times informed by the unexpected. In this sense, this work feels much more like a primary source than the work of a modern author writing almost 150 years after the events.

*Brent Nosworthy*

# PREFACE

Sentiment moves the world; man is nothing without it. He who feels no
pride in his ancestors is unworthy to be remembered by his descendants.
—MAJOR DAVID FRENCH BOYD, 9TH LOUISIANA INFANTRY

THE IRON BRIGADE. The Stonewall Brigade. The Irish Brigade. The Excelsior
Brigade. The Gibraltar Brigade. The Louisiana Tigers. These colorful military nicknames have come down through American history, although the
enlisted men and officers that bore them have all been dead for generations.
Yet, their exploits in the Civil War (1861–1865) live on. That tragic conflict
helped mold and shape the America of the twentieth century, and its ramifi-
cations and impact still resonate in our modern country. Even today, the war
generates new books, movies, magazines, and media coverage, and passions
at times still run deep in parts of the southern United States. Personalities
and places, weapons and tactics, soldiers and civilians, renowned regiments
and great generals—all have become a part of the lore of American history.

Among the most celebrated commands was the First Louisiana Brigade.
Over time, it became associated with the term *Louisiana Tigers,* a moniker
of a single company of controversial New Orleans infantrymen that came to
encompass a much larger entity. The brigade and its predecessor, Wheat's Tigers, have been the subject of legend and exaggeration, as well as scholarly
research and a few well-written books, particularly those by Terry Jones and
James Gannon. However, a detailed treatise of its complete activities during
the 1863 Gettysburg Campaign has been lacking, particularly in terms of the
brigade's nonbattle activities and movements through western Maryland and
south-central Pennsylvania in the week before the Battle of Gettysburg.

When I was researching the Gettysburg Campaign movements of Confederate Brigadier General John B. Gordon's brigade of Georgia infantry for

another book (*Flames Beyond Gettysburg: The Gordon Expedition, June 1863*),
I kept discovering parallel stories and incidents specific to Harry Hays' Louisiana Tigers. Several people encouraged me to expand my research on that
fabled brigade after completing my Gordon manuscript. The notes and documents generated through that earlier work formed the genesis for this book,
as well as several on-site visits to old campsites and battlefields the Tigers
would have known that summer.

I have freely used quotations from a wide variety of primary sources and,
in most cases, have slightly adjusted the original punctuation (and, at times,
spelling) for clarity for the modern reader, as well as adding pertinent material such as rank and given names for soldiers. In some cases, I have left the
original spelling intact when it adds color to the account. In addition to spelling and grammar issues, discrepancies exist in the soldiers' accounts of the
specific times associated with key events. Standardization of time zones was
unknown and synchronization of watches rare. I have used my best judgment
but recognize that the times assigned to events are debatable.

This book combines detailed accounts of the major battle actions of Hays'
Brigade at Second Winchester and Gettysburg with anecdotes from the grind
of long days of marching, as well as the diversions of camp life and visits to
towns along the way. I have tried to capture the flavor of the Louisianans'
interactions with the civilians they encountered, particularly here in Pennsylvania. I am fortunate enough to live in York County, an area rich in accounts
of the Louisiana Tigers' brief visit in the summer of 1863.

I come from a long line of American soldiers, men who fought for our
country in the Revolutionary War, the War of 1812, the Civil War, and both
World Wars. My inspiration was my late father, Staff Sgt. Robert E. Mingus, a decorated veteran of World War II's European Theater. He offered tremendous love, support, and enthusiasm for my past book projects. He and
my Mom gave me the early training and inspiration for a life of research and
study, both personally and professionally. I am proud of them and of all my
ancestors who helped make the American dream come true.

I am grateful to so many people for their assistance and support as I wrote
this book. First, and foremost, is my wife and best friend Debi, who has pa-
tiently put up with my endless babbling about the Civil War, endured several car rides to check out obscure locations associated with troop movements, and cheerfully endorsed the time I spent researching and writing all
my books. I also thank God for my children. Scott Jr. is a college history pro-

fessor and provided me with several useful suggestions. My son Tom frequently accompanied me to tour sites associated with this story. I also thank my daughter Melissa for her constant encouragement and support.

Several people critiqued parts of the manuscript, including my daughter-in-law, Rebecca Mingus, who proofread the text and made several valuable contributions, as did Rob Wynstra and Brent Nosworthy. I thank a bevy of researchers and contributors, including Louisiana historian N. Wayne Cosby, writer David Ward, and Jim McClure, the author of several popular local histories. Lila Fourhman-Shaull of the York County Heritage Trust provided leads on regional records and accounts of the Confederate invasion. Wayne Motts Jr. and Timothy H. Smith of the Adams County Historical Society shared articles written by Gettysburg residents pertaining to the Tigers' two stays in the area. The library of the Gettysburg National Military Park contains regimental histories, files, and other material related to Hays' Brigade.

The staff at the Pennsylvania State Archives helped me search through old records, including the microfiche collection of border claims from Franklin and York counties. I also thank Dr. Richard J. Sommers and the good folks at the U.S. Army Military History Institute in Carlisle, Pennsylvania, for their support in locating items in their collection. A few individuals granted permission to use materials from their private collections, including Ron Mesnard, a descendant of Luther B. Mesnard, whose diary I quote.

There is no substitute for touring on foot the ground trod by the Tigers. I am fortunate enough to live within thirty miles of Gettysburg, with easy access to their campsites and routes they marched. My frequent drives to Gettysburg nearly always follow much of their June 30 route back to Adams County after leaving York. Over the years, I have attended scores of guided battle walks at the Gettysburg battlefield, including several on East Cemetery Hill. My understanding of this chaotic struggle has been shaped and influenced by those tour leaders, including Wayne Wachsmuth, Chris Army, Brian Kennell, and several others. I have also been privileged to walk the XI Corps Day 1 field with such skilled discussion leaders as Eric Campbell, Phil Cole, Eric J. Wittenberg, J. David Petruzzi, Dr. Dave Moore, Troy Harman, Chuck Teague, and many others.

I am not a descendant of the Louisiana soldiers. However, for a few brief moments on a warm summer night on an obscure Pennsylvania hillside, my ancestors interacted with the fabled Louisiana Tigers. The Chambers boys of Marshall County, West Virginia, were among the soldiers of "Red" Carroll's

Gibraltar Brigade that encountered the Tigers around the Union artillery lunettes on East Cemetery Hill. Soldiers in the 7th West Virginia Volunteer Infantry, the Chambers lads were my great-great-uncles, with their little sister being my great-great-grandmother. I have artifacts of their service at Gettysburg, physical reminders of their part in the repulse of Harry Hays' Confederates that long-ago evening.

It is to the memory and valor of the Chambers boys, as well as their worthy foes from the Pelican State, that I dedicate this book. May their spirit of daring never be forgotten.

# THE LOUISIANA TIGERS IN THE GETTYSBURG CAMPAIGN
## JUNE-JULY 1863

# 1 | Hays' Louisiana Tigers

## The Reputation

FEROCIOUS. FEARLESS. POWERFUL. Determined. Unyielding. Untamed. These characteristics often are associated with tigers, wild animals that frequently are stereotyped as epitomizing fierceness and strength. The nickname *tigers* has been applied to intercollegiate and professional sports teams, popular athletes, celebrities, and other individuals and organizations that exemplify the characteristics of a tiger. During the American Civil War, the word *tiger* became associated with several military units in the Confederate States Army, including the First Louisiana Brigade of Brigadier General Harry T. Hays. The so-called Louisiana Tigers developed an early reputation for ferocity in combat and a prowess for foraging and drinking that became almost legendary within both the North and the South during the Rebellion. Southern writers often extolled the fighting ability of the Tigers, while the northern press pilloried the Louisianans as the worst example of Christian behavior.

*Thieves. Drunks. Uncivilized. Brutal. Wanton. Barbaric.* These are words found in the northern media of the period describing the Louisiana Tigers. It was an image perpetuated for much of the early part of the war, often based more upon rumors and reputation than on fact. The June 7, 1862, issue of a leading periodical, *Harper's Weekly,* was typical of this vitriolic (and often incorrect and exaggerated) portrayal of the Tigers.

> GENERAL [George B.] MCCLELLAN telegraphs that the "Fourth Michigan have about finished the Louisiana Tigers." We fancy we shall have some more dispatches of this tenor.
>
> These Southern bravoes, who call themselves "Tigers," and "Lions," and "Grave-diggers," and "Yankee-slayers"; who carry black flags, and refuse quarter to unarmed men; who dig up the corpses of our dead

soldiers, and send their bones home to their lady loves as trophies—these creatures, who are a speaking illustration of the brutalizing effect of the institutions among which they have been reared, and whose savage instincts would appall the most ferocious native of Dahomey or Patagonia—these fellows can never withstand the onset of a Christian soldiery. They are capable of assassinating a Union man, or of whipping a black woman to death; but when it comes to standing up in a fair fight against Northern men, in any thing like equal numbers, they run like hares. Brutality and manhood can no more coexist in the same individual than oil and water can mingle.

We are not sorry to hear that the "Louisiana Tigers" are "about finished." It is about time that some other of these Southern regiments, which have desolated the South and done their best to destroy the nation, were "about finished" too. A gentleman from Tennessee reports that in certain neighborhoods the rebel soldiers have not only destroyed crops and fences, but have wantonly torn down houses and barns, burned every thing that would burn, and so thoroughly obliterated every vestige of improvement from the land, that the wretched owners who are now returning to their homes, under cover of our flag, experience some difficulty in discovering whereabouts their houses stood. Others tell still more fearful stories of outrages—outrages nameless and horrible; of whole districts in which not a woman or a girl has escaped the fiendish brutality of the Texans and Louisianians. It is about time, in the name of God and humanity, that the authors of these atrocities should be "finished."[1]

Despite the desires of General McClellan and the poison pen of the *Harper's Weekly* correspondent, the Louisiana Tigers were far from "about finished"—very far indeed. In many ways, they were just getting started, and they and their reputation would remain prominent in northern press coverage and in the consciousness of much of America for most of the rest of the war.

The term *Louisiana Tigers* originated from the Tiger Rifles, the nickname of the zouave-outfitted Company B of the 1st Louisiana Special Battalion, a colorful five-company unit led by a Virginia preacher's son and former foreign mercenary, Chatham Roberdeau Wheat. Organized in June 1861, Wheat's "wharf rats" made quite an impression on those who encountered them. Bar-room brawls were common, and after a particularly nasty encounter in a New Orleans saloon with some civilians, the tavern was off limits. Some soldiers from the Shreveport Greys company found this punishment unbearable, crying, "Kill me, but don't take my whiskey!"[2]

The Louisianans traveled toward the front lines in Virginia, where, as they passed through Petersburg, one bystander opined, "In fact they were the most savage-looking crowd I ever saw." Another deemed them "a pack of untamed wildcats." Yet another fearful observer commented, "I got my first glimpse at Wheat's Battalion from New Orleans. They were all Irish and were dressed in Zouave dress, and were familiarly known as Louisiana Tigers, and tigers they were too in human form. I was actually afraid of them, afraid I would meet them somewhere in camp and that they would do to me like they did to Tom Lane of my company; knock me down and stamp me half to death."[3]

The four-hundred-man command fought at the First Battle of Manassas in mid-July, and the Louisianans' battlefield prowess and ferocity were evident to their peers and opponents. A member of the 7th Virginia wrote that as the Tigers closed with the enemy, they "threw down their muskets and rushed upon the enemy with bowie-knives. They were a dangerous, blood-thirsty set—at least so reputed." After Union forces had withdrawn into the safety of Washington, one federal soldier tried to explain the reason for the stunning defeat, uttering, "D——n those Louisiana Tigers—born devils, every one of them!"[4]

The southern press regarded highly the Tigers' propensity for thrill seeking and their love for danger. One Richmond newspaper editor penned, "It has been suggested—and I think the suggestion a good one—that in the event of a movement on Washington, a very handsome reward be secretly offered to some of the most daring and cunning of our troops, some such fellows as the Louisiana Tigers, for the capture of Lincoln; and a corresponding reward might be offered for Seward and Blair, or the rest of the Cabinet. I think we have the men who could bag some or all of these Yankee dignitaries."[5]

The Tigers never were sent after President Lincoln, but two men in Wheat's Battalion, after they assaulted one of their officers, had the dubious distinction of becoming the first soldiers executed in the Army of Northern Virginia. Civilians and soldiers alike were alleged or real victims of lawless Tigers. In November 1861, a Richmond newspaper reported, "G. W. Weeks, of Lynchburg, was robbed of $180 near that city in the open day, by five members of the Louisiana Tigers, on Monday last." Even their fellow Confederates were not immune. Private John R. Crawford of the 7th Virginia was guarding supplies and baggage stored at Fairfax Station when two Tigers tried appropriating the goods. Spotting them, Crawford ordered them to go away. When they persisted in their thievery, he reversed his musket and clubbed one of them over the head.[6]

In the spring of 1862, Wheat's Battalion was brigaded with the 6th, 7th, 8th, and 9th Louisiana Infantry under the leadership of Brigadier General Richard Taylor, son of former U.S. president and military hero Zachary Taylor. Their unruly reputation was growing, among both their peers and the Federal soldiers. During the Valley Campaign at Middletown, Wheat's boys captured a Federal supply train. General Taylor recalled, "The gentle 'Tigers' were looting quite merrily, diving in and out of wagons with the activity of rabbits in a warren; but this occupation was abandoned on my approach, and in a moment they were in line, looking as solemn and virtuous as deacons at a funeral."[7]

### Hays' Brigade

Uncivilized and rude behavior eventually became associated by default with many Louisiana soldiers on the Virginia Peninsula. Simply being in a military unit from the Pelican State became the only criterion needed to fit the stereotype. Hence, the nickname *Tigers* was perpetuated in the southern army long after Major Wheat's death during the Seven Days Campaign in June 1862 and the subsequent disbandment of his depleted battalion a month later. By late summer and the bloody northern Virginia and Maryland campaigns, the term *Louisiana Tigers* had become most commonly associated with the First and Second Louisiana Brigades. Brigadier General Harry T. Hays' First Louisiana Brigade primarily continued the legacy and reputation of Wheat's Battalion.

Harry Thompson Hays proved to be a fiery and volatile leader with a marked passion for his men. He was from one of the mid-South's most prominent families. His great-grandfather was a Scotch-Irish immigrant named John Hays who settled in Virginia in 1740. Hays' grandfather Robert moved to Tennessee and became prominent in farming and land speculation, amassing considerable wealth. He married a daughter of the founder of Nashville and operated a prosperous plantation near Little Cedar Lick in rural Wilson County. One of Robert Hays' brothers-in-law was the seventh President of the United States, Andrew Jackson.

Harry Hays' father Harmon served under the future Governor of Texas, Sam Houston, in the Creek Indian War and then under General Jackson at the Battle of New Orleans in January 1815. Elizabeth Hays gave birth to Harry on April 14, 1820, on the family's plantation. He was one of seven children, five of them boys. One of his older brothers, John Coffee "Jack" Hays, would become a well-known Texas Ranger and Indian fighter. They suffered through the emotional trauma of their parents' deaths from cholera a few weeks apart in 1833, which caused the younger children to be raised by various relatives. An uncle took Harry into his household in Wilkinson County, Mississippi.

A Roman Catholic, Hays graduated from St. Mary's College in Baltimore, Maryland, and then studied law. He moved to Louisiana in the early 1840s and established a law practice in New Orleans. When the Mexican War erupted in 1846, Hays enlisted in the 5th Louisiana Volunteer Cavalry and fought in several battles in Mexico. After the war, he resumed the legal profession and became active in Louisiana's Whig political party, serving as an 1852 presidential elector supporting General Winfield Scott. On July 13, 1854, Hays married Elizabeth "Bettie" Cage in Yazoo County, Mississippi. The couple would have five children.[8]

With the outbreak of war in early 1861, the forty-one-year-old Hays became colonel of the newly raised 7th Louisiana. He led his "Pelican Regiment" during the Manassas Campaign, catching the attention of his superior officer, Brigadier General Jubal Early, a crusty Virginian known for his mercurial temper and gruff nature. Hays' soldiers performed well as part of Richard Taylor's brigade in the 1862 Shenandoah Valley Campaign, serving in the division of Major General Richard S. Ewell. Hays suffered a painful gunshot wound to his left shoulder in the Battle of Port Republic on June 9. While convalescing in private quarters at Liberty Mills, Virginia, he received a promotion to brigadier general in July.[9]

Hays resumed field duty a few weeks later and assumed command of the battle-depleted brigade, replacing Taylor, who had been elevated to major general and sent to the Western Theater. Soon afterward, Hays' Brigade fought at Sharpsburg, where more than half of the 550 remaining men fell in less than thirty minutes of savage fighting. Each of the five regimental commanders went down in the relentless storm of Federal lead. Before the Battle of Fredericksburg in December, fresh recruits and the return of men who had recovered from wounds or illnesses replenished the ranks.

While near Fredericksburg, so many of Hays' men were involved in thievery and mischief that residents complained to division commander Jubal Early, who had replaced the badly wounded Ewell. The Virginia-born Early was a West Point graduate and former U.S. Army officer who had resigned in 1838 to become an attorney. The major general was "a man rather above middle age, heavily built, with stooping shoulders, a splendid head and a full gray-brown beard, sitting in his shirt sleeves on a camp stool, with one leg thrown over the other, his hands and apparently his every thought employed in combing out and smoothing a somewhat bedraggled black ostrich feather." Early was profane, quick-tempered, tough to please, and irascible. "Old Jube" also had a reputation as one of the hardest fighters in the Confederate army.[10]

Fed up with the complaints, Early persistently ordered General Hays to improve discipline, but he noted few results. Even fellow Confederates were becoming annoyed. John S. Apperson of the 1st Virginia wrote on November 28, "Everywhere we go, we hear of the depradations [sic] by the Louisiana Soldiers. I like the men for their bravery, but they are men of little principal [sic]." Under repeated pressure to control his troops, a frustrated Hays finally requested that he and his brigade be transferred elsewhere. The vitriolic Early responded by calling together Hays and all his colonels, and berating them for their inability to control their men and for the ill-advised request to leave his command. He bellowed, "No one in this army would have such a d——n pack of thieves but me. If you can find any major general in this army that is d——n fool enough to take you, then you may go." The brigade stayed put. At the May 4, 1863, Second Battle of Fredericksburg, the Tigers smashed two lines of Yankees and were driving them back. A jubilant Early excitedly threw his plumed hat on the ground and exclaimed, "Those d—d Louisiana fellows may steal as much as they please now!"[11]

Such was the reputation and battlefield prowess of the soldiers of the First Louisiana Brigade. Hard foraging, hard brawling, hard drinking, and hard fighting had cemented their reputation and, by the summer of 1863, Hays' Tigers were perhaps the most renown and feared brigade in the entire Army of Northern Virginia, at least according to the northern media.

## Hays' Tigers

New Orleans, the largest city in the South, was a melting pot of European immigrants who arrived almost daily in the busy port. As a result, the composition of many Louisiana military commands reflected this wide diversity of cultures, languages, traditions, and ethnic backgrounds. The five infantry regiments that comprised Hays' Louisiana Tigers during the 1863 Pennsylvania invasion reflected this dizzying array of personalities and ideals.

At the outbreak of the war, army recruiters solicited volunteers from New Orleans and nearby parishes. Most were sent to Camp Moore, the state's largest military training facility. Nearly one thousand men enrolled in the new 5th Louisiana Infantry, which mustered into service in May 1861 under Colonel Henry Forno, an aged veteran of the Mexican War. Not long afterward, the War Department assigned the 5th Louisiana to the Department of Virginia and sent the regiment to Richmond, where disease and desertion thinned the ranks. The 5th lost twenty-nine men at First Manassas in its first combat action. In July 1862, it was assigned to the First Louisiana Brigade and later experienced severe fighting at Sharpsburg.[12]

The 5th Louisiana marched into Pennsylvania under the command of twenty-three-year-old Major Alexander Hart, who was an anomaly in the Tigers' ranks. Not only was he American-born of German extraction, he was Jewish. A native of New Orleans, Hart was the oldest of twelve children of one of the founders of the city's first permanent synagogue, the Shangarai Chasset (Gates of Mercy). In May 1861, the store clerk enlisted as a noncommissioned officer in the Orleans Cadets militia, which in June became Company E of the 5th Louisiana. His comrades elected Hart as first lieutenant, and he progressively rose through the ranks to major. Hart suffered a severe wound at Sharpsburg that led to his capture by the Yankees. He recovered from his injury, received his freedom when exchanged for a Union officer, and subsequently resumed field duty.[13]

The 6th Louisiana was organized in May 1861 by Georgia-born Colonel Isaac G. Seymour, a prominent New Orleans newspaperman and Mexican War veteran. The recruits came from a wide variety of trades and occupations, with several newspaper employees and printers. The large regiment was soon nicknamed the "Irish Brigade" because so many of the volunteers came from the city's sprawling Irish shantytowns, where brawling and drinking were routine. Mixed in with the Sons of Erin were a significant number of German immigrants, many having traveled to Louisiana following the unsuccessful Revolution of 1848. Two-thirds of the thousand-plus recruits were foreign-born.[14]

Among them was twenty-three-year-old John Orr, who was born in Montreal, Canada, to Irish emigrant parents. As a youth, he ran away from home to go to sea, wanting to see the world. After spending time in South America and visiting relatives in Coleraine, Ireland, he settled in New Orleans. He worked for several newspapers until early 1861, when he enlisted in the service as a private. When the 6th Louisiana was organized, Orr was designated as the regiment's adjutant. He saw action at First Manassas, with Stonewall Jackson in the Valley Campaign, and in the Seven Days Battles around Richmond.[15]

After training, Orr and his fellow soldiers traveled to Virginia, where they guarded military supplies. In May 1862, the regiment was reorganized and sent to the Shenandoah Valley as part of Stonewall Jackson's force. There, another foreign-born volunteer joined the ranks. Edward Gunderson emigrated from Norway in 1859 when he was twenty-two years old, settling in Wisconsin and working in various lumber camps until the spring of 1860. Hearing about a major gold strike at Pike's Peak, he and a companion headed to Colorado to seek their fortunes. When they reached Hannibal, Missouri, the duo encountered several broke and starving miners who had returned empty-handed from the gold fields. Gunderson abandoned his quest and took a boat to St. Louis, where he worked at odd jobs for a few weeks before traveling downriver to New Orleans, where work was supposed to be plentiful. He held various jobs there until he enlisted in the 6th Louisiana in March 1862 and traveled to Virginia to join his regiment.[16]

Its ranks bolstered by fresh recruits such as Gunderson, the 6th Louisiana fought in the Peninsula Campaign. At the Battle of Gaines' Mill on June 27, the regiment was reduced to only fifty effectives. The popular Colonel Seymour was among those killed that day. He was replaced by Colonel William Monaghan, who rebuilt the regiment.[17]

Harry Hays had helped organize the 7th Infantry in May 1861 from the working class of New Orleans, as well as other southeastern Louisiana towns such as Baton Rouge, Livingston, and Donaldsonville. Of its nearly 1,000 original recruits, only 373 men were natives of the state. The majority of the others were foreign-born, with 331 hailing from Ireland, 50 from Germany, and 24 from England. The motley ranks also included volunteers from Sweden, Switzerland, France, Canada, and Scotland.[18]

Among the early recruits was James Benedict Roden, born in Dublin, Ireland, on February 14, 1837, to a working-class family. His father died less than a year later. Roden spent a few years as an apprentice in England and then, at the age of nineteen, emigrated to the United States. Arriving in Philadelphia in the winter of 1856, he decided to travel to the Deep South. Roden settled in New Orleans and found employment as a rigger and sail maker, serving on vessels on the Mississippi River and its tributaries. With the outbreak of war, he enlisted in May 1861 in the Crescent Rifles, which soon became Company E of the 7th. Because of his demonstrated skills with a rifle, Roden eventually joined the brigade's sharpshooter unit.[19]

During the Gettysburg Campaign, the 7th Louisiana was led by Colonel Davidson Bradfute Penn, who assumed command in July 1862 when Hays replaced Taylor as brigadier. Penn was born in Lynchburg, Virginia, and graduated from both the Virginia Military Institute and the University of Virginia. He moved to New Orleans in the 1850s and established a prosperous business. In the spring of 1861, he joined with long-time cotton merchant Honoré Doussan to recruit and organize a volunteer militia company, the Virginia Guard, which entered Confederate service as Company D of the 7th. Penn was elected as the captain, with Doussan as second lieutenant. Penn was promoted to lieutenant colonel on June 22, 1862, during the Peninsula Campaign, and then to colonel in July. He was captured at Second Fredericksburg, but rejoined his regiment after being exchanged.[20]

The 8th Louisiana Infantry Regiment was organized in mid-June 1861, with its ranks filled with men from several parishes, as well as a company from the city of Baton Rouge. The roster included a colorful array of names and nationalities, including twelve Scandinavians. Colonel Henry B. Kelly initially commanded the regiment, with future Louisiana Governor Francis T. Nichols as his lieutenant colonel. Along with several other Louisiana regiments, the 8th was transported to Virginia, where more than two hundred men soon died of typhus, dysentery, scurvy, and measles. The remaining soldiers were in reserve during First Manassas. After wintering in northern Virginia, the regiment moved into the Shenandoah Valley and saw considerable combat in Jackson's Valley Campaign and in subsequent battles on the Peninsula and in northern Virginia.[21]

Among the hundreds of volunteers who answered the call to arms were two brothers from the Rapides Parish town of Cheneyville. R. Stark Jackson, a sixteen-year-old student, was elected as the second lieutenant of Company I, and his twenty-one-year-old brother Warren became a sergeant in the same company. In August 1862, Stark was severely wounded in a battle at Bristoe Station in Virginia and went on extended furlough. Warren became a second lieutenant in March 1863. He kept in contact with his younger brother, sending him periodic letters and reports on the regiment's activities.[22]

Another early volunteer was Charles F. Lutz, who was a rarity in the Confederate army—a free black man. He was born in St. Landry Parish in June 1842 to a white father of Germanic heritage and a mulatto mother. Light skinned, he passed himself off as a white man and enlisted in the Opelousas Guards (Company F) in the hysteria after the bombardment of Fort Sumter. Lutz was wounded near Fredericksburg on May 3, 1863, when the regiment was defending Marye's Heights against the Union VI Corps. Along with more than one hundred other Tigers, he fell into federal hands and was imprisoned for two weeks before being paroled and exchanged. He traveled to the Tigers' camp near Fredericksburg in late May to rejoin his regiment.[23]

During the Gettysburg Campaign, the 8th Louisiana was commanded by the jovial Colonel Trevanion D. Lewis, with Creole attorney Alcibiades De Blanc as lieutenant colonel. Lewis mustered into the regiment in 1861 as a first lieutenant, but shortly after the 8th was mustered into Confederate service, he was elected as major. One of his enlisted men deemed him and a fellow officer as "the life of the Regiment" for their amiability and the integral part they played in the social fabric of the unit. He was promoted to colonel on April 6, 1863, when a partially disabled Colonel Kelly, unfit for further field duty, was appointed as judge of a military court. Lewis first led the regiment into action at Second Fredericksburg.

The 9th Louisiana Infantry was recruited mainly from the farmers and mechanics of rural northern and central Louisiana. They mustered in at Camp Moore in May 1861, and the new officers subsequently elected Richard Taylor as colonel. The regiment soon moved to Centreville, Virginia, where, unused to the climate and unsanitary conditions in camp, more than one hundred men perished from typhoid fever or measles.[24]

Typical of the soldiers in the 9th was Private Thomas Benton Reed of Company A, a twenty-four-year-old Alabama native who grew up in a rude cabin in northern Louisiana. The poor dirt farmer left his young wife Elizabeth and baby son to join the army in March 1862 when his two older brothers and their regiment were briefly home on furlough. He agonized over his decision to leave home and enlist, and "you have no idea how I mourned and grieved over the rash step I had taken, and often I went behind the house and kicked myself." Resigning himself to his choice of a soldier's life, he borrowed his father-in-law's two-foot-long butcher knife and believed "I was going to chop Yankees into sausage-meat." Instead, he suffered through his brothers' deaths and burials on the field.[25]

During the Valley Campaign, Reed and the 9th fought at Cross Keys and Port Republic. Transferred in late July to the Second Louisiana Brigade, the regiment was heavily engaged at Sharpsburg, where seventy-six men fell, including all eighteen active members of Company A. In October, in one of General Robert E. Lee's reorganizations of the Army of Northern Virginia, the 9th was transferred back to the First Louisiana Brigade, exchanging places with the 14th Louisiana.

During the Gettysburg Campaign, the 9th Louisiana's commander was Colonel Leroy Augustus Stafford, a wealthy forty-one-year-old cotton planter from Cheneyville. His father, the owner of the sprawling "Greenwood" plantation, had died when Stafford was thirteen. Leroy was educated in Bardstown, Kentucky, and attended college in Nashville. After graduation, he returned to Louisiana in 1843 and married a local girl, Sarah Wright. The couple would have ten children. For more than twenty years, Stafford operated several plantations in Rapides Parish. He served as the sheriff from 1846 until he left for the Mexican War the following year. He enlisted in a volunteer company known as the Rapides Volunteers and later served in the Texas Rangers under famed Captain Ben McCullough.

When Louisiana seceded from the Union, he formed his own militia unit, the Stafford Guards. It was the nucleus of what became Company B of the 9th Louisiana, with Stafford entering Confederate service as a captain. He gained a series of promotions and became the regiment's colonel when Taylor was promoted to brigadier general in October 1861. At Sharpsburg, he temporarily assumed command of William Starke's Second Louisiana Brigade after that general was killed. Stafford suffered a minor wound to his foot but soon recovered. His son George rose to the rank of captain in the 8th Louisiana.[26]

Stafford's lieutenant colonel was another colorful character, William Raine Peck, a huge man at six feet, six inches tall and weighing more than three hundred pounds. The forty-five-year-old native of Jefferson County, Tennessee, had moved to Louisiana in the early 1840s. He purchased land near the hamlet of Milliken's Bend in Madison Parish, on the opposite side of the Mississippi River from Vicksburg, fifteen miles to the southeast. His farm prospered and Peck acquired other land, piecing together a profitable cotton planting business. He subsequently built a large mansion known as "The

Mountain." A fiery secessionist and states rights advocate, Peck was a signatory to Louisiana's Ordinance of Secession in January 1861. With war looming, "Big Peck," despite his wealth and political prominence, enlisted as a mere private in the Milliken's Bend Guards. He rose steadily through the ranks to finish the war as a brigadier general.[27]

Another important officer in Hays' First Louisiana Brigade was William Johnson Seymour, who took a roundabout way to join the Tigers. The son of Colonel Isaac Seymour of the 6th Louisiana, he stayed home to edit the New Orleans *Commercial Bulletin* while his father marched off to war. In the spring of 1862, just months before his father's death at Gaines' Mill, Seymour accepted an appointment as a volunteer aide to his brother-in-law, Pennsylvania-born Brigadier General Johnson K. Duncan, who commanded New Orleans' defenses. Seymour was among those who surrendered at Fort Jackson on April 28 to Admiral David D. Porter of the Union Navy. Paroled, he walked back to New Orleans, which soon fell to U.S. forces. He kept the newspaper running during the federal occupation of the city, but Major General Benjamin Butler seized the offices and shut down the paper after Seymour printed a laudatory obituary of his father.

Seymour was imprisoned in Fort Jackson, but federal officials released him in October. He married Elizabeth Berthoud Grimshaw, and Butler finally allowed the young couple to leave New Orleans in December. The Seymours relocated to Macon, Georgia, where William eventually enlisted in the Confederate army, serving as an aide-de-camp to Harry Hays with the rank of captain. He joined the brigade in early 1863 and was present at the Second Battle of Fredericksburg. During the Gettysburg Campaign, he was Hays' adjutant, and kept a diary with extensive notes on his service.[28]

With hundreds of Irish Catholics in the brigade's ranks, one unofficial Tiger became a popular source of counsel. Born in 1819 in County Longford in Ireland, James B. Sheeran emigrated to Canada at the age of twelve. He later lived in New York City, McConnellsville, Pennsylvania, and Monroe, Michigan, where he taught at a boys' school. His wife died in 1849, and he became a priest six years later. He moved to New Orleans shortly before the war and served at its Redemptorist Church in 1861. Fervently pro-southern despite being northern educated, Sheeran volunteered as a chaplain in the 14th Louisiana.

He joined Richard S. Ewell's division in August 1862 and received a warm greeting from the general, who hoped the increased religious emphasis might improve discipline among the unruly Louisianans. Sheeran soon became a fixture in the Tigers' camps, becoming a particular favorite of the heavily Irish-Catholic 6th Louisiana. When his 14th Regiment was swapped with the 9th following the Maryland Campaign, he continued also serving Hays' Brigade, hearing confessions, celebrating Mass, and distributing Holy Communion.[29]

Father Sheeran was joined in his ministerial efforts by a variety of Protestant missionaries and preachers, including the assistant surgeon of the 5th Louisiana, Dr. William M. Strickler, who served as the regiment's acting chaplain. Early's divisional chaplain, J. William Jones, related, "It is no harm to say that Hays' Brigade, though as gallant fellows that ever kept step to the music of 'Dixie,' were noted for their irreligion."[30]

The Gettysburg Campaign in June and July 1863 would test the religion, reputation, and fighting ability of the First Louisiana Brigade, from its commanding general down to the lowest teamster and cook. To many, the fate of the war and the ultimate independence of the Confederacy rested upon the success of the summer fighting. Few doubted that Hays' Louisiana Tigers would play an important role in the upcoming combat. The motley collection of men with diverse personalities and backgrounds had meshed into one of the finest fighting forces within the Army of Northern Virginia. Although Jubal Early detested their lack of military decorum and discipline, he had come to rely upon the Louisianans as an aggressive command that could be trusted to carry out his orders on the battlefield. He would remain frustrated by their lack of self-control in camp and on the march, and their high desertion rate, but he had come to admire their spirit and martial skills. They would be put to the test in Pennsylvania.[31]

# 2 | Second Winchester

## Preparing for the Summer Campaign

IN THE SPRING of 1863, Confederate General Robert E. Lee was determined to take the offensive and move the main theater of operations from war-torn northern Virginia into unspoiled Pennsylvania, the North's second most populous state and a major source of materiel, troops, and food for the Union armies. "Marse Robert" had several goals in mind, and he was concerned to relieve Virginia farmers from the constant strain of supporting the two opposing armies. Pennsylvania offered an abundance of food, forage, cattle, and supplies to be collected and sent south for his army's future usage. An incursion into the Keystone State and a major victory on northern soil might spread panic throughout the Union and accelerate cries for peace.

Many in the Confederacy's highest levels believed the Yankees would strip significant quantities of troops from the Vicksburg Campaign to face this threat. The South did not have the soldiers, infrastructure, or natural resources to carry on a prolonged conventional war. Hence, it was now time to invade the North in hopes of ending the bloody conflict. The Federals thwarted an earlier attempt during the 1862 Maryland Campaign at Antietam, but this time Lee's army was stronger and better equipped.

With the death of Stonewall Jackson on May 10, Lee split his Second Corps into two smaller organizations, assigning these more manageable commands to newly promoted lieutenant generals Ambrose P. Hill and Richard S. Ewell. Some questioned these appointments. A. P. Hill was a proven fighter and his "Light Division" had performed well, but he had a contentious history with his superior officers, having been arrested at various times by both Longstreet and Jackson. The forty-six-year-old Dick Ewell had suffered a serious leg wound the previous summer and was just now getting back to the army, arriving on the train from Richmond. Marylander Randolph McKim noted his return: "On Saturday, the 29th, General Ewell arrived in camp with his wife—a new acquisition—and with one leg less than when I saw him last. From a military point of view, the addition of the wife did not compensate for the loss of the leg. We were of the opinion that Ewell was not the same soldier he had been when he was a whole man—and a single one."[1]

Harry Hays' Louisiana Tigers were encamped in a grove near the Hamilton's Crossing railroad station, about five miles south of Fredericksburg. One soldier penned a laudatory letter on May 29 expressing a different opinion about the new corps commander.

For some time past, considerable interest was manifested throughout the corps as to who would succeed the late and lamented General Jackson in command of the same. There were, of course, many surmises and much speculation on the subject. Early's division, firmly attached to their former commander, knowing and appreciating his valor and soldier-like qualities, espoused the cause of their favorite chieftain, Gen. R. S. Ewell, and, encouraged by the fact that Gen. Jackson, the sagacious and valiant leader, had in his last moments designated him as a proper successor, felt sanguine as to the result. Nor were they doomed to disappointment. On yesterday, reliable information reached camp of his promotion; today he arrived, and, as might have been supposed, was received more warmly and cordially. Lieut. Gen. Hill, Gen. Early, and the many officers of the army to whom he has during his military career endeared himself, were present to greet the hero once more returned to the service of his country. Gen. Hays's Louisiana Brigade was present in martial review to receive him, and claimed the honor of escorting their former and favorite commander to his temporary abode. Amidst deafening cheers and the rolling sounds of martial music, he was once more ushered into active service. May an all-wise Providence shield him, and give victory to the cause of which he is so glorious a champion.[2]

The daily monotony of camp life was broken again a few days later by a visit to Hamilton's Crossing by Louisiana Senator Thomas J. Semmes, whose brother Andrew was the regimental surgeon of the 8th Louisiana. Like many of the Tigers recruited from New Orleans, his home had been commandeered to quarter Federal troops occupying the city. Harry Hays formed the brigade to hear an "appropriate address" by the veteran politician, which was greeted with enthusiasm and applause. Then, the fiery Hays took front stage and brought the house down, playing on the emotions of the Tigers and stirring passions. A Richmond correspondent reported, "The affair was quite interesting—the feelings excited being the more heartfelt under the recollection that speakers and men were cut off from their homes, and far away from them were fighting the foe who had carried desolation and misery to those homes. Gen. Hays told them that though they had not the pleasure of fighting the enemy on their own soil, they could yet fight him here on a soil consecrated by the blood of a Seymour, a Wheat, and a host of brave Louisianians."[3]

### Into the Shenandoah Valley

Ewell's Corps comprised three divisions under major generals Edward Johnson, Robert Rodes, and Jubal Early. Hays' Louisiana Tigers were an integral part of Early's veteran division, along with the infantry brigades of generals John B. Gordon and William "Extra Billy" Smith, and the North Carolinians of Colonel Isaac E. Avery, who had temporarily replaced the wounded Brigadier General Robert Hoke. The last day of May brought ominous signs that the army would soon be embarking on a summer campaign. Early's men drew fresh clothing and shoes. Weapons were inspected, and those that were damaged or defective were replaced. Cartridge boxes were filled, and as one Georgian stated, "We knew *something was up*."[4]

On Wednesday, June 3, initial elements of the Army of Northern Virginia quietly broke camp near Fredericksburg and marched toward the designated rendezvous point at Culpeper Court House, several days away to the northwest. That same day, the 6th Louisiana received a boost in manpower and morale when fifty paroled and exchanged prisoners returned to the ranks. Signs indicated that Hays' Brigade would soon be on the road. Captain George P. Ring of the 6th Louisiana wrote that the Tigers were to "hold ourselves in readiness to move at a moment's notice." Private Thomas Benton Reed of the 9th Louisiana noted, "We are still on picket; no fishing allowed. We had very strict orders and we knew that something would happen soon." In preparation for the impending move, toward evening Harry Hays tellingly withdrew his pickets, who were replaced by men from Wright's Brigade of the Third Corps.[5]

The next night, Rodes' Division slipped away to avoid the watchful eye of Union observation balloonists. Portions of Jubal Early's 7,200-man division, including Hays' veteran brigade of five Louisiana regiments, prepared to depart Hamilton's Crossing and cooked three days' rations in the late evening.

Gordon's Brigade piled logs in heaps near their hillside camps and set the wood on fire, using the towering pillars of flames to mask their departure. Before midnight, the Tigers were also underway, leaving behind their sick and infirm comrades and those unable to withstand the rigors of prolonged marching. Captain Ring expressed the prevailing hope that this would be the final campaign.[6]

Early moved southwest over "a very rugged country" toward Spotsylvania Court House, followed by the division of Edward "Allegheny" Johnson. Along with other parts of Lee's army, they were to rendezvous near Culpeper. To mask their movements and delay any Federal pursuit, A. P. Hill's Third Corps was left to "watch and amuse" Major General Joseph Hooker's Union Army of the Potomac. The Tigers marched all night and camped in thick woods just before daylight. To avoid alerting the Federals to their presence, campfires were forbidden.[7]

At daylight on June 5, according to Hays' adjutant, Captain William J. Seymour, "The Yankee balloon was decried and the aeronaut must have discovered that our troops were on the march." However, despite the fears, the new campsite was not in view and the Confederates remained undetected as they lounged in the woods all day. After dark, Early's Division was on the road again. After a hard march of more than twenty miles, the First Louisiana Brigade camped just past Spotsylvania, with many men nursing sore feet and aching muscles. Weeks of relative inactivity had taken a toll, and it would be a few days before the Tigers regained their peak marching fitness. The trek to the Shenandoah Valley over the next week would be marked by alternating periods of hard rain and intense sunshine, and several Louisianans would drop from the ranks suffering from sunstroke and exhaustion.

The Tigers were on the road toward Shady Grove Church shortly after daybreak on June 6. About 10:00 a.m., after fording Catharpin Creek on a hot and dusty day, General Early received orders to halt his division and await further developments along the Rappahannock River, where elements of "Fighting Joe" Hooker's army threatened A. P. Hill's defensive line. The division remained stationary, enduring a driving rainstorm, until early the following afternoon when orders came to proceed to Culpeper. June 7 would see "a hard days march" of twenty miles on exceedingly dusty roads. The Tigers tramped through Old Verdiersville, a hamlet with a few scattered houses and a gold smelting facility marked by a tall brick chimney. Shortly after passing this landmark, the Louisianans splashed across the Rapidan River at Somerville Ford. Captain Ring wrote in his diary, "We rolled up our pants and into it we went." They passed within sight of Cedar Mountain, where many of them had fought the previous August, and camped two miles from Culpeper Court House.[8]

Among the ranks of the 9th Louisiana was Private White Murrell, a young farmer from Homer, Louisiana. His rough personality and lack of personal hygiene displeased his comrades. One of his Company A colleagues wrote, "This man was too trifling to feed dogs and no one would mess with him. When he drew new clothes, he would put them on and never take them off until he drew more, and when he drew rations—one, two or three days made no difference with White—he would go and cook it all up and sit down and eat it all, then starve or steal until next draw day."[9]

The odiferous Murrell and his fellow Tigers had a short day on Monday, June 8, passing through Culpeper and camping three miles to the west. Longstreet's First Corps and Hill's Third Corps were in the vicinity, as was Major General James E. B. ("Jeb") Stuart's cavalry. The next day at 2:00 p.m., Jubal Early received urgent orders to march northeast to the rail stop at Brandy Station, where a massive cavalry fight was underway. However, by the time the infantry arrived in the late afternoon after a seven-mile march, the battle was essentially over, so the Tigers pitched camp on the battlefield.

On the 10th, Early's Division returned to its campsites near Culpeper. Regimental returns taken that day indicated that Harry Hays' First Louisiana Brigade officially numbered 137 officers and 1,495 enlisted men. Several Tigers captured at Second Fredericksburg had returned to the ranks just before the campaign started, as well as dozens of men who had recovered from illness or injury or had been on detached duty. However, their numbers had been more than offset by soldiers who dropped out of the ranks after leaving Hamilton's Crossing because of illness, exhaustion, straggling, or desertion. At four o'clock in the afternoon, Hays' Brigade resumed the march, reaching Hazel Run before stopping for the night after a sixteen-mile hike.[10]

Rumors persisted that the Confederates might target Pennsylvania, and President Abraham Lincoln called for 100,000 new troops to repress this potential threat to the northern heartland. Pennsylvania's Republican governor, Andrew Curtin, began raising thousands of volunteers for the state's emergency militia. Union Major General Darius N. Couch, commanding the newly formed Department of the Susquehanna, worked with Curtin to mobilize the militia of neighboring New York and New Jersey to defend the state capital, Harrisburg, in case of a Rebel attack. The forty-year-old former commander of the Army of the Potomac's II Corps began developing plans to defend the vital Susquehanna River crossings.[11]

At sunrise on Thursday, June 11, Ewell set his Second Corps in motion for a full day's march, with Rodes' Division advancing on the Richmond Road toward Flint Hill. In a separate column, Early's four brigades followed Johnson's Division on a graded turnpike northwesterly through Woodville and Sperryville, which they reached in midafternoon. To keep the men relatively fresh, Ewell issued orders to halt the column after every two miles for a ten-minute rest break. One of John Gordon's Georgians recalled, "By doing this, we could march all day, and the boys who were well could keep up. We had but few stragglers. The wagon trains kept up and we drew rations regularly. We made excellent time."[12]

Jeb Stuart's troopers in the Loudoun Valley east of the Blue Ridge Mountains provided an effective cavalry screen, allowing the Rebel infantry columns to approach the lower Shenandoah Valley undetected by Union cavalry. In the evening, Early's Division tramped through the streets of Little Washington, the seat of Rappahannock County, where women and girls enthusiastically passed out water to the soldiers. Hays' Tigers, refreshed by the joyous parade and ringing cheers from the fairer sex, camped three miles beyond town. They settled into a grassy meadow for a night's rest, after another long hike of more than twenty miles. Ewell established corps headquarters to the east at Gaines' Crossroads.[13]

The Louisianans expected a battle within the next few days as they entered the Shenandoah Valley and neared the much-contested town of Winchester, where more than seven thousand Federal soldiers of the 2nd Division, VIII Corps blocked the Valley Turnpike leading northward to the Potomac River. Their commander was Major General Robert H. Milroy, an Indiana native who celebrated his forty-seventh birthday the same day Ewell's Confederates approached the valley. A graduate of a private military academy in Norwich, Vermont, Milroy captained a company of Indiana volunteers during the Mexican War but experienced little combat. He returned home and graduated from Indiana University's law school in 1851. After passing his bar examination, Milroy established a successful practice in Rensselaer, Indiana. He became an ardent abolitionist and early supporter of the state's fledgling Republican Party.[14]

Upon the outbreak of war, the strong Unionist recruited a militia infantry company. He was commissioned as colonel of the 9th Indiana in April 1861. He served in western Virginia under George McClellan later that year and commanded a brigade during the Valley Campaign and at Second Bull Run. "The Grey Eagle" subsequently received a promotion to major general of volunteers, dating from November 1862. The following January, Milroy arrived in war-weary Winchester and began improving or constructing several earthen fortifications that protected the main approaches to the important transportation hub. Pro-Confederacy residents soon came to resent his extreme harshness toward them, and many deemed him a tyrant.[15]

Richard Ewell knew that the seizure of Winchester, Federal-held Berryville (ten miles to the east), and Martinsburg (in West Virginia farther to the north) would open the lower valley to uncontested movement northward to Maryland and Pennsylvania. During Thursday evening, he hosted a council with generals Early and Johnson, along with famed topographer Jedediah Hotchkiss, to review detailed maps of the region and plan the best approach routes to Winchester and Martinsburg. Rodes, accompanied by Brigadier General Albert G. Jenkins' mounted infantry brigade, was to swing through Berryville and attack the Federal garrison at Martinsburg, while Early and Johnson marched northwest to seize Winchester. If successful, they would block Milroy's main line of retreat, and a decisive Confederate victory might be in the offing.[16]

Ewell's three divisions were on the road at daybreak on Friday, June 12, and soon approached the scenic Blue Ridge Mountains. One artilleryman recounted, "We heard, at first indistinctly, toward the front of the column continued cheering. Following on, it grew louder and louder. We reached the foot of a long ascent, from the summit of which the shout went up, but were at a loss to know what called it forth. Arriving there, there loomed up before us the old Blue Ridge, and we, too, joined in the chorus. Moving on with renewed life, the continued greeting of those following was heard as eye after eye took in its familiar face. We had thought that the love for these old mountains was peculiar to us who had grown up among them; but the cheer of the Creoles who had been with us under Jackson was as hearty as our own."[17]

In the late afternoon, Early's Division ascended Chester Gap, a pass noted for its magnificent vista of the Shenandoah Valley, the lush "Granary of Virginia." A trio of 9th Louisiana infantrymen stopped at a nearby farmhouse and requested a meal and a place to sleep for the night. One of them was Ole

Tristen, a Norwegian immigrant who spoke little English despite his having been in the Confederate army for more than a year. After eating, his comrades conversed with their hostess, who filled and lit a pipe lent to her by one of the men. She complained about a recent nasty encounter with several rowdy soldiers from Louisiana. Her guests said little until she asked them where they were from, to which the spokesman, Thomas Reed, responded, "We are Louisiana soldiers."

She turned pale as death, and then flushed as red as scarlet. The "pretty dame" cycled between white and crimson for a minute or so before regaining her composure. She exclaimed, "I tell you the very name of 'Louisiana soldier' is a horror to me, and I hope while you are under my roof you will behave yourselves." "Why, Madam, we propose to be gentlemen, and I will vouch for our behavior," responded Reed. "I know that our troops have a hard name, but I can assure you that there are as high-minded and refined gentlemen from Louisiana as there are in the State of Virginia, or any other state." The men obeyed her wishes, ate their meals, and quietly went to bed. In the morning, her husband, a cavalryman, brought out a decanter of apple brandy for the soldiers, and the Norwegian left with a wooden canteen full of the fruity alcohol. The three Tigers stuffed their pockets with ripe apples from a basket the woman offered to them.[18]

In the late afternoon, the long column of Confederates filed through the old Warren County town of Front Royal, a regional transportation hub at the confluence of the North and South Forks of the Shenandoah River. After marching almost 130 miles in eight days, they received a rousing reception from much of the remaining populace, who had chafed under Milroy's frequent raids for supplies. The enthusiasm was mutual. One young woman, Lucy Buck, wrote, "Oh how the gallant boys cheered and shouted. Ma and I went up on the house and when they saw us, they waved and hurrahed us. Oh! It was glorious!" Several townspeople encouraged the soldiers to catch Milroy soon and give him a good whipping.[19]

A spellbound young boy named Thomas Ashby watched as more than ten thousand Rebels marched through Front Royal. He remembered, "The men were in splendid condition and in high spirits. As they passed through the village, the soldiers closed up their ranks and the bands played as if on parade. The artillery and the wagons, interspersed between the different commands, added to the impressiveness of the occasion and gave a good idea of the details and appurtenances of war."[20]

After passing through town about 5:00 p.m. at the end of the lengthy procession, Gordon's and Hays' brigades and Lieutenant Colonel Hilary P. Jones' artillery battalion camped along the Front Royal Road on the east side of the South Fork. Avery's Carolinians and "Extra Billy" Smith's Virginians were farther north, after crossing both forks. Johnson's Division encamped beyond them at Cedarville, with Rodes' Division at Stone Bridge about five miles northeast of Front Royal. Ewell called a meeting in the late afternoon at Cedarville, where he explained his intended course of action to his subordinates. The next day, the corps would attack Winchester and Berryville, then take Martinsburg, and subsequently march to the Potomac before crossing into Maryland.[21]

During the day, Milroy's scouting parties had surprised several Rebels near Middletown, nearly eleven miles from Winchester. They seized more than three dozen prisoners, who indicated there were no other Confederate forces in the area. Milroy was convinced he only faced light opposition, ignorant that a much more powerful foe was approaching his defenses. The pro-Confederacy residents, so long under Milroy's thumb, were equally unaware of the oncoming liberators. Laura Lee wrote, "Our life is so monotonous that there is nothing to record from day to day but the same oppressions and tyranny. . . . It is still a mystery what has become of Gen. Lee's army, but all admit some great move is on hand." Federal troops, hearing reports that Rebels were in the valley, slept with their arms nearby.[22]

### Ewell Attacks Winchester

The terrain near Winchester is gently rolling, crossed by several meandering streams and dotted in 1863 with farm buildings. There are several low hills and ridges, none more than two hundred feet above the base terrain. To defend the town, General Milroy had several fortified positions, with three relatively large forts and seven smaller lunettes and redans. Trenches and roads connected the most important works.

A ridge line northwest of Winchester sported the largest redoubt, the "Main Fort" or Battery Number 2. Confederates had constructed it early in the war on the William Fahnestock farm along the Pughtown Road. In early 1863, Federals expanded and strengthened the bastion, rechristening it "Fort Milroy." It was also known as the "Flag Fort" because of the huge U.S. banner that flew overhead from a massive wooden pole. Commanding the western and southern approaches to Winchester, Fort Milroy bristled with

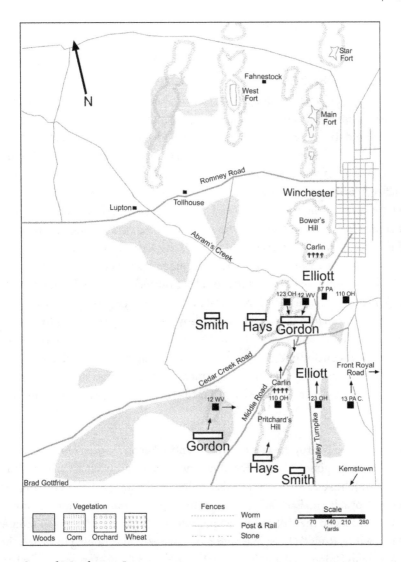

Second Winchester, June 13

six heavy guns (four 20-pounder Parrott rifles and two 24-pounder smooth-bore howitzers). It could hold more than two thousand troops along its parapets and accompanying entrenchments. Just to the north on a low hill beyond the Pughtown Road was Battery Number 3, or "Star Fort," an irregular eight-sided earthwork constructed by Union troops in 1862. Flanked by linear works along the crest, it could hold more than four hundred defenders and up to eight guns.[23]

A little more than a half-mile west of Fort Milroy and nine hundred yards southwest of the Star Fort, across the low ditch-filled ravine of a tributary of Red Bud Run, was the smaller "West Fort," or Battery Number 5. This unfinished lunette was open to the rear, allowing easy access and retreat, and could hold six light guns and five hundred men. A line of hillside rifle pits protected the southwestern approach. Work parties were still busy finishing the traverses and a flanking entrenchment, as well as felling trees to clear a field of fire. Nearby was a two-gun lunette, Battery Number 6, on a slightly higher elevation near the Pughtown Road. However, both fortifications were vulnerable, because a higher ridge line known as Apple Pie Ridge (part of the Little North Mountain range) dominated the western approach.[24]

Milroy's other prepared defenses included a series of linear earthworks about two miles south of Fort Milroy along Bower's Hill (also known as Milltown Heights because of its proximity to several large grist mills). However, due to the expanse of ground that Milroy needed to protect, his lines were not continuous, and a skillful opponent could potentially pick off the widespread forts one by one. To guard the southern approaches, he deployed five relatively inexperienced infantry regiments, along with cavalry and artillery. It was enough men in his estimation to fend off any small enemy raiding parties.[25]

Unknown to Milroy, he was facing the entire Second Corps of the Army of Northern Virginia. Richard Ewell planned a multipronged assault on Winchester. Johnson's Division would advance northward to the town using the Front Royal Road. Early's Division was to march behind them and then take a westward jog to the Valley Pike, which essentially paralleled Johnson's route. Meanwhile, Rodes' Division would move to Berryville, hoping to snatch the 1,800-man Union garrison there. Ewell augmented Early's force with two batteries of reserve artillery and Lieutenant Colonel James R. Herbert's mixed force of Maryland infantry and artillery. Early was to get into position on the ridges west of Winchester, where he could assault the main Federal forts to his advantage, while Johnson attacked from the southeast. Early left his supply train, except the regimental ordnance and medical wagons, at Cedarville with the 61st Georgia and prepared his division for serious fighting.[26]

Well before daylight on Saturday, June 13, Harry Hays broke camp along the Shenandoah River's South Fork and formed his brigade into column. Spirits in the Tigers' ranks were high, coupled with the usual nervousness as contact with the enemy loomed. The early morning weather was warm and balmy, and the roads in reasonably good condition. Shortly after wading across the North Fork at 3:30 a.m., the Louisianans soberly passed by the grave of Major Aaron Davis Jr., the brigade's former commissary officer, who died during the Battle of Front Royal the previous year. About 7:00 a.m., Hays' men reached the tiny hamlet of Ninevah, where they left the Front Royal Road and turned northwest onto the dirt road to Newtown (now Stephens City). Soon they rejoined the rest of Early's Division and turned north onto the Valley Pike. Clouds of dust kicked up by the soldiers, horses, guns, and wagons coated the lengthy procession with a fine powder.[27]

Four miles south of Winchester along the Front Royal Road, Milroy had posted a strong picket line at the Parkins Mill Battery, an earthen lunette that guarded the Opequon Creek crossing. Johnson's forward troops readily drove off the defenders about 8:30 a.m. An hour later, his lead regiment, the 16th Virginia, engaged in a series of skirmishes with the 12th Pennsylvania Cavalry along Hoge Run. Johnson maneuvered into position southeast of Fort Milroy, but its heavy guns finally stalled his progress shortly before noon. He held his place to await the arrival of Early while engaging in sharp skirmishing in Winchester's southern streets and dueling with Federal artillery posted on the heights south of town.[28]

Meanwhile, Early's progress on the turnpike was blocked just before noon by a sharp skirmish near Kernstown between Herbert's 1st Maryland Battalion and Federal cavalry and artillery. Captain W. H. Griffin's Baltimore Artillery unlimbered to support Herbert as the fray intensified. Farther north, Union cannon crowned Pritchard's Hill, a broad rise that commanded the three southwestern approaches to Winchester—the Valley Pike, Strasburg (or Middle) Road, and Cedar Creek Grade. General Early ordered Herbert to drive off the forward enemy skirmishers while he consulted his maps for options to best position his troops to attack the hill. After he "reconnoitered the ground carefully," Early rode to Harry Hays and conducted his brigade through a skirt of woods and a meadow to a country lane heading left from the turnpike. Leading from the village of Bartonsville on the Valley Pike northwesterly to the Cedar Creek Grade, the old dirt road offered a convenient way to advance against the Yankees on Pritchard's Hill.[29]

The Pritchard family had already experienced the trauma of warfare on their property. Fighting swirled about their farm in the Battle of Kernstown during the 1862 Valley Campaign while Samuel, his wife Helen, and their two small children huddled in the basement. After the combat ceased, the large three-story red brick house had been a temporary field hospital, and Mrs. Pritchard spent several days ministering to wounded Federal soldiers. Union Colonel Nathan Kimball had requisitioned seven of Pritchard's horses to replace battle casualties. Now, the Pritchard property was again a Union outpost, this time occupied by West Virginia artillery and elements of Brigadier General Washington L. Elliott's brigade, arrayed in a lengthy skirmish line across the knolls behind the home.[30]

Harry Hays led his column forward on the Bartonsville and Strasburg roads for perhaps half a mile toward the Pritchard farm before halting in mid-afternoon. He sent a courier galloping back to Early with word that the enemy had massed a considerable infantry force on the ridge to his left. In response to this unforeseen threat, Early immediately ordered Gordon's Georgians to follow the same road and clear the Yankees from the ridge line.[31]

Hays dispatched Colonel Leroy Stafford's 9th Louisiana into the fields in front as a strong skirmish line. The central and northern Louisiana farm boys deployed into battle line and steadily advanced toward Pritchard's Hill, taking cover behind clumps of cedar and pine shrubs, rock outcroppings, and bushes. Stafford ordered a charge and easily drove off Elliott's badly outnumbered Federals, including the 110th Ohio Volunteer Infantry, which was facing hostile fire for the first time. Buckeye Private Lorenzo D. Barnhart related, "We held them stubbornly and disputed every inch of ground. They were fighting us with a heavy skirmish line. At once they charged onto us with a whole Regiment on our light skirmish line. We gave them a volley from our skirmish line, then retreated toward our center. They pressed on. They now used cannons on us, and shot something at us: we thought it was pieces of railroad iron. It screamed and whizzed over our heads, and made a deathly noise. Some of these missiles went over our heads, and some lit on the ground. We could hear them thump."[32]

After the Union artillery (Carlin's Battery D, 1st West Virginia) abandoned Pritchard's Hill and galloped to the rear, Colonel Stafford dispatched a courier to inform Hays the hill was in Confederate hands. Hays advanced the rest of his brigade across the open fields onto the rise, where the Louisianans deployed into a lengthy battle line facing north. To his front beyond the hill were woods, which would provide cover for his advance skirmishers. He sent out six companies, including the brigade's sharpshooters, to occupy the woodlot to contest any enemy advance down the pike. Among the marksmen was Private James Benedict Roden, the Irish-born former Mississippi riverman. He and his comrades deployed among the rocks, trees, and bushes, and they kept a careful watch on the road.

A courier rode up the hill to Hays with orders from General Early to hold his line until Gordon's Brigade swept past the position and cleared the ridge to the left. Once the Georgians were in place to protect his flank, Hays was to advance in lockstep with Gordon toward the main Union line. Gordon "advanced handsomely, as directed," and engaged the inexperienced 12th West Virginia Infantry on the wooded Sandy Ridge. In conjunction with Colonel Penn's 7th Louisiana, Gordon's 13th and 31st Georgia drove the Federals from behind a stone wall, sending them stumbling through the open fields. Elliott's forces retreated to the Cedar Creek Grade and briefly counterattacked. They stalled Gordon and forced him back, but Jubal Early extended his line farther to the west, outflanking successive Union positions. In the meantime, Avery's and Smith's reserve brigades advanced to the front on each side of the Valley Pike past Kernstown.[33]

Under pressure from Gordon and Hays, by 4:30 p.m. the outnumbered Federals were falling back to their reserve position near Milltown. They slogged through the marshy lowlands around Abram's Creek to Bower's Hill, a broad rolling eminence just north of the stream. Teeming with Union artillery and infantry, the heights commanded both the Valley Pike and the Front Royal Road. The wetlands would slow any attackers, who would then have to ascend the steep southern slopes to reach the earthworks. A multi-building mill complex and a two-mile-long wooden millrace allowed protection for sharpshooters and skirmishers. Ironically, the Louisianans had occupied the same ground in May 1862 during Jackson's Valley Campaign.[34]

After inspecting the formidable position through his field glasses, Early called off any further assaults. He reformed Gordon's line across the Valley Pike near the tollgate about a mile south of Winchester, with Hays posted to his left on the ridge between the Cedar Creek Grade and Abram's Creek. Smith's Virginians were brought up and placed on Hays' left flank, along with some of Hilary Jones' guns. Union artillery boomed while the various elements of Early's Division reached their assigned positions. Early initially held Avery's troops in reserve in a position to support any renewed advance, but he soon ordered them back to Kernstown to guard the ambulances and ordnance and medical wagons, as well as to protect his artillery from any flanking movement around the left of the division's extended line. He ordered Herbert's Marylanders to swing around to Gordon's right to protect his flank.[35]

Early's men "lay here in the open fields under the bursting shells from the fort." On the extreme left of Gordon's line, many of the 31st Georgia had their eyes glued to the distant Union flag fort. Their attention turned to what Private Isaac Bradwell deemed "one of the most splendid spectacles I have ever seen. The sally port was open and out of it rode squadron after squadron of well-mounted cavalry, with their shining swords drawn and other equipment reflecting the bright sunshine. They formed as if to occupy the entire width of the pike, intending to cut their way out by a sudden and overwhelming dash through our lines. . . . The rattle of their steel scabbards, the clanking of their spurs, and the noise of the iron shoes of their horses as they struck the hard surface of the pike were awe-inspiring."[36]

Colonel Leroy Stafford of the 9th Louisiana sent Company A forward two to three hundred yards as advance pickets. They crouched behind a stone wall at an angle to the turnpike, ensuring a good field of fire to ambush the oncoming cavalrymen. Private Thomas Reed related that his captain moved up and down the line calmly remarking, "Now, boys, don't shoot until you hear the report of my pistol; then each man be sure he strips a saddle." Soon, the unsuspecting Union troopers were in range and the captain fired. Musketry crackled from behind the rock fence, and several Federals tumbled from their saddles. However, several Yankees returned fire, wounding Captain Montgomery Harrison and Private Manisco McGowen, a twenty-five-year-old Georgia-born farmer from Hillsboro Mills, Louisiana. Soon, the cavalry "stampeded" to the rear.

Georgia Private Bradwell commented on the cavalry's repulse. "In their headlong drive down the long slope they came into range of Hays's Louisianans, who poured into their ranks a few well directed shots that emptied a half dozen saddles and drove the rest back in a disorganized mass in to the fort. We were holding our guns in readiness for use at the proper time, but were disappointed by the too great haste of our Louisiana comrades."[37]

Despite their troopers' setback, many Yankees on Bower's Hill believed they had won a major victory in stopping the Rebels' advance. About 5:00 p.m., the 12th West Virginia dislodged Hays' forward picket line from behind the stone wall, capturing a prisoner and reinforcing the belief that the Confederates were whipped. Milroy's aide-de-camp later reported,

They [initially] proved too strong, and compelled him [Elliott] to fall back, flanking him three times, but his men fought the ground so obstinately, and his two pieces of artillery were so well handled, that their attempt to surround and take him proved abortive. They continued advancing, however, and when within reach of our guns on Milltown Heights, showed two long lines of battle, composed of a force of not less than 5,000 men, who all supposed comprised their entire force.

Our batteries opened on them, the infantry forces at the same time charging, and in less than fifteen minutes their entire lines were broken and their whole body retiring in the direst confusion. General Milroy superintended the placing and firing of the guns, and personally directed all the details of the fight. The rebels retired into the woods; our forces had successfully engaged them at all points; they everywhere had been repulsed, and we were fully convinced that the worst was over, and that their attack upon Winchester had proved a disastrous failure.[38]

Private Charles Lynch of the 18th Connecticut in Ely's Brigade was among those soldiers who did not share this optimism. He noted, "The sudden appearance of so large a force was a surprise . . . . It was plainly seen that a large force of Confederates were surrounding the town and that we were in a bad fix, as we could see the gray in all directions and knew that we were more than outnumbered."[39]

About 5:00 p.m., the 61st Georgia arrived at Kernstown, escorting Early's long train of supply wagons. Quartermasters and commissary sergeants distributed rations to the weary troops. Still arrayed in battle line, the Tigers settled down for the evening, eating their dinners and conversing before trying to catch some much-needed sleep. Many Confederates wondered what the morrow might bring, as the Yankees were not likely to go away in the night. Some Louisianans mourned the loss of friends and family members, for the day's advance had cost the brigade two men killed, three officers and eight men wounded, and three men missing.

One of the missing men proved to be valuable to the Federals. About 6:00 p.m., guards escorted a sullen Confederate prisoner to Milroy's headquarters. He identified himself as being from Hays' Louisiana Brigade of Ewell's Corps, which, together with Longstreet's Corps, was near Winchester. Soon afterward, a southern deserter confirmed the information. This was the first definite intelligence Milroy had received of the identity and magnitude of the Rebels now threatening his outer works. With his telegraph line to Harper's Ferry cut off at twelve o'clock, Milroy had no way to relay this important message quickly to Washington and the War Department. The news would not reach Lincoln until June 15, when General Hooker sent a telegram confirming the presence of Hays' Brigade (and Francis T. Nichols' Second Louisiana Brigade) at Winchester.[40]

The pro-Union civilians of the divided town were panic-stricken. Julia Chase recorded, "The town is all in an uproar . . . the secessionists very joyfully flocking to the sutlers, buying up all they can for their friends, while the Unionists are in an anxious state of mind. . . . God in his mercy, grant that Winchester may not be given up to the rebels; we dread their appearance."

After dark, concerned he did not have enough infantry to withstand a determined attack on Bower's Hill, Milroy began concentrating his forces inside a triangle defined by Fort Milroy, Star Fort, and the West Fort. He silently withdrew his artillery and main body of infantry, leaving a few skirmishers in the mills and hilltop fortifications to confront Early. No one was allowed to light campfires in the new positions to avoid tipping off the Rebels. Soon, he had reinforcements. Colonel Andrew T. McReynolds' brigade, harassed for hours by Jenkins' Confederate horsemen, finally reached Winchester after a roundabout march from Berryville. The weary soldiers filed into the Star Fort entrenchments. Milroy's soldiers had fought reasonably well during the previous afternoon, and the general was confident he could withstand renewed Confederate assaults for twenty-four hours until relieved by the Army of the Potomac.[41]

As rain began to fall and lightning flashed, Jubal Early finished arranging his division's dispositions southwest of Winchester. Escorted by Virginia cavalry, he rode across the countryside to consult with Ewell, but the thunderstorm became so violent and the night so dark that he had to turn back. However, his troops were now in position to attack Milroy's outer lines on Bower's Hill, while Johnson was poised to sweep into town from the southeast. Ewell ordered Rodes to advance on Martinsburg from Berryville to cut off Milroy's expected retreat in that direction. The noose was tightening.[42]

### The Fight for the West Fort

At daylight on Sunday, June 14, drumbeats woke the sleeping Tigers. The rain had ceased, but an overcast sky dimmed the morning. Privates Thomas Reed and Jackson Dawkins of the 9th Louisiana had camped in an open field,

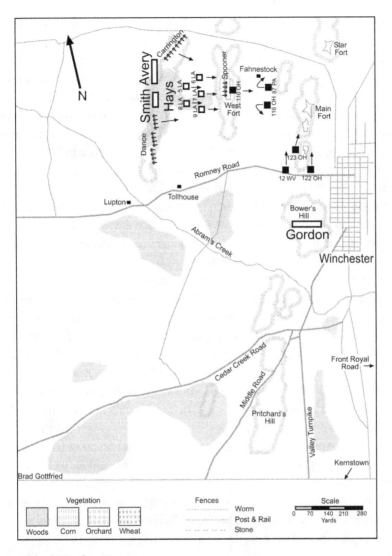

Second Winchester, June 14

and the thunderstorm had drenched their blankets. They decided to hang them over a fence to air dry, but Dawkins worried they might have to leave the blankets behind if the regiment hastily marched away. Reed, predicting success this day in defeating the Yankees, remarked, "Well, we will get some dry ones tonight."[43]

Shortly after dawn, brisk skirmishing erupted along Hays' front line, and

Captain Albert Dejean Jr. of Company F of the 8th Louisiana died in the exchange. About 7:00 a.m., General Early send orders to Hays and Gordon to each advance a regiment toward the enemy skirmish line around the millrace and probe the Federal defenses at Bower's Hill. In obedience, Hays sent forward Colonel D. B. Penn's 7th Louisiana, coordinating its movements with Gordon's men. At the same time, "Extra Billy" Smith's skirmishers advanced across Abram's Creek on their left. Soon, they cleared the mills and millrace of enemy skirmishers. Confederates swept up the steep hillside, driving off the few remaining defenders and easily seizing the earthworks. Concurrently, Early ordered Major William W. Goldsborough and his skirmishers from Herbert's Maryland battalion to advance off Hays' right flank into the outskirts of Winchester. However, fearing that Milroy's guns from the main fort might shell the town to clear out the skirmishers, the veteran general soon ordered Goldsborough to retire.[44]

Shortly after Early watched his men ascend Bower's Hill (likely by 9:00 a.m.), Lieutenant General Ewell and his staff rode up. Together, the two officers advanced to the crest in midmorning and reconnoitered the area from its height, which gave them "a very distinct view of the works about Winchester." To their surprise, the hill northwest of Winchester (Flint Ridge) that Early wanted to occupy to threaten Fort Milroy was now itself fortified and lined with Union troops. These would have to be driven off before any advance could be made on the main fort. The Confederate commanders' attention turned to a higher ridge line farther to the west that commanded the new works. Apple Pie Ridge offered a good jumping off point for an assault on the West Fort, and it would screen Confederate movements while they got into position.[45]

Ewell ordered Early to leave one brigade and part of his artillery to occupy the attention of the Yankees to his front. The remainder of the division, perhaps 3,600 men and twenty guns, would execute a wide flanking movement to get control of these heights, enabling the batteries to command Milroy's main fortifications. Early was to conduct this movement in secrecy to avoid alerting the enemy, who might shift troops to the threatened area. In the meantime, Johnson extended his line farther to the right against light opposition, and sharp skirmishing occurred in the streets of Winchester. That same morning, President Lincoln instructed department commander Major General Robert Schenck to order Milroy to remove his troops from Winchester to safety at Harper's Ferry. "He will be gobbled up if he remains, if he is not already past salvation." To reinforce the message, the commander-in-chief of the U.S. Army, Henry Halleck, wired Schenck, "If General Milroy does not obey your orders, remove him from command."[46]

While Milroy remained naively confident of his security, "Old Jube" was busy finishing his preparations for renewed fighting. He moved the rest of Gordon's Brigade to Bower's Hill and supported them with Herbert's Marylanders and Griffin's Baltimore Light Artillery. He dispatched Hupp's Battery from the corps reserve artillery to bolster Gordon's line and repositioned Jenkins' cavalry to watch the flanks. Satisfied these dispositions were strong enough to hold the Yankees in place, Early ordered his other three brigade commanders and the artillery to prepare to march. Hilary Jones would command a force of three batteries from his battalion, supplemented by Captain Willis J. Dance and eight guns from Ewell's reserve artillery, including the 1st Rockbridge Artillery. To guide the column into position, Early obtained the services of a "very intelligent and patriotic citizen" named James C. Baker, who had a son in the Confederate army.[47]

At 11:00 a.m., Early sent orders for Hays to withdraw the 7th Louisiana and his skirmishers, who were being relieved by elements of Gordon's Brigade. He was to reform his brigade on the Cedar Creek Grade. The Tigers formed ranks and trekked down an old country road. The cloudy day was becoming hot, so Hays ordered a short break once his men reached Cedar Creek Grade not far from the Bell homestead. When all was ready and his soldiers rested, Early ordered the advance and his column slowly headed west for a couple of miles, screened from Federal view by the heights. The Confederates crossed over the low Sandy Ridge, with Jones' artillery and the divisional ambulances trailing the column.

Guided by Baker, Early's force turned off the road and marched north across country through the Cloverdale Farm, jaunting across open fields and patches of light woods that allowed the passage of artillery limbers and caissons. The advance guard did not encounter any Federal patrols or pickets, although they did stumble onto two "very ordinary looking men," which raised some concern. Early ordered them to be taken along under guard.

The head of the column emerged from the woods and passed over the Romney Road. The Rebels paused at an eighteenth-century stone farmhouse known as "Walnut Grove," about three miles west of Winchester. Early consulted with the owner, Dr. John S. Lupton, an ardent southern sympathizer who informed the general that the Yankees had posted a picket force a half-mile down the road, and he believed the Federals were still present. To thwart any pursuit from that direction, Early dropped off the 54th North Carolina from Avery's Brigade to watch his rear. The remainder of the division, still guided by Baker, took a narrow, obscure country lane that led farther north-ward toward the rear of the high ridge line that Early sought to control. He left the two suspicious men behind at Lupton's house, with orders that the Tar Heels' provost keep a watchful eye on them.[48]

The long line of Confederates trudged along the relatively flat dirt road as the early afternoon temperature rose. Early did not find any Yankees block-ing his way, but he did encounter a young girl he estimated to be about thir-teen years old, riding on horseback while her younger brother walked behind her. The general recounted,

> She was carrying before her a large bundle of clothes tied up in a sheet, and when she unexpectedly came upon us she was at first very much frightened, but soon discovering that we were Confederates, she pulled off her bonnet, waved it over her head and 'hurrahed,' and then burst into tears. She told us that the enemy had been shelling the woods all around, firing occasionally into her father's house, and that she had been sent from home by her father and mother to get out of the way. She said that they had not been able to imagine what the shelling meant, as they did not know that any of 'our soldiers,' as she called us, were any-where in the neighborhood. It was not necessary to use any precaution as to her, and she was permitted to pass on, feeling much happier for the encounter.[49]

Early arrived between 3:30 and 4:00 p.m. on the reverse slope of Apple Pie Ridge not far from the Pughtown Road. Halting his column out of sight of the Yankees, he and his staff ascended the slope to observe the distant enemy po-sition and ascertain if indeed he could launch an assault from the heights. To his satisfaction, Early found that the pine-covered low mountain was perfect to form his troops secretly into battle line for the planned attack. It also of-fered a good artillery platform for a bombardment to soften the enemy's de-fenses prior to sending in the infantry. With battle looming, the civilian guide Baker thought it was wise to head back to his house near Winchester, so he excused himself. Early thanked him for his prudent and skillful method of guiding the division without attracting the attention of the Federals.

The Union commander indeed was ignorant of Early's whereabouts. Milroy had moved his headquarters from the town to the Main Fort during the night, and he had since established a lookout post in a basket raised high on the bastion's flagpole. Under a burning sun, he periodically ascended and anxiously scanned the vista through a pocket telescope for any signs of the enemy. He came to believe the main enemy body had moved toward Harper's Ferry, a misconception that was reinforced by the sound of heavy firing in that direction. His occasional artillery salvos fired at those Confederates who were in sight drew little response, leaving him to theorize the Rebels had left only enough troops and guns to engage him at skirmishing and occasional long-range artillery duels.

About 10:00 a.m., Milroy had ordered a scouting party of the 12th Pennsylvania Cavalry to circle the area around Little North Mountain and check for any Confederate activity. Captain Charles B. Morgan and his patrol found nothing suspicious. They returned to the general about 2:00 p.m., giving Milroy the false impression that there was no immediate danger from the north or west. Somehow, they missed spotting Early's flanking movement, perhaps by as little as half an hour. After his scouting party returned, Milroy had failed to post any videttes on or near the ridge and, as a result, his men in the West Fort were blind to the enemy threat.[50]

Unseen by Milroy, "Old Jube" continued to examine his new position. He was on a long ridge, the northern spur descending by the Pughtown Road. About three-quarters of a mile in front of him on Flint Ridge was the West Fort, his objective, and it would be within easy range of his guns once they deployed. The heights around him were crowned with a stand of rather heavy timber, but in places, the trees had been partially clear-cut. To Early's amusement, several notices tacked to the trunks proclaimed, "General Milroy orders all of the timber east of this point to be cleared off." The work had obviously not been finished, and the remaining trees would provide cover for his deployment and refreshing shade from the afternoon heat. His keen military eye indicated he could push a brigade forward unnoticed to within a short distance of one section of the enemy fortifications. That sector became the focal point of his planned attack.[51]

On the northern slope of Apple Pie Ridge, near the Pughtown Road, a large cornfield on Mrs. Brierly's farm offered enough concealment to move artillery secretly into the edge of the woods. Guns placed there would face southeasterly toward the West Fort. South of the Brierly farm, beyond the thick pine woods, was a mature, untended orchard and the remains of an abandoned farmhouse known locally as "Folk's old house," directly opposite the West Fort. Of military importance to Early, the eastern hillside in that section had been cleared, offering another excellent platform for Jones' guns. The two positions were perfect to bombard the enemy lines.

The general sent word back to bring up the troops. On this "exceedingly hot" day, Hays' Louisiana Tigers had marched nearly ten miles and were "very much exhausted," so Early hustled them under the canopy of woods behind the planned jumping-out point. Grateful soldiers packed into the welcome shade, stacked arms, and caught some much-needed rest. Early brought up Avery's North Carolina brigade and Smith's Virginians to support the assault, but the main attack would fall to the Louisianans.[52]

The Federals garrisoning the West Fort and Battery Number 6 were ignorant of the impending threat. Milroy had ordered these troops into the unfinished works just that morning. Their commander was Colonel J. Warren Keifer, a twenty-seven-year-old attorney from Clark County, Ohio, who would serve years later as speaker of the U.S. House of Representatives. He had at his disposal 323 men from his relatively green 110th Ohio Volunteer Infantry, led this day by Lieutenant Colonel William N. Foster. They were supporting Battery L, 5th U.S. Artillery—six 3-inch ordnance rifles and 99 men under Lieutenant Wallace F. Randolph. A little off to their right was the predominantly German Company C of the 116th Ohio, its northern flank somewhat in the air. Colonel Keifer recalled, "Quiet reigned in my front. The enemy appeared to be inactive." Private Barnhart added, "Everything was quiet on Sunday the 14th. The boys were laying on the parapets in the sun. We came to the conclusion the confederates had all went to Church to get Religion, but they were only fixing to kill all of us."[53]

Unseen by Keifer's dormant men, generals Early and Hays crept forward through the thick woods and carefully reconnoitered the enemy position, ascertaining the best tactical lines of approach. To their surprise, there were no pickets or lookouts posted. A few soldiers lounged outside the walls under the shade of a large tree. The Yankees "did not apprehend any danger in their immediate neighborhood." Instead, the Federals' attention was drawn to the south, where John Gordon's brigade had thrown forward skirmishers and was slowly advancing toward Winchester, while the Baltimore Light Artillery hurled shells at Milroy's position.[54]

Even as the West Fort garrison stared at the distant Rebels, a greater danger lurked to the west on Apple Pie Ridge. Lieutenant Colonel Hilary Jones had deployed his twenty guns on the reverse slope, preparing them to be hand-pushed forward into "excellent positions" once Early gave the requisite order. Twelve guns, commanded by Captain Willis J. Dance of the Second Corps reserve artillery, quietly rumbled up the slope to Folk's old orchard, about three-quarters of a mile from Keifer's position. The remaining eight guns, under Captain James Carrington of the Charlottesville Artillery, arrived on the left flank concealed by Mrs. Brierly's cornfield and halted behind a high stone wall. Gunners removed enough rocks to form embrasures for the muzzles, taking care to avoid detection while they loaded the guns. Runners brought extra ammunition forward from the caissons, and battery and section commanders chose their potential targets and estimated ranges. Carrington's position was the most vulnerable because it was open to partial enfilade from Battery Number 6.[55]

Early positioned Avery's 57th North Carolina to protect Carrington's two batteries from any Union movement from the Pughtown Road. He placed the other three Tar Heel regiments (minus the 54th North Carolina, which was still protecting the Romney Road at Dr. Lupton's house) in battle line a quarter of a mile directly behind Hays, along with Smith's Virginians. Early ordered Hays to rouse his men from their rest in the backside of the woods and move down the slope to the eastern edge, arranging their lines to be in position to quickly advance once ordered. The Tigers, still unnoticed by the Yankees, slipped forward through the heavy pine thickets. The stage was set, and the surprise complete.[56]

Colonel Keifer did not anticipate trouble because the Confederates had been inactive in his front all day. About 3:00 p.m., he rode three-quarters of a mile to the rear to meet with General Milroy. After arriving at the main fort, the Buckeye lawyer unsaddled his horse and requested that it be taken and fed. He found Milroy to be "in high spirits," and the general remarked that he did not expect a serious fight; the enemy was only "trying to scare him out of the Valley." Milroy referred to the quiet of the day as evidence of his opinion and mentioned that his cavalry scouting patrols had failed to see any signs of enemy activity in Keifer's front. After meeting for an hour or so, Keifer was dismissed. He visited with other officers and waited for his horse to be delivered to him for the leisurely ride back to the West Fort.[57]

Unknown to Keifer, at 5:00 p.m., Harry Hays received orders to form his brigade into battle line and ready it to charge the fort. Captain Samuel H. Chisholm of the 5th Louisiana recalled, "I have never seen men look so serious, but we knew that General Hays would lead the charge and we were willing to follow. I stepped back to my company and ordered the boys to throw off their blankets, etc. and in a moment all hands knew that the ironclad brigade had to make good again its name."[58]

Hays planned to attack in a double line, placing the 7th and 9th Regiments in the front, with the 6th Louisiana moving on their right to protect the flank against a Yankee counterattack. The 5th and 8th Louisiana would follow at a convenient distance in the rear as a second line, to be used on the flanks or in support, depending on how the front line's attack was progressing. Hays sent Adjutant Seymour to Early to report that his preparations were complete, and his brigade was ready to advance. Early instructed Seymour to return Hays and tell him to wait, as "he wished to dismount some of the enemy's guns before the attack by infantry commenced."[59]

As the afternoon wore on, the battle-ready Louisianans were "burning with impatience" as they anticipated the belated order to attack. Twice, Hays made ready to move, but both times he was detained by Early's orders. Early "could not believe but what the enemy were keeping a better look out than they did," and a third time he denied the anxious Hays' request to advance. The infantrymen surveyed the steep hill to their front, covered with recently felled timber, and the little bastion and the two lines of breastworks crowning the summit. The Tigers would be put to the test, as they "many times before enjoyed the honor of being selected for similar work."[60]

About 6:00 p.m., finally satisfied the enemy had not spotted his flanking movement, Jubal Early ordered a signal gun to fire, and a solid shot flew over the fort and whistled into downtown Winchester. The Federals were stunned that Rebels were now to the west. Within moments, "the whole posse of guns opened and kept firing as fast as possible." At the same time, south of town, Carpenter's Battery opened fire on the Union line in front of Gordon. Soon, much of Colonel William G. Ely's Federal brigade withdrew through Winchester toward Fort Milroy. The Union guns soon opened, and the thunder reverberated for miles.[61]

Jones' gunners hurled shells at a rapid rate at the West Fort, catching it in a plunging crossfire from his two positions, sixty feet higher in elevation. Private Lorenzo Barnhart of the 110th Ohio related, "All at once, Oh! Here came a shower of shot and shell. The boys tumbled off the parapets like turtles drop off a log into the water." To him, the distant pine mountain "fairly blazed with cannon," and it seemed like fifty to sixty guns were involved, instead of the twenty Jones actually had in action. Harry Hays recounted, "So well directed was this fire that in a few minutes the enemy were forced to seek shelter behind their works, and scarcely a head was discovered above the ramparts."[62]

In distant Front Royal, Lucy Buck and her family wondered, "There has been the heaviest cannonading heard in the direction of Winchester. I never have heard such a succession of rapid and heavy firing in my life—we all went out to listen and felt very anxious to ascertain the cause of it." The discordant roar was far louder closer to the action. From Ewell's hilltop headquarters near the Millwood Pike, partisan cavalryman Harry Gilmor marveled, "What a magnificent spectacle met my view! . . . The forts . . . belched forth fire . . . the firing was terrific." Winchester resident Kate Sperry worried, "Never heard such cannonading in all my life—am afraid our town will yet be blown to atoms." Another woman, Cornelia Peake McDonald, recorded that Union officers standing near her home initially believed the "blaze of fire from those western hills" marked the belated arrival from a rumored Federal relief column from Maryland. Shouts of "Mulligan has come!" echoed through Winchester's streets.[63]

From a hilltop northeast of town, a mounted staff officer in Johnson's Division leisurely surveyed the dramatic scene. "It was a picturesque battle. Early's Artillery opened vigorously on the north of the forts. We could see the flash of his guns, sixteen discharges per minute, while the Stars and Stripes waved defiantly amid the bursting shells in the rolling smoke, the sun sinking red and angry behind the western clouds, the advance and retreat of the skirmishers with the sharp crack of the rifle, while cavalry and artillery gallop into position and infantry file in column."[64]

In the Star Fort, Lieutenant William H. Beach of the 1st New York Cavalry had been enjoying a "perfect June day," peacefully surveying the "silent shimmering of the summer heat" over the verdant fields, woods, and hills surrounding the hilltop bastion. Now, the "holy calm of that sabbath day was broken" by the angry discord of warfare. He watched as enemy shells occasionally whistled overhead, landing amid the division's parked supply train. Teamsters feverishly moved the wagons to safer locations between the hills.[65]

To the south at Fort Milroy, Union Colonel Keifer was still waiting for his horse when the roar of artillery was heard coming from the low mountain beyond his uncompleted bastion. He was stunned by the opening fire "in broad daylight from a quarter where no enemy was known to be." He halted a passing wagon master and appropriated his horse. After a five-minute frantic gallop, Keifer arrived at the eastern base of Flint Ridge just below the West Fort. He dismounted and raced through "a storm of shot and exploding shell" to enter the stronghold's open backside.[66]

Louisiana Captain Seymour recounted, "Our artillery opened a rapid and well directed fire upon the redoubt; some of the shells explode over the work while others strike the parapet, tearing great holes in it and sending dirt high up in the air. . . . So taken by surprise were the Yankees that they made no response for several minutes, when, recovering themselves, they replied with considerable spirit." The incoming crossfire presented a major problem for the 5th U.S. Artillery's Lieutenant Randolph. If he focused strictly on his closest target, Carrington, Dance's gunners to the south took the opportunity to carefully sight their guns "with the greatest deliberation," almost assuring a hit even at a range of three-quarters of a mile. When Randolph turned his guns to fire at Dance, Carrington would shift positions and pound the Federals from in close. To Jubal Early, the resulting Yankee counterbattery fire was "in a very wild manner," and Hilary Jones believed his batteries' well-directed fire disrupted the enemy's aim, causing him to "shoot wildly over our heads."[67]

During one of Carrington's rapid movements, tragedy struck as his two batteries traversed a sunken farm lane. A pair of heavy stone gateposts flanked the path, but the gate itself and fencing were long gone. Only the two old posts stood as lonely sentinels as the octet of cannon and their limbers and caissons passed by. Most of the artillerymen climbed up the rough, steep slopes out of the lane to allow the horse-drawn vehicles unimpeded passage. However, as the Staunton Artillery lumbered through the gateposts, a crewman suddenly tried to squeeze through the narrow opening concurrent with the rear gun. With not enough room for both to pass, the impatient Confederate was caught between the unyielding stone pillar and the gun carriage. A cast iron washer hook "caught and tore open his abdomen, dragging the poor wretch along by his intestines, which were literally pulled from his body in a long, gory ribbon."[68]

Within ten to fifteen minutes after Jones opened up, Battery L, 5th U.S., was essentially wrecked. Ammunition caissons and limbers exploded or were knocked to pieces, and nearly four dozen artillery horses lay dead or dying. Randolph was down to two operational 3-inch rifles, with his other guns dismounted or their wooden wheels crushed. Carrington's skillful repositioning of his guns thwarted Federal attempts of counterbattery fire. New York Cavalryman William Beach watched as the Maryland gunners in the Star Fort "would now and then respond to some shot that would indicate the location of the enemy's guns."[69]

For perhaps forty-five minutes, the earth shook and the roar of artillery echoed through the woods where the Louisiana Tigers awaited the order to advance. With the success of Hilary Jones' prolonged gunnery in effectively suppressing the enemy guns, Harry Hays believed he had a favorable opportunity. Without waiting for confirmation from General Early, shortly after 6:30 p.m., he ordered the advance and his Tigers surged down the heavily wooded slope. Private Thomas Benton Reed of the 9th Louisiana recorded, "On we went, but when we got to the bottom of the hill our line was all broken, so we had to halt and form again. Then we moved, until we had gone half way, I suppose, when I heard Gen. Harry T. Hayes [sic] give the command: 'Hoist those colors in the Ninth!'"[70]

Clearing the canopy of trees at the eastern base of Apple Pie Ridge and emerging in the fading sunlight, Hays advanced his Louisiana brigade through three hundred yards of corn and wheat fields. Soldiers jumped over wooden fences and pushed their way forward. Union sharpshooters opened fire with Henry rifles, dropping a few Rebels. In the distance, Private Sam Buck of the 13th Virginia recorded, "After a heavy fire of half an hour, I saw coming out of the wood a half mile to my right, our old division moving in a line of battle by brigade front and marching as if on parade. Steel and shot tore through their ranks, but still they pressed on and on until within a short distance of the Fort."[71]

William Monaghan's 6th Louisiana approached a small stone house on the Samuel Yonley farm. Two stunned sisters, Alma and Lizzie, watched as Confederates streamed by "with banners flying and our own and the enemy's shells screaming over." Early's flanking movement had caught them, as well as Milroy's Federals, by total surprise. The younger sibling, Lizzie, later gushed, "The storming of those breastworks was the grandest sight my eyes ever beheld."[72]

At Ewell's headquarters near the Millwood Pike, Maryland cavalryman Harry Gilmor and others "crowded on the heights to see Early's charge. We could hear his skirmishers keeping up a continual rapid fire." The Tigers quickly pushed ahead, while Jones' artillery shells shrieked overhead toward the Federal entrenchments. Ewell, his staff, and Gilmor strained to see through the smoke that now obscured the area. "We could hear . . . occasionally a volley and a yell, as he charged some advanced position; and we could tell, by the coming in of the blue-coats that he was getting the advantage. Every piece seemed to be turned on him; but amid the thunders of thirty to forty guns, there broke on our expectant ears heavy volleys of musketry and the terrible, long, shrill cry of the two [lines] of the Louisiana Tigers." Further to the northeast, Lieutenant Randolph McKim of Johnson's Division noted, "The rebel yell of Early's men, as they charged position after position, could plainly be heard over the din of battle."[73]

Reaching the western base of Flint Ridge, Hays' Brigade began the ascent as Jones' artillery stopped firing to avoid hitting the Confederate infantry. Union Private Barnhart related, "Then they ceased firing off the pine mountain, and our officers gave us orders to fix bayonets and [get] our guns loaded, and watch over the fields in front of us. We would see the confederate infantry come out of the brush, out of a ravine." Colonel Keifer saw "at least five Regiments, in deep column of attack." He later claimed the Confederates' advance regiment pushed forward "carrying the United States colors." He added, "The enemy was able to come up under cover, to within one hundred yards of the works."[74]

Private Tom Reed described the *abatis* that slowed the front line. "On we went and when we were within about one hundred yards of the enemy's breastworks we came to a kind of stockade. This was made of trees fallen or dragged, with the tops of them outward, forming the breastworks, and the small ends of the limbs were cut sharp. Now, we had to pass through this mass of stuff before getting to the rifle pits, but this did not stop us."[75]

When Hays' front line reached the edge of the *abatis*, Keifer's nearly five hundred defenders immediately arose from behind their works. An expectant Barnhart added, "We would get to shoot only one shot, then use our bayonets and club with our guns." The inexperienced Buckeyes were outgunned and outnumbered but, for a brief instant, they held their own against their veteran enemy. Private Barnhart continued, "They came in desperate order. We gave them a volley low down in their legs. They dropped out of ranks. We made large gaps in their lines, but they did not stop, for they closed the gaps shoulder to shoulder." Unlike Barnhart and his inexperienced Ohio comrades, "They had been in such scraps before."[76]

Keifer later reported, with more optimism than fact, "The Infantry and Artillery opened fire on him with fearful effect, mowing down his advance Regiment almost to a man. My sharpshooters shot down the officers on horseback, but only for a few moments could we check the enemy's advancing column. . . . Many Confederate officers and men were seen to fall, and the head of the column wavered."[77]

The artillery rounds and the Buckeyes' deliberate low volley claimed a few oncoming Tigers, including several in the 6th Louisiana. A Minié ball slammed into Captain George Ring's left ankle, disabling him for eight months. Corporal James G. Barnett of the 9th Louisiana slumped to the ground. The thirty-two-year-old farmer from Livingston Parish would later be carried to the rear, where his leg was amputated. Captain John J. Rivera was shot in the side during the movement up the slope. As he neared the *abatis*, Tom Reed of Company A "looked and saw a man raising our flag. A shell had burst near and a piece of it had struck our flag-bearer, James Stewart, on the head and killed him instantly."[78]

After finally clearing the *abatis*, Hays gave the order to charge, and the Tigers "yelling like fiends" surged forward with such speed and determination that the Yankees only had time to fire off a few weak volleys that did little to stop the Confederates' momentum. Private Barnhart wrote, "They gave us a volley, then came onto us with bayonets and a yell like Indians." Captain Samuel Chisholm of the 5th Louisiana recalled that the Tigers did not fire "until within twenty steps of the breastworks." A few Buckeyes turned and sprinted for the rear as the wave of Louisianans closed.

From the heights south of town, Harry Gilmor and the corps command staff could discern the crest of Flint Ridge, despite thick clouds of smoke. He noted, "The enemy stood firm for a while, and Old Ewell was jumping about on his crutches, with the utmost difficulty in keeping the perpendicular. At last the Federals began to give way, and pretty soon, the Louisianans, with their battle-flag, appeared on the crests charging the redoubts." From an observation post high up on the Main Fort's flagpole, Robert Milroy watched the waves of Rebels enter his outer defenses. Perhaps to ease the sting of watching his men crumble so readily, he later claimed at least ten thousand men attacked Keifer's position, and that his officers counted seventeen Rebel colors in the main assault.[79]

Another interested observer was famed Confederate spy Belle Boyd. She and a wounded Rebel officer watched the combat from a hill near the Martinsburg Road. Several civilians, "for the most part mounted on emaciated horses and mules" not confiscated by Milroy's soldiers, soon joined the duo. The anxious spectators scattered when Union artillery suddenly lobbed a "hissing and shrieking" shell their way.[80]

Under the distant gaze of the fascinated onlookers, Hays' Tigers arrived at the West Fort. Four or five rounds of canister blasted out from Lieutenant Randolph's two remaining operational 3-inch rifles, but they "did not appear to have a particle of effect." With some difficulty, Louisianans scrambled across the ditches and up the steep dirt embankments. Tom Reed and the front line arrived at the parapets. "The Major of the 7th Louisiana regiment [J. Moore Wilson] was the first man to mount the works, and I was just behind him. He shouted out: 'Come on boys!' I shouted to him, 'I am here,' and mounted the breastworks."[81]

Harry Hays would later cite the "conspicuous gallantry" of Lieutenant John Orr, the Canadian-born adjutant of the 6th Louisiana, who was among the first Tigers to mount the enemy redoubt. As the twenty-three-year-old Orr crested the wall, he spotted a three-man Union color guard carrying off their banner. He leaped down, slashed the enemy wildly with his sword, and grabbed the flagpole. He received a severe bayonet wound in his side from one of the desperate defenders, who retreated with their colors. Orr would live, but he was out of action. The rest of Hays' front line spread across the position, and several more Ohioans began to fall back.[82]

The fight inside the fort was brief, violent, and at times, hand to hand. Private Michael Gleason of the 6th Louisiana died shortly after leaping from the parapet. Lorenzo Barnhart of the 110th Ohio Volunteer Infantry greatly exaggerated the Rebels' strength. "We used our gun stocks to [club] them [in] the front and to the rear. We clubbed them a while but to no use. Oh, we hurt some of them, but what could 80 soldiers do to 70 or 80 thousand." The two lines of screaming Confederates may have seemed endless to the young

Ohioan in his first battle. He added, "They overcrowded us, but we made it hot for them for a moment. [We] were clubbing with the butts of guns, and thrusting the bayonet at and through each other. For a moment it looked like H——l."[83]

As the Tigers swarmed through the lunette and its flanking entrenchments, they seized Lieutenant Paris Horney and sent him to the rear. One Louisiana infantryman badly wounded Sergeant Mathias McAnally by clubbing him in the head with a musket. Nearby, a Confederate major (possibly William H. Manning of the 6th Louisiana) demanded that Corporal John Rhoades surrender, but the defiant Buckeye bayoneted him. As Rhoades was withdrawing the bayonet from the fallen Rebel, he noticed another southerner swinging a rifle at him. He partially deflected the blow but suffered a severe gash in his scalp and fell to the ground. Dazed and bleeding, Rhoades slowly rose just as another Confederate took aim at him. However, a Rebel officer intervened and spared his life, although Rhoades became a prisoner of war.[84]

Within minutes of ordering the charge, Harry Hays watched as brightly colored Louisiana battle flags fluttered above the enemy fortifications. Yankees streamed out the open reverse side, throwing away accoutrements and abandoning their supplies, the guns, and battery wagons. After having three horses shot from under him, Battery L's Wallace Randolph fell with a severe wound and Second Lieutenant Edmund D. Spooner assumed command. From the now silent artillery line on Apple Pie Ridge, Confederate officer Robert Stiles, volunteering in the Charlottesville Artillery, watched the Tigers' bold charge and its aftermath. He later succinctly wrote, "The surprise was complete, the distance not great, and the effect overwhelming."[85]

Keifer realized his position was hopeless, and the West Fort would soon fall: "With terrible loss, he [Hays] effected an entrance into the works near the center of my Regiment, my men fighting him until he outnumbered us inside the works." He complained, "The trenches and breastworks were of such character as to afford no obstructions to the entrance of the enemy." Several years later, he reflected, "There was stubborn fighting over the low breastworks, and some fighting inside of them, but not until our exposed flanks were attacked did I order a retreat."[86]

The retreat quickly became a rout. Tom Reed of the 9th Louisiana gleefully commented, "The Yankees did not know that we were on them until they saw us standing over them. Then you ought to have seen those fellows run, and as they ran down the hill we poured it into them, but they soon scampered away and we were in possession of the breastworks." Captain Samuel Chisholm of the 5th Louisiana wrote, "But few of them dared to cross bayonets with us, the balance outrunning quarterhorses. All those who stood their ground were soon rolling in their own blood and many who ran were shot in the back." One 18th Connecticut soldier near Fort Milroy claimed he saw the Confederates "club the brains out of our men after they surrendered."[87]

Ohio Private Barnhart perhaps best summarized the sudden flight: "What could Co. B do to them, I thought? [We could] all get killed if we do not surrender. We did not surrender, we just quit and every man for himself. I seen my chance to get in a ravine close by and follow it. I did and then had to cross a level piece of ground to get our last resort and Fort [Milroy]. While crossing this, I was in plain view of them. They seen me get away. They sent the shot after me, but I would not halt. I went ahead towards the Fort with their bullets plowing the ground around my feet. I looked to be hit any moment, but I ran the Gauntlet all safe. My clothes were pierced with bullets, but my skin was not cut. I did not want to serve my time in a confederate prison." Barnhart eventually reached the safety of the protective guns of Fort Milroy and flung himself down on the ground just outside its earthen walls. He huddled down until nightfall.[88]

As Hays' Tigers secured possession of the West Fort, the few remaining Yankees along the flanking earthworks streamed to the rear as fast as possible. Many could not escape. Captain Frederick H. Arckenoe of Company C of the 116th Ohio was coolly firing his pistol at the swirling Confederates when a Tiger took aim at the Prussian immigrant and put a Minié ball squarely through his forehead. Arckenoe pitched to the ground, not far from Sergeant Oswald Heck, also a victim of Louisiana gunfire. Two privates fell wounded and Louisianans captured a third of the company, including Second Lieutenant Levi Lupton and twenty-seven enlisted men. The remaining men, now commanded by First Lieutenant James Mann, reassembled in the Star Fort.[89]

Keifer's rout was complete, but he managed to save all except forty to fifty men, who remained behind as casualties or prisoners. Under "tremendous pressure," the remaining regular artillerymen were among the last to leave the lunette. New battery commander Lieutenant Edmund Spooner claimed, "Not till the enemy had planted their colors upon the works did my men leave their guns." He and eighteen artillerists escaped to Fort Milroy while the Tigers were busy bayoneting those cannoneers who stayed in place trying to work the two remaining guns. Spooner later praised Keifer's infantrymen for their support in the face of overwhelming odds, declaring, "Men never fought better than those men did."[90]

Hundreds of fleeing Federals scrambled eastward across the ravine-filled valley. From the old orchard on Apple Pie Ridge, Captain Dance's gunners resumed fire and leisurely tossed a few shells at the distant Yankees, adding to the panic and confusion. Dance then turned his attention to the Main Fort and began bombarding it, while keeping some of his guns in position in case of any Union attempt to retake the abandoned West Fort.[91]

From his hilltop headquarters, the one-legged Ewell was beside himself with joy at the stunning results of Early's labor. He was almost dancing on his crutches and struggling to contain his excitement. Through his field glasses, Ewell thought he spotted the familiar form of the mounted Virginia general. His eyes welling with tears of exuberance, he hollered, "Hurrah for the Louisiana boys! There's Early; I hope the old fellow won't be hurt." Just then, a spent Minié ball slammed into Ewell's chest, almost knocking him to the ground. His concerned staff rushed to his aid, as did his medical director, Dr. Hunter Maguire. A quick examination revealed an ugly black bruise, but no serious damage. The doctor ordered the general to lie down and rest. Maguire took away his crutches and chided Ewell, telling him he "had better let those sticks alone for now." However, before long, the anxious Ewell was "soon on his feet again, or rather, on the only one he had left."[92]

On the smoky ridge under the distant eyes of his corps commander, a businesslike Harry Hays turned his attention to the secondary works, a small redoubt sporting a pair of 3-inch ordnance rifles about 150 yards above and to the left of the West Fort. The Yankee infantrymen had scrambled out from Battery Number 6 when they saw their comrades abandoning the primary works. The artillerists labored to carry off their pieces, and Hays quickly spotted an opportunity to capture the guns. He quickly faced the 7th Louisiana to the left. A volley rang out, dropping several limber horses and halting the section's retreat. Colonel Penn's boys soon possessed the guns, limbers, and accompanying caissons.[93]

Meanwhile to the south, victorious Confederates busily plundered the abandoned West Fort. Lieutenant J. Warren Jackson of the 8th Louisiana boasted, "We drove the Yankees pell-mell from their breastworks, capturing but few of them as they were rather too nimble for us." Perhaps more importantly to the young officer, he found "plenty of Coffee ready made & warm, soup & light bread. We evidently took [them] by surprise as they were just preparing their supper." The easy victory astounded Captain Seymour, who commented, "Our loss . . . was far less than anticipated."[94]

As Rebels raided the hastily abandoned food, the massive lieutenant colonel of the 9th Louisiana, William Raine Peck, laboriously climbed over the earthworks and collapsed against the dirt wall. One of the largest men in the Army of Northern Virginia at more than three hundred pounds and six-and-a-half feet tall, the dismounted Peck had failed to keep up with his swift-charging regiment. The wealthy cotton planter had struggled up the slope of Flint Ridge and was now wheezing and gasping for breath. However, "Big Peck" drew a mix of cheers and laughter when he managed to yell, "Bully! Bully! By God! Bully! For the old Ninth, by God!"[95]

Hays congratulated his men on clearing out the Yankees, but he wished that his triumph had been more decisive. "Owing to the difficulty experienced by my men in getting over the ditches and embankments after the works had been reached, and the precipitate flight of the enemy, the loss of the enemy in killed, wounded, and prisoners was very small. We captured one battery of the Fifth U.S. Artillery (regulars), of six guns, with caissons and trappings complete, and all the horses belonging thereto, save a few which we found it necessary to shoot in order to secure some of the guns."[96]

He did not have time to dwell upon his victory, however, as Federals were massing in three columns to his front, apparently aiming to retake the abandoned Flint Ridge fortifications and simultaneously push through Gordon's line to retake Bower's Hill. General Milroy had ordered the rest of the 116th Ohio, preceded by the 87th Pennsylvania, to reinforce the West Fort prior to Keifer's hasty withdrawal, and other troops from Ely's and Elliott's brigades were also forming. Hays reformed his infantry and turned two of Randolph's captured guns on the closest advancing Yankees, operating the pieces with infantrymen from the 5th and 6th Louisiana. He claimed that these impromptu gunners fired off "a few well-directed rounds" that compelled the enemy columns to retire to the safety of Fort Milroy. Early commented, "The force which had been advancing upon Gordon in the direction of Bower's Hill had retired precipitately, and the enemy's whole force seemed to be in great commotion."

Among the Federal columns was the 18th Connecticut, another regiment unused to combat. A thankful Private Charles Lynch wrote in his diary, "It was a hot place. The roaring of the big guns, explosion of shells, rattling of musketry, was something fearful. The charging of both sides was hot work. We drove the enemy back and they also forced our lines back. Darkness put an end to the carnage and I had passed through the battle unharmed. . . . The casualties were great as I could not help seeing. It gave me an opportunity to see what a horrible thing war really was."[97]

Wanting to finish off the Yankees with one last concerted push, Jubal Early consolidated his line on Flint Ridge and brought up his reserves. James Carrington's eight guns limbered and laboriously moved forward across the uneven valley. A couple of pieces careened around the West Fort earthworks, where they unlimbered in its open rear. The captain positioned the rest of his cannon in a level field on either flank and initiated an artillery duel with the remaining Federal-held forts. New York cavalryman William Beach watched as "some pieces of [enemy] artillery came into the works, wheeling and unlimbering in gallant style. The guns in the Star Fort greeted them with shell after shell planted among them with astonishing precision, and each one as it burst in the ranks of the enemy was followed by exulting cheers from the Union troops in the larger forts."[98]

Robert Stiles was acting as the Number 6 crewman on one of Carrington's guns, passing ammunition from the limbers to the loader. As enemy shells burst overhead, the Presbyterian preacher's son instinctively slammed down the lid of the ammunition chest to prevent hot fragments from prematurely detonating the lethal ordnance. He and other Confederate artillerists were at a loss to explain why the initial Federal counterbattery fire was so uncommonly accurate, until someone noticed a practice target marker standing in between two of their guns. It provided a perfect visual guide for the distant Union gunners, who presumably had practiced for such an occasion and predetermined how much to cut the fuses. The crews quickly moved the guns several dozen yards downhill, where Milroy's rounds began passing harmlessly overhead.

However, just before dark, a bursting shell mortally wounded one of Jones' battery commanders, Captain Charles Thompson of the Louisiana Guard Artillery, tearing off his left arm near the shoulder. He did not scream but instead calmly turned his horse toward his unsuspecting men so they would not see the magnitude of his massive injury. Calling out, "Keep it up boys! I'll be back in a moment," he slowly headed down the western slope toward the rear lines. However, before he had even reached the limbers behind his line of guns, he reeled in the saddle from shock and loss of blood. Without another word, Thompson pitched from his horse to the ground, lifeless.[99]

Inside the Star Fort, Lieutenant Beach witnessed the incident, recalling later, "A gallant officer on a spirited horse came riding out in front of the works that had been taken. A shell from one of Alexander's guns seemed to strike directly beneath the horse, bursting and raising a cloud of smoke and dust that enveloped the horse and the rider. Loud and long were the cheers that again broke from the Union men."[100]

While the guns thundered, Smith's Virginians, along with part of Avery's Brigade, arrived to support Hays. Jubal Early ordered Hilary Jones to move Captain Dance's twelve guns from Folk's orchard to Flint Ridge, but nightfall prevented further gains. Early galloped up to congratulate Hays, realizing the infantry fighting was over for the day. He apprehended, "The enemy's force occupying the works, and around them, was quite large, and deep and rugged ravines interposed between us and the two occupied works, which rendered an assault upon them from that direction very difficult." Seizing Fort Milroy and the Star Fort required careful coordination with the rest of Ewell's troops, something not readily accomplished until morning.[101]

Despite the annoying artillery bursts, Early's men began policing Flint Ridge. Armed guards escorted sullen prisoners to designated holding areas in the rear. Patrols scoured the captured fortifications, collecting weapons, accoutrements, supplies, and other equipment hastily abandoned by fleeing Federals. Many Tigers along Flint Ridge ate well, feasting on confiscated beef and other Yankee foodstuffs. Lieutenant Charlie Pierce of the 7th Louisiana found a fine sword, which he proudly carried for the rest of the campaign.[102]

Private Thomas Reed, the butcher-knife-wielding backwoodsman, decided to "look around a little, so off I went down the hill and found some [Union] caissons, which had some nice horses hitched to them. So I plundered through them, and found some clean underwear, two dry blankets that looked clean, and some stationery." He ascended the slope back to his regiment and was telling his comrades about the horses when Lieutenant Colonel Peck interrupted and offered him one hundred dollars if he would go back and get him one of the prized horses. Reed slipped back into the valley, where he "worked and tugged" to loosen a horse from its harness.

An enemy artillery round burst nearby, sending fragments whizzing by the Alabama native. He scrambled for safety but soon returned for another go at the horse. Yet another shell burst nearby, and Reed concluded he was its target. He raced back up the hillside to shelter. Finding "Big Peck," he related his adventure. The huge officer ruefully responded, "Well, you had better let the horses alone." Reed shared his newly acquired blankets with his friend Jack Dawkins, as he had predicted they would, that morning when they left their soaked ones hanging on the fence rail.[103]

The artillery dueled angrily into the night, their flashes producing "a lurid, weird effect." At one point, Federal chain-shot tore a portion of the roof from the Fahnestock house. In Front Royal, diarist Lucy Buck recorded, "The cannonade still continues without interruption." Winchester resident Cornelia Peake McDonald penned, "This was the time the firing was heaviest, and the terror so great." The prolonged exchange finally ceased about 10:00 p.m.[104]

Jubal Early planned to renew the bombardment in the morning, in conjunction with a general assault on the remaining Federal forts. He ordered John Gordon to advance northward and storm the main fort at daylight, with the rest of his division supporting the attack from the west. The astounded Georgian believed this to be a mistake, as it would be more prudent to bypass Milroy, cut his supply lines, and force him to fight in the open. He spent a sleepless night planning the assault and contemplating what he believed was his impending death.[105]

While Gordon brooded, other Confederates congratulated one another on Harry Hays' successful attack and the rich bounty of captured supplies and equipment. Jones' artillerists discovered a cache of artillery swords and distributed them to the battalion's sergeants. Lieutenant J. Warren Jackson of the 8th Louisiana gushed, "It was the best managed affair Hayes [sic] ever had anything to do with." Dick Ewell was so pleased with the ferocity and valor of the Tigers' attack on the West Fort that he ordered Flint Ridge redesignated as "Louisiana Heights" on all military maps of the area. He renamed Fort Milroy as "Fort Jackson" in honor of the fallen commander, and the West Fort became "Redoubt Hays."[106]

However, not all was joy in the ranks of the First Louisiana Brigade. Hays reported his losses as two officers and ten men killed, and eight officers and fifty-nine men wounded. The two days of sharp fighting near Winchester cost the Tigers fourteen dead, seventy-eight wounded, and three missing in action. The 6th Louisiana, which bore the brunt of the enemy fire from the earthworks and rifle pits, lost forty-three men. Fourteen more casualties were from the 9th Regiment. Still, from a military viewpoint, it was a relatively small price to pay to crush the Federal outer defenses and threaten the town and its nexus of roads.[107]

The two slain Louisiana officers were Captain Albert Dejean Jr. of the 8th Louisiana and Second Lieutenant Vitrivius P. Terry of the 7th. Terry's death was particularly bitter because several relatives also served in that regiment. A brother, Sergeant Orrin F. Terry, was convalescing in a Richmond hospital from a severe wound suffered at Second Fredericksburg. In the same fight, their older brother Thomas, the regiment's major, had been captured and subsequently incarcerated in Washington's Old Capitol Prison. After his parole, he had only recently rejoined the regiment. Yet another brother, Julius, was a private.[108]

Among Hays' dead enlisted men was twenty-one-year-old Private Julius D. Stall, a German-born shoemaker from Mount Lebanon who enlisted in 1861 in the 9th Louisiana. He had survived two prolonged bouts with illness, returning to active duty in April. His luck ran out in the surge toward the West Fort. Another victim was twenty-nine-year-old Irish-born Corporal Robert Cahill of the 6th Louisiana, who was struggling for life after a mortal wound. The antebellum New Orleans dance instructor died six days later. Ironically, he had been wounded in his right arm during the First Battle of Winchester in May 1862.[109]

Squads collected the dead from both armies, burying them hastily in shallow graves. More than a year later, surviving members of the 116th Ohio Volunteer Infantry would return to the area before the Third Battle of Winchester (or Opequon) and discover that their dead had been buried poorly. They dug up the decaying skeletons, took them to "a nice spot and buried them decently."[110]

Hays' wounded were taken to temporary field hospitals, including the Fahnestock house, where injured Louisianans mingled with wounded Yankees under the care of Mary Fahnestock. The surgeon of the 6th Louisiana, twenty-four-year-old Kentucky-raised Dr. Charles H. Todd, treated many of his regiment's wounded at Samuel and Maria Yonley's small stone farmhouse. Their two oldest girls, Alma and Lizzie, actively and generously ministered to their unexpected houseguests. Years later, Captain John J. Rivera recalled their unselfish kindness. "[Yonley's] devoted daughters, notwithstanding the bursting shells and the parental admonition to remain in a place of comparative safety, went about the stricken soldiers and ministered to their needs in every practical way. That entire night, they were zealous in their attentions, and for several weeks they kindly nursed several [men], the severity of whose wounds did not permit removal." Alma held his hand while the surgeon painfully probed his side for a bullet. Rivera would never forget "the cool serenity of her courage as he looked into her blue eyes beaming with sympathy and encouragement, while she unflinchingly aided the surgeon in his search. She was as tender and kind to the wounded in her care as she was brave under fire."[111]

Richard Ewell, correctly guessing Milroy would retreat during the night, ordered Johnson's Division to prevent the Yankees' escape by cutting the Charlestown Road. About 9:00 p.m., Johnson (with Steuart's and Williams' brigades and eight guns) marched north to the Berryville Pike and then west to Jordan Springs Road, where he turned toward Stephenson's Depot. About midnight, the Stonewall Brigade disengaged and joined the rear of the column, leaving Brigadier General John M. Jones' brigade astride the Berryville Pike east of Winchester.[112]

Milroy considered abandoning his entrenchments in a belated attempt to reach Harper's Ferry and called a council of war to discuss options. He and his subordinates unanimously decided to evacuate Winchester and, if necessary, cut their way through to Harper's Ferry in the moonless night. Soldiers and teamsters disabled the remaining supply wagons as time allowed, and all artillery pieces were spiked and their wooden carriages destroyed. Draft horses were unharnessed and led away as quietly as possible.

Between 1:00 and 2:00 a.m., the Union soldiers left their works so quietly that Early's Confederates on Flint Ridge did not know they were gone until morning. Cavalryman William Beach recalled, "It was a weird procession, passing in silence, without a spoken word, through the midnight darkness." Within an hour, Milroy's column massed in the low ground between the Star Fort and Fort Milroy and then moved undetected up the Valley Pike and the Winchester and Potomac Railroad. They marched toward the Charlestown crossroads, just south of Stephenson's Depot, and abandoned Winchester. Milroy left two thousand wounded Union soldiers in the town's sprawling military hospital to the mercy of the Confederates. Warehouses of supplies and foodstuffs were now unguarded, as were the remaining supply wagons.[113]

During the "intensely dark" night, Edward Johnson's division completed its flanking march and, before daylight on the fifteenth, cut off Milroy's line of retreat just north of Winchester at Stephenson's Depot. Stymied in his desperate effort to reach Harper's Ferry, Milroy escaped, but he lost more than 3,000 soldiers, 24 pieces of artillery, 300 loaded supply wagons, and 200,000 rounds of small-arms ammunition. The Hoosier general would face a formal court of inquiry in August to investigate his actions.[114]

As morning dawned, Jubal Early was unaware of the destruction of Milroy's force. Scouts reported the enemy had evacuated Winchester, leaving the road open to advance on Martinsburg, next in the line of Federal garrisons. He ordered Gordon to advance on the main fort. The Georgians to their surprise found the imposing fortifications unoccupied. They hauled down the large garrison flag, which Milroy had left behind. As Confederates filed into Winchester about 5:00 a.m., they were received with "the most rapturous expressions of delight" from many residents, who had "suffered terribly from the tyrannical acts of the infamous Milroy." Ewell would later send the captured flag to Richmond, escorted by some of Gordon's and Hays' infantrymen.[115]

Excited pro-secession citizens thronged the streets as Ewell's gleeful troops "liberated" Winchester. Laura Lee later wrote, "The people were perfectly wild with delight and excitement and the troops no less so. . . . Oh, this joyous day!" Women baked bread and passed out food and refreshments to the Confederates, and an atmosphere of gaiety soon filled the town. Emotional crowds laughed, sang patriotic songs, cheered the passing troops, and hurrahed the Confederacy. In turn, soldiers gave rousing cheers for the ladies of Winchester. A band paused in front of the Taylor Hotel to play *Dixie* and *The Bonnie Blue Flag*.[116]

For the pro-Union residents of the bitterly divided town, the day brought despair, gloom, and uncertainty. Julia Chase lamented, "And now we are in Dixie. Oh, what a sad, sad day this has been to us." Outside of town, Gordon's Brigade discovered several family members of Federal officers huddled together in a grove. Georgia infantryman Isaac Bradwell commented, "All the bright colors of the rainbow, all the finery displayed in the most fashionable shops of a city seemed assembled there in that strip of woods." Confederates took forty-seven women and children into custody around Winchester and escorted them to Richmond. Officials there freed the family members and arranged for their transportation to Annapolis.[117]

The stunning victory elated the South and elevated Ewell to celebrity. A Richmond newspaper soon crowed, "It is a glorious affair, however, and will be considered still more glorious if Milroy can be captured and hung. That scoundrel has been earning his portion of the gallows for six months, and it is most desirable that he should be paid." Confederate artillerist Robert Stiles later gushed, "This battle of Winchester ... was one of the most perfect pieces of work the Army of Northern Virginia ever did. .... I may add that the execution of the plan was committed largely to Old Jube, who certainly wrought it out and fought it out beautifully."[118]

**On to the Potomac!**

Discovering a large number of fully loaded Union supply wagons abandoned just outside of Winchester, Early detailed Colonel James B. Terrill's 13th Virginia of Smith's Brigade to guard them, as well as a considerable amount of warehoused supplies found in the town. He sent Gordon's Brigade ahead on the Martinsburg Road. Before resuming the march, hundreds of men took time to don new shoes and socks and exchange their worn-out ragged pants for new U.S. Army light blue trousers. Discarded equipment, weapons, hats, coats, blankets, and accoutrements littered the streets and roads, thrown away by Federal soldiers in their haste to escape. Quite a few Tigers now sported black leather knapsacks, most with stenciled Union regimental designations.[119]

Confederates replaced worn-out equipment from the Federal storehouses and stuffed their haversacks with food intended for Milroy's men. Sergeant Edmond Stephens of the 9th Louisiana wrote his parents, "Such plundering of the sutler wagons and fancy notions of the Yankees. Our soldiers were just turned loose & told to go [at] it." He scooped up "nice clothing," sugar, coffee, rice, and "everything else I wanted," including "Yankee paper, pens, ink & envelopes." He used some of his booty to write home.[120]

Once Avery's Brigade arrived and the supply and ammunition wagons were replenished, Early formed most of his division into column and headed northeasterly toward Stephenson's Depot. He left behind his sick and wounded, and those men too exhausted to continue. Among them was Private J. J. Anderson of the 9th Louisiana. Wounded in the fighting at Winchester, his comrades would never see him again. He later died from his injuries and was buried in the town's Stonewall Cemetery.[121]

One of Hays' regimental commanders would not make the subsequent trip to the Potomac River. Colonel William Monaghan of the 6th Louisiana had contracted an illness that rendered him unable to continue his duties, and he was left behind in Winchester. On the march northward, the star-crossed Lieutenant Colonel Joseph Hanlon, a recently exchanged prisoner of war, hustled to catch up with the regiment and assume command. The thirty-two-year-old Irish-born New Orleans newspaperman had joined the regiment at its inception as the first lieutenant of Company A, which had only three native-born Americans on its initial muster rolls. Hanlon had been shot through the body at Winchester in May 1862 and sent home. He never fully recovered (eventually dying after the war from lingering effects of his injuries), and it was nine months after his injury before he was fit to return to the field. However, with the chain of promotions within the regiment as field officers were incapacitated or killed, Hanlon was raised to major and then lieutenant colonel. He returned to active duty on May 3, 1863, but became a prisoner the next day near Fredericksburg. Gettysburg would be his first test in command of the regiment.[122]

After marching five or six miles, word reached Jubal Early that Johnson had captured the majority of Milroy's force, although the Federal commander and a small fraction of his command had escaped by mounting mules and horses taken from the wagons and artillery, much of which had been abandoned. Early called off any further pursuit, realizing that his foot soldiers could not catch the fleeing Yankees. Lieutenant Colonel Herbert's Maryland cavalry captured a few more straggling Federals, but Milroy's band was too scattered for any significant catches. The 9th Louisiana did seize Major Harry White of the 67th Pennsylvania. As he was escorted through enemy lines back to Winchester, White noted that the Confederates were "well equipped and supplied, confident of victory . . . and [I] heard all around, 'We're going on to Washington.'" After sending the prisoners to the rear, the Tigers bivouacked on a "very hot day" near Stephenson's Depot at Five-Mile Spring. Private Reed of the 9th Louisiana wrote in his diary, "This was as fine a spring and as good water as I ever saw. Here I washed and put on my clean clothes."[123]

In the meantime, Ewell sent Jubal Early back into Winchester to arrange for storing the captured supplies and processing the hordes of captured Yankees. Early dispatched Avery's 54th North Carolina and Smith's 58th Virginia to guard them. A captured colonel tickled Early when he declared the Rebels had lied about Stonewall Jackson being dead; "there was no officer in either army that could have executed that [hidden flanking] movement but 'Old Jack.'" After filling out the appropriate paperwork, Early sent the sullen Federals up the valley via Staunton and eventually to Richmond and prison.[124]

The Tigers remained in camp on the sixteenth, and left at two o'clock the next afternoon for a "very oppressive march" into West Virginia, as the temperature climbed. Ewell took with him Johnson's Division, Hays' Louisiana Tigers, Gordon's Georgians, and three regiments of Smith's Virginians. The orders to march had come suddenly and unexpectedly. The 8th Louisiana's Lieutenant Jackson had just settled down to read a letter from his younger brother Stark, still recuperating in Richmond from wounds suffered at Bristoe Station the previous August. He was "quite beside myself with joy" when he received the epistle, but for now, Jackson pocketed it and prepared to resume the northward trek. The Tigers marched nine miles unmolested toward Charlestown, where they camped for the night a few miles west of Harper's Ferry and its Union garrison. Captain Seymour remarked that it was a "dull, uneventful day," quite a change from the excitement of the previous few days.[125]

On the 18th, Hays' Brigade marched at daylight and camped in the early afternoon within four miles of Shepherdstown and the Potomac River. Torrents of rain fell that evening, swelling the river even higher and precluding safe passage across Boteler's Ford into Maryland, the only remaining local crossing since the highway bridge was burned earlier in the war. That same day, his task finished in Winchester, Jubal Early prepared to depart. He left Terrill's 13th Virginia in Winchester to guard the supplies and then followed Ewell northward to the river, leading the remainder of Avery's Brigade, Hilary Jones' guns, and the supply trains still guarded by Gordon's 61st Georgia. After pausing in Martinsburg to refill the wagons with captured Yankee supplies, he arrived in Shepherdstown the next day and reunited his division.[126]

For the next few days, the Confederates relaxed in their camps while waiting for the river to recede. Heavy rains on the 20th and 21st further delayed the planned crossing. Early's field return in camp on June 20 indicated he had 487 officers and 5,124 men still present for duty, even after leaving the three regiments behind in Winchester and permanently detaching Major Rufus H. Wharton's 1st North Carolina Battalion from Avery's Brigade to serve as provost guards for Ewell's Corps. Hays' Brigade that night numbered 119 officers and 1,281 enlisted men.[127]

Rebels foraged across a wide swath of farms for additional supplies and reflected on the campaign to date, which one soldier deemed a "summer picnic excursion." In the 8th Louisiana, Charles Lutz, the light-skinned black man, celebrated his twenty-first birthday on June 20. There is no record of whether supplies of local whiskey were involved, but Company F was known as a hard-drinking bunch. Captain Seymour took tea at the house of the nephew of the former governor of Georgia, William Schley. Ironically, Seymour's grandfather had wounded the politician years earlier in a duel. The First Louisiana Brigade's inspector general, Captain John New, had taken ill on the march, so Seymour temporarily assumed that role, in addition to his position as Hays' adjutant.[128]

With Milroy out of the way, the lower Shenandoah Valley now teemed with long columns of Confederates moving north to the Potomac. Lieutenant General James Longstreet's First Corps had arrived in the valley, followed by A. P. Hill's troops. Ewell's Second Corps remained at Shepherdstown, still delayed in its passage into Maryland by high water that rendered Boteler's Ford unusable. Soldiers loaded supplies foraged in the region into wagons and shipped them back up the valley for future Confederate usage. Drovers herded large numbers of beef cattle to the rear, while the Tigers and their peers feasted heartily.

With Confederates "raiding like banditti through the country," Union Major General Darius Couch, commanding the newly formed Department of the Susquehanna, took action and began organizing thousands of volunteers to serve in the state's emergency militia. He worked with Pennsylvania's governor, Republican Andrew Curtin, to mobilize the militia of adjoining New York and New Jersey to defend Harrisburg in case of an attack. Couch ordered the construction of forts to protect the riverside town's vital bridges and rushed troops via train to Chambersburg. He enrolled Major Granville O. Haller of the 7th U.S. Infantry, who had commanded McClellan's headquarters guard at Antietam, as his special aide-de-camp and dispatched him to Gettysburg. Couch instructed the veteran Indian fighter to plan and organize the defense of Adams and York counties should the Rebels turn east toward Gettysburg, York, and the Columbia-Wrightsville Bridge, the only span over the Susquehanna River between Harrisburg and the Mason-Dixon Line.[129]

While the Federal government scrambled to contest the expected invasion, the Louisiana Tigers finally took time to celebrate their recent accomplishments. They had marched hard, behaved well, and struck a telling blow that doomed Winchester's defenders to defeat. An exuberant Richard Ewell heaped praise upon Hays' men, telling Father James Sheeran that, next to God, he was indebted to the Louisiana Brigade for the almost bloodless victory at Second Winchester.[130]

# 3 | Pennsylvania

### Into the Land of Milk and Honey

BELIEVING THAT MAJOR General Joseph Hooker's Federal army not yet crossed the Potomac, on Monday, June 22, Robert E. Lee informed Lieutenant General Richard Ewell, stationary in northern Maryland, "If you are ready to move, you may do so. . . . I think your best course will be toward the Susquehanna." Lee stipulated, "If Harrisburg comes within your means, capture it," and that the "progress and direction will of course depend upon the development of circumstances." Lee closed with a benediction, telling Ewell that he was "trusting in the guidance of a merciful God, and invoking His protection for your corps."[1]

With that providential blessing, Lee set in motion his plan to invade Pennsylvania. Ewell would split his Second Corps, advancing through Chambersburg to Harrisburg with the divisions of major generals Robert Rodes and Edward Johnson. Major General Jubal Early's division would form a separate expeditionary force operating on the right flank. Ewell reiterated Lee's recent General Orders Number 72, which instructed the army to respect private property while they appropriated supplies deep in enemy country, and he gave additional orders aimed at Pennsylvania's residents. "Citizens of the country, through which the army may pass, who are not in the military service, are admonished to abstain from all acts of hostility, upon the penalty of being dealt with in a summary manner. A ready acquiescence in the demands of the military authorities will serve greatly to lessen the rigors of war."[2]

Ewell ordered Early to cross the Potomac River and proceed along the western base of South Mountain, a somewhat risky move because thousands of Union troops were to their rear. Early reported, "Maryland Heights and Harper's Ferry were both strongly fortified, and were occupied by a heavy force of the enemy, which we left behind us, without making any effort to dislodge it, as it would have been attended with a loss disproportionate to any good to be obtained. Our movements through and from Sharpsburg were in full view of the enemy from the heights." To augment Early, Ewell detached a regiment from Jenkins' Brigade, the 17th Virginia Cavalry, under Colonel William H. French.[3]

During the cloudy and sultry morning, Early's Division marched through Shepherdstown, forded the receded Potomac River "most boisterously," and entered Maryland. Captain William J. Seymour wrote, "The [river] was very high and it was very amusing to see long lines of naked men fording it— their clothing and accoutrements slung to their guns and carried above their heads to keep them dry." Lieutenant J. Warren Jackson of the 8th Louisiana remarked, "[We] waded across; the water was waist deep & quite swift. I fell twice in crossing and of course got wet." A significant number of Harry Hays' men who first crossed this ford in September 1862 during the Maryland Campaign were no longer in his ranks for this second incursion into the North. New recruits filled their places, as well as scores of men who returned to active duty after straggling on the autumnal march that had culminated in the Battle of Antietam.

After dressing and reforming into column, Hays' Tigers crossed over the Chesapeake and Ohio Canal and ascended the heights beyond using an old dirt road before turning onto the turnpike to Sharpsburg. A couple of hours later, they quietly marched through the town, where several residences, outbuildings, churches, and fences still exhibited scars from the September 17 combat. Jackson spoke for many of his comrades, "I did not have time or I would have gone over the battlefield." The long column marched past the Sunken Road and crossed Antietam Creek on an old stone bridge known as the Middle Bridge.

After a midday break, the Tigers tramped through Keedysville, which Lieutenant Jackson described as "a nice little village." Late in the humid afternoon, they entered Boonsboro, a quiet town of less than a thousand people nestled near the foot of South Mountain. Residents silently watched the lengthy procession, but there was no damage to civilian property and the Louisianans did not break ranks to seize liquor from the roadside taverns. Perhaps unaccustomed to marching after their extended sojourn at Shepherdstown, several Tigers struggled to keep up with the column during the tiring march. Lieutenant Jackson commented, "I came near 'playing out' that day— my feet were very sore and I straggled a little."[4]

During the 1862 Maryland Campaign, several Confederate leaders expected Marylanders to flock to the army once it crossed the Potomac, rushing to join the liberating force. Their belief that the secessionist attitude that pervaded Baltimore and eastern Maryland was also prevalent in central Maryland proved to be false. Few now held out any hope that this second invasion would have a different result. No Marylanders came into Hays' ranks to join the rebellion. A soldier in Rodes' Division penned a note to a Richmond newspaper describing the prevailing attitude of the locals. "All the stores and every house was closed; and every window, and even curtain, was down, as if the sight of a rebel could not be tolerated. . . . generally the women looked very glum, as if hesitating between a laugh and a cry, and the men looked serious, and were as mute as blocks of granite. All betrayed and evidenced fear."⁵

Early's Division camped for the night three miles beyond town on the Hagerstown Pike near the tiny hamlet of Benevola. Campfires crackled with fence rails taken from nearby fields, and the Tigers wearily cooked rations and nursed their tired legs and sore feet. Foraging patrols fanned out through nearby farms to collect supplies, horses, and livestock. Federal scouts reported, "The rebel forces in and around Sharpsburg are exclusively employed collecting plunder in Pennsylvania and Maryland. A large train just passed the Shepherdstown Ford into Virginia, and also a large drove of beeves. This plunder is guarded from Shepherdstown by infantry, which, after a short absence, returns."⁶

On Tuesday, June 23, Early's Division arose at daybreak and assembled into march column in the morning rain. The soldiers left the Hagerstown Pike and headed northward through the Cumberland Valley on a series of rural roads parallel to South Mountain. Early split his force into two columns, with Gordon protecting the left flank using roads through Hagerstown and Leitersburg. To the east, Early's column passed through the small towns of Beaver Creek, Cavetown, and Smithsburg, where the Rebels finally found a "good meney [sic] Secesh" as they paraded through at midday. Cheering residents lined Smithsburg's streets and Confederate flags hung from several houses. Unknown to Jubal Early, two of the onlookers were busy counting his regiments and artillery and estimating his strength. They informed Hiram Winchester, a Frederick schoolmaster-turned-spy, who relayed the useful intelligence to Federal authorities.⁷

Encouraged by the unexpected public expression of Secessionist sympathies, the Southerners marched through Ringgold before reaching the Mason-Dixon Line in midafternoon. According to Lieutenant Jackson, the Louisiana Tigers crossed the line about 3:30 p.m. He added, "We shook the M[aryland] dust off our feet and marched into the union to the tune of 'Dixie.' The men were quite lively & joked [with] the citizens by telling them that we had eaten up the last mule we had, and had come over to get some beef & bacon." Other Tigers sarcastically jabbed they were "going back into the Union at last." A few soldiers, including Lieutenant William Guss of the 5th Louisiana, were returning to the state of their birth.[8]

While the jubilant Confederates celebrated their arrival into the North, hundreds of terrified refugees crowded the roads ahead of them. They included scattered groups of Milroy's defeated Pennsylvania soldiers who had escaped the Winchester debacle. Many of the Federals were unarmed, having flung aside weapons and knapsacks during the frantic effort to avoid capture. They crossed the Pennsylvania border and hustled through the streets of Waynesboro, a Franklin County village of some 1,200 people about two miles into the Keystone State. Desperate to return home, they pushed their way through throngs of badly frightened citizens without pausing to assist them, much to the consternation of townspeople who expected Union soldiers to show more backbone.[9]

Civilian scouts soon raced into Waynesboro, just four miles north of Smithsburg, with the alarming news that Rebel infantry was approaching. A few townsmen, fearing maltreatment or capture, hid themselves in attics, cellars, and other out-of-the-way places. Other residents locked their doors, bolted their shutters, and stayed indoors. Only a few hardy souls remained on the sidewalks to watch for the arrival of the lead elements of the feared Army of Northern Virginia.[10]

Waynesboro was decidedly more pro-Union than the secessionist-sympathizing Smithsburg, and most houses proudly waved the Stars and Stripes for travelers coming up from the South. Earlier in the war, the local newspaper had urged "every worthy citizen . . . to show his colors openly to his neighbors and to the world by displaying at his own dear home the glorious old flag of his country." However, by common consent, residents now took down all flags in town and tucked them away in dark corners and other hiding places in case the oncoming Confederates searched the houses. Albert Jenkins' Rebel cavalry had visited the town just a few days before, and residents' nerves were on edge as the enemy infantry approached.

Shortly before noon, Early's advance cavalry arrived, followed in the late afternoon by the head of the infantry column, marching four abreast into the town. Officers quickly dispatched pickets to guard the streets while the brigades tramped through town to their assigned campsites. One observer commented, "The soldiers were well armed, in perfect discipline and moved as one vast machine. Not many stragglers were to be seen. . . . The Southern soldiers were supposed to be uniformly clothed in grey, but not these soldiers who came through Waynesboro. Their dress consisted of every imaginable color and style. Some even wore blue clothes, which they had doubtless stripped from the Union dead in former battles. Most of them were of necessity ragged and filthy, showing that they were sadly in need of new outfits."[11]

As the dreaded Confederates arrived, a few leading townspeople fled for safer environs. Captain William Seymour wrote, "In Waynesboro, the people are strongly 'Union' in their proclivities, and their countenances and actions did not indicate much joy at our arrival." One local woman recalled, "Again the rumor that a large force of the enemy were crossing the Potomac echoed through our streets, and for a day and night we watched the usual mad rush to get beyond their reach. At last the rumor appeared to be well founded. On June 23, 1863, just before noon, we found our streets swarming with gray-clad men. That which we had so long anticipated with dread had happened, and the enemy was at our gates—indeed, he was within them."[12]

John Philips, cashier of the First National Bank, hastily gathered up the bank's money and valuables and placed them in his carriage. He headed east with his wife and son across the Monterey Pass to Fairfield in neighboring Adams County. There, he encountered Major Granville Haller, the commander of the Department of the Susquehanna's district of Adams and York counties. Phillips excitedly informed him that three thousand Rebels now occupied Waynesboro. Haller rode back to his headquarters in Gettysburg to telegraph the alarming news to his superior, Major General Darius Couch, in Harrisburg.

While Phillips was racing out of town with the bank's assets, Jubal Early arrived in the Center Square with his staff and escort. After establishing headquarters in the town hall, he placed Waynesboro under martial law. Soon, a bright Confederate flag fluttered atop the building, and military bands merrily played in the square. Early stripped Chief Burgess Jacob R. Welsh and the town council of their civil authority, transferring it to his provost marshal. He instructed former Union soldiers and local "stay-at-homes" to search the town for bread and meat for his Confederates. Women began baking bread for his hungry soldiers as Early established guards to ensure that his demands were enforced. A deputation of citizens informed him that thousands of men in that part of the state were opposed to the war. Many belonged to a secret society known as the Knights of the Golden Circle, "who had their distinctive signs, grips and countersigns; all of which were imparted to the General, who in turn, gave them to his officers."[13]

Early's trailing brigades, artillery, and supply wagons began arriving in the "unpretentious village." Staff officers directed them to their respective campsites near Little Antietam Creek, which provided a source of fresh water for the men and horses. Burgess Welsh's sixteen-year-old daughter Lida watched the Rebels as they marched through Waynesboro. "They filled the town with their gay music, prancing horses, glittering musical instruments, bayonets and other bright equipment, and their banners—such beautiful banners—made by mothers, wives, sisters, and sweethearts in the South. Ah, the tears and sighs, hopes and fears, stitched into their silken folds."

She added, "The men all seemed cheerful. They spoke kindly to the children on the porches; no doubt many of them were fathers of little ones. When a two-year-old boy, left alone for a short time, stood on a rocking-chair and rocked with all his tiny strength until the chair moved along to the very edge of the porch, a dozen men broke ranks and rushed to save the little fellow."[14]

Lieutenant J. Warren Jackson recalled, "We went on, passed through Waynesboro—a very pretty little town & camped near it. Some of the company went out foraging and got apple butter, light bread, chickens, milk." Miss Welsh watched the Tigers as they arrived. "A long-legged, long-necked Shanghai rooster that almost lived on the street fearlessly threaded his way between their feet, and occasionally a man would take him and carry him a few yards until a watchful officer ordered his release. That rooster paraded long after the last gun of the Confederacy was silenced." Part of the First Louisiana Brigade camped along South Church Street on the grounds of the Union Church. Tom Reed recounted that the 9th Louisiana "camped on a high hill, in a nice piece of woods."[15]

As the Charlottesville Artillery passed through one town, perhaps Waynesboro, a thirsty Major Robert Stiles rode up to the front fence of a prosperous-looking house. Spotting an elderly lady sitting on the porch, he asked if he could get a drink of water from her well. After quenching his thirst, the northern-raised officer sat on the porch and engaged in a "friendly and pleasant conversation" with her. Learning he had a sister in New Haven, Connecticut, the woman gladly consented to mail a letter for him. She had a table, pen, ink, paper, and stamps brought out to the porch. As Stiles finished penning his epistle, his hostess's daughter came to the door, exclaiming that her little son was missing. Searching the house, the two ladies soon emerged onto the front porch, dragging a pale and violently trembling five- or six-year-old boy. He had been hiding between a mattress and feather bed in an upstairs bedroom, terrified of the bloodcurdling stories he had overheard about the Rebels' cruelty and ferocity.

Soon, the genial Stiles made friends with the child, who was sitting on his lap when the frantic mother realized that she had not seen her elder son for some time. Suddenly a "bright boy of ten or eleven summers" burst into the gate, breathless with excitement and wonderment, and gasped out, "Mother, mother! May I go to camp with the rebels? They are the nicest men I ever saw in my life. They are going to camp right out here in the woods, and they are going to have a dance, too!"

The Louisiana Tigers were passing by the house at the time, and the mother was taken aback by her older son's new companion, "a bowing, smiling, grimacing, shoulder-shrugging Frenchman, who promised, in rather broken English, that he would take the best possible care of him." The mother hesitated, but, trusting Stiles by now, she decided to allow her son to accompany the friendly Creole to the dance. The youth returned home with a happier attitude toward the Tigers, who had greatly entertained him with their song and dance.[16]

Curious townspeople ventured cautiously from their homes to see the Confederates. Early's provost marshal informed Chief Burgess Welsh the Confederate troops were "under complete control," and residents should not fear any depredation, as General Early had given strict orders that no people or private property were to be molested, and no soldier could enter the citizens' houses. "But," he added, "we may be repulsed, and if we have to retreat we may not have complete control. Tell your people, in that case, for their own safety, not to taunt or offer our troops any insult. I advice you also to have all intoxicating liquors put out of reach."[17]

The "complete control" was not absolute. Some Confederates accosted twenty-seven-year-old Josiah F. Kurtz on the steps of the National Hotel and demanded that the prosperous farmer furnish the names and addresses of

Waynesboro's wealthiest citizens. When he stubbornly refused to comply with the directive, an officer angrily drew a sword and attacked Kurtz, leaving a severe gash in his hand. Kurtz hastily left town and stayed with relatives in his native Somerset, a hundred miles away, until the invasion was over.[18]

Early ordered the bars closed and all whiskey supplies destroyed. Several distillers in Washington and Quincy townships attempted to hide barrels of whiskey in out-of-the-way places and, in some cases, resorted to digging pits to bury their inventory. Confederate officers discovered most of the hidden stash and smashed in the barrelheads. However, several Louisiana Tigers found "quantities of liquor," and their commanders had trouble keeping them in the ranks. Several miscreants robbed citizens of clothing, money, watches, and possessions. A few Tigers accosted two men walking along Main Street and forced them into an alley, where they robbed them and ordered the terrified duo to remove their clothing, hats, and shoes. The Rebels donned the civilian clothes and left "a few lousy rags" for their victims.

Some Southerners took "great sport" in forcing the men of Waynesboro to exchange headgear and shoes with them. Outdated high hats, which many of the older gentlemen still wore, were a particular target for the Rebels' jests. They taunted the civilians with chants of "Hats are so dear and the cows all dead, so the old man wears the churn on his head," according to Lida Welsh. She added, "One old gentleman whom I had never known to wear a low hat did so because he got tired of being invited 'to come down out of that hat' and being told that they 'knew he was in it, for they saw his toes wriggle.'" A sympathetic, early-twentieth-century Waynesboro historian wrote, "Our men of seventy years ago were not cowards, but they submitted gracefully to these incivilities because the soldiers carried guns, which were instruments of persuasion, although it is a fact that never a shot was fired."[19]

The Confederates elicited a variety of emotions from townspeople during their stay. Miss Welsh remembered,

> Not only did we observe the visitors, but they observed us—with mixed emotions. As my brother sat on our porch steps an artillery officer dismounted, gave his horse in charge of an orderly, and came across to our porch. After introducing himself—I have forgotten his name and rank—he said that he would like to ask a few questions. Getting my brother's consent, he said: "This is the first Pennsylvania town we have

entered, and I am surprised to see so many able-bodied young men on your streets. Is this town a fair sample of the reserve force of the northern States?"

My brother assured him that it was. [The officer] looked very grave for a moment, and then remarked that he could not have heard anything more discouraging. "Why aren't you in the army?" he asked. My brother told him of his first enlistment for three months, when it was the general belief that the war would all be over in that time, and of his re-enlistment for nine months. The officer then asked what battles he had been in, and when Fredericksburg was mentioned he said he had been there too, he had commanded one of the batteries on Marye's Hill. My brother told him that he had been with the troops that made the charge on that hill. The officer then remarked, "I've been in many battles, but have never seen the bravery of that charge surpassed."[20]

Another woman recalled, "These southern boys were polite and courteous, but ragged and dirty." Several ladies received small keepsakes and remembrances from southern officers, and some baked bread and prepared other food for their uninvited guests. However, for years, they "remember[ed] the Louisiana Tigers, who were much dreaded.... There is no record that the soldiers harmed any one along the line of march, but they needed food, and a chicken or a pig running at large was not safe during this invasion."[21]

Lieutenant Jackson wrote, "The people were very much afraid of us and gave the men every thing they asked for." Another Rebel officer admitted his part in relieving some of the "dreadfully frightened" locals of their footwear. "They expected they were to be the victims of the most atrocious barbarity. In Waynesboro, we made the people hand over what boots and shoes they had, also other articles that were needed for the comfort of the soldiers."[22]

One hungry Confederate infantryman stopped at a house near the camp of the 7th Louisiana and asked the housewife for bread and milk. After inviting him to take a seat at the table while she fetched the food, she casually inquired his regimental affiliation. When he replied "the 7th Louisiana," the lady fainted and dropped to the floor. Concerned, the bewildered soldier rushed to her side and tried to revive her. At that moment, her husband entered the room. He demanded an explanation as to why the two were on the floor together.

The soldier, embarrassed at his suggestive position, quickly explained the situation, commenting that he did not know why she had fainted when he merely mentioned he was from the 7th Louisiana. The old man replied, "Oh, that explains the matter." He told the soldier that when the cavalry had passed through, they had "told everybody that the La. Tigers would kill, burn & destroy every thing & every body in the country." The woman soon revived and stood up. Still, "it was some time before Mr. 7th could convince the lady that he was not a cut throat and a [thief]."[23]

It saddened the 8th Louisiana's J. Arthur Taylor to see the women crying and wringing their hands at the sight of the Confederates. Wary of the invaders, they watched from a distance "with every appearance of fear, very much in the same manner as the wild beeves of Louisiana gather around a person creeping through the grass in hunting ducks." Out of fear, citizens opened their larders and pantries to the Rebels, giving them whatever they asked for, in an effort to avoid having their property destroyed or damaged. One resident later stated the Confederate officers "were apparently very careful to give receipts for all horses, cattle and other property confiscated and told our people that if they won the war, their government would pay their bills and redeem their currency in gold, but if they lost the war, the Federal government would be obliged to make settlement."[24]

As night settled over the quaint valley town, martial bands serenaded Waynesboro's residents as Confederates celebrated their first night in Pennsylvania. Some soldiers billeted in area homes, but many slept in open fields and yards. Young Lida Welsh heard hundreds of men "singing familiar old hymns" in a field at the end of her street. Her neighbors heard chaplains leading their men in prayer. Despite the religious services, many citizens had trouble sleeping with so many enemy soldiers in their midst.[25]

### Into the Heart of the Cumberland Valley

At seven o'clock the next morning, Wednesday, June 24, Early departed Waynesboro after leaving a guard detachment to retain possession of the town hall, above which a Confederate flag still fluttered. To Lida Welsh, the "steady tramp of the men and continuous rumble of artillery and heavily loaded wagons over our narrow stony street became almost intolerable, and we were relieved when the last straggling soldier and the last rumbling wagon had vanished over the hill north of town." West of Early's route, Ewell's column marched through Chambersburg. "There was but little confusion or

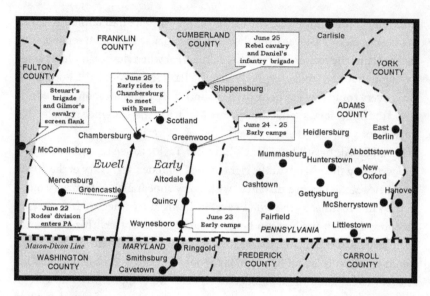

Confederate infantry invades Pennsylvania, June 22–25

noise, nothing but the tramp, tramp of thousands of feet," reported a local newsman, "and the continual monotonous rattle of canteens and equipment."

With the Rebels gone from Waynesboro, the terrified men who had remained hidden throughout the Confederate occupation emerged from their cellars and attics. To their chagrin, they discovered their cowardice was unnecessary, for "the women and children, as well as the [other] men, who did not take these precautions were not harmed. When these frightened men came out of hiding, they looked rather sheepish and were the butt of much good-natured fun among those of their neighbors who had been courageous enough to watch the great parade from the roadside."[26]

Early's Division headed northeasterly from Waynesboro on Black Gap Road, a route that generally paralleled the South Mountain range off to the east. The Rebels marched through the rural farming villages of Quincy and Altodale, where some curious residents gawked at the lengthy procession, while others scrambled to hide their horses and livestock. A few soldiers snatched hats from the heads of bystanders. One lad was busy chopping wood by the side of the road when an infantryman leaned from the ranks and grabbed at the youth's hat. He missed and kept walking. The boy turned, menacingly raised his axe, and dared the Rebel "to try that again!"[27]

Foraging parties stripped that part of the Cumberland Valley, which was among the most prosperous agricultural regions in Pennsylvania. One Confederate recounted, "Our quartermaster and commissary departments took every cow, sheep, horse, mule and wagon that they could lay their hands on, besides bacon and flour. Foraging was strictly prohibited among the men in line. The cavalry and commissary department did the work. We boys, with guns, had more strict orders here than we ever had in our own country; we just had to stay in line, and sometimes we almost suffered for water."[28]

The long column of thirsty and tired soldiers stopped briefly for a rest break near the Caledonia Iron Mines, a large ore-mining operation owned by firebrand Pennsylvania attorney and politician Thaddeus Stevens, whom Captain Seymour termed "one of the vilest, most unprincipled & most fanatical of the Yankee Abolitionist Congressmen." Jubal Early granted permission for his soldiers to take revenge. Seymour added, "Our men took pleasure in helping themselves most bountifully to the products of his broad and fertile acres."[29]

After a march of sixteen miles that day, Early finally halted his troops at Greenwood, a rustic village eight miles east of Chambersburg on the western approach to South Mountain. There, they camped near the macadamized turnpike that ran westward to Chambersburg and eastward to Gettysburg. The 9th Louisiana was east of the main camp, toward Black Gap. Regimental bands played in the evening, entertaining the soldiers and several locals who came out to see the much-ballyhooed Rebels.[30]

While Early's jubilant men camped and entertained the mountain folk, they were being watched by unpaid volunteer civilian spies under the direction of David McConaughy, a Gettysburg attorney. These "scouts" monitored the movements of the Confederate columns and relayed information to the nearest telegraph stations, where the latest news was wired to Harrisburg. In response, Major General Darius Couch shifted his hastily organized Pennsylvania militia to contest the Rebels' presumed routes to the state capital and the Susquehanna River.

One full regiment, the 26th Pennsylvania Volunteer Militia (P.V.M.), was sent via train to Major Haller in Gettysburg to protect the nexus of roads. Couch dispatched Colonel William Thomas's 20th P.V.M. to York County to guard the railroads that connected Harrisburg and Philadelphia with Baltimore and Washington, while Colonel Jacob Frick's 27th P.V.M. moved to

Columbia to protect the vital mile-and-a-half-long covered bridge across the Susquehanna at that location. Additional Pennsylvania and New York militia regiments manned the recently constructed earthworks now protecting the southern entry to Harrisburg.[31]

In his Greenwood camp, Jubal Early was unaware of this rapid movement of Union militia. He reported, "There were no indications of any enemy near us and the march was entirely without molestation. We were now in the enemy's country, and were getting our supplies entirely from the country people. These supplies were taken from mills, storehouses, and the farmers, under a regular system ordered by General Lee, and with a due regard to the wants of the inhabitants themselves, certificates being given in all cases. There was no marauding, or indiscriminate plundering, but all such acts were expressly forbidden and prohibited effectually."[32]

On the 25th, the Tigers "laid in camp all day cooking rations," according to Lieutenant Jackson. They heartily enjoyed the bounties taken from Winchester and the previous day's foraging on Congressman Stevens' lands. Captain Seymour's diary entry reflected the deep satisfaction felt by many in the brigade: "In camp all day, luxuriating on old Thad's provider and good things generally."[33]

Curious country folk came out in droves to see the Rebels and visit their various camps. According to Colonel Clement Evans of Gordon's Brigade, the locals were awestruck by the artillery pieces, as they had never seen cannon before. Many Confederates were considerably surprised at the profane language of the Pennsylvania women. To those officers and gentlemen who had never heard a rough word escape the lips of a proper southern belle, it was "very strange" to hear even young females of this "poor class of people" cursing repeatedly. The residents evoked Evans' curiosity: "We find them generally living in pretty good style, but coarse, uneducated, and apparently having little knowledge of the outside world."[34]

That morning, General Early rode to Chambersburg's Franklin Hotel to consult with Richard Ewell and receive his orders for the next step in the campaign.

> In accordance with instructions received from General Lee, General Ewell ordered me to move with my command across the South Mountain, and through Gettysburg to York, for the purpose of cutting the Northern Central Railroad (running from Baltimore to Harrisburg),

and destroying the bridge across the Susquehanna at Wrightsville and Columbia on the branch railroad from York to Philadelphia. Lieutenant Colonel Elijah White's battalion of cavalry was ordered to report to me for the expedition in addition to French's regiment, and I was ordered to leave the greater portion of my trains behind to accompany the reserve ordnance and subsistence trains of the camps. I was also ordered to rejoin the other divisions at Carlisle by the way of Dillstown [Dillsburg] from York, after I had accomplished the task assigned me.[35]

A few Marylanders from Rodes' and Johnson's divisions who were familiar with the York and Gettysburg regions were temporarily reassigned to Early's Division as guides. Early and his staff and escort returned to the Greenwood camp in the midafternoon, and he explained Ewell's plans to Harry Hays and his other three brigade commanders. He stripped the division to fighting trim to enable it to march faster, unencumbered by the lumbering supply trains, which were soon sent off westward to Chambersburg. Hays' Louisiana Tigers would not see their supply wagons for the next three weeks and they would have to live off the land, foraging or purchasing food and supplies along the way. Fifteen empty wagons would accompany the column eastward, along with the ambulances. Each regiment could take only one medical wagon, one ordnance wagon, and one wagon with cooking utensils. The officers, including the generals and division staff, had to leave behind their personal baggage, except what they could carry on their backs or horses.[36]

### First Contact at Gettysburg

On Friday morning, June 26, a cold northeast intermittent rain delayed Jubal Early's departure for Adams County until midmorning. One of his infantrymen wrote, "We had orders to leave at day break but it was a raning so hard we dident leave untell about 8 oclock and it dident Still sease raning but raind all day." In the rear, the Tigers did not get on the road until nearly ten o'clock, according to Lieutenant J. Warren Jackson; Adjutant Seymour stated it was closer to eleven before all the men were on the road on this "most disagreeable day." The division slogged eastward toward South Mountain with more than six thousand men, including the four brigades of infantry, Hilary Jones' quartet of artillery batteries, Lieutenant Colonel Elijah White's cavalry battalion, and Colonel William French's 17th Virginia Cavalry.[37]

When the head of the column reached Congressman Stevens' Caledonia

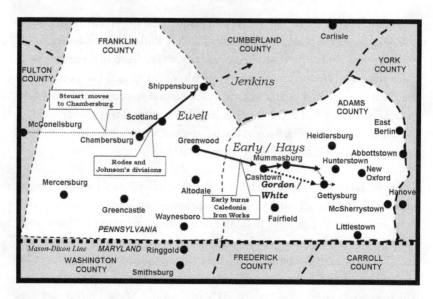

Tigers reach Gettysburg, June 26

Iron Works on South Mountain, Early ordered his pioneers to torch the main buildings and several smaller facilities and storehouses, although he spared the workers' barracks and homes. Early personally ordered the destruction of this private property in retribution for Stevens' open advocacy of similar tactics by the Union army in the South.

Shortly after navigating Cashtown Gap, Early split his division while descending the eastern slope of South Mountain. Scouts had informed him that felled trees partially obstructed the turnpike leading through Cashtown to Gettysburg, a town rumored to be defended by a Federal force, although Early could get no definite information as to its size. Wanting to pin the Yankees in place, he sent Gordon's Brigade and White's cavalry battalion ahead on the turnpike to "skirmish with and amuse the enemy in front." He led the rest of his division to the left on a dirt road through Hilltown and Mummasburg, planning to get on the Yankees' flank and rear in order to capture the whole force. Heavy overnight rains had since diminished, but the road was still muddy, drastically slowing Early's column.[38]

A few miles to the east, Gettysburg was in confusion. Hearing scouts' reports that Confederate infantry was approaching, several residents left town, taking their horses, wagonloads of furniture, heirlooms, and other valuables to safety. The postmaster and railroad telegrapher fled, as did a few other officials. Government supplies were hastened to the next county, and members of the hastily organized state militia prepared to defend the town as best they could with their limited training.

Gordon moved quickly on the macadamized turnpike and sent Elijah White's advance cavalry to contest enemy skirmishers deployed on a ridge west of Gettysburg near Marsh Creek. Soon, he sent a courier back to inform General Early that the main Yankee force was hastily retreating through the fields between Mummasburg and Gettysburg. In response to the welcome news, Early sent most of William French's "wildcat" 17th Virginia Cavalry trotting off in pursuit. Soon afterward, the long column of muddy and tired infantry began arriving in Mummasburg, with the Tigers in the lead slogging through the slop. Jubal Early instructed Hays to keep marching, heading southeast toward Gettysburg. Smith, Avery, and the rest of the column halted and set up camp just outside Mummasburg.[39]

Unknown to Early, Gordon, after chasing off the 26th Militia, had marched down the Chambersburg Pike into Gettysburg and halted his Georgians along the sidewalks lining the main street. In the meantime, Jubal Early led the road-weary Tigers from Mummasburg toward Gettysburg, arriving in the vicinity in the late afternoon. When couriers informed him that Gordon had already taken possession of the town, Early ordered General Hays to halt and camp along the Mummasburg Road, a little more than a mile northwest of Gettysburg. Tigers began ripping down the wooden fences near Oak Hill and preparing campfires to cook their rations. Soldiers filled canteens and pails with fresh water from Willoughby Run.

Early dispatched two of Hays' five regiments to the northeast toward the Hunterstown Road to help catch the fleeing militia but, slowed by the mud and exhaustion, they were unable to catch up with them. The task of rounding up prisoners fell to Colonel French's horsemen. Adjutant Seymour exaggerated the Tigers' role in dispersing the newly recruited state militiamen, "who no doubt had previously resolved to die if need be in the defense of their homes and friends, changed their minds when they caught a glimpse of our two little regiments in the distance and most precipitately and ingloriously fled the field. Darkness coming on, our men returned to camp, weary from their long and useless march in the rain and mud."[40]

Before heading back to camp, several Tigers from these two forward regiments, as well as some of French's cavalrymen, stopped at a farmhouse where eighteen-year-old Sue King Black lived, about four miles north of Gettysburg. She reported, "I counted a hundred who came into the yard; got tired [of] counting and quit. One young fat fellow, sitting on the porch steps, bare footed and footsore was in a bad humor; said he belonged to the Louisiana Tigers. One of them gave me a big Jews harp."[41]

Not long after Gordon occupied Gettysburg, "a few Irish soldiers" from Hays' Brigade stacked arms, walked into town, and strolled down Baltimore Street to its southern outskirts. There, they found residents, also of Gaelic descent, who sold them liquor. Soon, a brawl began as drunken Louisianans quarreled with locals. Private Isaac Bradwell of Gordon's 31st Georgia, the designated provost regiment, reported that the Tigers were busy "beating up the old citizens" when the guards finally arrived to stop the brawl. They did not arrest any of the riotous Irishmen or townspeople.[42]

Shortly before 4:30 p.m., General Early, escorted by his staff, rode into town to confer with the victorious Gordon. Early dispatched a courier to David Kendlehart's house to summon the council president so he could levy a tribute on the town. "After matters had been satisfactorily arranged between our Burgess and the Rebel officers," recalled Fannie Buehler, "the men settled down and the citizens soon learned that no demands were to be made upon them and that all property would be protected. Some horses were stolen, some cellars broken open and robbed, but so far as could be done, the officers controlled their men. The 'Louisiana Tigers' were left and kept outside of town."[43]

The Tigers were encamped northwest of Gettysburg along the Mummasburg Road near Willoughby Run, with French's Virginia cavalry posted nearby. However, the Louisianans and the rest of Early's Division were not idle. They scoured the countryside, sending wagonloads of corn, oats, hay, meat, and other supplies back toward Chambersburg. They also appropriated "every farm animal that walked." Thomas B. Reed stopped at a house near Gettysburg looking for food or supplies. A "little Dutch woman" answered and begged the Tiger to help himself to her property but spare her household. He recalled, "She was the worst scared woman I had ever seen." When she learned that all he wanted was food, she nervously ushered Reed into her home while she collected food items for him to take back to camp. Other soldiers arrived and asked for food, and, by the time the Tigers were lining up at the doorway, "the little woman was almost crazy." Reed consoled her as much as he could and then left with his food. He later wrote, "I never knew how she got along with those other fellows." He and his friend Jack Dawkins "had a good supper that night and slept well, for Oh! we were so tired."[44]

A Harrisburg reporter detained by the Rebels earlier in the day had received a pass for safe passage through Confederate lines to the Cumberland Valley. He stopped at a tavern near Cashtown, where he later encountered "three wild Rebel Irishmen," stragglers from Early's force. They had filled their canteens with whiskey and "had evidently been indulging in their national proclivities." The journalist judged them as a "fair example of the lower order of rebel soldiery." Emboldened by the liquor, one of them philosophized on the war. "What the divil are yer fiting us for? You may hate us now, but you'll niver put us down. By my sowl, we'll fight until the last man ov us is kilt, and then, be jabbers, the women will take a hand at it. You may fight us for all eternity, and thin we won't be whipped afther all!" The amused newsman later related to his readers, "Such is a specimen of the language and sentiments of these misguided people. They said that they had been with Stonewall Jackson in all his campaigns, and had never been whipped yet, and what was more, the Yankees could never raise men enough to do it."

The correspondent continued to quiz the inebriated trio, who related that General Early was no particular favorite. They mentioned the army disliked him greatly, and there were several fellows who would shoot him as freely as a "d——d Yankee" if they had the proper opportunity. However, they spoke of Ewell in glowing terms. When the reporter pressed them as to their destination, one of them replied, "I don't know where the army is going, and I don't care a d——n. Old Lee is the boy to lead us into a scrape or to get us out of one, and we don't care a d——n."[45]

As darkness fell, the majority of Hays' Tigers returned to their campsites, their fires fueled by rails taken from fences along Mummasburg Road. Hays allowed each man a pint ration of whiskey taken from Gettysburg taverns. Some of the Tigers were able to procure more or borrow from friends, and soon, many Louisianans were inebriated. Lieutenant Jackson recalled, "The whole brigade got drunk. I never saw such a set in my life."[46]

In Early's next objective, the prosperous borough of York, two days of rumors that the Rebels might invade that part of south-central Pennsylvania seemed to be coming true. Refugees from Franklin and Adams counties streamed eastward through York, headed for safety across the Columbia-Wrightsville Bridge over the broad Susquehanna River. By nightfall, frightened travelers brought word that Gettysburg had fallen to the Confederates,

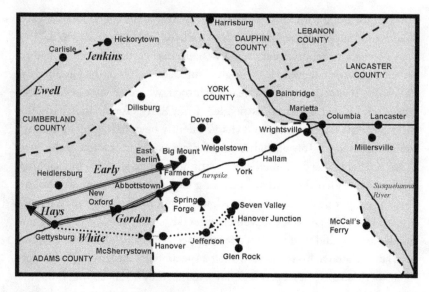

Tigers march into York County, June 27

and Jubal Early with five thousand men now occupied the town. When some of the state militia that had been guarding Gettysburg arrived in York after midnight and reported the day's events, fear turned to reality. Townspeople and civic authorities hotly debated various options to prepare for the imminent arrival of the Rebels.[47]

## On to York!

About 6:00 a.m. on Saturday, June 27, Early's main column departed Mummasburg, heading east toward neighboring York County and its rich prize, the region's largest and most prosperous town, York. By seven o'clock, the rain abated after nearly 1.3 inches had fallen. Hays' Brigade backtracked from their camp near Gettysburg westward to Mummasburg and then headed east on the road toward Hunterstown. They left behind an incapacitated infantryman on the David Schriver farm along the Mummasburg Road. Private John W. Shackleford of the 9th Louisiana had been feeling ill, and now the Rocky Mount farmer was unable to continue the march. His comrades lost track of him after they headed across the rolling hills of northern Adams County.[48]

While an exhausted Shackleford managed to find shelter in Schriver's barn, his comrades in the Louisiana Tigers marched toward York County, finally catching up to the rear of Early's column near Hunterstown in the late morning. Several of Hays' men were in no condition for the long hike across the undulating muddy roads. According to Adjutant Seymour, "The men having had too much free access to liquor, of which there are large quantities in Gettysburg, many of them were drunk and caused me much trouble to make them keep up with the column." Thomas Reed of the 9th Louisiana wrote, "You should have been with us. The boys were nearly all full, and such a time as we did have."

A frustrated Seymour finally ordered the most obstreperous ones to be confined in the supply wagons that held the cooking utensils, where they suffered through "a disagreeable ride" while sitting on the sharp edges and projecting legs of the various iron pots and kettles. This action "sobered them speedily" and they "begged most piteously" to be allowed to get out of the wagons and walk.[49]

Private Reed's 9th Louisiana was in front of the column this day, with his Company A at the rear of the regiment and the 7th Louisiana immediately behind them. Two Irishmen in the latter regiment, their attitudes influenced by the whiskey, had been loudly bickering all morning. When General Early called a halt about 10:00 a.m. for a ten-minute rest break, Colonel Davidson B. Penn rode back to find the two quarrelers. He asked a captain to point them out and then ordered some soldiers to rip down a nearby "very stout rail fence." Two Tigers fashioned the rails into an impromptu boxing ring, and Penn ordered the arguers to "get in there and fight it out." The duo slugged it out for several rounds, cursing and swearing at one another until Penn finally halted the spectacle. He ordered the bloodied bullies to go down to a nearby branch, wash themselves, and get ready to march. They squatted near each other at the creek and soon were laughing about their fight.[50]

By noon, Early's column, slowed by the muck and mire, passed through Hunterstown and paused to rest, eat, and regroup. Lieutenant J. Warren Jackson reported, "The mud [was] nearly Knee deep & [men were] straggling by the hundreds." As the day wore on, Early's Division slogged across Adams County on country roads through the villages of New Chester, Hampton, and East Berlin, which Private Charles Moore Jr. of the 5th Louisiana deemed "a beautiful place."[51]

A few stragglers never rejoined the ranks. Private Robert Boyd of the 9th Louisiana slipped away from his regiment near East Berlin and deserted; he was "not heard of again." Federal records indicate he was captured on June 28 "at Berlin" and subsequently imprisoned in Fort Delaware. He took the Oath of Allegiance on July 7. The fate of another Tiger remains a mystery. German-born Corporal Charles Brown of the 8th Louisiana was "absent without leave since June 27th, 1863"; he had "straggled on the march from Gettysburg to York and [was] supposed to have been killed by the citizens of Penn."[52]

Captain Seymour claimed, "During our march, the inhabitants were treated with the greatest kindness and consideration." While the Tigers were adept at foraging, they invariably offered to pay for the food, livestock, and other goods they confiscated, although at times the locals refused to accept the worthless Confederate scrip. Seymour added, "Stragglers would sometimes make predatory excursions into barnyards and dairies belonging to persons who were disposed to be inimical and unaccommodating—this was unavoidable; but I did not hear of a single instance of a citizen being insulted or his property damaged." However, soldiers stopped at John Snowden's place in New Chester and carried off a large assortment of new shoes. Cattle, horses, and mules were particular favorites of the raiding parties.

General Early had heard in Waynesboro that thousands of people in south-central Pennsylvania were members of the secret Knights of the Golden Circle and would welcome the invading army with special hand signals that indicated they were friends. Seymour commented, "Much to our surprise, hundreds of people in the towns through which we passed greeted us with these signs and we joyfully accepted them as proofs of the anti-war feeling that pervaded the country."[53]

Gossip and stories had spread throughout this prosperous agricultural region regarding the outlandish behavior of the Louisiana Tigers. Several residents fled, taking their horses and valuables to protect them from Confederate foragers. However, Huntington Township resident George Schmick was too late, and a pair of Early's scouts stopped at his farm and rode away leading two of his horses. Most refugees headed through the borough of York, where they created a panic by reporting the Confederates were coming that way. Soon, several Yorkers joined the exodus toward the Susquehanna River, taking their livestock and horses.[54]

After a march of about twenty-one miles, Early finally halted three and a half miles past East Berlin. In the early evening, he established camp near Big Mount, a farming village in rural western York County. Gordon was encamped south of Early's column at the tiny rural hamlet of Farmers, with White's cavalry farther south at Spring Forge, protecting the right flank in case of any Federal movement up from Maryland.[55]

After Jubal Early oversaw the placement of his brigades for the night, he sought shelter for himself and his staff, because their camp equipment was back in Chambersburg with the baggage wagons. Near the road was a corn-field, where he directed Colonel French's 17th Virginia Cavalry to turn loose their horses to graze. Not far away, he spotted a large barn. Riding over, he approached the frightened farmer, who could (or would) not speak a word of English. A frustrated "Old Jube" eventually gave up the idea of quartering with him and rode on a little farther into the hamlet of Big Mount, where he found "a decent looking" brick house with a good-sized front porch that he and his staff could use for shelter.

As the Rebel horsemen rode up, the owner, a German widow named Mrs. Zinn, came out to the gate in great trepidation. She exclaimed in broken English, "Are you goin' to destroy us, are you goin' to take all that we've got?" Early calmly reassured her, "No madam, and to give you the best protection possible, I will stay with you, with my staff, and no one shall trouble you." He directed his staff to take possession of the property, stating that the porch would do for sleeping. Early then rode southeast four miles with a small escort to give Gordon his final instructions about entering York the next day. Earlier in the evening, a delegation of York's leading citizens met with General Gordon at Farmers and discussed the terms by which the town would accede to Confederate occupancy. By midnight, the city officials had returned to York to inform waiting residents that on Sunday morning, the Confederates would march into town unmolested.

General Early did not return to Big Mount until 9:00 p.m., and then he discovered that his staff had already eaten supper. However, the old lady had saved a very plentiful meal for Early, with about fifteen varieties of food— meats, vegetables, coffee, and milk. While he was eating, Widow Zinn, no longer fearful, was instead very talkative, wanting to discuss the merits of Stonewall Jackson, among other topics. She gave Early a good clean bed, and the well-fed general enjoyed an excellent night's sleep.[56]

Despite the late hour, news spread rapidly in downtown York about how close the Confederates were to the prosperous regional railroad, manufacturing, and agricultural center. Refugees from western York County, hustling through town to the long bridge over the Susquehanna River at Wrights-

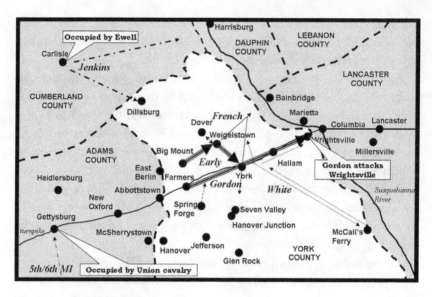

Tigers march to York, June 28

ville, verified the Rebels indeed were approaching "with an immense force." According to resident Cassandra Small, York's women and children were "dreadfully terrified." They were particularly concerned about the arrival of the ballyhooed and unpredictable Louisiana Tigers.[57]

## York Under the Rebel Flag

On a bright sunny Sabbath morning, June 28, the Tigers broke camp at sunrise and departed Big Mount. Early's Division, split into three columns, resumed the eastward march toward the prosperous borough of York. Lieutenant Colonel Elijah White's partisan Virginia cavalry battalion screened the right flank, with orders to raid the important telegraphic communications and rail center at Hanover Junction. Gordon's Georgians, William Tanner's Courtney (Richmond) Artillery, and Company C of the 17th Virginia Cavalry comprised the center column, marching through thick clouds of choking limestone dust on the macadamized York Turnpike. Farther to the north was Early's main force, consisting of the bulk of William French's 17th Virginia Cavalry and the infantry brigades of William Smith, Isaac Avery, and Harry Hays. The rest of Hilary Jones' batteries and the wagons trailed the lengthy column.

Gordon departed Farmers and marched about ten miles across the dusty turnpike into York, with bands blaring martial airs and battle flags unfurled. Meanwhile, Jubal Early led his other three brigades over the Canal Road across the lower part of Dover Township toward York, thirteen miles from their Big Mount campsite. He had issued strict orders that morning that no man could leave the ranks with his gun. The command had been sent down through the ranks, and company leaders such as Captain Reuben A. Pierson of the 9th Louisiana relayed it to the noncommissioned officers and enlisted men. The regiment had only traveled a short distance when the antebellum schoolteacher discovered that one of his men was somewhat intoxicated. Pierson assigned a sober soldier to keep on eye on him. A half-mile down the road was a large mud puddle from the previous day's rain. The drunken man climbed over the fence alongside the road into a nearby field to circumnavigate the mud hole. Spotting the incident, Colonel Leroy Stafford immediately arrested Pierson for allowing the enlisted man to violate the orders.[58]

Curious to see the storied Confederates, several villagers sat on a fence along the road a few hundred yards south of Davidsburg. Among them was John B. May, who held a York newspaper in his hand. General Early, with his staff, was riding near the head of his column. When he saw the civilian with the newspaper, Early requested that it be given to him. He scanned it as he rode along, loudly stating, "This is just what I wanted!" From the paper, he garnered information about the Union troops in the area.[59]

When he arrived at Weigelstown, Early sent Colonel French and a two-hundred-man cavalry detachment eastward to the mouth of the Conewago Creek at York Haven to burn the pair of railroad bridges there, which they accomplished about noon after driving off the 20th Pennsylvania [Volunteer] Militia. The division marched on country roads north of York to Emigsville and the Harrisburg Turnpike and then turned southward. Early dropped off Smith's Brigade, the Louisiana Guard Artillery, and Hays' Tigers a couple miles north of York and ordered them into camp. He then led Avery's Brigade and the remaining two batteries of Jones' battalion down George Street across a stone bridge into downtown York, arriving in the Center Square a few hours after Gordon's triumphal parade eastward.

The First Louisiana Brigade went into camp in the early afternoon northeast of York, along the railroad tracks near Codorus Creek, a meandering stream that provided water power for two large flour mills. Hays posted guards at the doors of the prosperous businesses, which contained nearly two thousand barrels of stone-ground wheat flour, much of it for the export markets of Cuba and South America.[60]

Hays' Brigade camped on various nearby farms, including the sprawling property of Samuel Hively in Spring Garden Township. Hively would later file a claim with state officials citing considerable damage to his farm, including the loss of 1,500 fence rails burned by the Rebels in their campfires, as well as 75 cords of firewood. His fields of ripening wheat and oats were ruined, trampled flat by the Confederates. Nearby, farmer John D. Baisch reported that Hays' infantry flattened a wheat field and took from his property 50 bushels of wheat, 125 bushels of corn, 160 bushels of oats, and 12 tons of hay, as well as stealing a harness from his barn.[61]

Near the Tigers' position was an eminence known to locals as Diehl's Hill. Captain William Seymour marveled at the expansive view from this commanding position, crowned with the Louisiana Guard Artillery, their barrels pointing south from hastily dug earthworks at the borough. The view was tranquil and the countryside unspoiled by war, unlike much of northern Virginia. Seymour commented, "The surrounding country was in a high state of cultivation and from our camp presented a beautiful appearance with its immense fields of golden grain that flashed in the sunlight—dotted here and there with neat little cottages and large substantially build barns which were literally bursting with wheat, oats, & corn. Most of the barns in this section of Pennsylvania are larger and more finely built than the dwellings of the farmers; the Dutch lords of the soil invariably bestow more care and attention on their crops and stock than they do on their families."[62]

One of Early's first acts after occupying York was to post armed guards at every drinking house to prevent his troops from indulging in one of their favorite pastimes. He sent detachments to guard the flour mills, several stores, and potential areas where trouble might occur. He deployed the Staunton Artillery on Webb's Hill south of town and ordered Carrington's Charlottesville battery into the local fairgrounds in reserve, along with part of Avery's Brigade (the rest camped at the sprawling U.S. Military Hospital at Penn Commons immediately south of York).

Early rode to the county courthouse and established his headquarters in the sheriff's office. A few hours later, the general emerged and ordered the courthouse bell to be rung to assemble the townspeople. He demanded 100,000 dollars, 2,000 pairs of shoes, 1,000 hats, 1,000 pairs of socks, and three days' rations for his troops. He ordered stunned civic authorities to fulfill the requisition, delivering the designated items to his quartermaster. The town's Committee of Safety met in emergency session and decided to comply with as much of Early's ransom as possible. Ward committees went door to door soliciting cash and informing citizens that the borough would assume the overall debt and would later reimburse the donors for their contributions. The prosperous firm of P. A. and S. Small agreed to furnish all the groceries and flour requested by Early, and hatters and shoemakers were pressed into service to provide hats and footwear for the Rebels.[63]

Several residents grew concerned that Early's intentions might prove sinister, and that, at any moment, the ominous cannon on the hills might start shelling the town. Uncontrollable Confederate soldiers might forcibly take what they wanted. Mary Fisher, the wife of Judge Fisher, later wrote, "We knew not how soon might come a signal to unleash the dogs of war in our midst and give our homes as prey to the invader."[64]

In the Tigers' camp along Codorus Creek, soldiers relaxed and entertained guests from the town. Private Charles Moore Jr. of the 5th Louisiana commented about the particular hospitality of Mrs. Dr. Codwise and Miss Georgia Bird and noted the Copperhead sentiment of the people who came out from the town, which he deemed a "lovely place."[65]

In the humid late afternoon, patrols of sweating Tigers and Louisiana Guard artillerymen roamed the countryside north of York, foraging and searching for horses and mules. They rounded up dozens of animals and turned them over to the quartermasters for distribution to the batteries and wagon masters. Captain Seymour noted numerous farmers who apparently were open Confederate sympathizers, greeting the passing column with friendly words and unusual hand signals, which he took as signs of welcome. He quickly learned the truth: "When we reached York, we found that these professions and demonstrations were hollow and hypocritical."

Seymour soon discovered the reason. "Just in advance of our army, two Yankees from one of the New England States traveled through the country, professing to be high officers of a New York lodge of the 'Knights of the Golden Circle' and that they were empowered to receive any number of persons as members of the Order, on payment of the small fee of five dollars per capita." The shysters purported that their northern branch of the society was closely aligned with a similar group in the South, and all members and their property would be respected by the Confederate army. He added, "Thousands of people were induced to pay their money for the privilege of being accounted as friends of the South; hence our apparently cordial greeting along our line of march. A shrewd Yankee trick, that."[66]

Early agreed. "As we moved through the country, a number of people made mysterious signs to us, and on inquiring we ascertained that some enterprising Yankees had passed along a short time before, initiating the people into certain signs, for a consideration, which they were told would prevent the 'rebels' from molesting them or their property, when they appeared. These things were all new to us, and the purchasers of the mysteries had been badly sold."[67]

Several leading citizens opened their homes and larders to Early's officers. According to young Republican lawyer James W. Latimer, "Some of the Copperheads were very much alarmed . . . , but others gave them all the aid & comfort in their power. Reb officers said they had many sympathizers here; that they could get any information they wanted. One Copperhead, hearing a Union man asked by an officer for a Map of York Co., which was of course refused, volunteered to take him to his house and give him a map. Early was informed by someone who the prominent Union Men were; and they were marked."[68] A farmer rode into York to report that Rebels had seized his mules. A picket referred him to a nearby infantry captain who would listen to his complaint. The officer inquired, "How many did you lose?" The angry countryman replied, "Two." The Rebel retorted, "Two mules! What an example of the patriotism of these Northern heroes! I have staked everything on this issue—houses, lands, negroes, money, everything I have in this world, and you complain of two mules!" With that admonishment, the captain sent the farmer off to divisional headquarters at the county courthouse, stating, "Tell your wrongs to General Early. I think you can get your mules." Early gave the requisite orders, and the mules were indeed eventually restored to the farmer.[69]

Toward evening, Early rode to Wrightsville to check on Gordon's progress in seizing the militia and the covered bridge across the Susquehanna. He was disappointed to learn that the Yankees had escaped and burned the mile-and-a-half-long bridge behind them. Returning to York after dark, he accepted a dinner invitation from an elderly Copperhead attorney. After his late meal, Early turned in at the Metzel House, a prominent hotel owned by the widow Metzel. Throughout the night, guards from Avery's Brigade patrolled the streets, with orders to keep out unwanted visitors, presumably including the Louisiana Tigers.

Early on Monday morning, June 29, disturbing reports filtered back into York that unruly Louisiana Tigers had ransacked the two Codorus flour mills during the night, dumping large quantities of flour and wheat into the millraces and causing "great damage" to the property. The rumors of the Tigers' wanton destruction of the prosperous mills and Early's excessive demands for groceries and flour had caused considerable consternation for the owners, Samuel and Philip A. Small. One observer, attorney James Latimer, later wrote, "Philip Small was excessively frightened—in fact I think he was quite demented for a while."[70]

A concerned Samuel Small Jr. immediately sought out General Early to inquire as to the validity of these claims. Early listened to him and stated, "It cannot be correct. My troops dare not waste and destroy the wheat and flour, or tear down the buildings. Go out yourself to tell General Hays, who commands the brigade, that his men must obey my orders." The general added that, if the stories proved true, the offenders would be identified and executed at once.[71]

Small, alarmed at the thought of riding a couple of miles through enemy-controlled roads, objected. He exclaimed, "I cannot go alone." Early responded, "You *must* go, but I will give you a pass. . . . Take one of our horses and ride out there." Anticipating an emergency such as the Confederate occupation, Small had previously hidden a horse in an out-of-the-way stable behind the drug store of Charles A. Morris. He asked for permission to ride his own horse out to the camp to interview General Hays. Aide-de-camp Lieutenant William G. Calloway penned the order, and Early dismissed Small. The businessman ducked into the stable, moved the boxes and barrels hiding the horse, mounted the animal, and rode off to investigate the damage. The pass enabled him to ride safely through Avery's outer pickets northward, although several times they stopped him and challenged his right of way. Confederates offered to swap their played-out mounts for his fresh horse, but Early's signature prevailed.[72]

Soon, Small anxiously approached Harry Hays' picket line along the Codorus Creek, where the Louisianans allowed him free passage to inspect his sprawling mills. To his relief, he found that the rumor was untrue. Everything was indeed safe, and armed Confederates stood guard at the doorways to prevent unauthorized entry to the mills.[73]

Meanwhile, throughout the morning, civic leaders scurried about York trying to raise the cash demanded, as well as the food and supplies. If the citizens complied with his request promptly, Early agreed to spare all private property; otherwise, he would take what he could find and would not be responsible for the conduct of his troops while they foraged through the town. The authorities believed there was no other alternative, so they collected the supplies and money and delivered them to the quartermaster. By Monday afternoon, ward officials had amassed $28,610 in U.S. currency from door-to-door solicitation and delivered it to Major Charles E. Snodgrass, Early's quartermaster.

Young lawyer James Latimer "very foolishly" gave $100, half the cash he had on hand. He questioned whether the town should have so readily acceded to Early's demands. To a shamed Latimer, "Authorities behaved so sheepishly in regard to the surrender." The prosperous firm of P. A. and S. Small, already charged with providing flour and vegetables, raised $2,502. However, the cash raised was far less than the one hundred thousand dollars Early had demanded.[74]

To Early's disappointment, Snodgrass reported that the required number of shoes could not be produced. Mayor David Small assured Early there were no more shoes to be had, and this was all the money that could be raised. The banks and wealthier citizens had previously sent most of their funds and valuables off to Philadelphia for safekeeping in the event of a Confederate invasion. Early later commented, "I believed that he had made an honest effort to raise the money, and I did not, therefore, take any stringent measures to enforce the demand, but left the town indebted to me for the remainder." A small portion of the ransom money was paid back to Yorkers to buy beef cattle, a commodity that "could be found much more readily when they were to be paid for than when [Confederate voucher] certificates were to be given." Snodgrass turned over the majority of the remaining cash to Colonel James L. Corley, the chief quartermaster of the Army of Northern Virginia, to be used for future purchases.[75]

Early may not have "taken any stringent measures," but he did try extortion. He threatened to burn the railroad complex north of town, and he summoned Judge Robert Fisher and demanded all the keys to the courthouse,

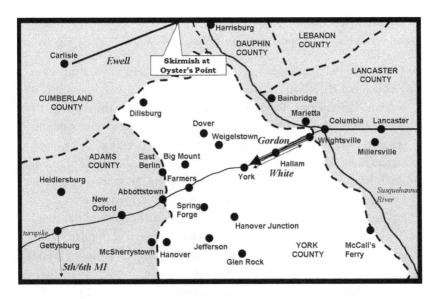

Tigers encamped near York, June 29

stating he would torch the county's records if the rest of the money were not delivered. A stunned Fisher responded that Early had promised (through General Gordon's negotiations the previous night with the town fathers) that the Confederates would not destroy personal or public property.

An undeterred Early remarked that if he did so, it would be in retaliation for a similar act that Union troops had perpetrated earlier in the war on the county courthouse in Fairfax, Virginia. "Two wrongs would not make a right," Fisher argued, and he pleaded with Early not to burn the vital records. The general finally acquiesced.[76]

While Early was negotiating the full collection of his demands, his camps were being inspected by James Gall Jr., a relief agent for the United States Sanitary Commission, a charitable organization that served the needs of soldiers. Commission leaders feared that a battle would occur near York, and they had sent Gall to prepare the way for relief efforts in that event. On Saturday, the relief worker had traveled from Harper's Ferry via train to Parkton, Maryland, where he found that he would have to proceed on foot because the Northern Central Railway had been severed by Rebel cavalry. He left Parkton at 9:00 a.m. on Sunday and arrived in York at four o'clock in the afternoon.

On Monday morning, Gall visited Ike Avery's men at the fairgrounds. He commented on their appearance, condition, and habits.

Physically, the men looked about equal to the generality of our own troops, and there were fewer boys among them. Their dress was a wretched mixture of all cuts and colors. There was not the slightest attempt at uniformity in this respect. Every man seemed to have put on whatever he could get hold of, without regard to shape or color. I noticed a pretty large sprinkling of blue pants among them, some of those, doubtless, that were left by Milroy at Winchester. Their shoes, as a general thing, were poor; some of the men were entirely barefooted.

Their equipments were light, as compared with those of our men. They consisted of a thin woolen blanket, coiled up and slung from the shoulder in the form of a sash, a haversack swung from the opposite shoulder, and a cartridge-box. The whole cannot weigh more than twelve or fourteen pounds. Is it strange, then, that with such light loads, they should be able to make longer and more rapid marches than our men? The marching of the men was irregular and careless; their arms were rusty and ill kept. Their whole appearance was inferior to that of our soldiers.[77]

Riding out to the camp of "a Louisiana Brigade, situated a mile from the city," about lunchtime, Gall reported:

The supply wagons were drawn up in a sort of straggling hollow square, in the center of which the men stacked their arms in company lines, and in this way formed their camp. There were no tents for the men and but very few for the officers. Their whole appearance was greatly inferior to that of our soldiers. The men were busy cooking their dinner, which consisted of fresh beef, part of the York levy, wheat griddle cakes raised with soda, and cold water. No coffee or sugar had been issued to the men for a long time.

The men expressed themselves perfectly satisfied with this kind of food, and said they greatly preferred the bread prepared in the way they do it, to the crackers issued to the Union soldiers. I asked one of the men how he got along without a shelter tent. His answer was, "First rate." "In the first place," said he, "I wouldn't tote one, and in the second place, I feel just as well, if not better, without it." "But how do you manage when it rains?" I inquired. "Wall, said he, me and this other man has a gum blanket atween us; when it rains we spread one of our woolen blankets on the ground to lie on, then we spread the other woolen blanket over us, and the gum blanket over that, and the rain can't tech [touch] us." And this is the way the rebel army, with the exception of a few of the most important officers, sleeps. Everything that will trammel or impede the movement of the army is discarded, no matter what the consequences may be to the men. . . .

In further conversation with the Louisiana officer, I ascertained that this was the corps which moved down through the Shenandoah Valley, surprised Milroy at Winchester, and was the first to cross the Potomac River at Shepardstown [sic] into Maryland. He informed me that his corps and the North Carolina brigade were entirely armed with Enfield Rifles taken at Winchester after Milroy's defeat.

In speaking of our [Union] soldiers, the same officer remarked: "They are too well fed, too well clothed, and have far too much to carry." That our men are too well fed, I do not believe, neither that they are too well clothed; that they have too much to carry, I can very well believe, after witnessing the march of the Army of the Potomac to Chancellorsville. Each man had eight days' rations to carry, besides sixty rounds of ammunition, musket, woolen blanket, rubber blanket, overcoat, extra shirt, drawers, socks, and shelter tent, amounting in all to about sixty pounds. Think of men, and boys too, staggering along under such a load, at the rate of fifteen to twenty miles a day.[78]

Gall knew about Early's ransom, and he added that the general "scrupulously kept his word, order being strictly enforced, and private property left untouched." Squads of North Carolinians burned a few railroad cars but did not proceed with his threat to torch the buildings. When one of Avery's squads approached a particular railcar to burn it, one of the railroaders protested, stating that it was the property of the Presbyterian Church, and the lumber inside was destined to be used in the construction of a new sanctuary. Hearing that the church owned the wood, the squad's captain ordered his men to back away. He explained that he was a member of the Presbyterian Church in Durham, North Carolina, and no harm should come to church property.[79]

In the late morning, Samuel Small Jr. returned to York and reported that all was well at his family's flour mills. General Early ordered him to show his quartermaster the route to the mills. Small, accompanied by "a Louisiana colonel," another officer (likely Major Snodgrass), and several empty wagons, returned to the mills in the early afternoon. Meanwhile, regimental quarter-masters distributed the available shoes, hats, and socks to Early's men. While the supplies were being dispersed, Hays' patrols exchanged gawks with curious civilians, very few of whom had previously seen a Confederate. A few infantrymen overheard one young child ask, "Why Papa, I thought the Rebels had horns. Where are they?" Several soldiers turned to the child, pointed to their bayonets, and exclaimed, "*Here* are our horns!"[80]

Enjoying the pleasant early summer weather and a rare day off from marching, many Confederates strolled through the town as their officers allowed. One popular attraction was Captain James Carrington's guns parked on the fairgrounds. An appreciative Carrington recounted, "In that city we were treated with much kindness by many of its citizens, and there I met friends and acquaintances who were cordial and hospitable." Early and his staff visited the various brigade camps in the late morning and early afternoon, and the general called upon the sister-in-law of his superior, Richard S. Ewell.[81]

During the afternoon, Captain William Seymour visited downtown York. He deemed it a

pretty place. . . . Some of the public buildings were exceedingly tasteful and imposing structures. All the stores were closed and I was disappointed in not being able to purchase articles of clothing of which I stood in great need. Through the kindness of my friend Major [Samuel] Hale, of Gen. Early's staff, who was acting Provost Marshal, I got into the back door of a very large fancy store, where I purchased a bottle of old Cognac brandy and a few other articles.

The proprietor of the establishment was a Baltimore woman, who appeared to be greatly rejoiced at the advent of Confederate troops and declared her willingness to accept Confederate money in exchange for anything contained in her store. The inhabitants professed to be 'Copperheads' and opposed to the Federal Conscription Act and further prosecution of the war. Not much faith to be placed in their professions; they are a mean, selfish, sordid people who would profess or do anything to save their money & property.

Seymour's close friend and brother-in-law, Brigadier General Johnson K. Duncan, had died of malaria in Tennessee in mid-December. The West Point graduate was a native of York and much of his family still lived there, including his sisters. Seymour decided to call on Margaret Duncan Beitzel. As he rode up to her house, her husband "darted out of the back door in a painful state of trepidation, leaving his wife to do the honors." Seymour received a *"frigid* reception" but remained awhile conversing. His prolonged presence finally drew curiosity of Beitzel, who returned home and was "hugely relieved and rejoiced" at finding that the Southerner's visit was not for a hostile purpose.[82]

Soldiers visited old acquaintances, relaxed, cleaned equipment, or visited York's retail shops, at times forcing proprietors to open them. They "scattered their counterfeit trash around freely, paying $5 or $10 for a couple of cigars, and waiting for change." Rebels entered Charles Spangler's dry goods store, buying notions, ginghams, calicoes, stationery, gloves, and other merchandise with Confederate scrip. Hungry Southerners visited Jacob Sechrist's grocery store and appropriated 30 pounds of cheese, 5 pounds of tea, 30 pounds of sugar, and 8 pounds of coffee, as well as 6 pairs of men's drawers, 5 undershirts, and a new suit of clothes. N. Lehmayer and Brother lost 225 coats, 100 hats, 387 shirts of various styles and colors, 50 undershirts and drawers, 50 pairs of suspenders, 50 pocket handkerchiefs, and 50 pairs of woolen socks.[83]

One clothing merchant had concealed most of his inventory. An officer from the Louisiana Tigers knocked on the door, and the old man responded that he had nothing left to sell. The Confederate offered gold for some fresh shirts, and the storekeeper opened his locked store and allowed the Rebel to select what he wanted. The Southerner returned to his quarters and declared to his men where they could obtain shirts. Several Tigers headed into downtown York, stopped at the old man's store, and asked for shirts. The merchant refused to sell any to them for worthless Confederate scrip, so the Rebels pushed him aside and entered the store to check for themselves. They found the shirts, as well as a supply of aged whiskey and other choice liquors.

When the merchant refused to give them any alcohol, the Tigers locked him out of his store and proceeded to "indulge in a great spree." Soon, a crowd of onlookers huddled outside his windows, peering at the commotion inside. The soldiers emerged with their arms loaded with large quantities of merchandise and asked the shopkeeper to tally the bill. They handed him Confederate currency, leaving him with a "rueful countenance, notwithstanding the assurances of the officers that the day would come when he would be *glad* to have some Confederate money in his possession.[84]

The identities of the Tigers involved in the escapade are unknown, but it is possible they were Private Thomas Benton Reed and some of his merry friends from Company A of the 9th Louisiana. He wrote in his diary, "We lay still today, and some of the boys made a raid on the merchants of York and got a lot of hats and shoes. I got a nice hat, which I was very proud of." Upon returning to camp, he went on picket duty. A group of Irishmen in Company E drank too much and soon became intoxicated from the effects of "Old Red Eye." Soon, a brawl broke out in camp and one lieutenant was "badly used up." Reed and other pickets finally broke up the fight and placed several of the brawlers under guard in the "Bull Pen." The Irishmen soon dozed off and slept off the effects of the York County whiskey.[85]

One captain, perhaps also emboldened by alcohol, made a loud speech downtown that drew a large crowd. He rambled on about the merits of southern independence and exhorted local Democrats to rise up and assert their rights. The officer defended slavery as a "divine institution" and mocked Lincoln's policies as trampling on the Constitution. He finished his emotional monologue by denigrating the foreign-born soldiers in the Union army: "There is one unpleasant feature to the war, that is, the enlightened South is compelled to fight the low, degraded scum of other nations."[86]

Fresh horses were of particular interest to the Southerners, especially to pull their heavy wagons, caissons, and limbers, and General Early authorized his quartermasters to scour the countryside to procure suitable animals. Many residents previously had taken their horses and livestock across the Susquehanna River into neighboring Lancaster County, where they were presumably safe from Confederate predators. However, hundreds of York Countians failed to heed repeated warnings that the Rebels were coming. Foraging patrols freely roamed the countryside, and residents took belated precautions to protect their horses from seizure. Some rural folk came into town, angrily seeking the New York con artists who had sold them the worthless tickets purported to spare their horses and livestock from Confederate confiscation. The farmers were shocked to learn that it was a ruse to separate them from their money.[87]

Other Pennsylvanians hastily took measures to protect their horses, including hiding them in cellars, haylofts, out-of-the-way ravines and hollows, and even within their houses. One woman went as far as smearing fresh cow dung all over her horse to dissuade the Rebels from taking it. Other citizens tied strings tightly around their horses' legs to make them appear lame and unfit for military service. Still others placed fresh crocks of butter, wheels of cheese, baked goods, and other food at their gates in a vain effort to bribe the soldiers or keep them occupied with eating instead of searching for hidden animals.[88]

Hays' acting quartermaster, Major John G. Campbell, heard that a particular farmer had a large draft horse. He stopped at a large, finely furnished house, but the owner denied having such an animal. However, the sound of neighing from an adjoining room soon confirmed its presence. Campbell quietly opened the door to the parlor and discovered a massive Conestoga plow horse standing beside an expensive rosewood piano. With some difficulty, the major led the horse away. The chagrined farmer was left with a fistful of worthless Confederate currency and a parlor that smelled like a barnyard.[89]

George and John B. Rutter owned a Manchester Township farm not far from the Tigers' campsite. Hays' men raided the barn, stealing a horse, three mules, several harnesses, halters, collars, traces, and a wagon whip and riding saddle. They took other personal property and destroyed it. Another squad of Louisianans visited a gristmill owned by Josiah E. Myers. Breaking in, they stole eight barrels of stone-ground flour, fifteen bushels of corn, and fifteen meal bags. Rebels filled their haversacks with twenty-five bushels of flour at Zechariah K. Loucks' mill and took sixty bushels of corn and fifty bushels of wheat. They burned his fencing for firewood and destroyed twenty acres of grass and grain while camping on his farm.[90]

One group of Louisianans discovered a knot of civilians trying to hide several horses in a field along Trout Run. They accosted John C. Hake, Adam Hake, and John B. Rutter and took a large seven-year-old bay horse, as well as a bay mare and a roan. Nearby, John F. Hake lost two horses and a mare, along with a harness. Near Pleasureville, several Tigers overtook a horse-drawn wagon being taken to safety by the Jacob Kessler family. They forced the farmers to drive into the Confederate camp, where they released the men, but kept the wagon and all five mules. The Kesslers walked home to discover that their bay stallion and a favorite riding horse were missing from the stable, as well as several bushels of oats, shelled corn, and horse feed.[91]

The wanton thievery appalled at least one Confederate. Private William

B. Hockett, a thirty-six-year-old Quaker conscientious objector, had been drafted into the 21st North Carolina in May and forced against his will to join the regiment for the march into Pennsylvania. He met up with Company M shortly after Second Winchester but refused to take up arms. Officers placed him under arrest for defying orders. Staying with the brigade's wagon train in downtown York, he wrote in his journal Sunday evening, "My heart is sick, seeing the roguery our men are up to; taking horses, cattle and provisions of all kind. Nothing that they see escapes their grasp, and they are thrown away because men cannot carry them."[92]

In the late afternoon, wagonloads of requisitioned flour from the Smalls' mills rumbled into the Confederate campsites. Other deliveries brought sides of fresh beef. Regimental quartermasters and commissary sergeants such as Louis M. Rambin of the 9th Louisiana accepted the foodstuffs and added them to their stores of provisions. Fires soon were roaring, and hundreds of Tigers enjoyed the first hot meal they had eaten in several days. They quickly devoured huge quantities of roasted meat and mountains of bread.[93]

The idyllic times would soon end. A cavalry patrol thundered into downtown York from the northwest while Early was conferring with businessman Philip Small, who agreed to post a $50,000 bond toward the $71,400 shortfall in tribute money. The horsemen were accompanying Captain Elliott Johnston, General Ewell's aide, who dismounted and sought out Early. He delivered a copy of a note from Robert E. Lee to Ewell stating the enemy's army was moving north and directing that the various corps were to concentrate on the west side of South Mountain. Johnson relayed verbal instructions from Ewell that Early was to move back to rejoin the rest of the corps.

Early began preparing to leave York. He instructed the editor of the *Gazette* to print a handbill notifying the citizens that he would not burn the railroad buildings as threatened. In his opinion, he would have been perfectly justified applying the torch, "but we do not war upon women and children." At 9:00 p.m., Early withdrew the guards from the hotels and taverns, and shortly thereafter, Avery's North Carolinians departed the fairgrounds and army hospital. They marched westward to the Carlisle Road, where Gordon's Georgians were camped. Smith and Hays posted extra provost guards to try to stop their men from deserting or wandering back into town to take advantage of the unguarded liquor stores.[94]

A few Tigers were still in town, having missed the orders to return to their regiments. Lieutenants William C. McGimsey and J. Warren Jackson of the 8th Louisiana had slipped out of camp earlier in the day for an unauthorized "French leave" visit to York. Jackson, a confirmed teetotaler (a rarity in Hays' Brigade) later wrote that York had "some magnificent buildings in it, the streets are very regular & well paved. The people are mostly Dutch and were very friendly. Confederate money was taken *at par* and I shall ever remember York with pleasure. . . . Had lots of fun, saw some pretty girls and amused ourselves extensively until 10:00 p.m."[95]

Another absentee was Private Charles Moore Jr., who remarked in his diary, "Detailed for patrolling and feasted on cherries." He watched Avery's men apply the torch to several railroad cars at the freight yard and then went sightseeing with a friend. "Lieutenant [George H.] Henchey and I spent the evening at Mrs. Codwise's and tramped around town. The town clock struck 12, then we left for camp."[96]

Early retired to the widow (Hannah) Metzel's hotel and spent a quiet evening conversing. Meanwhile, Hays and the other brigade commanders "and their subordinate officers slept very little that night, for they were laying plans to countermarch at a given signal." Shortly after midnight, Hays' five regimental leaders began spreading the news to their company line officers to prepare for the march, and the men prepared two days' rations. Chagrined lieutenants Jackson and McGimsey "got back into camp that night & and found that we would have to march before day."[97]

### Westward Once Again

Before daybreak on Tuesday, June 30, Early's Division broke camp and prepared for another day of marching. Drumbeats roused Hays' Louisianans at 4:00 a.m. in a light rain and fog. After hastily cooking some breakfast, they were on the road within two hours, marching through Weigelstown to the Canal Road, rejoining the main column on the way. Early and his staff were among the last Confederates to leave York, departing about 7:00 a.m. On the march, Colonel Trevanion Lewis of the 8th Louisiana placed lieutenants McGimsey and Jackson under arrest for their clandestine visit to York and forced them to ride in an ambulance.

The bulk of the division backtracked from Weigelstown through East Berlin in the general direction of Heidlersburg, a route that gave Early the option to move either to Shippensburg or to Greenwood by way of Arendtsville, "as circumstances and enemy movements might dictate." The day was

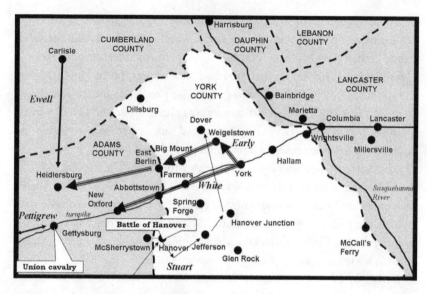

Tigers march toward Heidlersburg, June 30

cloudy with calm winds as Hays' Louisiana Tigers essentially retraced their movements of June 27 and headed west toward an unknown destiny. They progressed slowly on the winding, hilly dirt roads in western York County, averaging perhaps two miles an hour during the morning.[98]

The retrograde movement was a clear indicator to the officers and men that a battle loomed. For days, rumors of Yankee movements had circulated, although none seemed consistent or reliable. The Pennsylvania militia that had "skedaddled" out of Gettysburg and then York was no longer a concern, as they were now east of the Susquehanna River and had shown no signs of any aggressive action. Somewhere off to the south was the Army of the Potomac, but exactly where was unclear. What was clear was that the senior commanders expected to fight a decisive battle on northern soil. The leisurely, almost picnic atmosphere of the days of foraging and sightseeing was now over. This westward march was different, for battle loomed. Confidence remained high, tinged with the uncertainty of individual fate. Lieutenant Michael Murray of the 6th Louisiana wrote, "We turned back towards Gettysburg, where important business awaited us."[99]

Meanwhile in York, the U.S. Sanitary Commission's relief agent, James Gall, observed that the Confederate provosts' efforts had not been successful in preventing soldiers from straying into the unguarded bars: "The city is now clear of rebels, except some stragglers who purposely staid [*sic*] behind, or were too drunk to go with their commands." Federals picked up one straggler, English-born Private George Dearie of the 5th Louisiana, near East Berlin the next day.[100]

Residents took stock of their losses during the brief two-day occupation. Staunch Republican attorney James Latimer penned a lengthy letter to his younger brother recounting Jubal Early's stay in the borough. He added a telling postscript, "Afternoon. No rebs here. The County people are beginning to come in. They were plundered indiscriminately particularly by a Louisiana brigade. Horses and mules taken, houses broken open, and everything the thieves fancied stolen." Among these victims of the Tigers was Pleasureville merchant Emanuel G. Keller, whose dry goods store was robbed of large quantities of shoes, hats, pencils, pens, and other sundries. Spring Garden Township farmer Samuel Stevens reported losing four hams, seventy-five barrels of lard, three sides of leather, nineteen crocks of apple butter, bed clothing, men's and women's clothing, chickens, garden produce, dishes, and pieces of furniture that were taken from his house and smashed. The Rebels also destroyed a bureau and a barrel of vinegar.

The Tigers had once again lived up to their fearsome reputation, and York Countians would long remember their visit. Jubal Early would never forgive borough officials for not paying the full amount of cash he requisitioned. More than a decade after the battle, he complained, "We were compelled to get our provisions from the country we were in. Ewell's corps was pretty well supplied for a few days, my division best of all, for which the town of York is not yet done paying."[101]

While his comrades in Company D of the 9th Louisiana were marching back toward Adams County, the ill Private John D. Shackleford was still lying in a barn on the David Schriver farm along the Mummasburg Road west of Gettysburg. Discovering his unexpected guest, Schriver summoned Dr. John W. C. O'Neal, a Virginia-born physician who had graduated from Gettysburg College and the Maryland Medical School. After practicing in Baltimore and then Hanover, Pennsylvania, O'Neal had moved to Gettysburg that February.

Hearing that a sick man needed attention, O'Neal headed his carriage out of town to the farm. He spoke to the prostrated soldier and managed to get his name, address, and his mother's name, Mary. The doctor examined his patient and prescribed medication. However, Shackleford did not respond to the treatment. Instead, he weakened considerably and died, to O'Neal the result of being "overmarched." The Schrivers buried the Confederate alongside the road. The Tiger, only nineteen years old when he enlisted in 1861, was likely the first Confederate buried in Gettysburg during the campaign. He would not be the last Louisianan whose fate was a grave in the rich topsoil of Pennsylvania.[102]

About noontime, Early's Division stopped less than a mile west of the tiny hamlet of Davidsburg and began cooking more of the York levy. The major general stopped at a roadside hotel and tavern owned by William Julius, where he ordered meals for himself, his staff, "Extra Billy" Smith, and Harry Hays. While the proprietor's family prepared the food for twenty Confederates, Early and his brigadiers conferred in a small room, speaking in low tones and discussing the military situation. Their staff officers sat in a front room, some of them reading pocket Bibles, for they all knew a desperate battle was soon to take place. When the food was ready, they sat around a long table for half an hour quietly eating their midday meal, which they all seemed to relish. There was very little conversation at the dining table, for "a serious air seemed to pervade the entire room all the time they remained." As Early and Hays walked out the front door, they heard the distant booming of cannon toward the southwest. "I suppose a battle has begun," Hays remarked as Early mounted his horse, held by the proprietor. Before leaving, Early handed William Julius four five-dollar Confederate notes in payment for the twenty dinners that he had ordered.[103]

The division was back on the road by two o'clock in the afternoon. Colonel French's 17th Virginia Cavalry screened Early's westward march. Near East Berlin, the mounted infantry briefly skirmished with cavalry from the Army of the Potomac. They captured a Federal, who turned out to be twenty-six-year-old Hamilton McKinney Bell, a native of Washington County, Pennsylvania, and now a commissary sergeant in Company B of the 1st West Virginia Cavalry. Guards escorted the former grocer and millwright into East Berlin to General Early's headquarters.

There, Jubal Early peppered the captive with questions concerning the past and present movements of the Federal army. However, Bell refused to volunteer anything of value to the enemy leader, only replying, "I am not commanding the Army of the Potomac." He stared at Early and asked the gray-clad general if he knew the nature of the oath a United States soldier was required to take upon enlistment. When Early sarcastically replied that he did, Bell solemnly retorted, "It was not befitting either a gentleman or a soldier to endeavor to get a prisoner of war to perjure himself by giving the enemy any intelligence of the movements of an army that he knew of." A frustrated Early gave up and remarked, "I will not ask him any more questions." The uncooperative prisoner was turned over to the provost of the 5th Louisiana for safekeeping. He would march with the Tigers for the next few days before being paroled after the Battle of Gettysburg and sent to Carlisle.[104]

While Early paused in East Berlin, a courier dashed into town with a dispatch from General Ewell, stating that he was moving with Rodes' Division by way of Petersburg to Heidlersburg. Early's Division was to march to the same place. The column resumed its westward trek, finally halting after marching nearly twenty-six miles since leaving York. The Louisiana Tigers camped about three miles east of Heidlersburg, not far from the farming village of Round Hill. They were near the source of the sluggish Plum Run, where fresh water and forage for the horses were plentiful. Campfires soon blazed with fence rails taken from nearby fields, and more of the York ransom was consumed.[105]

Spirits were high that night. The drunken binges at Gettysburg and York were still fresh in the minds of many men. Now, the focus was on the imminent meeting with the Federal army in the next few days. Captain William Seymour believed "it was inspiring to see the spirits of the men rise at the prospect of a fight. We all knew that, were Meade's Army to be defeated, the roads to Washington, Philadelphia and Baltimore would be open to us."[106]

Early and his escort rode through the crossroads village to see General Ewell, finding him encamped a mile north of town with Rodes' Division along the Harrisburg Road. Several officers attended the meeting, including a supernumerary major general, Isaac Trimble, who, after recovering from a wound, had hastened north to catch up with the army. He had been assigned temporarily to Ewell's Corps. Ewell informed them that Lee wanted to concentrate the corps at or near Cashtown at the eastern base of South Mountain. His division was to travel there the next morning by way of Hunterstown and Mummasburg, while Rodes would take a more northerly route through Middletown (now Biglerville) and Arendtsville.[107]

In the early evening, a message from General Lee gave Ewell the option of bringing his two divisions to either Cashtown or Gettysburg, depending on circumstances. A second courier brought a note from Third Corps commander General A. P. Hill stating that his troops were in and around Cashtown. Neither message said anything about enemy troops in Gettysburg. The generals and their troops settled down to a night's sleep. The clouds had cleared by 9:00 p.m. and stars twinkled high above the pastoral campsite. For a few of Harry Hays' Louisiana Tigers, the peaceful slumber in the verdant pastures east of Heidlersburg would be their final night on earth.

# 4 | Gettysburg

## Day 1

### A Promising Beginning

SUNRISE ON WEDNESDAY, July 1, brought the promise of another day on the road for the Louisiana Tigers, but one that could result in contact with the Yankees. Confederate cavalry patrols had encountered their counterparts from the Army of the Potomac the previous day, a telltale sign that the enemy infantry was no longer deep in Virginia. A significant battle loomed, but no one was certain of where and when it would occur. Major General Jubal Early prepared his veteran division to march. His orders were to march through Hunterstown toward Cashtown or Gettysburg, depending upon the circumstances.

When everything was ready, his division moved out, with John Gordon's Georgians in the lead heading westward on the Berlin-Heidlersburg Road. Harry Hays' First Louisiana Brigade brought up the rear of the miles-long column this day, marching behind the supply wagons as a rear guard. According to Charles Moore Jr., the 5th Louisiana "camped all day until 9 o'clock, then took up our line of march for Gettysburg, where a battle had begun."[1]

The sky was overcast throughout the morning, with cumulostratus cloud cover and temperatures in the low seventies. A gentle, warm breeze blew from the south as the Tigers headed deeper into Adams County, an area they had last visited on June 27 when they camped just northwest of Gettysburg. Now, they were several miles northeast of the borough.[2]

In a short distance, Early reached Five Points, where the road he was supposed to take to Hunterstown meandered off to the southwest. The general gruffly noted that this "road" was nothing more than a rutted farm lane with several twists and turns, which offered a "very rough and circuitous" path. On his own initiative, he changed his route, staying on the graded road to Heidlersburg and then turning southward at the crossroads onto the Harrisburg Road, a much higher quality roadbed. This route intersected a few miles to the south with the road to Mummasburg that he was originally to use to head toward the designated Cashtown rendezvous. This latter road traveled north and west of Gettysburg and offered several intersections with roads leading directly to that town should he be redirected there.[3]

Not long after passing through Heidlersburg, Early received a dispatch from Ewell informing him that generals Hill and Rodes were moving toward Gettysburg against an enemy force and directing him to lead his division there as well. The distant roar of battle could be heard echoing off the verdant Pennsylvania hills. The prospect of a good scrap excited many of the Tigers, who naturally widened their strides in anticipation as Hays urged them on. According to one of Rodes' staff, "When it was announced that a battle was on hand, Hays' Louisiana Brigade could scarcely be controlled; they shouted, and breaking ranks, were about to rush forward, when the influence of Generals Gordon and Hays restored order."[4]

The Confederates quickened their pace as they neared Gettysburg and its Union defenders. Adjutant William Seymour recorded, "the heavy booming of cannon told us that the conflict had begun and we pushed on with great rapidity." In Major Alexander Hart's 5th Louisiana, spirits were high as his infantrymen approached Gettysburg. Following the division's occasional brushes with the state militiamen, who had run off when challenged, the boys believed the day would be short and decisive. One enlisted man explained, "They fully believed they could clean up the Army of the Potomac in about four hours and put an end to the war." The results of the recent Chancellorsville fight only reinforced this prevailing attitude of invincibility.[5]

Rodes' Division filed off to the southwest onto Herr's Tavern Road toward the Carlisle Pike and followed a ridgeline somewhat parallel to Early's line of approach. His specific foe's identity was unknown as Early neared Gettysburg, but lead elements of the Army of the Potomac had arrived. West of town along the Chambersburg Pike, part of A. P. Hill's corps had already clashed with Brigadier General John Buford's cavalry and the I Corps, killing Major General John Reynolds early in the fight.

One-armed Major General Oliver O. Howard had taken command of the field, with Howard's XI Corps falling to Major General Carl Schurz, a politically important ally of President Lincoln in securing the support (and vote) of the burgeoning German-American population. The corps had been maligned in the press and the army for perceived cowardice at the Battle of Chancellorsville, and many of the soldiers and officers were seeking redemption this day. Most of Schurz's men were arrayed in the relatively level fields a mile north of the borough to protect both the Harrisburg Road and Carlisle Pike, with the remainder in reserve on Cemetery Hill, which dominated Gettysburg's southern outskirts. Blocking Early's line of approach was Brigadier General Francis C. Barlow's 2,500-man First Division, composed of the veteran brigades of Colonel Leopold von Gilsa and Brigadier General Adelbert Ames. They were posted immediately west of the pike around a low, lightly wooded rise known locally as Blocher's Knoll.

At the base of the hill, to Barlow's front was the swollen Rock Creek, its steep, underbrush-lined banks slippery from recent rains. Von Gilsa's New Yorkers and Pennsylvanians formed the front line, with most of Ames' Brigade in support. Once aware of the Confederate threat, Major Allen G. Brady and four companies of the 17th Connecticut Infantry would extend the line east of the road into gently rolling terrain (mostly open farm fields and pastures lined with wooden fences). Two sections of nineteen-year-old Lieutenant Bayard Wilkeson's Battery G, 4th U.S. Artillery crowned the knoll, the gleaming muzzles of four bronze smoothbore Napoleons pointing northward.[6]

Barlow had moved his division forward to this location without obtaining permission from his corps commander. It was a slightly curved defensive position that would elicit controversy in the years to come, isolated and exposed well in front of Barlow's original designated position. His right flank dangled precipitously in the air, although veteran Federal cavalry under battle-tested Colonel Thomas Devin was in the vicinity to contest any flanking movement on the York Road. Barlow's left flank loosely connected with the extended right flank of the division of Major General Carl Schurz, which, in turn, was to provide support for the I Corps on Oak Ridge to the west.

Peering through his field glasses from a ridge north of Barlow's position, Jubal Early surveyed the battlefield. Rodes was already in action, opposing a "very large force which overlapped his left, and seemed to be pressing back that flank." Skirmishers from Brigadier General George Doles' Georgia Brigade were pulling back as fresh Union troops moved forward. Well to the south, Early noted that Union artillery on the distant Cemetery Hill could sweep his approach on the Harrisburg Road, as well as the York Pike should he try a wide flanking maneuver. Despite staring for some time at the hill,

Early could not determine if the guns had any substantial infantry support, as Cemetery Hill was higher in elevation than the low ridge on which he and his staff were standing.[7]

The immediate concern was the enemy infantry massed on the rise near the creek. Early would need to deal with that before he could move back into the town he had tried to ransom less than a week ago. Despite Robert E. Lee's orders to avoid a general engagement, the stage was set for the decisive battle north of the Mason-Dixon Line for which many in Richmond had clamored. Early began deploying his column into battle line, with Gordon immediately to the right of the road. Ike Avery's depleted brigade was to the left rear, supporting three of Jones' batteries, which unlimbered about 2:30 p.m. (by his estimation) on a low rise northeast of the Federal guns. Smith's Brigade was behind Avery, with his line facing the distant York Pike. The rear of Early's column was not yet up, so he delayed his infantry attack until Hays was in position.

Confederate gunners prepared for action. They estimated ranges, cut fuses appropriately, and rammed rounds into the muzzles. Early gave the order, and the earth shook as the big guns thundered, sending shells shrieking toward Barlow's position. Jones' efforts attracted the attention of the long-range 3-inch rifles General Howard had previously stationed on Cemetery Hill. Buffalo-born teenager Bayard Wilkeson's six Napoleons on Blocher's Knoll also roared in reply to Early's divisional artillery.[8]

A handful of artillerymen and horses on both sides were soon incapacitated or dead. One of Jones' guns, a 12-pounder Napoleon belonging to Garber's Staunton Artillery, was disabled when a solid shot smashed into the muzzle and bent the tube, permanently taking it out of action. The Confederate gunners themselves knocked out a 10-pounder Parrott rifle in Green's Louisiana Guard Artillery. Anxious crewmen loaded a shot that was too large for the inner diameter of the barrel, and it lodged halfway down the tube. Repeated attempts to finish ramming it into position failed, and crews withdrew the gun. A similar problem with mismatching ammunition temporarily disabled two other cannon. However, the remaining guns created havoc around Wilkeson's position.[9]

After marching some twelve miles from their Plum Run campsite, the Louisiana Tigers arrived northeast of Gettysburg shortly after 2:30 p.m. As Hays surveyed the terrain in his front, he discovered that Early had left a space in the center of the division battle line for the Louisianans. Gordon's and Avery's brigades were already arrayed in a long sweeping battle line, with Gordon's 26th Georgia detached to support Jones' artillery. Smith's Virginians were in reserve a half-mile to the north in a field east of the road. Near them, Carrington's Charlottesville Artillery parked alongside the road, awaiting orders to gallop to the front to exploit any breakthrough. Captain Carrington and his crews clamored for a chance to join in the fray. "While these batteries were this engaged, I and my men became a little impatient, and General Early passed by towards the front. He paused for a moment, and I playfully stated this to him. He replied to me good-naturedly that I need not be impatient, that there would be plenty for me to do after awhile."[10]

The Tigers quickly filed into the fields on either side of the pike. Hays formed his line with the 7th and 8th Regiments and the left wing of the 9th Louisiana to the east of Harrisburg Road and the right wing of the 9th Louisiana and the 5th and 6th Regiments west of the road in a skirt of woods behind Rock Creek. As the 9th deployed, a solid shot struck the turnpike fifty yards in front of the regiment and ricocheted into the trees to their right. It was a grim reminder that the days of picnicking in Pennsylvania were now over. Hays ordered the men to load their muskets and prepare to advance upon his order.[11]

Deployed on the extreme left of the brigade on a broad plateau, Lieutenant J. Warren Jackson of the 8th Louisiana, no longer under arrest, "could see Rodes on our right driving the Yankees like sheep before him." He later informed his brother, "It was the prettiest sight I ever saw." The excitement was infectious, and the Tigers itched to join the action. The crest of the distant Oak Ridge, beyond which the brigade had camped on June 26, cut off Jackson's eastward view. None of the men in Company D of the 9th Louisiana could have possibly known that their friend John Shackleford lay in a fresh grave there along the Mummasburg Road, having died the day before in David Schriver's barn.[12]

About 3:00 p.m., Early ordered Gordon's Brigade to advance. With battle flags unfurled and waving in the gentle breeze, the Georgians moved forward through fields of ripening wheat and waist-high corn, their right flank supported by Doles' Georgia brigade, which was again advancing after its earlier temporary setback. As Gordon approached the abrupt and rugged banks of Rock Creek, Early sent word to Hays to also advance.

Lieutenant Jackson placed the time of the Tigers' advance as 3:05 p.m.

Hays' left wing—Colonel Davidson Penn's 7th Louisiana and Colonel T. D. Lewis's motley 8th Louisiana, and half of Colonel Leroy Stafford's Central Louisiana farm boys—pressed onward through the Rebert and Bender farms. Jackson mentioned that they "marched slowly in line for 1 ½ miles before we got to any Yankees." There, Avery's and Hays' advance skirmishers encountered Major Brady's four companies from the 17th Connecticut. Occasional artillery shells burst overhead, adding to the danger from the whistling Minié balls. Confederate blood began to be spilled in the fields, and a handful of Tar Heels and Louisianans trudged to the rear, nursing wounds.

Private Thomas Reed of the 9th Louisiana commented, "Company A was sent out skirmishing. We found the enemy. . . . My dear friend, L. B. Bonnard [Barnard], went into this fight wearing a three-story white silk hat, and he was shot to death on the picket line; he did not get into the general engagement." Private Barnard may have been the first Louisiana Tiger shot during the Battle of Gettysburg. If not, he was among the first. He expired on July 4.[13]

On the right, Major Alexander Hart's 5th Louisiana, Lieutenant Colonel Joe Hanlon's Irish Tigers of the 6th Regiment, along with the 9th's right wing under Lieutenant Colonel William R. Peck, stayed in line through the Josiah Benner farm, supporting Gordon's fight on Barlow's Knoll. Gordon finally pushed the Yankees off the hillock, and Early gave the order for Hays and Avery to drive forward. Hays' right wing followed Gordon's victorious troops in sweeping across Rock Creek. There, the Tigers' right flank swept past the flotsam of battle on the knoll, teeming with dead and injured soldiers from both armies. Among them were young artilleryman Bayard Wilkeson and division commander Barlow, both grievously wounded.

Hilary Jones had to watch his fire carefully to avoid hitting Early's infantrymen while they swept forward on the flatland south of the knoll. "On the advance of General Gordon's brigade from our right, we directed our fire farther to the left, on the disordered masses of the enemy that were rapidly retreating before our troops. This was continued until the advance of our men rendered it dangerous to continued firing from that position."[14]

Soon, the limbered Charlottesville Artillery received orders to leave its reserve position north of Rock Creek, and the Virginia gunners followed immediately behind Gordon's battle line, crossing the Rock Creek bridge one gun at a time and turning into the fields beyond Blocher's Knoll. For much of their advance, Jubal Early accompanied them. Captain James Carrington took time to watch his division commander: "General Early was silent as we rode together, most of the time, his attention being absorbed by what was going on in front. He was perfectly cool, but manifested the deepest interest." Within "ten or fifteen minutes," the youthful Carrington watched as "Hays' Brigade made their appearance upon our left," and soon he heard the "wild Confederate yell," which he took as an indication of victory. Robert Stiles, in charge of one of Carrington's pieces, recalled, "We drove the enemy pell-mell over rolling wheat fields, through a grove across a creek, up a little slope and into the town itself. The pursuit was so close and hot that, though my gun came into battery several times, yet I could not get in a shot."[15]

Several Yankee guns stopped periodically on hillocks and low rises to fire off a few rounds at the advancing Confederate infantry and then limbered and withdrew before Carrington could reply. Wilkeson's Battery, now under Lieutenant Eugene Bancroft, had a particularly hard time avoiding the rapidly advancing Rebel infantry. "During this engagement the battery was separated into sections or half batteries, and its struggle to maintain itself was very severe and persistent."[16]

After Gordon's Brigade shattered the Federals' hastily improvised second line at the sprawling Adams County Almshouse complex, Jubal Early ordered the exhausted Georgians to halt in a shallow depression near the John Crawford house. Nearly out of ammunition, Gordon's men refilled their cartridge boxes, but their fighting was done for the day. Hays' line inexorably swept southward still bisecting the Harrisburg Road, his right wing slowed somewhat by the Almshouse complex and its orchard and in passing through Gordon's stationary line. The Tigers and George Doles' Georgia brigade to their right steadily pushed the retreating Yankees toward the town. Union Brigadier General Adelbert Ames, commanding the XI Corps' First Division since Barlow went down, bemoaned, "The whole division was falling back with little or no regularity, regimental organizations having become destroyed." A gleeful Jubal Early reported, "the rout soon became general."[17]

Colonel Andrew L. Harris of the 75th Ohio, now temporarily commanding Ames' Brigade, frantically tried to keep his battered regiment together. "If a man straggled, he was certain to be captured, and this was the case with many who were attempting to get off their wounded friends, and chose to die with them rather than leave them to the foe." One of his Buckeyes, Private William Southerton, recalled, "Giving the word to retreat, Colonel Harris led the way back through town. Confusion was everywhere, and the Johnnies were right at our heels. Some of the boys took refuge in cellars when they were overtaken. Colonel Harris . . . was as anxious to get away as any of us.

We were much like a parcel of schoolboys turned loose. The order was to follow Colonel Harris, stick close to him. Those who did made it through the town safely. And I was one of them. I was right at the colonel's heels."[18]

Major Allen Brady's four companies of Connecticut skirmishers had remained in the fields east of the Harrisburg Road to slow the Confederates. Ames sent an aide with orders for Brady to head into Gettysburg and assume command of his regiment, because Lieutenant Colonel Douglas Fowler was down. Brady and his men abandoned their position and hustled downtown in a circuitous route using the York Road to avoid the Confederate lines.[19]

Now free from the annoying skirmishers that delayed their left wing, the Tigers surged forward. Harry Hays later called his brigade's movement across the undulating open fields toward Gettysburg "rapid and impetuous." An admiring Major Campbell Brown of Ewell's staff recalled, "Then came one of the most warlike & animated spectacles I ever looked on. Gordon & Hays charged across the plateau in their front, at double-quick, sweeping everything before them & scattering the extreme right of the enemy." A few Tigers fell, including Captain Frederick Richardson of the 5th Louisiana.[20]

A few impetuous Louisianans entered homes on Gettysburg's northern outskirts and began shooting at knots of retreating Federals. Lieutenant Lewis Fischer of the 74th Pennsylvania was leading several Union soldiers back toward the town. Just south of Pennsylvania College was a small stone bridge that crossed over a small nameless brook. The bridge's arch raised the roadbed in the center several feet above the ends of the span. Word was passed from man to man to bypass the bridge and instead trudge through the deep mire around the brook, as Rebel infantry hiding in several houses east of the bridge were raking it with rifle fire.

Second Lieutenant William Roth scorned the idea of any Rebel actually hitting him, and he defiantly marched onto the bridge, against the advice of his comrades. He made a perfect target when he reached the arch's full height. His comrades heard the distinctive dull thud of a Minié ball striking flesh and watched as Roth reeled and then sank to the ground. Fischer decided to avoid presenting a similar target, so he ducked through the miry ground and safely crossed the brook.[21]

In Gettysburg, Dr. John W. C. O'Neal recorded about 4:00 p.m., "Our army is believed to be falling back, and the fighting is getting nearer. There is intense excitement among our citizens." Federal reinforcements rushed forward to slow the Confederate advance. Colonel Charles Coster's reserve brigade moved toward Avery and Hays' left wing, and the four 12-pounder Napoleons of Captain Lewis Heckman's Battery K, 1st Ohio Artillery galloped to the front and unlimbered east of Pennsylvania College near the Harrisburg Road. Second Lieutenant Charles M. Schiely's section aimed at an oncoming Confederate regiment within easy range. The subsequent blasts of canister slowed the Rebels but did not stop them. Within short order, Second Lieutenant Columbus Radamour's section joined in, spewing wide arcing swaths of canister balls at the enemy.

"We commenced giving them our best wishes in the shape of shell and canister, which mowed them down like wheat," recalled quartermaster sergeant Cecil C. Reed, a twenty-year-old Clevelander. "But on they came, closing up their ranks wherever they were torn asunder by our shots, and they were not idle all the time either; they were pouring in their volleys with telling effect. Our men were falling fast and they were coming so close that some of their skirmishers were literally blown to pieces from the muzzles of our guns." Over a period of thirty minutes, Heckman fired 113 rounds, mostly canister, but lost 13 men and 9 horses.[22]

One member of the 8th Louisiana, twenty-year-old Second Lieutenant T. Laizer Broussard, was wounded by a canister ball that passed through his buttocks. Another member of the regiment, Private Charles L. Comes of Company K, was killed, as was Sgt. Jefferson B. Smith, a Pennsylvania native. Captain Seymour was thankful about his own fate, "In this charge, I had a very narrow escape from a shell which burst near my head and almost stunned me; two fragments struck my horse on the head and neck, but only wounded him slightly."[23]

Well to Heckman's left, across Carlisle Street, Bancroft blasted away at Doles' line. They may have also taken a few shots at the 5th Louisiana, just off Doles' left flank. Part of Captain Hubert Dilger's Battery I, 1st Ohio Artillery also unlimbered farther west, near Washington Street, and tried to arrest Doles' progress. Harry Hays later gave credit to the Federal artillery as his men pushed southward toward the Gettysburg Railroad. "In my progress to this position, the fire to which my command was subjected from the enemy's batteries, posted upon well-selected rises of the ground, was unusually galling."[24]

Several survivors from the XI Corps' Second and Third divisions reformed near the guns and blazed away at the Confederates. Lieutenant Colonel

Adolphus Dobke of the 45th New York mentioned, "In a short time all sorts of missiles found their way through houses, fences, and gardens, and it was evident that to stay much longer would be certain destruction."[25]

To their left was a knot of 100–150 men from Colonel Wladimir Krzyzanowski's shattered brigade. Major Frederick C. Winkler rallied thirty-two men from the 32nd Wisconsin, including two soldiers from Company B who had saved the colors during the regiment's frantic retreat. The odds were against him, but Winkler was determined to try to protect his isolated position. The twenty-five-year-old Bremen, Germany, native later reflected, "I formed my little band in two ranks and had them sit down in the road. It was useless, of course, to try to resist the long rebel forces that were then approaching, but we could delay them and thus ensure a safe retreat to the rest of our troops." However, as the Confederates came closer, many of the other Federals supporting the guns began to pull back. Winkler, a Milwaukee attorney before the war, used his oratory skills and managed to keep his badly shaken group from routing. He stood in the road beside the crouching soldiers watching the riveting action unfold to his right.[26]

Meanwhile, Hays' left wing had swept forward, moving steadily through the maze of fence-lined fields and splashing across Rock Creek and Stevens Run, the latter just above Gettysburg. During the advance, Avery's right flank had drifted in front of Hays' left, forcing the 7th and 8th Louisiana to slow down. The Tar Heels and Louisianans approached the town's northern outskirts, where they encountered Howard's rear guard. He had hastily thrown forward the brigade of Colonel Charles R. Coster, a New York City native who had served in the state militia and then the 12th U.S. Infantry regulars before becoming colonel of the 134th New York.

Directed into position at the double-quick by Major General Schurz, Coster deployed three regiments in battle line to the right of Stratton Street, keeping his fourth regiment, the 73rd Pennsylvania, in reserve downtown near the railroad station. He lined approximately one thousand men behind a wooden fence near John Kuhn's brickyard. They knelt and fired a volley at the advancing Confederates, who were perhaps two to three hundred yards away cresting a rise in a wheat field when Coster finished his deployment. An awestruck Private Charles McKay of the 154th New York wrote, "I shall always remember how the Confederate line of battle looked as it came into full view and started down toward us. It seemed as if they had a battle flag every few rods."[27]

The 27th Pennsylvania was near Kuhn's hemisphere-shaped brick kilns, with the 134th New York on its left. In its haste to get into position, the 134th had left a large gap beside the 154th New York. Spotting the problem, Lieutenant Colonel Lorenz Cantador of the 27th ordered his second battalion to be thrown into the breech but, owing to the din and confusion of the battle, the order was only partially executed. Only about fifty men under Lieutenant Aldolphus F. Vogelbach reached the desired position, as the battalion suffered severe losses while crossing an open field that was swept by the fire of Early's advancing troops.[28]

It was too late. By the time Vogelbach deployed, Avery's 57th North Carolina had swung to the open flank of the mispositioned 134th and decimated the New Yorkers. Almost simultaneously, many of Hays' Tigers climbed over a wooden fence without halting and attacked. Confederates soon turned the flank of the scattered 27th Pennsylvania, while the 8th Louisiana and hundreds of Carolinians struck the 154th New York. Coster began to withdraw as the pressure mounted and his isolated position became hopeless.

The Yankees "raised up like a flock of blackbirds" and skedaddled into town, just as the Rebels poured "a terrible fire" into the fleeing New Yorkers. Tom Reed of the 9th Louisiana wrote, "I ran down to a plank fence and the Yankees were running across an old field and looked to be as thick as you ever saw black birds fly, and as they ran I took three fair cracks at them. I don't know whether I killed one or not, but I hope I did not." Several Confederate witnesses denigrated Coster's fight, but Private J. Arthur Taylor of the 8th Louisiana later credited the Yankees in his front for making a better stand than he had ever seen before.[29]

Panic set in among some Federal leaders who were unable to find a quick way to escape the Confederate onslaught. Hays' adjutant Captain Seymour recorded, "On we pushed, driving the enemy in great confusion upon the town, taking whole regiments belonging to the 11th Corps. . . . One Dutch colonel at the head of about 250 men came up to me and cried out that he surrendered. . . . I made him throw his sword upon the ground and sent the whole party back to our rear guard under the escort of only one Confederate soldier." Coster's small brigade lost 575 men, the overwhelming majority as prisoners.[30]

From his vantage point in the middle of the Carlisle Road, Major Winkler watched as Confederates overran Coster's position and approached the isolated Union guns. The rest of his brigade had already withdrawn toward

Gettysburg, and Winkler pondered what to do, because he had not received instructions to do likewise. Spotting one of Colonel Krzyzanowski's aides going by, he shouted to him for orders. The reply came to fall back, and Winkler complied. He noticed a "little white cottage where the little remnant of our brigade went into the yard and from there fired another volley at the advancing line of the right flank. My men went in, fired, and then followed the rest, running into the city."

The Wisconsin officer watched his little band disintegrate in the face of Hays' and Doles' advance:

> It was useless to attempt—useless to hold them—useless to stay there, but I was enraged; I felt furious when I saw [Ames'] 1st Division all crowding the sidewalks; think of it, it was a northern village. I had ridden up and down its streets from one end to the other three times that day and everywhere there were manifestations of joy; handkerchiefs were waving everywhere, and ladies stood in the streets offering refreshments to the soldiers as they passed. It seemed so awful to march back through those same streets whipped and beaten. It was the most humiliating step I ever took.[31]

As their infantry supports collapsed and ran "pell mell through and beyond the town," Heckman's and Bancroft's gunners frantically managed to get off several rounds of canister before retreating. The 6th North Carolina, free to advance when Coster withdrew, turned to the west. They flanked Lieutenant Schiely's section of Napoleons, shooting down horses, severely wounding Schiely, and claiming his two guns, but not before the Ohioans had "well spiked" the pieces. The remainder of the badly mauled battery moved toward Cemetery Hill minus the guns and nine horses, as well as several crewmen. Captain Heckman lost his horse, grabbed his saddle and remounted, and then rode back through a hail of gunfire to make sure none of his wounded had been left behind.[32]

The situation was becoming critical. Gettysburg physician John O'Neal recorded at 4:20 p.m., "It is feared the First and Eleventh Corps have been defeated. They now are hurrying through the town, artillery and infantry, in wildest confusion. Our citizens are terror-stricken."[33]

James Carrington's Charlottesville Artillery had closely followed Hays' Brigade into Gettysburg's northern extremities. The captain unlimbered three of his guns on the Harrisburg Road, placed canister rounds near their muzzles, and prepared to sweep the streets of residual Yankees, who darted into alleys and gardens to avoid the expected blasts. One of Hays' men, a six-foot-tall muscular Irishman named Burgoyne, had a habit of slipping away when his regiment supported the artillery so he could help work the big guns. Seeing Carrington's crewmen prepare for action, he wandered over, seized the sponge staff, and rammed home a charge, "giving vent to his enthusiasm in screams and bounds that would have done credit to a catamount."

Standing sullenly near the gun was a recently captured Union soldier, of Irish ancestry like Burgoyne, but with an even bigger and more strapping frame. Catching Burgoyne's thick brogue, he mockingly asked him what he was doing serving in the Rebel army. The Louisianan retorted that, as a free Irishman, he had just as much right to fight for the Rebs as the other man did for the Yankees. The prisoner taunted Burgoyne, "I know ye, now you've turned your ugly mug to me. I had the plizure of kicking yez out from behind Marye's wall, that time Sedgwick lammed yer brigade out o' there!" Tempers flared as the other soldiers watched in amusement, and Burgoyne shouted, "Yer a d——n liar, and I'll jist knock yer teeth down yer ugly throat for that same lie." He vaulted over the cannon and went after the impudent Yankee. The two men squared off and the first fist flew. Just as the two closed for the brawl, artillery officer Robert Stiles noticed that the right fist of the "Federal gladiator" was gory, bleeding from the stumps of two shattered fingers sustained earlier during the military battle. Despite the pain, he was preparing to slam the mangled fist into Burgoyne's face.

Stiles cried out to Burgoyne, "Hold! Your man's wounded!" Instantly, Burgoyne's fists fell, and he turned sympathetic toward his opponent. "You're a trump, Pat; give me your well hand. We'll fight this out some other time. I didn't see you were hurt." The brawlers shook hands and went their separate ways. Not long afterward, one of Early's staff members galloped by, shouting orders for the battery to retire to the rear, as it was no longer needed at the front. Captain William Tanner's Courtney Artillery had arrived to relieve Carrington's Battery, which pulled back a mile north of town and redeployed on a hillock.[34]

The brief stands by members of the XI Corps at the Almshouse, Pennsylvania College, and Kuhn's brickyard had failed to halt the advancing Confederates, although their progress was somewhat retarded. Harry Hays recounted, "Here I found the enemy in considerable strength. I still continued to move on." His casualties to this point had been remarkably light, much to the general's surprise and relief and despite the Yankee artilleryman's overenthusiastic claims that they "mowed them down like wheat." Among the few Tigers killed so far was Private George H. Jemison of the 8th Louisiana, an Orleans Parish resident who died in the fields near the Harrisburg Road during the advance on Coster. Later, his body would be recovered and buried behind the Crawford house, north toward the Almshouse along a wooden fence.[35]

Hays halted briefly to reform his brigade at the tracks of the Gettysburg Railroad, which ran east to west through northeastern Gettysburg. He noted a large body of Union troops approaching his right flank—the remnants of Brigadier General Alexander Schimmelfennig's Third Division, which was retiring in good order from the fields to the northwest. Hays immediately changed the front of the 5th, 6th, and the right wing of the 9th regiments to face the threat. Several "well-directed volleys" dispersed the Federals "in full flight through the streets of the city." He bemoaned, "But for this movement on my flank, I should have captured several pieces of artillery opposite the left of my line, upon which the Seventh Regiment was advancing in front and the Eighth by a side street at the time I halted."[36]

Among the recipients of Hays' volleys was the 119th New York. Major Benjamin A. Willis reported, "At this juncture, with an enemy in front [likely Doles' Brigade] and on either flank, not only threatened with, but experiencing, a heavy enfilading fire, we retired in good order [down Washington Street]."[37]

One courageous Federal officer tried to slow the Tigers' progression into the town. "A little to the left of Hays, a tattered Federal regiment faced about and tried to make a stand, led by a mounted officer, who, riding among them, waved his hat and sword, shouting, 'Don't run, men, none but cowards run.' Some of the Confederates, admiring his pluck, cried out, 'Don't shoot that man'; but a volley brought him down, and his heroic command was scattered by the advancing battalions of Hays and Avery." Another eyewitness recorded, "General Hays, who was near at the time, expressed his deep regret when the gallant hero fell." The fallen officer may have been thirty-five-year-old Colonel James S. Robinson of the 82nd Ohio, who was shot in the chest as his regiment entered the town.[38]

XI Corps commander Major General Carl Schurz reported, "The Third Division . . . fell back toward the town in good order, contesting the ground step by step with the greatest firmness. . . . The retreat through the town, protected by part of our artillery, was effected as well as could be expected under such circumstances, the streets being filled with vehicles of every description and overrun with men of the First Corps. A considerable number of men, who became entangled in cross streets and alleys, were taken prisoners by the enemy, who entered the town immediately after us." Michael O'Connor, a thirty-seven-year-old Irish-born captain in the 6th Louisiana, recalled, "We drove them back and captured the town." The former New Orleans storekeeper believed the Yankees in front of his regiment had showed "stubborn resistance" before falling back.[39]

Having disposed of the Third Division, the First Louisiana Brigade swept into downtown Gettysburg in close pursuit of Schurz's fleeing Federals. They faced little organized resistance, except for a couple of isolated Union units. Shirkers, retreating batteries, ambulances, wagons, and retreating infantry filled the narrow streets. To protect the Union rear, Lieutenant Clark Scripture's section of Dilger's Battery paused in the town square, unlimbered, and fired rounds of canister up Carlisle Street to slow the Confederates. Terrified Gettysburg citizens who had not fled with the arrival of the armies huddled in their cellars as the din of battle swept through their streets.[40]

In the confusion of maneuvering through Gettysburg's streets while trying to locate the easiest route to the rallying point on Cemetery Hill, many Union troops inadvertently ran straight into other retreating Federals or, even worse, into the oncoming Confederates. The 45th New York of Schimmelfennig's Brigade entered town on Washington Street but soon encountered retreating I Corps columns coming in from the west. Turning several times in an effort to find a clear passage, Lieutenant Colonel Aldolphus Dobke finally led his regiment into an alley. Unfortunately, it emptied into a spacious yard surrounded by large buildings, with no exit except one small doorway in a distant fence. Confederate sharpshooters had piled a barricade of dead Union soldiers in the street in front of the door. Dobke and about one hundred of his men finally extricated themselves from the trap, ran through a gauntlet of Louisiana lead, and finally arrived safely at Cemetery Hill.[41]

The late afternoon shadows lengthened as the sun dipped toward the South Mountain range. It had been forty-five to fifty minutes since Hays first advanced against well-defined enemy positions. Now, he faced mobs of terrified Yankees who seemed to be everywhere, many throwing down their weapons and begging for mercy. J. Warren Jackson of the 8th Louisiana recorded, "We shot them down, bayoneted them, and captured more prisoners than we had men." In some places, the town's public gardening lots, dozens of small plots each surrounded by board fences, impeded the Union troops' line of retreat and added to the confusion and panic.[42]

Private Thomas Reed of the 9th Louisiana recalled, "While we were chasing the Yankees and getting in behind the houses, I saw their flag fall nine times. We would shoot it down and they would grab it up and run, till finally them scoundrels got it behind the houses and were gone. I will say right here that a man will stay longer and stick closer to his colors than he will to his brother."[43]

Hays' leftmost regiment, Colonel D. B. Penn's 7th Louisiana, had pushed into the eastern part of town. There, it encountered part of the 9th New York Cavalry of Devin's Brigade, which earlier had been positioned off of the Union right flank. Colonel Devin later wrote, "The enemy, having gained the York road, entered the town immediately after my pickets retired, and, passing through with their sharpshooters, attacked the flank of the brigade, killing and wounding several men and horses. I immediately dismounted one squadron of the Ninth New York, who with their carbines, drove them some distance into the town, punishing them severely."[44]

Major Allen Brady's 17th Connecticut of Ames' Brigade turned to face the Confederates, who were advancing rapidly through the town. He immediately deployed his regiment along the sidewalks and fired several volleys, retarding Hays' advance long enough for an artillery section to unlimber. However, the guns deployed in the wrong position and were thus unable to support Brady properly. Louisianans rushed up York Street and soon compelled the outnumbered Connecticut infantrymen to fall back, "which we did reluctantly, but not without contesting the ground inch by inch. As we retreated, we loaded, halted, and poured destructive volleys into their ranks, which cleared the main street of them several times, but we found the enemy too many for us. They poured in from every street in overwhelming numbers, which broke our ranks."[45]

Between 4:30 and 5:00 p.m., with no further organized resistance, Hays' Louisianans advanced through Gettysburg, clearing the streets of residual enemy troops and collecting prisoners "at every turn." J. Warren Jackson, caught up in the excitement of the chase, related to his brother a few weeks after the battle, "We ran them thro the town & and caught hundreds of them in the houses and cellars."[46]

Tigers entered one house at the corner of Baltimore and Middle streets and rousted a dozen cowering Yankees. The magnitude of surrendering Yankees was staggering, but Harry Hays, unwilling to reduce his combat strength by detailing guards, simply ordered the chagrined captives to walk to the rear. Many took the Carlisle Road, where they encountered Rodes' troops. In Hays' estimation, "I am satisfied that the prisoners taken in the above-mentioned movements by my brigade exceeded in numbers the force under my command."[47]

Abraham Stout, the assistant surgeon of the 153rd Pennsylvania of von Gilsa's Brigade, was the only doctor accompanying the regiment after the surgeon was captured at Chancellorsville. The Bethlehem native had been among the last men to leave the collapsing Union line, and he was taken prisoner by the 7th Louisiana as he headed for Gettysburg. As a guard escorted Stout through town, Colonel D. B. Penn spotted the doctor and dismounted. He walked by his side until they came to the German Reformed Church on High Street in the southeastern part of town. Penn remarked, "You ought to take this church for a hospital." Dr. Stout agreed, but only if the doors were unlocked. Penn responded that if it was locked, his men could soon open it. However, the church was indeed unlocked, and the doctor entered and set up a temporary field hospital. Within half an hour, wounded Union soldiers filled the structure.[48]

Jubal Early had ridden forward in the assault with Carrington's Battery, directing and coordinating the movements of his brigades. Now, he called for Smith's reserves to come up and for Jones' remaining artillery to limber and advance toward Gettysburg, where there were good opportunities for flank shots on Union troops (most likely Brigadier General John C. Robinson's late retreating I Corps division) "passing to the right of the town towards Cemetery Hill." However, before the batteries arrived, the Federals were out of reach. Early later wrote, "Elated with the success, I rode into the town, past the prisoners streaming to the rear with scarcely any guard, and found Hays forming line along a street on the left of the town."[49]

The stunning victory thus far had come at a relatively modest price—Hays would report his losses on the day as one officer and six enlisted men killed, four officers and thirty-seven men wounded, and fifteen men missing. Among the dead was twenty-two-year-old Private David T. Moore, a Georgia-born farmer from Homer, Louisiana. The bachelor had enlisted in 1861 in Company A of the 9th Regiment and had served in several battles. He had survived two prolonged bouts with illness, returning to active duty in April before the Chancellorsville fight. His luck ran out in the fields along the Harrisburg Road north of Gettysburg.

Hays proudly added, "The loss of the enemy cannot be known with exactness, but it was apparent from an inspection of the field that his loss exceeded ours by at least six to one." Some of his regiments were relatively unscathed, with the 6th Louisiana reporting only five men missing and none wounded or killed.[50]

### Cemetery Hill—A Squandered Opportunity?

The Union rallying point was Cemetery Hill, a twin-crested rise extending in a southwest-northeast direction for about seven hundred yards south of Gettysburg. It was named for the borough's Evergreen Cemetery, which had been established just a decade before the battle. Before that time, the eastern crest, named Raffensberger's Hill for one of the landowners, had been a popular picnic spot. The cemetery's brick gatehouse was its most prominent landmark at the time of the battle, and its tiny rooms and stone basement provided shelter for dozens of wounded Federal soldiers while surgeons ministered to their needs. Less than a week before, Jubal Early's cavalrymen under Lieutenant Colonel Elijah White had visited the same gatehouse, begging food and water from the cemetery keeper's wife, Elizabeth Thorn. The troopers shot and killed a local cavalry picket, George Washington Sandoe, less than a mile south of the hill.[51]

Three key roads ran across Cemetery Hill—the Emmitsburg and Taneytown roads that joined on the low southwestern slope, and the Baltimore Pike to the east that followed a saddle between the primary summit and East Cemetery Hill. These roads led south into Maryland and offered access to the Federal rear supply and communication lines if the Rebels could secure the hill. Holding these avenues was vital to Meade's army remaining in Gettysburg, and Oliver Howard called Cemetery Hill the "only tenable position for my little force." In the late morning, he had established his headquarters on the northern summit and posted a sizeable reserve force of XI Corps infantry and artillery facing Gettysburg.[52]

Relatively devoid of vegetation in 1863 except for some low trees, wheat and corn fields, a small orchard, and an imposing poplar that was visible for miles, Cemetery Hill rises about one hundred feet above Rock Creek, with relatively gentle slopes to the north, west, and south. However, the eastern approach is significantly steeper, dropping off sharply into a pastoral bottomland cut by ditches, creeks, springs, and low ridges. Farther east is Wolf's Hill, a heavily wooded natural buttress choked with thick underbrush. Its very steep slopes and underbrush precluded any significant military presence on the rugged heights. However, the soggy bottomland between East Cemetery Hill and Wolf's Hill concerned General Howard and other Federal commanders. The broad ravine formed a perfect corridor for enemy movement toward Culp's Hill, immediately southeast of Cemetery Hill. Control of the two hills meant control of the vital roads.[53]

Earlier in the day, Howard had posted his reserves on Cemetery Hill, including Colonel Orland Smith's 1,600-man brigade and Captain Michael Wiedrich's New York battery. Between 4:00 and 5:00 p.m., XI corps survivors assembled there, as well as the shattered remnants of the I Corps, which had lost its commander and nearly one-third of its men in a series of attacks by A. P. Hill's Third Corps. Colonel Charles Coster scattered his relatively undamaged reserve regiment, the 73rd Pennsylvania, among the houses and outbuildings on the extreme southern side of Gettysburg to delay any oncoming Confederates.[54]

In the early afternoon, Army of the Potomac commander George Meade had dispatched Major General Winfield S. Hancock to take command of all Union forces at Gettysburg. Now, Hancock, Howard, cavalry Brigadier General John Buford, and Chief of Engineers Brigadier General Gouverneur K. Warren began repositioning the exhausted troops as they reached the hill. Staff officers turned the XI Corps to the left on East Cemetery Hill and Major General Abner Doubleday's I Corps to the right. A series of long stone walls running east-west offered protection and a useful way to reform and steady the shaken troops. Howard ordered the men to throw up hasty works and start digging rifle pits, expecting a follow-up attack at any minute. However, the distant Rebels were still busy collecting prisoners and reforming in the fields beyond town.

Hancock corralled artillery Captain Greenleaf T. Stevens and ordered him to deploy his guns (5th Independent Battery [E], Maine Light Artillery) on a small open knoll on the western spur of Culp's Hill on the James McKnight farm. After unlimbering, Stevens faced north, his guns covering any enemy approach up the Rock Creek ravine. In support were survivors of Brigadier General James Wadsworth's I Corps division, including remnants of the famed "Iron Brigade," shattered earlier that day on the ridges west of Gettysburg by Major General Dorsey Pender's determined attacks. Wadsworth's tired men began constructing breastworks along the brow of Culp's Hill.[55]

Artillery commanders repositioned their batteries, and soldiers began digging earthen lunettes to protect the guns and crews. The limbers and caissons were sheltered in a natural depression on the southeastern slope, where they would be relatively safe from enemy fire. The artillery west of Baltimore Pike was placed under Major Thomas W. Osborn, commander of the XI Corps artillery, while those batteries east of the road were assigned to Colonel Charles S. Wainwright, Osborn's counterpart for the I Corps. Heckman's badly damaged Ohio battery retired to the rear, out of the battle.[56]

By late afternoon, Gettysburg was free of organized Yankee resistance. As Rodes' Division entered the borough from the northwest, Harry Hays finished his search for Yankee stragglers and rested his weary but jubilant Tigers. However, he kept them in battle line ready to advance, placing his right flank along Middle Street. A few Federal guns (most likely Wiedrich's) played on the exposed part of Hays' new line, but without significant effect despite blasts of canister. Confederate officers posted a battery along the York Road to counter this threat. Early reasoned, "It was very apparent that a force was there which had not participated in the fight below [the plains north of Gettysburg]."[57]

Union sharpshooters fired on Hays' left from houses on the southern outskirts of town, as well as from the northern foot of Cemetery Hill. Confederate pickets moved from house to house to get closer to the Federals, hoping to drive them off, and sporadic sniping continued as afternoon turned to evening. Rebels occupied several houses along Breckinridge Street on the south side of town, including the home of tanner John Rupp. Less than 150 yards to the south, Union snipers maintained an advance outpost in the Wagon Hotel and other nearby buildings.

Lieutenant J. Warren Jackson of the 8th Louisiana was ordered to take his Company I and form a skirmish line in the open fields south of Gettysburg.

"The enemy was posted on Cemetery Hill about 600 yards from town & had command of every place near town or around it. Our position was a poor one and as we deployed we were subjected to a galling fire from their sharpshooters. Nobody hurt and we soon laid low in the grass, but their position was such a good one that they could see us." The Cheneyville native added, "I spent about 2 hours as miserably as I ever did in my life."[58]

Many Confederates clamored for a renewal of the attack, judging that the day's victory was incomplete with Cemetery Hill crowned with the shattered remnants of two supposedly demoralized Union corps. Ewell's men implored their commanders with cries of "Let us go on!" but no orders were forthcoming. One of Avery's Tar Heels recounted, "There was not an officer, not even a man, that did not expect that the war would be closed upon the hill that evening." An angry Tom Reed of the 9th Louisiana expressed, "We charged and routed the Yankees and drove them through Gettysburg, and if the General in command had pursued them a little farther our victory would have been complete." Captain Seymour claimed, "Here we all felt the loss of Gen. Jackson most sensibly. Had he been alive and in command when we charged through the town, I am sure he would have given his usual orders under like circumstances, 'Push on the infantry,' and time would not have been afforded the enemy to make their position impregnable."[59]

Jubal Early repeated orders for Smith to advance to support Hays and Avery, and then rode through town to find Ewell or Rodes to urge an advance "at once upon the hill in our front, before the enemy could reform." He reasoned that the decisive attack should come from the right, an easier route to Cemetery Hill than what Hays and Avery faced. The Virginian found some of Rodes' men in the western part of Gettysburg reforming into battle line, but he did not locate General Rodes. Frustrated, Early sought out Ewell to urge "an immediate advance upon the enemy before he could recover from his evident dismay." However, he could not find the Second Corps commander either.

A messenger galloped in from the eastern outskirts from General Smith reporting that a strong column of Yankees was "advancing on the York Road." Early later claimed that he had no faith in the report but, worried about the effect on his men's morale should Federals appear in their rear, he took action. He dispatched Gordon's weary Georgians to assist Smith in blocking any enemy flanking movement from that direction, and placed John Gordon in command of both brigades, his confidence in "Extra Billy" gone. Smith, a former Virginia governor and U.S. Congressman, had likely witnessed the movements of Brigadier General Thomas H. Ruger's First Division of the XII Corps, which had demonstrated south of Hanover Road, heading in the general direction of the York Road, before withdrawing. The threat to Early's vulnerable flank subsided well before Gordon's Brigade arrived, but half of Jubal Early's division was no longer available to support a follow-up attack should Rodes advance.

Unable to find General Rodes, Early encountered a staff officer from Pender's Division and sent him westward along Chambersburg Pike to urge A. P. Hill to press the issue. Returning to Hays' line, Early was met by Colonel Abner Smead of Ewell's staff, who had been dispatched to tell him that Johnson's Division was en route to Gettysburg, and to ask Early where he would advise them to deploy.[60]

Concurrently, Union guns on Cemetery Hill and McKnight's Knoll "commenced a furious fire." Avery's Brigade had crossed the railroad tracks and swung farther to the east to determine if the way to Culp's Hill was free. Crossing open fields, the Rebel column was plainly visible to Captain Stevens' Maine gunners and to Michael Wiedrich on Cemetery Hill, who wheeled his six guns to the northeast. He estimated the yardage to the enemy column and ordered his long-range 3-inch rifles to open up. The ensuing explosions shattered the late afternoon calm, and a thick cloud of white smoke enveloped the position. In the distance, Avery halted as shells whistled over his troops. He moved his three regiments back toward town, where they crouched in the rolling fields on the Louisianans' left flank, protected by a low rise.[61]

Meanwhile, Early met with Ewell and Rodes under a shade tree on the town square. The corps commander repeated his message concerning where to place Johnson's oncoming division when it arrived in Gettysburg. Early pointed out Culp's Hill as the correct place for Johnson to occupy, as it commanded the Federal position, and he urged Ewell to order an immediate attack on Cemetery Hill. In response, Ewell asked Early to ride to the southern part of town to reconnoiter the Union position. As they rode down Baltimore Street, they came into range of the pesky Federal snipers. The generals and their escorts had to duck into an alley and then take High Street to avoid them. From the low plateau in southeastern Gettysburg, they carefully observed Cemetery Hill, which they estimated now held forty cannon and a full brigade of infantry. Distant Union sharpshooters spotted the officers and opened fire, forcing Ewell and Early to withdraw deeper into town.

Ewell was not willing to launch a risky attack. Rodes had lost 2,500 men so far, and Early was down to only two brigades with Smith and Gordon out on the flank. Ewell wanted to wait until Johnson arrived and was in position. Meanwhile, reports were "constantly coming in" that Yankees were advancing on the York Road. Elijah White's cavalry battalion earlier in the afternoon had reported seeing some Federals in that vicinity, but these recent messengers were mainly stragglers from Jeb Stuart's cavalry, who Early later believed were "waifs from the battle-field of Hanover." (Stuart had fought a relatively large cavalry battle with Judson Kilpatrick's division in the southwestern York County borough the previous afternoon.)

While waiting for Johnson's arrival, Ewell, Early, and Rodes rode a short distance out of Gettysburg to look down the York Road to see if there were indeed any Yankees in the vicinity. From their vantage point on the plateau, they could see two miles to the east but noted no indications of enemy activity. To Early, the lack of any visible threat reinforced his opinion that the rumor had no foundation, "but Rodes was inclined to believe it, while Ewell seemed at a loss as to what opinion to form."

Early recalled,

> While we were discussing the matter, a line of skirmishers was seen away out on our right of the York road, as we stood apparently advancing towards us, when Rodes exclaimed: "There they come now!" To this I replied in somewhat emphatic language, that it could not be the enemy; that Gordon was out there; and if the enemy was advancing he would certainly be firing on him. It must be recollected that it was very hard to distinguish between the blue and the gray at a distance, as both looked dark. To resolve the doubt, Lieutenant T. T. Turner, of Ewell's staff, and Robert D. Early, of mine, were sent to ascertain the fact. It turned out that the skirmishers were some General Smith had sent out, which Gordon was having moved back to post differently. All this consumed time, and Johnson had not yet arrived.

Turner and young Early found the hill unoccupied upon their arrival.

Harry Hays' Tigers had first entered Gettysburg sometime after 4:00 p.m., and by now, it was dusk. Hays and some of his colonels insisted they should be allowed to attack the hill while there was still time and sent word to Early, who sympathized, but refused to disobey Ewell's orders to halt. Early rode back into Gettysburg to visit Hays and Avery, who agreed the Federals were determined to hold the position on Cemetery Hill. At Hays' "urgent request," Early sent a courier back to General Ewell, who took some time to arrive at Early's headquarters. To their dismay, the commander laughed at Hays and asked if his men would "never get a bellyful of fighting." Hays answered that he wanted to prevent the slaughter of his men, who would throw their lives away uselessly if they waited to attack the heights after they were fortified.[62]

While their senior commanders repeatedly conferred and debated their next actions, the Louisiana Tigers and Tar Heels "despondingly" settled down, ate their dinners, and took stock of their lost comrades. Patrols scoured through the fields north of town to locate those wounded men who were too badly injured to make it to the rear. Early's medical staff had established temporary field hospitals at the Almshouse and the John Crawford property, and surgeons were busy ministering to the wounded.

In the downtown streets, soldiers stacked several thousand Union muskets taken from surrendering Yankees or collected from the fields, sidewalks, and roads. Rebels collected hay and straw from area stables and barns and spread them across the brick sidewalks along Middle Street, and soldiers began to cook rations. Ten-year-old Gates D. Fahnestock recalled, "We boys watched them from the second story through the slatted shutters and could hear parts of their talk. They were elated at the result of their first day fighting and talked confidently of the results of the next day and what they would do to the Yankees then." Townspeople were wary of their southern "guests." Sallie Myers commented, "'The Louisiana Tigers' were feared the most, because of their reputation for lawlessness, and so the people avoided them as best they could."[63]

Several soldiers sat on the curb in front of the William McLean house and rummaged through captured Federal knapsacks while McLean furtively peeked from his window. They were opening the Yankees' letters and reading them aloud for amusement. McLean was horrified when his little five-year-old daughter began loudly serenading the Rebels with her rendition of "We'll Hang Jeff Davis from a Sour Apple Tree," a popular northern patriotic war ditty. Expecting the Confederates to storm his house, McLean was relieved when they simply ignored the girl. They also ignored a bucket of water he had earlier set out for the passing Union troops, perhaps fearing it was poisoned.[64]

One wounded Union prisoner of war, Private Justus Silliman of the 17th

Connecticut, recalled, "The rebels occasionally came in bringing sheep, chickens, etc captured at neighboring farm houses . . . some of the rebs would come up from the city with carpets, collars, shoes, and other articles taken from the stores." The captive conversed with several Louisianans at the brigade's field hospital. "They all seemed perfectly confident of success as they were concentrating nearly the whole of their army of [Northern Virginia] at this place. . . . [They] seemed anxious to close the war and all were anxious to see Jeff Davis and Abe Lincoln hung and many looked forward to our next presidential election in hopes that it would either bring about a reconstruction of the union or come to some terms of peace."[65]

As the Tigers ate their meals and showed off their newly acquired store goods, they could not be aware that other Confederate troops were capitalizing on their dreaded name and fearsome reputation. During the day, fighting had raged on the sprawling Emmanuel Harmon farm west of Gettysburg. Harmon lived in Baltimore, where he could keep an eye on his prosperous mercantile business. In 1861, when talk of secession had divided loyalties in the city and created instability and danger, he sent his fourteen-year-old daughter Amelia to live on the farm with his fifty-three-year-old sister Susan Castle. Now, two years later, the war had come unexpectedly to Gettysburg, trapping the two women in their home while soldiers were shooting each other in their fields. They watched the action unfold from the cupola of the farmhouse.

As the fighting intensified, they moved from the cupola to the cellar. When the 80th New York retreated, the 47th and 52nd North Carolina regiments surged through the property. Amelia Harmon and her aunt peered at the advancing Rebels from the narrow windows in the cellar. They saw smoke pouring from their barn and soon heard the heavy footsteps of men upstairs. Coming upstairs, they saw Rebels piling books, rugs, and pieces of furniture on a pile of burning newspapers on the floor. The two women tried to put out the fire and begged for help, "but there was no pity in those determined faces. They were 'Louisiana Tigers,' they boasted, and tigers indeed they were." Unable to prevent the Confederates from destroying their house, the women fled. They would be convinced for some time that the famed cutthroats had torched their house and barn.[66]

While most of the real Tigers relaxed along Middle Street, to the south, Lieutenant J. Warren Jackson and his skirmishers of Company I maintained their desultory fire against their Union counterparts. The gathering darkness allowed him to reposition his men. "We posted some advance skirmishers & placed the reserve behind a plank fence near town & there we had to stay—if anyone shewed themselves or a hat was seen above the fence, a volley was poured into us." To reinforce Jackson, Hays dispatched Lieutenant William N. McGalliard and Company E, the Franklin Sharpshooters, to join the skirmish line. Two men from that company were slightly wounded later that night.[67]

The sniping finally ended after dark. Gettysburg's residents slowly emerged from their cellars as skirmishers from both armies put down their guns and belatedly ate their dinners. Teenager Tillie Pierce recalled, "At night, when all the folks had gone up stairs, these sharpshooters would enter the cellar in search of eatables. On these occasions, as was observed from the windows above, they carried milk and cream crocks, preserves, canned fruit, etc., out into the side street; and seating themselves on the pavement, and along the gutter, no doubt had an enjoyable feast, and a hilarious time over the newly captured provisions. They did not call it stealing in war times."[68]

Alice Powers noted, "What a scene of desolation and confusion were the streets and yards of our town that night; fences down and the well made gardens trampled in the stampede of retreat; dead men and horses lying in the streets; all sorts of household goods and [possessions] scattered, with shot and shell everywhere. No wonder hands were wrung and tears flowed at the dismal sight, for many depended in a great measure on these large gardens for a living."[69]

Late in the evening, Richard Ewell summoned Jubal Early to yet another meeting, this time in the arbor of John Crawford's sturdy brick house along the Harrisburg Road. Robert Rodes was there, as was Robert E. Lee, who by now had arrived in Gettysburg. The topic of renewing the assault was not on the agenda, as "all idea of advancing to the attack of Cemetery Hill that night had been abandoned, for it was apparent to all that the time for that had passed." After his subordinates had updated Lee on the day's results and the condition of their troops, the commander inquired, "Can't you, with your corps, attack on this flank at daylight tomorrow?"

Early was the first to speak, because he had examined "more thoroughly and critically" than the others the enemy's position east of Gettysburg. His two brigades immediately confronted it, and he believed "it was peculiarly my duty" to render his opinion. When he had visited Gettysburg the week before, he noticed the general character of the surrounding terrain. Early had observed that the ascending slope on Cemetery Hill was much easier and gentler on the right than on the other side.

Lee, concerned about a Federal counterattack, floated the idea of withdrawing to the west to consolidate the army. Early's negative response may have influenced the outcome of the next two days, as it helped convince Lee to keep his existing battle lines in their general positions. Early later wrote,

> My men, who had marched to the Susquehanna and returned without serious opposition, were very much elated with the success of the day, and I shared their feelings. I know what a damper it would be to their enthusiasm to be withdrawn from the position they had gained by fighting, as it might appear to them as if a reverse had occurred somewhere and we had not gained much of a victory after all.
>
> Moreover, there were some of my wounded not in a condition to be removed, and I did not like the idea of leaving those brave fellows to the mercy of the enemy; and there were a great many muskets stacked in the streets of Gettysburg which I did not want to lose. So I replied at once to General Lee, and assured him that he need not fear that the enemy would break through our line, and that we could repulse any force he could send against us. The fact was, that on that part of the line it was more difficult for the enemy to come down from the heights to attack us than for us to ascend them to attack him, as difficult as the latter would have been.[70]

Night fell with the Tigers still in battle line facing Cemetery Hill, silhouetted by a full moon. Tom Reed recorded, "Well, we slept on the streets with our guns in our arms." Most Confederates fully expected another attack in the morning, but some feared their chances of success as the disturbing sounds of axes and shovels emanated from the shadowy heights. They could hear distant rumbling as the enemy's heavy artillery arrived and deployed.

Federal commanders had taken advantage of the unexpected and sustained lull in Confederate activity to adjust their lines to optimize their firepower. Near dusk, Captain Michael Wiedrich had received orders for one of his three sections to take a new position west of the cemetery to provide additional artillery support in case of a Rebel attack from the west. He dispatched Lieutenant Christopher Schmidt and the left section, thus reducing his firepower to the north and northwest, territory his remaining two sections would have to cover.[71]

Shovels, axes, bayonets, tin cups—all were being methodically utilized by the men to dig in. With Chief of Engineers G. K. Warren present, the works were becoming more formidable by the hour. A contemporary historian recounted, "There was no time to build a fort, for which the ground was admirably adapted. [Warren] accordingly threw up lunettes around each gun. These were not mere heaps of stubble and turf, but solid works of such height and thickness as to defy the most powerful bolts which the enemy could throw against them, with smooth and perfectly level platforms, on which the guns could be worked."[72]

William Seymour and other Louisiana officers expressed concern that the Yankees were fortifying their position instead of running away as many expected or hoped. "All night long, the Federals were heard chopping away and working like beavers." Many Federals also would have trouble sleeping that night, reliving the harrowing narrow escapes of the day, mourning lost or missing comrades, and worrying what the morning light might bring. Lieutenant Albert W. Peck of the 17th Connecticut was among them. "We were posted in an apple orchard close to the edge of town, with our videttes posted along by a board and rail fence. . . . I don't think I got any sleep that night."[73]

All was quiet in the town except for the moans and cried of the wounded and the movement of sentries and pickets. Once, a brief flurry of gunfire shattered the stillness, waking the Tigers and the adjacent men of Rodes' Division. Lieutenant Franz Ehrlich of the 75th Pennsylvania (Krzyzanowski's Brigade) cautiously led a patrol of men from the 58th New York into Gettysburg's southern extremities. They had orders to ascertain the condition of wounded Union soldiers left behind during the hasty retreat through town. Rebel pickets spotted them in the moonlight and opened fire, scattering the patrol and sending the Germans retreating to Cemetery Hill without fulfilling their mission. Ehrlich claimed to have killed or wounded several Confederates without losing a man.[74]

A few Tigers took advantage of the bright moonlight to search for fallen comrades. Charles Moore Jr. and some colleagues from Company F of the 5th Louisiana returned to the trampled fields north of Gettysburg and located the body of Captain Frederick Richardson. They "buried him at midnight" under a cherry tree on the Alexander Spangler farm.[75]

Meanwhile, several dead Yankees lay near the Presbyterian Church. Resident Alice Powers recounted, "These dead soldiers lay on the sidewalk until Saturday morning as the squad of Louisiana Tigers who guarded the street would not permit the citizens, who begged that privilege, to bury them at night. . . . Restless and uneasy we slept in our clothes that night getting up often to watch that no harm came to the dead who lay in sight of our doors."[76]

About midnight, a courier rode up to Harry Hays, saluted, and delivered an order from Major General Early instructing him to reconnoiter the ground between his line and the enemy on the commanding heights. Hays, "after a careful examination of the locality indicated," about two o'clock in the morning of July 2, roused his troops and moved them left and forward into an open field between the borough and the base of a low intervening ridge that screened his force from enemy fire from Cemetery Hill. Hays' new position was several hundred yards closer to the Union lines. He anchored his right flank in the fields in front of the German Reformed Church on High Street, and his line crossed several rolling fields eastward to a point in front of the Henry Culp farm buildings. To his front, the low rise offered some protection, and a sluggish stream at its northern base, Winebrenner Run, offered a source of fresh water. He threw out pickets to his front, and Tigers crept forward in the shadowy moonlight to take position behind fences and thickets.[77]

Still on the forward skirmish line directly south of Gettysburg, lieutenants Jackson and McGalliard's men hugged the ground in the tall grass, unaware that their brigade had changed position. Tired of being exposed so dangerously to the enemy skirmishers, the two 8th Louisiana line officers decided they should make a run for the rear. "While lying there late in the evening, we concluded to back out of our position and go to the Regt. We had to crawl about 60 yds in the bushes, then jump and run . . . for about 30 yards. We all got to town & round to the regt. which had advanced and was posted behind a hill about 600 yards from the enemy."[78]

It had been a long day for the soldiers of the First Louisiana Brigade. They had risen in the lush fields along the Berlin-Heidlersburg Road, marched more than a dozen miles, engaged in a sweeping attack that carried them into Gettysburg, pursued and collected more than two thousand prisoners, and then moved their line forward into position to renew the hostilities if directed. Their success elicited admiration from their peers in the Second Corps. A field correspondent for the Richmond *Enquirer*, writing from a Confederate camp near Hagerstown, Maryland, on July 8, spoke to several veterans about the fighting exactly one week before. He summed up their beliefs, "The conduct of Gordon's and Hays's brigades is said to have been very fine."[79]

The exhausted Tigers finally caught a couple hours of much needed sleep in the early morning hours, with the disconcerting sounds of axes and shovels on Cemetery Hill ringing in their ears. For many of Hays' men, so far from their Louisiana homes, the morrow would bring injury or death.

# 5 | Gettysburg

## Day 2

### The Calm Before the Storm

THE SUN ROSE on Thursday, July 2, at 4:44 a.m. Harry Hays' Tigers rose not long afterward and began preparations for the day, while Major General Jubal Early took breakfast with generals Rodes and Ewell at John Crawford's house north of Gettysburg. The sky was covered with a layer of cumulostratus clouds, with a warm, gentle breeze blowing from the south at two miles per hour. The temperature was a clement 74 degrees at 7:00 a.m.[1]

Several hundred yards south of the Tigers, Jacob Smith of the 107th Ohio Volunteer Infantry was also enjoying daybreak. "This morning was fresh, balmy and pleasant. The sun shone mildly through an atmosphere still smoky from yesterday's conflict giving it the appearance of a huge ball of fire. All the world was quiet and at rest. There was nothing outside of our immediate surroundings that would indicate . . . the dreadful struggle that was not long in starting."[2]

Ordinarily, it would have been a delightful early summer morning, except the country was at war and, unlike their Yankee counterparts on the stone wall–lined hill, the Louisianans were not in a position to enjoy the pastoral Pennsylvania scenery. With the growing daylight, they took stock of the new position they had reached during the night. They were on the southeast outskirts of Gettysburg, encamped along a small, sluggish tributary (known to locals as Winebrenner's Run) of Rock Creek that offered fresh water for morning coffee. However, they were now four to seven hundred yards away from the enemy position on East Cemetery Hill, which bristled with artillery.

To the left of Hays' line were the Tar Heels of Colonel Isaac Avery. Well behind the Tigers were John Gordon's Georgians. Smith's Brigade was nowhere to be seen, as it was still out on the extreme left flank, protecting the York Road from any enemy flanking movement in the absence of Stuart's cavalry and the tactical deployment of Ewell's supporting cavalry elsewhere. Hilary Jones' gunners were in reserve, well to the rear, as they had no suitable artillery platform from which they could easily reach the enemy positions.

A few men were more concerned about personal gain than preparing to attack the Yankees. Gettysburg resident Catherine Foster and her family were "undisturbed till break of day, then we heard an effort to break open the back door, and to prevent them from breaking in I hastened to open it. Two toughs, supposed to be Louisiana Tigers, stood there and demanded a light to 'search for the Yankees.'" She remonstrated, stating that officers had searched the house the previous day, and no Federals were found (one was indeed hidden in their cellar). When she went to fetch a light, James Foster came into the room to confront the Rebels, one of whom pointed his gun at him and demanded fifty dollars. When informed that there was not fifty dollars in the house, the Rebel angrily ordered, "Give me what you have!" Foster took out his pocketbook and handed over its contents, three dollars. Swearing at him, the Rebels left.[3]

On Cemetery Hill, hundreds of eyes strained to the north, watching for any signs of an impending Confederate attack, which men on both sides, including Jubal Early, expected to commence soon. During the night, several Louisiana skirmishers had worked their way to the town's southern extremities. They scrambled into buildings and hid behind fences and sheds as they moved toward Union skirmishers that had deployed in the fields on the northern slope. Confederates erected a barricade across Baltimore Street so they could move back and forth without drawing Union fire. Their movements were evident to Dr. John W. C. O'Neal, the Gettysburg physician who had treated the dying John Shackleford on June 30. He penned in his journal at 6:00 a.m., "All is quiet at this hour. We can see the enemy in the streets of the town and their main line of battery about a mile distant. . . . Confidence is once more restored and great hopes expressed that we may today compensate by a victory for our defeat of yesterday."[4]

Gunfire soon shattered the morning calm as Louisiana skirmishers and sharpshooters started the day's unpleasantries. A Pennsylvania newspaperman was enjoying the peace of the early morning. "I strolled out to the cemetery where the dew was not yet melted from the grass, and leaned against a monument to listen to the singing of birds. One note, milder than the rest, had just broken from the throat of an oriole in the foliage above me when the sullen rattle of musketry on the left told that skirmishing had begun."[5]

Lieutenant Albert Peck of the 17th Connecticut observed, "As soon as it was light . . . , we could see the Johnnies moving along the fences in our front, keeping out of sight as much as possible." "It was not long before 'zip' came the bullets from them, and our boys promptly returned their fire, although it was difficult to see them. Our boys took shelter behind the rail and board fences and apple trees, and once in a while the bullets would peel the bark from the trees, and there were a good many close shaves."

The air whistled with Minié balls as Major Brady's Connecticut skirmishers dueled with Hays' Louisianans. Men ducked for cover, reloaded, changed positions, and fired, all the while hoping to avoid getting shot by opponents using the same tactics. Peck continued, "[Sergeant] George Shaw, who was stationed behind an apple tree, and the Johnnies had got a range on him and were trying their best to sting him—their bullets cutting bark from the tree—but they did not hit him, and he was blazing away as fast as he could load and fire." Second Lieutenant Peter Hare deployed Company K of the 6th Louisiana as skirmishers "under a heavy fire from the enemy's sharpshooters."[6]

While the skirmishers banged away at one another in their deadly cat-and-mouse game, Confederate commanders peered through the haze at Cemetery Hill, their field glasses bringing into sharp focus what Hays and his officers had feared. During the night, the Yankees had dug in, instead of slinking away in the darkness. Freshly dug lunettes protected tiers of guns. Union infantrymen crouched behind fresh rifle pits and low trenches, and the low stone walls had been reinforced with fence rails, knapsacks, crates, and other hastily improvised protection. Loopholes had been made in the stone walls and hasty works to shelter a man when he fired his musket. A line of *abatis,* or felled timber, blocked easy ascent to the crest and the lunettes and would slow down any attacker. Additional Federal reinforcements had arrived in the night, and now batteries of long-range 20-pounder Parrott rifles crowned the hill in and around the cemetery itself.

According to Hays' adjutant William Seymour, when Ewell saw how formidable the hill now appeared, he "expressed great anxiety to withdraw our brigade, but this could not be done without immense loss in the face of the powerful batteries on the hill which could . . . sweep the field over which we would have to pass in retiring." Hays' right two regiments, presumed to be Major Hart's 5th Louisiana and Lieutenant Colonel Hanlon's 6th Louisiana, were particularly exposed, as they lay in the tall grass along Winebrenner Run without the cover of the intervening ridge enjoyed by the bulk of the brigade. Seymour continued, "So we had to remain there more than five hundred yards in advance of Ewell's main line of battle—hugging the ground behind a very low ridge which only partially covered us from the enemy's fire. It was almost certain death for a man to stand upright." A few Tigers went down when they poked their heads too high.[7]

Unknown to General Ewell and his commanders, Cemetery Hill now formed the curved apex of a strong Union defensive line roughly in the shape of a large fishhook, with Culp's Hill as the barb. Any concentrated attempt to take Cemetery Hill would require simultaneous action on the western, northern, and eastern slopes—no easy task considering that Gettysburg blocked easy movement and deployment of troops.

Adelbert Ames had ascended to command of the First Division with Frank Barlow's wounding. His two brigades formed the northern portion of the East Cemetery Hill defensive line. Ames had no more than 1,300 men left in the ranks, probably many fewer. Badly mauled on Blocher's Knoll and during the subsequent retreat, more than one-third of the division was now gone. The stone walls, rifle pits, and the sloping terrain on the hill offered protection for the battle-weary survivors. Supporting Ames in the multitiered defensive line upon the hillside were five batteries, totaling twenty-three guns.

Colonel Andrew Harris of the 75th Ohio now commanded Ames' Brigade, which included three heavily depleted Ohio regiments—the 25th, 75th, and 107th—as well as the 17th Connecticut. The future governor of Ohio positioned his men between the Baltimore Pike and the stone wall–lined brickyard, or Winebrenner's, lane. Much of Major Allen G. Brady's 17th Connecticut, down to perhaps 225 men, still manned the forward skirmish line.

The 179 survivors of the 107th Ohio, a veteran regiment composed primarily of German immigrants from the Cleveland region, were positioned behind a stone wall facing north toward Gettysburg. Adjutant Peter F. Young now led the battered regiment because Colonel Seraphim Meyer was arrested on July 1 for failing to obey an order to reform his troops to face the enemy after the Buckeyes arrived on Cemetery Hill. To their right was the tiny 25th Ohio, a Scotch-Irish regiment from east-central Ohio, extending its sixty-man line to cover an area that stretched toward the brickyard lane.

The brigade line then refused, or bent, to the right in an inverted L-shape to follow the brickyard lane at the base of East Cemetery Hill. Facing eastward along the stone wall–lined lane was the 75th Ohio, a predominantly German regiment from the Cincinnati area. With Colonel Harris's elevation to brigade command, twenty-one-year-old Captain George B. Fox now commanded the regiment, which had been reinforced during the night by a part of a detachment that had been on scouting duty and missed the fighting on July 1. Still, as morning broke, Fox counted only ninety-one men in his depleted ranks.[8]

To the right of Fox was Ames' other brigade, that of Colonel Leopold von Gilsa, who counted perhaps seven hundred men still in his ranks. He commanded four predominantly German regiments—the 54th and 68th New York, 153rd Pennsylvania, and the 41st Pennsylvania, the latter regiment having arrived during the night after missing the July 1 fight. To their front was rolling bottomland covered with fences and stone walls, with a small woodlot that offered cover for an attacker. Their right flank was unoccupied for several hundred yards to where the lane bent to the west to connect with the Baltimore Pike.

Behind Ames in the multitiered defensive alignment was a mixture of artillery batteries from the I and XI Corps, all on higher elevation than Ames' infantry. Battery I, 1st New York Light Artillery, a German battery from Buffalo, was about one hundred yards northeast of the cemetery. The commander, forty-two-year-old Captain Michael Wiedrich, was born and raised in eastern France and had immigrated to Buffalo in 1840 at the age of twenty. Four of his guns pointed north and east toward the Confederate lines. To Wiedrich's right, facing east, were the four rifled guns of Captain James H. Cooper's Battery B, 1st Pennsylvania. To Cooper's right, completing the first gun line, was Lieutenant George Breck's Battery L, 1st New York, and its five rifles. Breck was new to battery command, with Captain Gilbert H. Reynolds a casualty earlier in the battle.

On slightly higher ground behind Cooper were the four remaining 12-pounder Napoleons of Lieutenant James Stewart's Battery B, 4th U.S. Artillery, the only regular battery posted on East Cemetery Hill. The pieces faced north in case of a sudden advance from the town along the Baltimore Pike. The fifth battery east of the turnpike was Captain Greenleaf Stevens' 5th Maine Battery, with its six gleaming 12-pounder Napoleons.

To Ames' left, west of the Baltimore Pike, were the depleted brigades of Colonel Wladimir Krzyzanowski and Charles Coster of Carl Schurz's division (Schurz was back in charge of the Third Division, with Howard returning to corps command after the arrival of Hancock and army commander

George Meade the previous night). Brigadier General Adolph von Steinwehr's Second Division manned the western slope. The two divisions had a combined strength of perhaps 4,300 effectives. Seven batteries with more than thirty guns faced north and west to assist in repelling any enemy attacks from those directions.[9]

Schurz peered through his field glasses at the Confederate positions, which were now noticeably closer than the previous evening. He later reported, "The sun of the 2nd of July rose brightly upon these two armies marshalling for battle. Neither of them was ready. But as we could observe the field from Cemetery Hill, the Confederates were readier than we were. The belts of timber screening their lines presented open spaces enough, in which we could see their bayonets glisten and their artillery in position, to permit us to form a rough estimate of the extent of the positions they occupied and of the strength of their forces present."[10]

Emotions were mixed that morning among the rank and file of both armies. Many Confederates were still smarting over their leaders' failure to finish the job the previous evening, well before the Yankees' shovels and axes made the task much more challenging. Several men on both sides were apprehensive, realizing the fight would be desperate. New York artillery Lieutenant George Breck was among the scores of soldiers who wrote letters home during the unexpected lull in combat. He expressed what thousands of men in both armies were thinking—today's results might end the war. "We were completely overwhelmed yesterday by superiority of numbers. Our army is now concentrating here, and I think the great battle, if not decisive battle of the war, will be fought here. We are pretty tired, as you can imagine. But I presume we shall be kept engaged, till the battle is decided, one way or the other. Appearances look as if the issue of the war, the success or downfall of the rebellion, would be determined in this state."[11]

Skirmishing and occasional artillery duels, sometimes heavy in nature, continued throughout the warm morning into the early afternoon. Private James Benedict Roden and Hays' other sharpshooters worked their way into the fields opposite the base of Cemetery Hill and were firing from behind fences and thickets. Snipers in the houses along Breckinridge Street and other avenues on the southern side of Gettysburg maintained a ready eye for opportune targets amid forward Union skirmishers and the enemy line on the northern slope of the hill. They managed to pick off fourteen men in the 25th Ohio throughout the day, as well as a few officers and gunners.

In the 17th Connecticut's skirmish line, Lieutenant Albert Peck was fed up with the "Johnnies" in his front. "We were all under an apple tree, excepting one man who stood as an outpost. We were annoyed very much by the frequent shots striking the ground around us, and also the tree under which we were. No one was hit as yet, but we did not like to be shot in that way and not know where it came from."

The twenty-five-year-old Fairfield native schemed to lure the enemy snipers from their nest.

> Finally we decided that the shots came from what appeared to be a hog-pen situated at the rear of a house about two or three hundred yards distant. . . . So it was decided that four of our party should load and fire a volley into that hog-pen, and one of us reserve his fire to see the effect of the fire. As I was on the outpost, it was left for me to hold the reserve fire. As the smoke from the volley cleared away, three or four rebs were seen to clamber out of that hog-pen. Just as the last one was throwing his leg over the top board, I sent a "minnie" after him, and he went over sooner than he intended.[12]

It almost became a sport, as Tigers placed their hats on sticks and raised them to draw enemy fire, enticing the Yankees to reveal their firing positions. Hays would lose forty-five men during the day from the enemy skirmishers, and the Federals probably lost at least as many skirmishers, as well as dozens of men on Cemetery Hill who foolishly exposed themselves.[13]

Among the favorite targets of Hays' concealed marksmen were the gunners of Michael Wiedrich's Battery, who were prime candidates to be shot if they were careless in their movements. The New York captain reported, "All the loss we sustained was from their sharpshooters, who were secreted in the houses of the town, and who molested us continually for two days." He decided to take action to quiet one of the enemy sniper nests. "The sharpshooters in the church steeple were very annoying, having wounded several of the men and two of the officers, viz., Lieuts. Nicholas Sahm and Christian Stock, and killed some of the horses. The gunner of the third piece, notwithstanding the orders not to fire into the town, loaded his gun with a shell and fired it at the steeple; it had the desired effect."[14]

Several Tigers had crept into Samuel McCreary's brickyard, just northeast of Colonel Harris's 75th Ohio. Sheltered by the hemispherical kilns and stacks of molds and processed bricks, they peppered the flank of Lieutenant J. Clyde Miller's skirmishers from the 153rd Pennsylvania of von Gilsa's Brigade. A frustrated Miller sent a runner back toward Cemetery Hill to request some artillery fire on the brickyard. Dodging a gauntlet of Confederate bullets, the messenger made it to Union lines, and soon a round from one of the big guns sent the Louisianans scampering to safety.[15]

Harry Hays' hidden sharpshooters were not the only targets of Federal artillery that morning. Colonel Charles S. Wainwright directed his gunners' attention to the northeast, where they "opened at times on small bodies of infantry passing our north front toward Culp's Hill." From midmorning until 3:00 p.m., Captain Wiedrich's crews, the northernmost battery, occasionally exchanged rounds with two Confederate batteries that deployed during the night directly to his front. Their resounding booms periodically broke the stillness of the day, but few took this desultory cannon fire to signal any major troop movement.[16]

Wiedrich's duel probably kicked off in earnest in midmorning, according to Gettysburg housewife Sarah Broadhead, while Louisiana sharpshooters were still busy in their deadly intercourse with the Connecticut boys. She noted, "The cannonading commenced about 10 o'clock, and we [she and her husband Joseph, a Gettysburg Railroad engineer] went to the cellar and remained a little until it ceased. When the noise subsided, we came to the light again, and tried to get something to eat. My husband went to the garden and picked a mess of beans, though stray firing was going on all the time, and bullets whizzed about his head in a way I would not have liked. He persevered until he picked all, for he declared the Rebels should not have one."[17]

Captain Stevens' 5th Maine Battery spent part of the day carefully registering the ranges from their position on McKnight's Knoll to particular landmarks, so that if an attack came up the ravine to their front, they would be able to hit their marks with each salvo. Stevens' French ordnance glass enabled him to judge accurately the distance to his potential targets. With Colonel Wainwright's permission, he verified the range with a few rounds of solid shot. However, one of Ike Avery's advance sharpshooters deployed in the valley drilled him through both legs with a well-aimed shot, and Stevens was carried to the rear. Command of his battery fell to Lieutenant Edward N. Whittier, the senior section leader.[18]

From late morning through early afternoon, the battlefield was essentially quiet, except for the occasional sharp report of the skirmishers' muskets as

the lethal cat-and-mouse game continued. With the opposing soldiers relatively idle, several Gettysburg residents returned to some semblance of nor-
malcy, among them Sarah Broadhead. "I baked a pan of shortcake and boiled
a piece of ham, the last we had in the house, and some neighbors coming in,
joined us, and we had the first quiet meal since the contest began. I enjoyed
it very much. It seemed so nice after so much confusion to have a little quiet
once more.[19]

Among the wounded Yankee prisoners held in town was James Patrick
Sullivan, an Irishman in the Iron Brigade's 6th Wisconsin. He recounted,
"Hays's Brigade of Louisiana Tigers was stationed in Gettysburg, and they
felt very jubilant over yesterday's battle, exultingly told that 'you uns' were
whipped and they were going to take Washington, Baltimore, and Philadelphia and end the 'wah.'" Defiantly, the Westerners responded that if it took
half the Rebel army just to beat part of the I Corps yesterday, they would find
a "very different job" today when Meade's entire army was on the field. They
added sarcastically, "If Howard [XI Corps] spent his time running, there
were plenty of fighting men in the Army of the Potomac ... [who] would serve
Lee worse than at Antietam." Sullivan noted that this retort "took the brag
out" of the Tigers. Not long afterward, he observed General Early riding by,
whom he described as a "short, pussy, gray haired, bull-headed Reb with no
great amount of intelligence in his look." Some of Hays' men responded that
Early was a "fighting devil."[20]

Early periodically rode through Gettysburg, conversing with staff officers
and encouraging his troops. Residents overheard him exclaim, "Wait a day
or two and we will show you what rebels can do. We have a small job at hand
that will only take a few hours to attend to, viz: to dispatch the remnant of Joe
Hooker's broken down army. That done, then hurrah boys! Then Baltimore
is ours! Washington is ours! Harrisburg and Lancaster fall into our hands,
and Philadelphia becomes our headquarters! Then we will make the Quak-
ers howl!"[21]

### Preparing for the Assault

As the skies cleared, the temperature rose, reaching 81 degrees at 2:00 p.m.
Prone in the grass behind Winebrenner Run without any shade, Hays' Louisiana Tigers broiled in the summer sunshine. A few men lay prostrated by
heat exhaustion or sunstroke. Concurrently, Union soldiers on Cemetery
Hill suffered from hunger and thirst. In several regiments, food was scarce

because the supply wagons had been left in Westminster, Maryland. Many men last drew rations before arriving in Gettysburg on July 1 and had since devoured the meager contents of their haversacks. Soldiers in the 17th Connecticut had "nothing to eat but what scraps of food we could pick up by foraging during lulls in the battle."

With three sides of the hill controlled by enemy sharpshooters, forays to Rock Creek to fill empty canteens could be fatal. Confederates controlled Winebrenner Run and the borough's water supplies. Some Union commanders sent patrols southward on the Baltimore Pike to fetch water for their men and horses, but most soldiers suffered in the unrelenting sunshine and heat, their thirst only occasionally quenched. A Connecticut officer related, "what water we had to drink came from a well which was constantly dipped dry, and was in so much demand that it was necessary to wait several hours before we could fill our canteens."[22]

Jubal Early instructed General Hays to hold his brigade in position and ready it for a charge on the enemy works now crowning the summit of Cemetery Hill. The Virginian added that there would be a general advance of the entire line at the same time. Hays' preparations soon came under the gaze of several prisoners. During the previous afternoon, Early's provost had collected several dozen wounded Yankees and escorted them to buildings in southeastern Gettysburg. These temporary field hospitals included a large brick school and the nearby German Reformed Church, both on High Street in the southeastern part of town. From the second-story windows in the church, Private Reuben F. Ruch of the 153rd Pennsylvania in von Gilsa's Brigade "had a grand view of the greater part of the battlefield."[23]

Other prisoners peered out of the school's second-story windows, including 17th Connecticut infantryman Justus Silliman. He had a bird's eye view of the skirmishers. "The La Brigade were in a hollow in front of us, where they lay close until nearly dark though they had their skirmishers out nearly all day. They were occasionally picked off by our sharpshooters. Bullets frequently whistled around our hospital, but I have not heard of anyone being injured by them." His view was sweeping and magnificent: "We are in full view of the battlefield, the Confederate line of battle being within a few rods of our hospital. Our own line is also in full view. They occupy a line of hills which they have fortified." Hays' men "stretched on the ground under cover of a low ridge and spent the afternoon in eating, sleeping and card playing."[24]

Another Yankee prisoner watched Hays' medical team prepare for battle.

During the previous day's fighting, Colonel Roy Stone, a brigade commander in the I Corps, had been wounded and carried into Gettysburg. When the corps retreated to Cemetery Hill, Stone's acting assistant adjutant general, Captain John E. Parsons, remained behind enemy lines to minister to his stricken commander. During a lull on the morning of July 2, Parsons helped carry Stone to a house north of the Baltimore Pike. The lieutenant noted, "The house had been deserted by the family and was in a sad condition; portions of the floor torn up for plunder, the beds ripped open and feathers scattered over the house, and the hand of the spoiler visible on every side." That afternoon, Hays' surgical staff took possession of the stone house as the brigade's field hospital for the anticipated attack on Cemetery Hill.[25]

While the Tigers sweltered in the withering sunshine awaiting the call to advance, many Union soldiers were enjoying the weather and relaxing as best they could while waiting to see what the distant Rebels were planning. Whitelaw Reid, a field correspondent for the Cincinnati *Gazette*, was on Cemetery Hill taking advantage of its vista of the battlefield while watching the persistent distant skirmishing off to the west. He wrote, "The afternoon passed in calm and cloudless splendor. . . . Everywhere quiet, the men stretched lazily on the ground in line of battle, horses attached to the caissons, batteries unlimbered, and gunners resting on their guns . . . it seemed as if the sun might set in peace over all this mighty enginery of destruction, held in calm, magnificent reserve."[26]

While their counterparts on Cemetery Hill relaxed, Lieutenant Peck and the skirmishers of the 17th Connecticut were still sparring with their enemy counterparts. For some time, the Confederates had been trying to outflank the Yankees to force them to abandon their tenacious grip on the apple orchard. Peck later recalled, "The Johnnies finally got a cross fire on us from the vicinity of the old tan yard and it got so hot that we were finally relieved and moved back to our old position" along the north-facing stone wall on East Cemetery Hill, where they reformed in battle line between the 25th and 75th Ohio.[27]

As the hot afternoon wore on, the Tigers' orders to advance did not come, despite a brief but violent artillery duel that shattered the calm. Confederate Major Joseph H. Latimer unlimbered four batteries on Benner's Hill northeast of Hays' position, and soon his sixteen guns began firing at the higher elevation of Cemetery Hill, about a mile away. Joe and Sarah Broadhead's peaceful afternoon disappeared as the guns thundered. "The quiet did not last very long. About 4 o'clock P.M. the storm burst again with terrific violence. It seemed as if heaven and earth were being rolled together. For better security, we went to the house of a neighbor and occupied the cellar, by far the most comfortable part of the house. Whilst there, a shell struck the house, but mercifully did not burst, but remained embedded in the wall, one half protruding."[28]

One newsman in Evergreen Cemetery penned, "Altogether the city of the dead was a very lively place; but very soon after the artillery became warm, it was deserted by all but the generals, whose headquarters were there, and the men necessary to hold the place." Colonel Adin B. Underwood of the 33rd Massachusetts observed, "The sharp flashes ran all around the encircling ridges which seemed to throb with fire and smoke, and the hills roared with heavy echoes . . . splinters of gun carriages, pieces of tombstones, even human legs and arms and palpitating flesh were flying about in every direction." A huge roar erupted when a parked Federal caisson exploded from a direct hit, adding to the chaos. Cincinnati reporter Whitelaw Reid hastily noted, "Trains are hurried away on the Baltimore pike; the unemployed *débris* of the army takes alarm, a panic in the rear seems impending. Guards thrown hastily across the roads to send the runaways back, do something to repress it."[29]

While the big guns roared, Hays and Avery's sharpshooters were still engaged in their deadly game, adding to the Federals' woes. Private William Southerton of the 75th Ohio later wrote, "A few too many shells on Benner's Ridge came our way, and a few too many balls from sharpshooters' rifles. Thunder and lightning!"[30]

During the shelling, Harry Hays began to form his lines for the impending attack on Cemetery Hill. Most of the 5th and 6th Louisiana assembled along the streets of Gettysburg. Mrs. Robert Sheads lived in one of the houses not far from their position. The Louisianans were talking in loud enough voices for her to overhear their conversation through her open window. "Boys, we are going to take that hill where the graveyard is. It will be a steep climb, but we will do it or die." Another of the Rebels remarked, "Yes, we are going to take that hill and capture the guns that have been shelling our lines all day." Sheads recoiled in fear and spent the afternoon praying for a Union victory.[31]

In a little more than a half-hour, well aimed Federal counterbattery fire from Cemetery Hill and Culp's Hill silenced several Confederate guns and mortally wounded Major Latimer. About 5:30 p.m., Union Major Thomas Osborn withdrew Wheeler's Battery, which had lost some caissons the day before and had since exhausted its remaining ammunition.[32]

A New York *World* correspondent traveling with the Army of the Potomac recorded, "About 6 o'clock p.m., silence, deep, awfully impressive, but momentary, was permitted, as if by magic, to dwell upon the field. Only the groans, unheard before, of the dying and wounded, only the murmur—a morning memory of the breeze through the foliage, only the low rattle of preparation of what was to come, embroidered this blank stillness." Huddled in the Winebrenner Run ravine, many Louisianans realized that any subsequent infantry assault would go in without artillery support, unlike their victorious charge on Winchester's West Fort two weeks earlier.[33]

Most remaining Gettysburg residents had taken shelter in their cellars while the artillery dueled. Joseph and Sarah Broadhead were ensconced in a neighbor's basement when Latimer's remaining guns withdrew. "About 6 o'clock, the cannonading lessened, and we, thinking the fighting for the day was over, came out." Throughout Gettysburg, in places where it was safe from the sharpshooters' duels, citizens emerged and compared stories.[34]

Shortly after the cannonry ended, a fresh replacement battery from the Army of the Potomac's reserves wheeled into position, replacing Cooper's Battery. Reserve Artillery battalion commander James Huntington ordered Captain R. Bruce Ricketts' 1st Pennsylvania Light Artillery, Batteries F/G to leave the artillery park and report to Colonel Wainwright on Cemetery Hill. Ricketts had graduated from seminary just before the war erupted and had consequently canceled plans to attend Yale Law School to enlist instead in Battery F as a private. Short and slight in body, the twenty-four-year-old had previous combat experience as a section commander, but this was his first opportunity to lead the combined battery into action.

The Pennsylvania artillerists rode up the Taneytown Road past Meade's headquarters at the Widow Leister house and parked just south of Cemetery Hill. When the order came to advance, the battery crested the hundred-foot-high prominence, where Ricketts unlimbered on a protruding slope east of the Baltimore Pike. His left gun was adjacent to one of the stone walls, with Wiedrich's New York battery farther to the left. General Ames informed him of the "absolute necessity" of holding his important position. Wainwright, temporarily commanding all Federal artillery on Cemetery Hill east of the pike, was standing nearby. He added, "In case you are charged, you will not limber up under any circumstances, but fight your battery to the last."[35]

Even as Ricketts deployed, soldiers on Cemetery Hill and their prone Louisiana opponents along Winebrenner Run could hear the roar of battle to the south, where James Longstreet's First Corps had engaged the III Corps, as additional Federal troops rushed in as reinforcements. The New York reporter watched the distant assault take shape. "Then, as the smoke beyond the village was lightly borne to the eastward, the woods on the left were seen filled with dark masses of infantry, three columns deep, which advanced at a quickstep. Magnificent!"[36]

The sound of battle rolled ever northward as each wave of Longstreet's *en echelon* attack met Union defenders along Devil's Den, the Wheatfield, and the Peach Orchard. As the fighting south of Cemetery Hill waned about 6:30 p.m., trouble was brewing to the east. Federal gunners spotted Confederates (Johnson's Division) forming on Benner's Hill around the wrecked batteries, preparing for an apparent assault on Culp's Hill. Colonel Wainwright sent orders for his batteries to fire. In Gettysburg, Sarah Broadhead was concerned. "Then the noise of the musketry was loud and constant, and made us feel quite as bad as the cannonading, though it seemed to me less terrible. Very soon, the artillery joined in the din." The Broadheads beat a hasty retreat back into their neighbors' cellar, where they stayed until the shooting stopped late in the day.[37]

Seeing the distant attack on Culp's Hill and not sensing any supporting attack from the north, about 7:00 p.m., First Division commander Brigadier General Adelbert Ames ordered the 17th Connecticut to shift farther to the right. Major Allen Brady's men marched a few hundred yards southward along the dirt lane, where they redeployed left of von Gilsa's brigade.[38]

However, this movement created a large gap in the defensive line. To rectify the situation, Colonel Andrew Harris stretched his already depleted Ohioans even farther. He later wrote, "This left my line very thin and weak. [Every man] could get to the stone wall, used by us as a breastwork, and have all the elbow room he wanted. . . . I rode along the line, and gave the men all the encouragement possible, and told them of the importance of our position, and that we must hold it at all hazards." He added, "Before I could make any arrangements to remedy this breach in the line, the attack of the enemy on Cemetery Hill was made."[39]

## Hays' Initial Assault

In the late afternoon, Jubal Early rode into town to meet with Richard Ewell. He received orders to "advance upon Cemetery Hill with my two brigades that were in position as soon as General Johnson's division, which was on my left, should become engaged at the wooden hill on the left, which it was about to attack." The time had finally come for the long anticipated assault. Early's understanding was that "the advance would be general, and made also by Rodes' division and Hill's division on my right." In the field hospitals, regimental surgeons, including Alexander Semmes of the 8th Louisiana and Charles Todd of the 6th, grimly prepared for the night's casualties.[40]

Meanwhile, Harry Hays was concerned about whether he would be fully supported in the anticipated attack. He dispatched Colonel William H. Swallow, one of Rodes' staff officers who had accompanied Early's Division for several days on its march to York, back to Rodes to "ask him to rally on our division and assist us in the attack." The Marylander found his old commander "completely choked up in the narrow streets of the town with his division, and consequently he could not aid us."[41]

Captain William Seymour watched "Old Jube" ride back to meet with Hays to give him the final instructions for the attack. "Just before dark, the solitary figure of old Gen. Early is seen emerging from the streets of the town and riding slowly across the field in the direction of our position; the little puffs of dust that rise from around his horse's feet show that the Federal sharpshooters are paying him the compliment of their special attention. Presently the old General reaches us and after inquiring whether we are ready, gives the order to charge."[42]

Shortly before sunset (7:41 p.m.), Hays received the belated order to advance, with the North Carolinians going in on his left from their position on the Henry Culp farm. Hays was assigned overall command of the two-brigade assault. With the 54th North Carolina left behind in Virginia and Major Wharton's battalion serving as Ewell's provost guards, Avery's Brigade was under strength, with perhaps nine hundred men in its ranks. The 57th North Carolina lined up on the far left, with the 21st in the center, and then the 6th. To the right, the twelve hundred Louisianans were deployed in a roughly eight-hundred-yard battle line essentially facing south/southeast, with Trevanion Lewis's 8th Louisiana presumably on the far left (eastern) flank, then D. B. Penn's 7th, and Leroy Stafford's 9th Louisiana in the center. Next likely was Joe Hanlon's Irish 6th, with the right flank of Major Alexander Hart's 5th Louisiana resting in Gettysburg's outskirts.[43]

Hays began preparing his men for what some hoped would be the final assault of the war. In the ranks of the 9th Louisiana, Company D's newly promoted Captain Richard J. Hancock watched the former Whig politician try to encourage the men. "Gen'l Harry Hays, who was no man to deceive his men nor any one, rode along the line about dusk and told his men that Gen'l Early had said we must go to Cemetery Hill and silence those guns and Gordon would reinforce us and hold them."[44]

The sudden flurry of activity along High Street and in the Winebrenner Run ravine attracted the attention of the Union prisoners locked up in the schoolhouse, on the plateau behind Hays' line. The 17th Connecticut's Justin Silliman was among them. "Just at dusk we saw those infallible La Tigers make preparations for a charge. They stealthily formed in line under cover of a hill." Several Confederates stretched their cramped legs and jogged into position.[45]

Peering from the second story of the adjacent German Reformed Church, Pennsylvania Private Ruch noted, "A little before sundown I saw a stir and a moving about of the Rebels under the window where I was sitting, as if they were getting ready for some kind of move. I also saw them drinking out of a barrel. The head of the barrel was knocked in. One would get a tin cup full and three or four would drink out of the same cup until it was empty. It could not have been water, for a tin of water would not have had so many drinks in it. It was straight whiskey, and they were getting ready to charge the Eleventh Corps." He watched the Rebels form in low ground near the town's old prison, as well as behind a ridge he estimated was six to eight feet high. He reported they were aligned in three distinct lines of battle.[46]

Not having the protection of the low ridge to shield them while forming for the assault, Avery's Brigade was exposed to Union observers, who through the twilight strained to watch the advance. Artillery Colonel Wainwright was among the first to spot the Rebels forming, and he sent an aide galloping to McKnight's Knoll with instructions for the 5th Maine Battery to open fire. Lieutenant Edward N. Whittier, elevated to command following Captain Stevens' wounding, readied his six Napoleons with case shot. All the hours of carefully estimating ranges would soon pay off handsomely.

The Portland native commented, "It was about 7:30 or 7:45 p.m.; the sun had dropped behind the Cumberland mountains, and the dusk of evening was creeping through the valley of Rock Creek, when we made out the lines of the enemy at a distance of 1,000 yards, forming near the house and farm buildings of William Culp, on the outskirts of town. Up went the limber-chests, the fuses were cut in another moment, and the guns were loaded as if on drill."[47]

With the farthest distance to reach East Cemetery Hill, the Tar Heels jumped off before the Tigers. At Hays' command, Colonel Avery gave the order, a single bugle blared, and his line moved out. The Carolinians did not have long to wait for a response from the Yankees. When they were eight hundred yards away from McKnight's Knoll, Whittier gave the command to fire. "At once there was the flash and roar of our six guns, the rush of the projectiles, and along the front of the enemy's charging line every case shot . . . burst as if on measured ground, at the right time and in the right place above and in front of their advance." Several other batteries were soon in action, and they "made the ground tremble with their volleys" as their shot and shell began "plowing through the lines of the enemy."[48]

In the narrow valley below Whittier, the 33rd Massachusetts had just taken position behind a stone wall facing northward when the artillery opened fire. Colonel Adin Underwood "had no knowledge, the evening was so far advanced, of any artillery near me, when right over my head, it seemed to me, there was a flash of light, a roar and a crash as if a volcano had been let loose." The ground trembled, and fire belched from the muzzles of the cannon.[49]

From behind his line, Harry Hays described it as "a most terrific fire." As shells burst overhead in the twilight sky, it was soon the Tigers' turn to advance. Battle flags were unfurled, and officers and file closers took their assigned positions. Shouts of "Fix bayonets!" rang down the line. Harry Hays gave the order to advance, and the skirmish lines moved out. Lieutenant Jackson was concerned about his fate: "I felt as if my doom was sealed, and it was with great reluctance that I started my skirmishers forward." Adjutant Seymour, positioned near the center of the brigade line with the 9th Louisiana, observed his fellow Tigers. "The quiet solimn [sic] mien of our men showed plainly they fully appreciated the desperate character of the undertaking; but on every face was most legibly written the firm determination to do or die."[50]

Within moments, the Louisianans' main battle line surged forward, the men stooping and leaning forward as if it were raining. Seymour wrote, "At the word, up spring our men, and away they rush over the little ridge behind which they had so long laid, and down into the Valley which separated it from the dreaded 'Cemetery Hill.'" After watching the assault commence, Jubal Early sent a courier galloping off to inform Rodes that his two brigades were moving. Prisoner-of-war Justus Silliman watched as the Confederates "slowly and in excellent order advanced toward our lines." An officer in von Gilsa's Brigade, Lieutenant Benjamin F. Sheldon of the 134th New York, marveled at how few the attackers seemed: "Evidently they deemed themselves sufficiently strong for us, as they advanced upon us in splendid style."[51]

As the Tigers crested the rise, they became visible to the Union artillery on Cemetery Hill and McKnight's Knoll. Harry Hays related, "I had gone but a short distance when my whole line became exposed to a most terrific fire from the enemy's batteries from the entire range of hills in front, and to the right and left." Explosions rocked the air and gaps appeared in the Tigers' line. On East Cemetery Hill, Colonel Andrew Harris witnessed, "When they came into full view in Culp's meadow our artillery . . . opened on them with all the guns that could be brought to bear. But on, still on, they came, moving steadily to the assault." Several bleeding and mangled men soon lay on the grassy ridgeline.[52]

Another spellbound observer was the 153rd Pennsylvania's Private Ruch, still a prisoner in the German Lutheran Church a couple hundred yards behind Hays' line. He watched the sudden spectacle from his second-story vantage point.

Between the Rebel and Union positions was a ridge six or eight feet high. The Johnnies started stooped over, scattered like a drove of sheep, till they got to this ridge. Then every man took his place, and giving the Rebel yell; by this time our grape and canister began to plow gaps through their ranks. They closed up like water, and advanced at the double quick. This was a very interesting sight for me, for I was sitting back and looking on . . . no one can see much of a fight if he is in it. To see grape and canister cut gaps through the ranks looks rough. I could see hands, arms, and legs flying amidst the dust and smoke. . . . It reminded me much of a wagonload of pumpkins drawn up on a hill, and the end gate coming out, and the pumpkins rolling and abounding down the hill. . . . The slaughter was terrible.[53]

Confederate Lieutenant Jackson related, "But 'Old Harry' shouted forward and on we went over fences, ditches, [and] through marshy fields." Despite the early carnage, Hays pushed his brigades forward into the low fields past the Winebrenner Ridge, where a shallow depression offered momentary respite. Captain Seymour caught his breath. "[We] are down in the valley in a trice, the Yankee missiles are hissing, screaming and hurtling over our heads, but doing very little damage." Alabama-born Captain R. J. Hancock of the 9th Louisiana concurred, "The enemy's cannon lighted up the heavens but most of the charges shot over us but even at that we suffered terribly."[54]

Union officers were more optimistic about the effect of the cannonade. Colonel Underwood of the 33rd Massachusetts recorded, "The darkness is lighted up with the flames from the cannon's mouths that seem to pour down in streams onto them. The roar and shriek of the shot and shell that plow through and through their ranks is appalling. The gaps bravely close up and still they advance."[55]

The aerial display in the night sky and the thundering booms were noticeable throughout the area. As he returned to his XII Corps lines, a 3rd Wisconsin soldier noted a lurid glow illuminating the sky ahead of him toward Cemetery and Culp's hills. Van R. Willard recalled, "The smoke had settled down so thickly that the flashes of artillery could only be seen glaring red as blood through it. The thick clouds settled down over the hills, fields, and woods like a pall, illuminated at times with the crimson fire of the artillery as it flashed and burned across the sky." Mesmerized by the deadly light show, he termed the colorful exhibit "magnificently grand."[56]

Townspeople huddled in the cellars had endured the rumbling of the afternoon's fighting south of Gettysburg and the even louder resonance of the guns on Cemetery Hill dueling with Latimer's artillery on Benner's Hill. Now, another torrent of noise tormented their nerves, as the sound from the big guns and resulting shell explosions reverberated through the town. Thirteen-year-old Billy Bayly was among the country residents watching the display from a safe distance. He was awestruck. "I had the sensation of a lifetime. . . . There was a thunder of guns, a shrieking, whistling, moaning . . . of shells before they burst, sometimes like rockets in the air." From his vantage point north of Gettysburg in the dusk, he could see little of what was transpiring around Culp's and Cemetery hills. "No results of the conflicts would be noted; no shifting of scenes or the movement of actors in the great struggle could be observed. It was simply noise, flash, and roar, the roar of a continuous thunderstorm and the sharp angry clashes of the thunder-bolt."[57]

Most of the First Louisiana Brigade encountered a series of fences separating fields of Timothy grass, and the line wavered briefly as soldiers crossed each impediment. The left two North Carolina regiments, the 21st and 57th, picked their way through an orchard, slowing their initial progress. As Hays' lines emerged from the depression, the former U.S. Army officer and Mexican War veteran was grateful for the late start of the attack. "Owing to the darkness of the evening, now verging into night, and the deep obscurity afforded by the smoke of the firing, our exact locality could not be discovered by the enemy's gunners, and we thus escaped what in the full light of day could have been nothing else than horrible slaughter."[58]

Unfazed by the rain of jagged metal fragments from the timed shells and the solid iron shots that occasionally bounded toward their lines, few Confederates broke ranks. Avery's advance skirmishers climbed the next slope and briefly engaged in a firefight in Culp's southern fields with Lieutenant Miller's 153rd Pennsylvania skirmishers. The Keystoners were soon in reverse, but in a controlled manner as they harassed the Rebels. Miller recalled, "Towards sundown, their skirmishers appeared, followed by two lines of battle in the rear. We commenced falling back: I remember halting three times and firing." The series of small arms exchanges slowed the Tar Heels' progress. Miller's men double-quicked toward the rear as Avery approached the next advance Federal defenders.[59]

Volleys soon came from the seven hundred men of the 41st New York and 33rd Massachusetts, which General Ames had positioned behind a stone wall on a wooded hillock approximately five hundred yards beyond the brickyard lane. Having slowed the Rebels, the two Federal regiments pulled back to the lane and extended von Gilsa's right flank. Avery was further slowed by the uneven terrain, marshy depressions from recent rains, and several fences and stone walls that impeded the attackers' progress. Confederates simply kicked aside several loosely constructed Virginia worm fences, but other sturdier fences required scrambling up and over.

To Lieutenant Whittier on McKnight's Knoll, the sweeping Rebel lines seemed to be taking considerable time crossing the fields.

> Delayed by the twilight obscuring the ground in their front; delayed
> by the difficult passage over rolling farm lands and fields shut in by
> stone walls breaking up their alignments; delayed by loading and firing

as they advanced, for as soon as they felt the annoyance from the few sharpshooters and skirmishers in our front they opened fire along their whole front; delayed by the fire of the sixteen guns from East Cemetery Hill directly in their front, and six smooth bores on Culp's Hill on their flank; nearly an hour was consumed in passing over the 700 yards between their starting point and the fields within short range of our infantry behind the walls at the base of East Cemetery Hill.[60]

Hays' eight veteran regiments advanced steadily over the rolling terrain. Gaps occasionally appeared in their long lines when Federal artillery shells exploded nearby and knocked down several men. To most Union observers, the isolated attack appeared to be in support of the larger concurrent assault on Culp's Hill. Few realized Jubal Early's true target. Colonel Andrew Harris later wrote, "It was a complete surprise to us. We did not expect this assault as bravely and rapidly made. In fact, we did not expect any assault. We would not have been much more surprised if the moving column had raised up out of the ground among the wavering Timothy grass of the meadow."[61]

In the growing darkness and with the terrain impediments, the western part of the Louisiana Brigade's line was not visible to many Union officers on Cemetery Hill, whose primary focus was on Avery's steady progress up the ravine toward the knoll. There, the 5th Maine Battery and the survivors of the battered Iron Brigade steeled for the expected impact. Harris, mesmerized by the Rebels' unwavering march across Henry Culp's meadows, reported, "But on, still on, they came, moving steadily to the assault, soon the infantry opened fire, but they never faltered. They moved forward as steadily, amid this hail of shot shell and minnie ball, as though they were on parade far removed from danger."[62]

To the Federals' surprise, about 8:30 p.m., the Rebel column began a long, sweeping right wheel through a cornfield and several rocky and uneven pastures. File closers closed the Confederate ranks, and they pressed forward through the soggy bottomland, crossed three stone walls, and swung in a wide arc to the southwest to face Cemetery Hill. This movement exposed the left flank of the 57th North Carolina to enfilade from Lieutenant Whittier's gunners on McKnight's Knoll. He wrote, "The enemy swept past the left flank of the 5th Maine Battery with such rapidity that the right half battery could not be brought to bear upon their lines hastening to gain a new position and re-form on ground from which they could more successfully charge the crest of the hill."

Although this was his first time commanding an entire battery, the veteran Whittier reacted quickly. "The trails of the guns of the left battery were swung sharp and hard to the right; the right half battery was limbered to the rear and in the darkness hurried into position on the left of the guns remaining in the works." When all six guns were in position, he opened up on Avery's flank at close range "with double canister, pouring a most destructive, enfilading, demoralizing, fire into a confused mass of the enemy, struggling in the uncertain shadows of the crest of East Cemetery Hill." Shotgunlike blasts from Federal guns blew huge holes in a couple of companies, sending several Tar Heels of the 57th North Carolina sprawling and their lines wavering. They were forced to refuse their left flank to face the knoll, essentially ending any chance for the regiment to reach the brickyard lane with the rest of the brigade. Thick clouds of acrid white smoke soon covered the area, and visibility became poor in the fading light.[63]

Ike Avery went down during or shortly after his brigade's pivot maneuver. Severely wounded in his neck, the thirty-four-year-old former railroad contractor pitched from his white horse into the grass. In the darkness, few of his men saw him fall. Aides rushed to minister to him, but Avery was now partially paralyzed and unable to speak. There is no record that anyone notified Hays of this sudden change in his left brigade's leadership. Command of the North Carolina Brigade should have devolved to the next most senior officer, Colonel Archibald C. Godwin, but, in the confusion, noise, and darkness, he was not notified until much later. The Tar Heels were advancing now without a central leader, but they were veterans fully capable of executing the difficult maneuver under the control of their regimental and line officers.

Avery and his Carolinians were not the only casualties during the wheel maneuver. One of Lieutenant Whittier's Maine gunners, Private John F. Chase, suffered a crippling wound. He recalled, "My battery was enfilading the charging column as it dashed up the hill. Our shot, shrapnel, and canister were doing such terrible execution that the Confederates opened three or four batteries on us, and made the shot rattle around us pretty lively. One of those shrapnel shells exploded near me and forty-eight pieces of it entered my body. My right arm was shattered and my left eye was put out. I was carried a short distance to the rear as dead, and knew nothing more until two days later."[64]

Union officers now realized that von Gilsa's Brigade and Harris's right flank would withstand the brunt of this shifted Confederate assault. Behind Harris's extended line, Colonel Wainwright was busy directing his batteries. "As the enemy advanced, we commenced firing canister, depressing the guns more and more, until it was one continual shower straight down the hill. . . . The smoke lay so thick that you could not see ten yards ahead; seventeen guns vomiting it as fast as they can will make a good deal of smoke." The shelling from Cemetery Hill slackened as Avery's Brigade reached a final depression before the foot of the hill, where Federal gun barrels could not depress enough to hit them. Shells whistled again harmlessly over their heads before Wainwright finally ordered his guns to cease firing.[65]

Friendly fire from the Federal artillery claimed at least one life. Lieutenant Milton H. Daniels of the 17th Connecticut had led his Company C, as well as Company D, forward into the open fields to act as skirmishers on the regiment's left flank. His advance position proved hazardous, as "the battery in our rear was giving them a warm reception with grape and canister, firing over our heads. I remember the lead wadding from one shot killed one of our men, which demoralized us worse that the enemy in front."[66]

In the twilight, Avery's right flank and the Louisianans' left approached Major Brady's repositioned Connecticut line. One soldier recounted, "We had two men, one on Company 'C,' George Wood, Jr., the other William Curtis, who were particularly noticeable for their coolness. . . . While the Tigers were coming across the meadow, George and Bill were sitting down behind the stone wall, and you would have supposed they were shooting at a target. I saw Bill shoot from a dead rest, and heard him say, 'He won't come any farther, will he, Bill?' Then Bill shot and said, 'I got that fellow, George.' And they kept it up that way perfectly oblivious to danger themselves."[67]

The situation concerned Brady. Confederates were advancing rapidly upon his right (Avery's 6th and 21st North Carolina), with a full brigade (Hays) obliquely on his left. In short order, several Louisianans from the 7th and 8th Regiments chased in Daniels' skirmishers and subsequently poured through the gap to his left and began ascending the steep hill to his left rear. His bigger concern was the charging southerners to his front, who were wildly yelling and coming quickly. When they were within 150 paces, he ordered an opening volley that thinned their ranks and temporarily checked their progress.

The respite was brief. Harry Hays noted a "simultaneous rush from my whole line." His adjutant, William Seymour, accompanied the center regiments as they approached the brickyard lane. The captain reported, "Skirting the base of the Hill is a stone wall, from behind which a heavy line of Yankee infantry greet us with a destructive volley, and many of our noble fellows go down before it, killed or wounded; but our little command is not delayed by this impediment more than a minute."[68]

Brady's men feverishly reloaded their Enfield rifles and began firing volleys by battalion, but soon Hays' yelling Confederates slammed into their line and the adjacent troops of von Gilsa. In the ensuing melee, diminutive Captain Henry P. Burr seized a Rebel flag out of the grasp of a color bearer twice his size. After savage hand-to-hand conflict for several minutes, the 17th held its ground, and the Confederates withdrew a short distance, with the 21st North Carolina having lost four color bearers in the attack. Brady went down with a wounded right shoulder that would limit his arm's mobility the rest of his life.[69]

Just to the south, hundreds of Tar Heels and several Louisianans had reached von Gilsa's strong skirmish line in front of the brickyard lane line, and "a brisk musketry fire ensued." Captain Frederick Otto von Fritsch, a German-born baron, reported the Rebels were screaming, "We are the Louisiana Tigers!" as they advanced through a cornfield. Lieutenant J. Clyde Miller and the skirmishers of the 153rd Pennsylvania loaded and fired as they fell back. Reaching the brickyard lane, they double-quicked back to their regiment. As other shadowy figures approached in the twilight, Lieutenant William Beidelman yelled "Fire!" and the entire regiment opened up. Standing on the slope, Colonel von Gilsa started screaming for his men to cease fire, assuming the oncoming force was part of his skirmish companies. "No, General," came Miller's response, "They are the enemy, and charging in two lines."[70]

The shrill Rebel yell rang out as Hays' Confederates charged toward the stunned Germans defending the stone wall. The 54th and 68th New York, two relatively new regiments with little combat experience, broke suddenly, and terrified soldiers raced uphill to the rear as the Carolinians surged toward them. Artilleryman Whittier watched in horror as "von Gilsa's Brigade, Eleventh Corps, behind the stone wall at the foot of Cemetery Hill, disappeared at the first approach of the enemy and left their front open." Captain von Fritsch of Colonel von Gilsa's staff frantically tried to stop several men, but he tumbled senseless to the ground when a panic-stricken soldier savagely whacked him in the chest with the butt of his musket.[71]

Some of Major Samuel Tate's 6th North Carolina poured through the resulting gap and headed up the steep hill toward the guns of Bruce Ricketts, who had been ordered to "fight your battery to the last." That time would soon come. To stop the charging Rebels, the captain "expended every round of canister in the battery, and then fired case shot without the fuses." His respite would be momentary.[72]

Many of von Gilsa's terrified Federals scrambled uphill "in the greatest confusion." They raced through the spaces between Ricketts' lunettes, but for some, the confusion and darkness had tragic results. The young Pennsylvanian later claimed these men were "so panic stricken . . . that several ran into the cannister fire of my guns." He would never forgive the foreigners who fled and exposed his battery to an enemy infantry attack, berating their cowardice and equating it with their ethnicity. A few of his crewmen were caught up in the growing panic and started for the rear, but most returned after Ricketts exhorted them to halt. Only promoted to captain in May when Battery G was added to his Battery F, he bellowed, "Die on your own soil boys before you give up your guns." One of his men begged off, telling the captain he was "awful sick" and needed to go to the rear. An angry Ricketts thundered, "If you don't take your place, I'll make you sicker!"[73]

A stunned Colonel Wainwright watched in disbelief as Rebels pushed toward his batteries. "I pitied General Ames most heartily. His men would not stand at all, save one." In the confusion, he believed that the entire division supporting his guns had given way, although some of Ames' regiments were still standing firm in the smoke and darkness. "I believe that not a single regiment of the Eleventh Corps exposed to the attack stood fire, but [instead] ran away almost to a man. [Lieutenant James A.] Stewart stretched his men along the road, with fence rails to try to stop the runaways but could do nothing. Officers and men were both alike. Stewart's men however got a supper (they had been without food all day) for when they knocked a Deutschman down, they took his haversack from him."[74]

### The Fight for the Crest

In addition to the 17th Connecticut's stubborn fight along the brickyard lane, an embattled Colonel Andrew Harris had other significant problems. Off to Major Brady's left, Leroy Stafford's 9th Louisiana, the center of the Tigers' five-regiment line, slammed into the thin line of the 75th Ohio Volunteers. The Buckeyes' first intimation of impending trouble had come several minutes earlier, although in the darkness, no one knew where the Rebels were headed. Private William Southerton had just settled down behind the stone wall "when a horrible screaming and yelling arose from the lowlands [west] of

Rock Creek," and the tiers of artillery behind them on the hillside suddenly unleashed their projectiles. Southerton could see, lit briefly by the flashes of the exploding shells, the oncoming distant enemy soldiers. "The screaming hordes came rushing at us. Frantic warnings could not be heard in that confusion. We didn't need warnings. We knew."[75]

Another Ohioan, First Lieutenant Oscar D. Ladley, recalled, "They came on us about dark, yelling like demons, with fixed bayonets. We opened on them when they were about 500 yards off, but still they came, their officers & colors in advance." Not far away, Private Southerton recorded, "[Wiedrich's] battery on the crest above us poured grape and cannister right into midst of the fiendish horde." His comrades in Company B were soon busy. "The crackle of our rifle fire was incessant. What a furious gnawing of cartridge paper!" Within short order, the Louisianans were at the wall and engaged in a furious tussle. A Tiger grabbed hold of the man standing next to Southerton, Private John North, and yanked him over the wall. Corporal George C. Humphrey went down with a gunshot; a handful of Hays' men hauled him to the rear as a prisoner.[76]

Lieutenant Ladley's Company G prepared for the onslaught. "We lay behind a stone wall and received them with our bayonets. I was standing behind the wall when they came over. A Rebel officer made at me with a revolver with his colors by his side. I had no pistol, nothing but my sword. Just as I was getting ready to strike him, one of our boys ran him through the body [and] so saved me." The twenty-three-year-old former dry goods clerk from Yellow Springs, Ohio, lamented his fallen foe, "There was a good man killed in that way." Thirty-nine-year-old Private William Wesley Raike died behind the stone wall from a Rebel bayonet thrust deep into his groin. Ironically, his prewar occupation had been butcher, and now he was slaughtered by Rebel steel.[77]

As the Tigers struggled with the Buckeyes along the brickyard lane, Confederate Major Henry L. N. Williams fell, mortally wounded. The twenty-seven-year-old field officer hailed from Alabama, and he co-owned a store in Mansfield, Louisiana. When he went off to war in 1861, he left his partner in charge of the business. The spring of 1863 had not been kind to the major. Captured near Fredericksburg in early May, he endured a brief stay in the Old Capitol Prison in Washington D.C. Paroled on May 18 and exchanged, Williams rejoined his regiment at Hamilton's Crossing before the Gettysburg Campaign.[78]

One unidentified Buckeye colorfully described the swirling chaos in which Williams received his death wound. "There stood the major of the Tigers! Right on top of the wall! He carried their flag! A flash of steel! Lorenzo Fowler stabbed the major through with his bayonet. The rebel fell headlong over the rocks as a force of his men sprang to the top of the wall."

With Williams and much of the color guard down and the Ohioans savagely bayoneting Confederates as they leaped over the wall, the 9th Louisiana briefly withdrew down the hill. The unknown writer continued, "A lull for a moment or two. The Tiger's flag! What a scramble as the flag was torn to pieces! Our boys pounced on the rag as if a piece of it would be the greatest badge of bravery they would ever get their hands on. [Private] Andrew Jackson got the biggest piece. He shoved it into his pocket. He kept it as long as he lived, and gave it to one of his sons."[79]

The Buckeyes' respite was only momentary. The second charge by the Louisianans quickly overran two of the 75th's companies, and Confederates seized the Cincinnatians' flag and several prisoners. Dozens of Yankees scrambled up the slope for safety. The unidentified Buckeye lamented, "Within an instant another charge by the Tigers! The wall, as far as I could see, was ablaze! Our color bearer was killed. We lost our flag and never got another." A Rebel bullet smashed the right thigh of Color Sergeant William B. Spears, and his colors disappeared into the night in the hands of a Confederate.

Tigers (likely the left companies of the 6th Louisiana) overran one of the 75th Ohio companies stationed at the salient. Captain Ben Fox, temporarily commanding the depleted regiment, stood blocking a small gap in the wall. He later wrote his father, "A 1st Lieut[enant] was first to enter. I had no pistol and not having my sabre drawn, I hit him with a rock. He not over ten feet at the farthest from me. A private of Co. D was ready for him with cold steel, or the bayonet, and making a lung[e] at him, ran it through up to the hub, putting an end to the Lieut. The Reb Colors next came with a lot of mad men—did not stop. Up and on they went, the battery was what they wanted."[80]

Maine artillerist Whittier related, "The remainder of the 75th Ohio changed front to the rear on the third company (now on the right of the regiment), and held firm place," despite the flood of Rebels passing through the gaps to their left and right. Lieutenant Ladley was concerned: "They [the Tigers] had driven back the Dutch Brig[ade] on our right and had got behind us, and rebels & Yankees were mixed up generally." Ladley's Company G was all but destroyed in the melee. One man was wounded and nine taken prisoner, more than half of the remaining men.[81]

Louisianans soon overran Company B as well. Private Southerton recalled, "My company was caught in the onslaught, [some men were] killed, wounded, captured. Others were lost in the crazed mob and were swept right up to [Wiedrich's] battery." Teenaged Private Andrew Jackson, still with the big piece of the 9th Louisiana's flag in his pocket, "wriggle[d] in reverse," slipped over the wall, and disappeared farther down the hill in the darkness. He found a convenient hiding place in a nearby locust thicket.

Sergeant John A. Starrett of Company B dropped to the ground and played dead to avoid capture. "I lay as limp as I could be. One of the rebels yelled at me, 'Get up there! I'll run this bayonet right through you!'" A terrified Starrett slowly began to rise as a prisoner of war when a shell burst overhead, scattering Tigers in every direction. He ran back over the wall to the rear, as dozens of Colonel Harris's men fled for safety or huddled in fright along the reinforced stone wall along the brickyard lane.

Southerton watched the Rebels sweep up the hill to the next defensive line: "The Johnnies, pushing, crowding, gained our first epaulements [flanking rifle pits and earthworks] in spite of our efforts to block the way. It was almost impossible to distinguish who were Union, who were Confederate, to shoot and not kill our own men." Several men in the rifle pits had to hold their fire as the mixed lot of panicking Federals and charging Louisiana Tigers overran the line of hillside defenses.[82]

An embattled Andrew Harris rode up and down his line, trying to restore order. Amazingly, he escaped unharmed. He later wrote, "About dusk the enemy attacked the regiment in the front and on the flank and rear at nearly the same time, having come through the space vacated by the earlier redeployment of the 17th Connecticut Volunteers. From this attack, but few [of my men] escaped, and only those in the darkness and smoke; the greater portion were no doubt made prisoners."[83]

His Confederate counterpart, Harry Hays, recounted, "We passed such of the enemy who had not fled, and were clinging to the wall, to the rear, as prisoners." Knots of Stafford's men rushed uphill, cleared the *abatis* of felled timber, and headed toward Ames' second line in the hillside rifle pits. Partisan cavalryman Harry Gilmor, bored with scouting duties and eager for a fight, had left his troopers and volunteered to join the assault on the heights. The major recounted, "There was a perfect network of rifle pits to be taken before reaching the intrenchments; and, although the brave boys fell in piles, they charged and took them one after another." Many frightened Buckeyes simply threw down their guns and surrendered. General Hays would order these prisoners escorted to the rear, taking some of his attackers out of the fight as guards. He and his staff started uphill on foot behind his troops.[84]

As scattered groups from the 9th Louisiana approached the crest, Colonel Stafford sprinted to the top to be the first Confederate to occupy the position, but the honor instead went to the more fleet-footed Captain John J. Hodges of Company D. Regimental officers struggled to keep control of the regiment in the subsequent rush for the artillery lunettes. At some point in the assault, Captain Richard J. Hancock, an Alabama native who moved to Bossier Parish in 1858, went down with a severe gunshot wound to his hip. Among the 9th's enlisted men to fall that day was twenty-five-year-old Private John McClannahan, a Georgia-born bachelor from Filemon, Louisiana. Ironically, his pre-war occupation was as a gunsmith. Now, Federal gunfire ended his brief life. Casualties mounted and the organizational structure had disappeared, but Stafford's Tigers were still in decent fighting shape when they reached Wiedrich's lunettes.[85]

Major Gilmor recalled, "On reaching the main works, the brigade was a good deal scattered, but still bravely went forward. I was the only mounted man in the whole command, not caring to attempt to ascend on foot, and I had no trouble in leaping the trenches and keeping well up to the front. There were fifteen guns mounted in those works, all pouring a deadly avalanche of shell and canister down upon the Louisianians, who never quailed but pressed on until they scaled the works." Wiedrich's gunners expended their canister rounds and began firing "rotten shot," spherical case shot loaded backward and fired without fuses. It would explode in the gun barrel, spewing deadly missiles downrange.[86]

From his observation post near Gettysburg, Jubal Early strained to see in the darkness. Guided by the flashes of gunfire, he watched Hays assault the Federal lines. He sent a series of couriers to General Rodes, each time urging him to go forward, but there was no evidence of a supporting attack from west of town. Early bitterly complained, "but he did not start. I have nothing to say in regard to the causes of his delay, except that I imagine that he and the division commander on his right were discussing the question as to whether the latter should also move, while the time was passing when they could advance with chances of success."[87]

Gettysburg residents huddled in cellars as the sound of musketry rolled through town. Young Albertus McCreary recalled the assault: "What a racket that did make! It was an infantry charge, and the sound was as if a million boys with sticks were beating on a board fence."[88]

Hays' rightmost regiments, the 6th and 5th Louisiana, had been sheltered for much of their movement by the Winebrenner Run ravine running obliquely to the Federal lines and a high stone wall at the northern base of Cemetery Hill that ran all the way to the Emmitsburg Road. A knee-high cornfield and a small knoll on the northeastern slope also helped block the Federals' line of sight. One of General Ames' staff officers, Lieutenant Edward Culp of the 25th Ohio, wrote a few days later, "On they came, with their wild, diabolical yells, up to our first line of stone fence . . . and the carnage began. I cannot describe the scene that followed. Nothing would stay the progress of the rebels."[89]

A surprised, but combative Colonel Harris related, "The right of Hays' Louisiana brigade [struck] my brigade just between the 107th and 25th Ohio. At that point, and all along my whole line the fighting was obstinate and bloody. The bayonet, club-musket, and anything in fact that could be made available was used." Lieutenant Culp added, "The smoke of battle was so thick that with the increasing darkness it became difficult to distinguish friend from foe."[90]

The thinly stretched and badly outmanned 25th Ohio lost eight color bearers in Hanlon's sudden attack on the salient. The battle-weary regiment had lost nearly half its strength and went through several commanders on July 1. Lieutenant Colonel Jeremiah Williams had been captured and Captain Nathaniel J. Manning was gunned down. Second Lieutenant William Maloney led the Cincinnatians in their initial defense of the stone wall until he too was a casualty, a victim of a Louisianan's bullet in the darkness. Lieutenant Israel White took over for the rest of the battle, becoming one of the few officers of that grade to command a regiment at Gettysburg. He would later call the bitter melee at the stone wall an "obstinate engagement."[91]

The 6th Louisiana's flag bearer, Sergeant Phillip Bolger, went down with a severe wound. He had assumed the dangerous role of color sergeant following the death of his predecessor at Sharpsburg. Now, Bolger lay bleeding on the northern slope of East Cemetery Hill from injuries to his arm and lung. The New Orleans laborer would survive but never fight again. Captain Louis A. Cormier fell mortally wounded while leading the advance of his St. Landry Guards (Company C). Lieutenant Jefferson D. Van Benthuysen took a bullet in the head that blinded his right eye. One of the merry New Orleans Irishmen, Sergeant Patrick McGuinn of Company B, fell; his body would never be identified. Among the many wounded enlisted men was Edward Gunderson, the native of Solør, Hedmark, in eastern Norway.[92]

However, the sheer numbers of Confederates soon spelled disaster for the undermanned 25th Ohio. George S. Clements of Company H was among the Buckeyes caught up in the rush of Rebels pouring into the position. He recalled, "[They] put their big feet on the stone wall and went over like deer, over the heads of the whole . . . regiment, the grade being steep and the wall not more than 20 inches high." After a relatively brief engagement, Lieutenant White and most of his surviving men fell back from the stone wall. However, several Buckeyes broke under the nighttime assault and began scampering up the clover field to the perceived safety of the artillery lunettes and accompanying rifle pits. Rebels rushing up the hill scooped up several prisoners.[93]

Hays' rightmost regiment, the 5th Louisiana, contacted the right flank of the outgunned 107th Ohio Volunteers. "They were all bent over as they charged up the hill," observed one of the Germans, Silas Shuler. Sergeant Frederick Nussbaum claimed, "We mowed the Tigers down as they came up the hill." Private Shuler was perhaps more accurate that the understrength Buckeyes' fire yielded more modest results: "They kept coming up the hill right into the flat area in front of our position. Then we opened up our fire on them. Some of them fell." The flurry of musketry took a toll among the 5th's officers. Major Alexander Hart went down and Captain Thomas H. Briscoe of Company K temporarily assumed command. Several other officers soon were incapacitated and out of action.[94]

The 5th's color bearer, Robert F. Wilson, perished and dozens of men were hurt, including Charles Moore Jr., who wrote in his diary, "At twilight we charged the heights of Gettysburg. I was wounded in the charge. I came to a Yankee Hospital and a Yankee surgeon extracted the ball from my foot and dressed my wound. Our ambulance came for me & Capt. [St. Clair] Johns and took us to our Brigade Hospital."[95]

The Tigers' mass and momentum soon forced the 107th "in some disorder" back up to a stone wall in front of the north-facing section of Wiedrich's 1st New York, Battery I (another section faced east, and the third section had been redeployed to western Cemetery Hill the previous night). Supported by the Buckeyes, the Buffalo gunners stood firm at their now silent guns, which had stopped firing not long ago. The smoking barrels could not be depressed enough to hit the Confederates when they reached the base of the hill.

The sudden Rebel onslaught from the north surprised James Stewart's Battery B, 4th U.S. Artillery in their lunettes to Wiedrich's left rear. Confederates "swarmed up the bank of the little ravine and over the stone wall" and charged, "yelling like demons." They came "within 10 or 15 rods" of the regulars, but to the artillerymen's amazement and relief, they did not set loose a lethal volley that might have devastated the helpless gunners. Instead, the Rebels came on "with the cold steel alone." Stewart's veterans quickly recovered, and a "solid sheet of flame" erupted as they opened up with canister, temporarily halting the Louisianans' advance. Several surviving Tigers would later find their clothing scorched by the exploding powder from the Union guns.[96]

First Division commander Adelbert Ames, with his career perhaps hanging in the balance, frantically rode from spot to spot to rally his beleaguered troops, and "with extraordinary exertions, arrested a panic." The 107th Ohio, now commanded by the adjutant, twenty-three-year-old, Prussian-born Lieutenant Peter F. Young, reformed at the wall to face the Tigers, but Stewart's guns had slowed the enemy. Young's concern suddenly shifted to his right, where a mixed mob of both fleeing Yankees (from the 75th Ohio) and Confederates now were advancing directly uphill at his position.[97]

Much of Colonel Trevanion Lewis' 8th Louisiana and parts of the 9th had poured through the gaps in Harris's brickyard lane line and ascended the clover-covered hillside. They carried with them the entangled remnants of Captain Ben Fox's tiny 75th Ohio regiment, and likely some of the 6th Louisiana as well. Formal organizational structure had long since evaporated in the confusion for both the Yankees and Confederates. Fox later wrote, "All of us that got out safe [from the collapsed brickyard lane line] were among the Rebs when they advanced up the hill—about 100 yards high—it being a clover field. . . . I was among them going up the hill. [It] was so smoky and dark that one could hardly be distinguished." He and Lieutenant Ladley would be the only two officers in the shattered 75th to return to camp that night; everyone else was lost in the chaos.[98]

The charging Tigers were soon entangled in a disordered melee with the

107th Ohio and a few of Fox's men along the stone wall immediately to the left of Wiedrich's guns. One Louisianan described the confused swirl of individual combat: "here we had a hand to hand fight, the Yankees on one side and we on the other side of the wall—knocked each other down with clubbed guns and bayonets." The color bearer of the 107th, Sergeant Christian Taifel, sprang onto the wall and defiantly waved his flag at the Confederates. He was shot down, and the silk banner tumbled to the ground on the opposite side of the rocks. It had scarcely touched the ground before Adjutant Young, a pre-war Cleveland dry goods salesman, leaped over the wall and snatched the colors out of the hands of an oncoming Rebel.[99]

The 8th Louisiana lost its flag to the Buckeyes during a savage encounter that several witnesses later described. Lieutenant Jackson related, "We 'botch up' at a stone wall behind which mr. yank posted himself and he did not want to leave. With bayonets & clubbed muskets we drove them [the 107th OVI] back, by this time it was dark & we couldn't tell whether we were shooting our own men or theirs. Some of our men went on up to the battery. [Arthur E.] Duchamp, the Color Bearer, was wounded & Leon Gusman carried the colors up to the battery and planted them on the breastworks. He was then wounded or taken & our colors lost."[100]

Maryland cavalryman Harry Gilmor watched the swirling and confused twilight melee on East Cemetery Hill, once a peaceful picnic area for the locals. "I saw one of our color-bearers jump on a gun and display his flag. He was instantly killed. But the flag was seized by an Irishman, who, with a wild shout, sprang upon the gun, and he too was shot down. Then a little bit of a fellow, a captain, seized the staff and mounted the same gun; but, as he raised the flag, a ball broke the arm which held it. He dropped his sword and caught the staff with his right hand before it fell, waved it over his head with a cheer, indifferent to the pain of his shattered limb and the whizzing balls around him. His third cheer was just heard, when he tottered and fell, pierced through the lungs."[101]

Sergeant Frederick Nussbaum recorded the same incident from the Union perspective, spotting the Rebel colors being boldly waved from the leftmost lunette. "I called the attention of Adjutant Young to this demonstration, and there being about seven of us, we at once, by command of the Adjutant, fired a volley and advanced toward them, scattering the color-guards in every direction. The color-bearer, being severely wounded, dropped on one knee holding to his flag with such a firm grip, that Adjutant Young who was trying to wrench it from him could not do it." Buckeye Private Shuler added, "Our Adjutant asked their Captain, 'Will you surrender?' 'No, Sir!' So the Adjutant shot the Captain." Nussbaum continued, "The color-bearer had a large navy revolver in his right hand. I saw him pull the trigger and shoot the Adjutant through the shoulder blade; the Adjutant in turn planted his sabre in the color-bearer's breast. The color-bearer held on to the flag and sabre with a firm grip until he dropped over dead, never loosening his grasp until he drew his last breath."[102]

Another Ohioan later wrote, "The color-bearer of the Eighth Louisiana 'Tigers,' in his enthusiasm dashed gallantly forward, waving his flag as he advanced, seeing which, Adjutant Young, revolver in hand, seized the staff and shot the color-bearer in his tracks. But he too was shot—a minie-ball passed through his left arm and pierced his lung. A Confederate officer aimed a fearful blow at his head, which was skillfully parried by Lieutenant [Fernando C.] Suhrer, and reeling to his regiment, still clinging to the [Confederate] flag, [Young] sank into the arms of Sergeant-Major [John] Brinker and was saved." Soldiers carried Young to the rear to the Evergreen Cemetery Gatehouse, "where refreshing water somewhat allayed the burning fever and saved my life." Young entrusted the captured flag to Sergeant Brinker and turned over command of the 107th OVI to a Bavarian-born Cleveland shoemaker, Captain John M. Lutz, who had been lightly wounded on July 1 but had stayed in the field.[103]

High cirrus clouds and a thick canopy of smoke darkened the night, and combatants could only see each other by the bright flashes from the gun muzzles when the powder discharged. One Buckeye remembered, "For a time, the opposing forces were much mixed up together, and with the uncertainty of the light, in the dusk of evening it was difficult to distinguish friend from foe." Eventually, Captain Lutz and the 107th OVI was forced back farther, leaving the gun crews to fend for themselves as the Louisiana Tigers surged into the guns.[104]

While chaos reigned on the northern slope and summit of East Cemetery Hill, the wounded Major Brady's Connecticut Yankees were still gallantly holding their tenuous grip on their part of the brickyard lane. Lieutenant Milton H. Daniel related one incident as his men struggled to hold their ground. "Corporal George Scott, who was [the] acting orderly, had it hand to hand with the enemy as they charged the fence. He shot a fellow and took a captain prisoner. He had caught a Tiger; we did not know what to do with him; it was dusk and we had not the men to spare to send him to the rear, and I never knew how he was disposed of; I have often wondered."

Men grappled with each other, discarding weapons and openly brawling in a desperate contest of strength. Captain Henry Burr "grabbed a 'Johnnie' by the collar of his coat during the fight, drew him over the wall, and made him a prisoner." Ironically, Burr himself had been captured at Chancellorsville in May and had only recently been exchanged. Perhaps balancing Burr's seizure of the Tiger, a Confederate won a wrestling match with Private Moses Wheeler of Company C, dragging him across the wall and escorting him through the meadow to the rear.[105]

The 17th Connecticut would be one of the few regiments in Ames' Division to stand firm and not yield its position. Lieutenant Daniel proudly stated, "Only about half a dozen of the enemy broke through, but the dead in front were in heaps." One of the Confederates' problems in attacking Brady's position, as well as the right of von Gilsa's Brigade, was the uneven terrain bisected by stone walls. Colonel Godwin wrote, "In this charge the command had become much separated, and in the darkness it was now impossible to concentrate more than forty or fifty men at any point for farther advance."[106]

To the 17th's right, men from the left regiments of von Gilsa's line continued to stream panic-stricken uphill to the rear, where, along the Baltimore Pike, Stewart's gunners wielded fence rails to halt the fleeing infantrymen. Other terrified soldiers ran northward along the brickyard line behind the 17th Connecticut and 75th Ohio, threatening to destabilize their already wavering lines. Officers from other regiments tried to arrest the growing panic. Lieutenant Oscar D. Ladley of the 75th OVI fumed, "They [the Confederates] had driven back the dutch Brig[ade] on our right and had got behind us, and rebels & Yankees were mixed up generally. They (the 'dutch') commenced running as usual. My sword was out and if I didn't welt them with it my name ain't O.D.L. It was the only good service it has done me yet, and if I live to see it home, I will have the satisfaction of knowing that if it never killed a reb, it came mighty near laying out a dutchman!"[107]

Charging through von Gilsa's gap, scores of Confederates headed uphill toward Ricketts' Battery, receiving a few last blasts of canister when they emerged into the six Napoleons' arc of fire. Colonel D. B. Penn's 7th Louisiana, as well as a contingent of Major Tate's weary North Carolinians, attacked the combined Pennsylvania battery, which to that point had fired its guns with relative impunity. Several Tigers lined up at the stone wall on the left of Ricketts' lunettes and discharged their muskets, dropping a few crewmen in the enfilade. However, as the terrain dropped sharply past the left section, the remaining gunners were relatively safe as the Confederate bullets merely whizzed overhead. A few Tigers jumped over the wall and charged the battery, which was supported by a few infantrymen from von Gilsa's Brigade, including Lieutenant J. Clyde Miller and part of his skirmish company. Miller later deemed the bitter fighting as "certainly a hot time in the old town of Gettysburg."[108]

One gunner witnessed,

A Confederate lieutenant dashed boldly up and seized the battery's guidon. Private [James H.] Riggin, its bearer, drew his revolver and shot him dead. At the same time, a minie-ball severed the staff and Riggin fell a corpse with that of his adversary. Lieutenant [Louis] Worcester, Seventh Louisiana, charged into the battery, and laying his hand on a gun, demanded its surrender, but was instantly brained by a blow with a handspike in the hands of one of the gunners. Here, at the third gun from the wall, a Confederate sergeant, musket in hand, sprang upon Sergeant [Richard S.] Stratford and demanded his surrender. He was quickly answered by Lieutenant [Charles B.] Brockway of the battery, who coming quickly behind, with a stone he had seized, felled him to the ground.

He continued, "Stratford caught the musket and fired, wounding him severely; and in the fury of the moment clubbed the gun and but for the interposition of Captain Ricketts, would have killed him on the spot." The dying Riggin cried, "Help me, Captain!" and staggered against Ricketts for support before falling to the ground. The left sleeve of Ricketts' coat was drenched with his color bearer's blood. Ricketts' left three guns were all overrun, and his crewmen engaged in hand-to-hand fighting for several tense moments before Union reinforcements starting arriving.[109]

Lieutenant Brockway's postbellum recollection of his role in the incident was more detailed. He had been on the right of the battery when his attention was drawn to the chaos in the left section. He hurried there and found himself "in the midst of a tussling, struggling, swearing, yelling mass of soldiers, bluecoats and butternuts all mixed up together." The Rebel "rascals" successfully spiked one gun, but the cannoneers were busily "whirling their handspikes, swinging their rammers, and using their fists." Brockway could see the muzzle flashes from the Confederate rifles, and he felt all was lost. "I was so desperate that I did not care what came to me personally in the battle, so I pitched in with all my might."

He spotted a Rebel clutching the battery guidon and leading a captured Federal horse. In the darkness and chaos, "the fellow was trying to make off with both. I felt for my revolver, but found it gone just when I needed it most. I determined that I would not let that fellow steal our flag nor capture the horse, so I picked up a stone and knocked him to the earth with that." Brockway continued, "I pounced on him and grabbed the flag out of his hands, and as I lifted it up into the air, the staff was shot in two while I waved it aloft. I did not care for the stick, but I was mighty glad to save that guidon."[110]

Major Samuel Tate of the 6th North Carolina claimed, "75 North Carolinians of the Sixth Regiment and 12 Louisianians of Hays's brigade scaled the walls and planted the colors of the Sixth North Carolina and Ninth Louisiana on the guns. It was now fully dark. The enemy stood with tenacity never before displayed by them, but with bayonet, clubbed musket, sword, pistol, and rocks from the wall, we cleared the heights and silenced the guns."[111] Rebels seized three of Ricketts' men in the "bedlam of terror" for his leftmost piece. They escorted their sullen captives down the hill to the rear with other prisoners, and placed them under the watchful eye of Hays' provost guards. However, before the gun was abandoned, crewmen managed to spike it.[112]

Major Tate mentioned that only seventy-five men from his regiment made it to the crest of East Cemetery Hill. The rest of the 6th North Carolina, and most of the 21st, had been repulsed finally by Brady's 17th Connecticut. The 57th North Carolina, battered by artillery flank shots, had not been able to penetrate the line of the 153rd Pennsylvania, 41st New York, and 33rd Massachusetts, the regiments that were out in the fields contesting the middle stages of the Tar Heels' advance. Perhaps the semiliterate Sergeant Bartlett Y. Malone of the 6th North Carolina best summed up the confusion in Avery's Brigade and the reason why so few made it up East Cemetery Hill. "It was soon so dark and so much smoke that we couldent see what we was a doing. And the enemy got to geather again and we had no reinforcement and we had to fall back to our old position."[113]

While Ricketts' Pennsylvanians were fighting for their lives and their guns, a similar melee continued to their left at Wiedrich's position. According to one Buffalo artilleryman, the attack "was so sudden and so violent that the infantry in front [the 107th OVI] gave way, and the enemy got within the battery; but only for a moment." In the pandemonium, the shrill Rebel yell mixed with deep guttural shouts in English and German from the gunners, who had grabbed pickaxes, shovels, fence rails, handspikes, rocks, and whatever other things they could use as weapons. "One Rebel planted his colors on the lunettes of the first section (which was on the left), and demanded the surrender of the gun. He was promptly knocked down with a handspike."[114]

As Private William Southerton of the 75th Ohio ran back up the hill after passing the line of rifle pits, he noted that Rebels ahead of him had reached the lunettes. "Artillerists fought with ramrods, wielding them like ballbats. Our guns were not spiked. So infuriated were the Tigers that they jabbed with their bayonets. Fought with rocks. A tall rebel shoved right at my elbow, a huge rock raised to dash it at [Captain Benjamin] Fox. I jabbed with my bayonet. A burst of fire! The rebel fell, shot through the head. The rock crashed upon one of his screaming comrades."[115]

As the 153rd Pennsylvania of von Gilsa's Brigade rallied, they witnessed a wild melee between the Rebels and the crews of Wiedrich's Battery. One daring southerner allegedly reached a field piece and draped himself over the muzzle, while crying out to the remaining gunners "I take command of this gun!" A sturdy artillerist, in the act of firing the gun, curtly replied, "Du sollst die haben" ("You can have this!") and yanked the lanyard. A second later, the brave but reckless Tiger disintegrated.[116]

A Louisiana officer brandished his sword and triumphantly screamed, "This battery is ours!" One of the gunners smashed in the Confederate's skull with a devastating blow from his sponge-staff, all the while exclaiming, "No, dis battery is unser!" An artilleryman snatched a musket from a Confederate's hands and savagely drove the bayonet through a nearby Rebel captain. A grudgingly admiring Colonel Charles Wainwright, commanding the guns east of the Baltimore Pike, later reported, "the Germans fought splendidly, sticking to their guns."[117]

The 8th Louisiana's charismatic colonel, Trevanion D. Lewis, fell among the lunettes. The "life of the Regiment" soon died, and the campfires would not be as merry in the days to come. Lieutenant Colonel Alcibiades De Blanc also went down, never to return to the regiment, and Major German A. Lester temporarily assumed command. His men highly respected the fallen De Blanc, deeming him a "perfect gentleman and an excellent officer. . . . All respected, obeyed and loved him."

Another popular officer, Second Lieutenant William McGimsey of Company A, fell with a severe wound; Yankees would later take him prisoner. He was one of the two officers that Colonel Lewis had placed under arrest during the June 30 march from York to Heidlersburg, along with J. Warren Jackson. Lieutenant W. N. McGalliard, who commanded Company E's forward skirmishers, also was now out of action. Comrades carried Captain Victor St. Martin to the rear; he would soon die.[118]

Among the enlisted men to fall was twenty-one-year-old Private Charles F. Lutz of Company F. Born in St. Landry Parish, he was one of the few mustered black men in the Army of Northern Virginia. He had been captured at Chancellorsville and exchanged in time to rejoin the Tigers in camp at Hamilton's Crossing shortly before the Gettysburg Campaign. Now, he would again be a Union prisoner, suffering from a severe gunshot wound to his left forearm.[119]

The Buffalo gunners may have lost their guidon in the confusion. Confederate Lieutenant Jackson recorded, "Willis had a hand to hand fight with a Yank and took his colors from him." The proud new owner of the Union flag was Private Nathan Holmes Willis, a twenty-eight-year-old Alexandria, Louisiana, engineer who had been born in Canaan, New Hampshire. The flag may have been cut up for souvenirs. One week after the attack on East Cemetery Hill, Private J. Arthur Taylor of Company F wrote his father a brief synopsis of the results. "We took the hill and the artillery, but having no support were obliged to fall back. Our Regiment lost its flag, but brought out a yankee flag in return, a piece of which I enclose in this letter." Hays later mentioned his men captured four flags in total, but exactly what flags remains unclear.[120]

Fierce hand-to-hand fighting continued for perhaps fifteen to twenty minutes among the Federal batteries. Just downhill of the chaos in the lunettes, an anxious Harry Hays and Adjutant Seymour continued to look for the promised reinforcements.

### The Repulse

The sharp Confederate attack surprised most Federals. Sergeant E. B. Taylor of the 14th Connecticut, along the stone wall on Cemetery Ridge, recorded, "That night as we lay, our knapsacks plumb up to the base of the stone wall and pillowed our heads thereon . . . , we sought for the rest and sleep we so much needed." He was drifting off to slumber when "suddenly there rang out the volleys of musketry, the roar of artillery, and the rebel yells. . . . Every vestige of sleep was dispelled and every man on the *qui vive*, for there is something weird, mysterious, and almost unearthly about a sudden night attack."[121]

Major General Oliver Howard stood near the Evergreen Cemetery Gatehouse talking with his highest-ranking subordinate, Carl Schurz, the former German revolutionary. With the darkness and persistent sounds of the concurrent fighting on Culp's Hill, they had not discerned Hays' and Avery's movement toward East Cemetery Hill until the attack hit home. Schurz knew the moment of crisis was at hand:

> It was already dark when we on Cemetery Hill were suddenly startled by a tremendous turmoil at Wiedrich's and Ricketts' batteries placed on a commanding point on the right of Cemetery Hill. General Howard and I were standing together in conversation when the uproar surprised us. There could be no doubt of its meaning. The enemy was attacking the batteries on our right, and if he gained possession of them he would enfilade a large part of our line toward the south as well as the east, and command the valley between Cemetery Ridge and Culp's Hill, where the ammunition trains were parked. The fate of the battle might hang on the repulse of this attack.[122]

Schurz instinctively seized the initiative. "There was no time to wait for superior orders. With the consent of General Howard, I took the two regiments nearest to me, ordered them to fix bayonets, and, headed by Colonel Krzyzanowski, they hurried to the threatened point at a double-quick. I accompanied them with my whole staff. Soon we found ourselves surrounded by a rushing crowd of stragglers from the already broken lines. We did our best, sword in hand, to drive them back as we went."[123]

Even as unseen Union reinforcements rushed forward to relieve the beleaguered batteries, Harry Hays and his Confederates were flushed with apparent victory. However, to his anguish, his promised supports were missing. He later reported,

> I captured several pieces of artillery, four stands of colors, and several prisoners. At that time every piece of artillery which had been firing upon us was silenced. A quiet of several minutes now ensued. Their heavy masses of infantry were heard and perfectly discerned through the increasing darkness, advancing in the direction of my position. Ap-

proaching within 100 yards, a line was discovered before us, from the whole length of which a simultaneous fire was delivered. I reserved my fire, from the uncertainty of this being a force of the enemy or of our men, as I had been cautioned to expect friends both in front, to the right, and to the left, Lieutenant-General Longstreet, Major-General Rodes, and Major-General Johnson, respectively, having been assigned to these relative positions; but after the delivery of a second and third volley, the flashing of the musketry disclosed the still-advancing line to be one of the enemy.[124]

Hays ordered his men to open fire, temporarily checking the Federal re-inforcements. William Seymour exulted that the "Yankee line melted away in the darkness," keeping the dream of a decisive victory alive for a few more moments. However, to Hays' dismay, a second line was also moving his way, and in the dim light, he could discern a third line in its rear. Reality dawned slowly—this was not going to be a repeat of the Tigers' success in sweeping through the guns and their defenders from the West Fort at Second Winchester. This time, the First Louisiana Brigade was in trouble.[125]

The oncoming Federal reinforcements were primarily commands whipped on July 1 now looking for redemption, including remnants of Colonel Charles Coster's three regiments shattered the previous day at Kuhn's brickyard. Lieutenant Colonel Lorenz Cantador's 27th Pennsylvania, a German regiment from the southeastern part of the state, was particularly effective in stopping Hays' remaining momentum, charging toward the Rebels' right flank and scattering the 5th and 6th Louisiana.[126]

Major General Schurz and two regiments from Krzyzanowski's Brigade also rushed up in the darkness to engage the Confederates. The Polish-born Krzyzanowski personally led the 119th and 58th New York eastward toward Wiedrich's Battery. As they arrived, Schurz found "an indescribable scene of *mêlée* . . . the cannoneers defended themselves desperately." It was all over in minutes. "Our infantry made a vigorous rush upon the invaders, and after a short but very spirited hand-to-hand scuffle tumbled them down the embankment." Behind them, although too late to make any material difference, came three other regiments from von Steinwehr's Division. With the Louisianans pushed back from their lunettes, Wiedrich's gunners began filtering back to their silent pieces and collecting the tools needed to operate the weapons.[127]

With no help forthcoming from Rodes or Gordon, and his position now tenu-ous at best, Harry Hays reluctantly gave the order to retire back to the stone wall at the bottom of the hill. His men "quietly and orderly obeyed." Lieu-tenant J. Warren Jackson recounted, "Harry soon gave the order to fall back, which we did in tolerably good order." Perhaps simultaneous with Hays' order, another significant Union counterattack crashed into the isolated Confederates.[128]

In the early evening, Major General Winfield S. Hancock, commander of the Union II Corps along Cemetery Ridge, had grown concerned about the sounds of combat emanating from East Cemetery Hill less than a quarter-mile to his right rear. He ordered one of his division commanders, Brigadier General Alexander Hays (no relation to Harry Hays), to move the bulk of the "Gibraltar Brigade" from its position on the low ridgeline to counter the threat. Colonel Samuel "Red" Carroll, a fifty-five-year-old Ohio-born, river town hotelkeeper, led the brigade. The 8th Ohio, on detached skirmishing duty well in front of Cemetery Ridge, was not available. Carroll's three re-maining regiments, the 4th Ohio, 14th Indiana, and 7th West Virginia, had spent the afternoon plugging various gaps in the line as other II Corps troops shifted southward to repel Longstreet's *en echelon* assault.

Carroll, also known as "Old Bricktop" for his red hair and stubbornness, was highly regarded by the army's senior command. Hancock trusted him and relied upon his judgment. Oliver Howard deemed Carroll to be "a young man of great quickness and dash," capable of delivering "energetic help." Han-cock had picked the right leader for the counterattack.[129]

Major J. M. Norvell, Alexander Hays' adjutant, instructed Carroll to move immediately to the assistance of the XI Corps, and one of Howard's aides would lead him into position. The promised guide failed to appear in a timely fashion, so Carroll bellowed "clear ringing orders," and the brigade surged forward. His men fixed bayonets and gave a loud cheer. Due to space limita-tions caused by the massed Federal batteries, Carroll could only advance by the width of a single regiment, a space no wider than seventy-five yards. The 14th Indiana led the way in two successive lines, with the 7th West Virginia following and eight companies of the 4th Ohio in its rear. With no one to guide him in the darkness, Carroll headed toward the roar of battle. His men double-quicked through Evergreen Cemetery as bullets splattered against the gravestones.

There, reserve artillery Captain James Huntington directed Carroll to the

Rebel lines. The 7th West Virginia moved left of the gatehouse, with the other two regiments south of it. The men could see muzzle flashes, directing their path as they rushed forward in the darkness to a scene of "wildest confusion." First Sergeant Joseph L. Dickelman of the 4th Ohio related, "We started for this point at the double-quick, which soon became a dead run; many of our men throwing away their knapsacks and blankets in order to keep up with the mad dash."[130]

The Gibraltar Brigade stormed onto East Cemetery Hill about 9:00 p.m. Carroll's immediate goal was to cross the Baltimore Pike and drive several dozen Rebels from Ricketts' guns. They almost ran down several men of the XI Corps in the process. Private Luther B. Bresnard of the 55th Ohio in Orland Smith's brigade on western Cemetery Hill had been ordered to the rear following a severe wound to his arm. As he ran back across the crest trying to reach the aid station on the Baltimore Pike, he looked to his left and through the smoke noticed Rebels engaged in hand-to-hand fighting amid the guns. He noted, "I came near being run over by some reinforcements just coming in. Dear me, but that was a terrible place just at that time!"[131]

The 14th Indiana arrived at Ricketts' lunettes and assisted the beleaguered defenders in finally driving off Colonel Penn's 7th Louisiana. A small knot of forty to fifty Tar Heels rushed forward in a last desperate attempt to re-capture the guns. They were too few and too late to make any difference. The Indianans easily drove them down the hill and over the stone wall along the brickyard lane. The Hoosiers followed them down to the wall, where they fired two or three volleys that forced the Carolinians to withdraw farther into the dark pastures to safety. There, some Tar Heels discovered their mortally wounded colonel, Isaac Avery. Directed by Major Samuel Tate, his aide-de-camp and antebellum business partner, they carried their commander back to Culp's farmhouse. There, his right hand useless from partial paralysis, Avery used his left to scribble, "Major, tell my father I died with my face to the enemy."[132]

To the Hoosiers' left, Carroll's other two regiments were subjected to a severe crossfire from Rebels ahead of them on the hilltop and along a stone wall to the north. Carroll reacted quickly, ordering the 7th West Virginia to change its front to face this threat: "Halt! Front face! Charge bayonets! Forward, double-quick! March! Give them H——l!" Bugles and drums signaled the advance and the mountaineers pushed forward. The 7th's colonel,

Jonathan H. Lockwood, had his horse shot from under him. He was soon out of commission, badly bruised by a shell fragment.

With relative impunity, Stewart's regular battery had been pouring canister at the 5th and 6th Louisiana, who were "isolated and unsupported on either flank," according to one artilleryman. Finally, the Confederates withdrew to the small ravine and the nearby stone wall, where they regrouped and "began a spattering of musketry." Given time, this gunfire might have been destructive to the battery, but the veteran gunners suddenly heard cheers to their right rear. Out of the darkness came Carroll's "splendid brigade," and elements of it swept past the excited artillerymen and started driving back the Rebels from their front and right flank. Lockwood's mountaineers "charged straight at the wall and ravine, from which they routed the Rebels pell-mell." While they cleared out the Confederates with relative ease, it may have been concurrent with Harry Hays' orders to withdraw.[133]

Hays' 8th and 9th Louisiana reluctantly withdrew from Wiedrich's guns and headed downhill toward the brickyard lane. The gunners rushed back to their pieces and quickly loaded them. Captain Seymour commented, "Had it not been for the darkness, the enemy would have, no doubt, cut us up terribly with his re-captured artillery as we fell back down the hill." Krzyzanowski's 58th and 119th New York followed the retreating Tigers, at one time flopping to the ground in front of some of Wiedrich's guns so they could fire one last round of canister at the retreating Rebels. After the blasts did their work, the Federals leaped up and scrambled down the steep slope, where a sudden volley out of the darkness halted them. Dead and severely wounded New Yorkers now lay beside Buckeyes and Louisianans in the blood-soaked clover field.[134]

At the rock wall at the base of East Cemetery Hill, Harry Hays and many of his remaining Tigers regrouped and rallied for a brief period. Still full of fight, they turned to face their pursuers. However, with no supports in sight and Federals still threatening his front, Hays decided to finally call it quits and head farther to the rear. His survivors collected as many of their wounded as they safely could and then fell back in decent military order across the open fields to a wooden fence some seventy-five yards behind him. There, they awaited further developments. Hays rued the fact that he did not have enough men to safeguard the array of Yankees captured during the attack. "The prisoners sent to the rear, being under charge of no guard, escaped in the darkness; 75 were brought back by my men in retreating from the hill." Dozens of Ohioans and New Yorkers, as well as some of Brady's embattled Connecticut Yankees, managed to slip away and rejoin their respective regiments.[135]

The Tigers' reverse movement across the wall into the meadow east of the brickyard lane came in view of Private Andrew Jackson of the 75th Ohio. He had slipped over the same wall minutes earlier when the Tigers attacked and had cowered in a locust thicket during the mad scramble up the hill. A day later, when all was safe, he recounted his second experience with Hays' Tigers. "I saw a chance . . . in all that yelling and screaming. My ammunition was gone. It was dark. No one could see me crawling through the brush along the fence where I went before." He had used this same route to evade the Rebel sharpshooters' notice in the afternoon when his company was moving out to the meadow on skirmish duty.

Now he was back in the same thicket he had used for cover to fire at Hays' skirmishers. "I knew there would be a lot of dead Johnnies there. The place was thick with dead bodies. I pulled one dead Johnnie, then another, up against me for protection and went through [their] pockets. I got all these watches. And some money, too. [As] I started back [to the lane], I didn't know if I could make it or not. When I was part way up the hill, the Tigers started to come back. Like wild beasts! They ran right over me. When I reached the wall, I climbed over it in a hurry." He informed his listeners, "I've been down there twice now. I'll never go again, never." He hated the sight of his pilfered watches and traded them for greenbacks.[136]

On the crest of East Cemetery Hill, artillery commander Charles Wainwright believed "the attack was now evidently over." He began ordering his batteries to cease fire to allow the smoke to clear. He passed the word down the line of lunettes and cautioned the battery commanders to prepare for a second attack. An infantry lieutenant colonel rode up, saluted, and informed him that Carroll's Brigade was going to charge down into the valley along his front to try to take the Rebels on the flank. However, Wainwright questioned the movement: "I did not think he would find many live rebs there." He was correct in his assessment. Hays and Godwin had disappeared into the night shadows. Carroll eventually collected perhaps a hundred prisoners in his ill-advised foray but failed to locate Hays' flank for a decisive blow.[137]

Sergeant Joseph Dickelman of the 4th Ohio was among those chasing prisoners. Eight companies of his regiment had reached the stone wall along the brickyard lane and fired a fruitless volley into the night at the distant Rebels.

The Buckeyes were startled in the darkness by a booming voice with a thick Irish brogue calling, "Hould on, byes, I'm wan ov yoursilves. Don't shoot me!" Dickelman instructed the man to jump over the stone wall and surrender. The Irish Tiger slapped his thigh with his hand and exclaimed, "Thank Jasus, I'm in the Union again." He was escorted to the rear, glad to be alive and his long campaign over. The regiment captured thirty-four men and picked up nearly two hundred Confederate rifled muskets to replace their old smoothbores.[138]

News of the Union victory was already spreading throughout the area, and hurrahs echoed in the air. At 9:00 p.m., Dr. John W. C. O'Neal jotted in his journal, "A tremendous attack has just been repulsed on East Cemetery Hill at a point held by Ricketts' Battery."[139]

Meanwhile, Harry Hays discerned in the dissipating smoke and brightening moonlight that the Federals had moved back down the hill and were reoccupying the stone wall along the brickyard lane. He was contemplating retreating to a better position when his brigade quartermaster, Captain John G. Campbell, informed him that Gordon was coming to his support. Hays immediately dispatched a staff officer "to hasten General Gordon with all possible speed." However, the messenger soon rode back, stating he had not been able to locate Gordon.

Frustrated by the lack of reinforcements, Hays went back to seek General Gordon. To his dismay, long battle lines of Georgians were not coming to his assistance. Instead, he found Gordon's Brigade stationary in the exact creekside location from where Hays had launched his futile attack not long ago. Realizing that even if the Georgians started forward now, they would be too late to make a difference, Hays believed his only remaining option was to withdraw across the fields and reform in the rear. Shortly after 9:30 p.m., he returned to his men still huddled at the fence line.

Seymour recalled, "Two columns were heard advancing on upon our flanks, threatening to surround and capture our little Brigade and the few men of [Avery's] Brigade who charged with us. Gen. Hays, perceiving the imminent danger he was in and having given up all hope of a supporting force coming to his rescue, was obliged to give up his hard earned captures and marching by the right flank he led his Brigade back towards town." The remaining Louisianans marched behind a hill to avoid fire from the Federals, and Hays conducted them back to a spot just to the right of his original position, arriving about 10:00 p.m.[140]

Before Hays and his band reached the safety of the Winebrenner Run ravine and the High Street plateau, perhaps as many as three hundred surviving Tigers, primarily from the 5th and 6th Louisiana, remained isolated near the extreme northern slope of Cemetery Hill. They had found a temporary respite from the Federal fire by huddling together for protection behind a little knoll not far from the southern outskirts of Gettysburg. The low mound had sheltered their approach earlier in the evening, and now the Tigers again were using it as cover from Federal muskets, as well as Lieutenant Stewart's now silent regular artillery and the north-facing section of Wiedrich's Battery.

In the confusion and low hanging smoke, a few Yankee prisoners managed to escape from the Tigers and make their way back to the restored Union lines on East Cemetery Hill. There, they informed Federal officers of the location of the hidden Confederates. Word reached the one-armed General Howard, who wanted to seize all of the enemy combatants. With Carroll's men now gone from the summit into the valley below, the emotional corps commander was frantically trying to find "two strong regiments to push down the hill near the town" to cut off the line of retreat for the disordered mass.

The nearest available "strong regiments" would have most likely been from Krzyzanowski's Brigade. However, when he was ready to order the charge, Howard could not scrounge up any subordinate officer of rank to lead the effort. Colonel Wainwright matter-of-factly asked him, "Why don't you have them shot?" A frustrated Howard snipped, "I should have to shoot all the way down; they are all alike." The Confederates eventually slipped away without significant further damage. Regimental commanders Lieutenant Colonel Hanlon and Captain Briscoe managed to regroup their scattered men in Gettysburg along High Street. Most of the Louisiana boys stacked arms and wearily lay down to rest. It had been a long day.[141]

The sudden stillness when Colonel Wainwright ceased his artillery fire was noticeable to the troops on both sides, as well as to the townspeople who were listening from the safety of cellars and the farmers and country folk watching the aerial fireworks from distant hillsides. Young Billy Bayly was among the latter group of Adams Countians who had not fled the area when the armies arrived. He noted, "The firing had ceased ... uncanny in its silence as the noise had been satanic in its volume." Captain Ricketts' memory of the night focused on the one peaceful thing he could recall. "I never knew how long the fight lasted on the evening of the 2nd, but I remember that after everything had become quiet, the full moon was above Culp's Hill."[142]

As the smoke began to clear and the moonlight brightened, the Union prisoners still being held in the German Reformed Church and the nearby brick school watched as Hays' men returned to their old positions. Private Justus Silliman of the 17th Connecticut peered out from a second-floor schoolhouse window. "The clash was tremendous, but short, and [Stonewall] Jackson's picked men retreated back panic stricken and with their ranks terribly thinned." The captives were "gladdened by the cheers" of the victorious Yankees on distant East Cemetery Hill.[143]

In the blood-soaked pastures past the brickyard lane stone wall, "Red" Carroll's victorious II Corps troops had given up chasing the Rebels after collecting a few dozen prisoners. Along with other Union soldiers, they now were busy filling their canteens at a cold spring just beyond the brickyard lane. They introduced themselves to Stewart's grateful gunners, who had also descended the hill to renew their water supply. Up until then, the regulars had no clue as to the identity of the "splendid brigade" that had swept past them and driven off the howling Confederates.[144]

No one was sure how long the confused and swirling fighting on East Cemetery Hill had lasted. Captain John Lutz, commanding the battered 107th Ohio, estimated the entire Confederate attack to be ninety minutes. Other estimates varied from one to three hours. What was clear was that the toll to attack and defend East Cemetery Hill had been staggering. Shrieks of pain and low moans mingled in the night air, still acrid with the smell of freshly burned gunpowder. Soon the loud reports of gunfire again rang through the night as the pickets and snipers regained their positions and methodically resumed their deadly work, exchanging unpleasantries in the dim moonlight until nearly midnight.[145]

In the 75th Ohio, more than half the men were missing, taken by the Tigers back down the hill into the meadows. Captain Ben Fox reported, "Half an hour after the engagement, many of the men are prisoners—at least we did not find very many left on the field." A few men would trickle in during the night; either soldiers who had run away or those prisoners who managed to escape their captors and return to Union lines.[146]

## Taking Stock

"Within thirty minutes from the time the charge was made," commented one 25th Ohioan, "the smoke had cleared away and the moon had risen with great brilliancy, flooding the battle field with mellow light. It was a ghastly battle field." With the firing apparently done for the night and the dense clouds of gunsmoke finally dissipated, a patrol from the 58th New York under Lieutenant Carl Schwarz probed the front for signs of the enemy. He found nothing but the dead and wounded.[147]

All along East Cemetery Hill, exhausted soldiers slumped to the ground to catch some rest, with the fighting over for the night. With the welcome news that all was clear and the Rebel infantry indeed was gone, relief crews scurried about seeking what wounded men they could locate in the brightening moonlight. "The ground was covered with the groanings and moanings of the wounded," wrote Major General Howard. "While the soldiers were sleeping, the medical men with their ambulances, aided here and there by a chaplain or a member of the Christian Commission, were going from point to point to do what little they could for the multitude of sufferers." Colonel Andrew Harris, relieved the crisis was finally over, reported, "We gathered up the dead and cared for the wounded of both friend and foe."[148]

Private Andrew Diembach of the 73rd Pennsylvania encountered "one poor fellow clad in gray, who was shot in the head. We carried him to the pump back of the cemetery gate. He was moaning piteously and rubbing his hand over gaping wound from which his brains were oozing. How we pitied the poor wounded man—ten minutes ago a foe, now a helpless comrade needing our care! One of our boys, with tears in his eyes, put his gum blanket under the sufferer's head, and said, in a choked voice, 'There, my poor fellow, that will make you rest easier;' and other comrades moistened his feverish lips with water from the pump."[149]

Likewise, Harry Hays' medical stewards and other volunteers scoured the fields over which they had recently traversed looking for fallen comrades. Ambulance drivers such as Private B. J. Smith of the 6th Louisiana were busy transporting the wounded to the rear to a barn hastily improvised as a field hospital, although the relief parties dared not get too close to the regenerated Union lines. As a result, scores of Tigers and Carolinians lay suffering for hours in a light rain shower. Dr. William Robertson and other regimental surgeons worked through the night, and amputated limbs soon piled high.[150]

On East Cemetery Hill, Federal parties collected those Louisiana soldiers too badly wounded to walk and carried them behind Union lines for treatment. Many Tigers faced weeks or months of recuperation, some in hospitals and some in prison camps. Corporal Ulysses W. Fisher of the 6th Louisiana had recovered from a gunshot wound suffered in his foot at Sharpsburg. Now, he lay grievously wounded in the thigh; he would never rejoin his comrades in Company C. He would eventually be transported to the Davids' Island Military Reservation at the western end of Long Island Sound in New York, where he died in early September.[151]

Several soldiers of the 107th Ohio located the body of the defiant color bearer of the 8th Louisiana, who had died in the memorable struggle with Adjutant Young. They counted seven bullet holes in the corpse. His canteen contained a mixture of whiskey and gunpowder, which the Federals "judged accounted for his desperate bravery." Corporal Frederick Nussbaum appropriated the dead Tiger's knapsack, "which was a very neat one, made of leather with a goat-skin cover; and which contained a single biscuit lately baked yet warm; being minus my own knapsack, I carried it a while, but [my] Comrades made so much fun of me that I threw it away, for which I have been sorry ever since."[152]

Long after dark, an artilleryman from Cooper's Battery encountered a Louisiana Tiger, who had been wounded and knocked down, possibly from being clubbed in the head. The man's behavior was so erratic that Lieutenant James Stewart of Battery B, 4th U.S. commented to Captain Cooper, "The man is either drunk or crazy." Guards finally escorted the delirious prisoner to the rear.[153]

The Tigers' loss was relatively heavy—21 killed, 119 wounded, and 41 missing. Among the dead were Colonel Trevanion Lewis, Captains Victor St. Martin and Louis Cormier, and Lieutenants Wallace P. Talbot, Auguste Randolph, and Richard T. Crawford, adjutant of the 9th Louisiana. Dozens of other line officers were wounded, and many of the missing were in all likelihood among those killed. Among those Tigers never heard from again was Corporal Michael Henry of the 5th Louisiana. Severely wounded and captured at Antietam, he had just rejoined his regiment in the spring.[154]

Hays and Early were both frustrated that Rodes' Division had failed to advance. "General Early's indignation was great," recorded Lieutenant Thomas Turner of Ewell's staff. "He rode to Gen. Ewell's Headquarters bitterly commenting on Rodes' failure to fulfill his promise to support him." General Rodes later rationalized, "I would attack at dark just at dark, and [I] proceeded to make my arrangements; but having to draw my troops out of the town by the flank, change the direction of the line of battle, and then traverse a distance of 1,200 or 1,400 yards while General Early had to move only half that distance without change of front, the result was that, before I drove the enemy's skirmishers in, General Early had attacked, and had been compelled to withdraw." Coupled with information on the strength of the defenders in his front and the nature of the terrain he would have to cover, as well as the increased darkness, Rodes convinced himself that "it would be a useless sacrifice of life to go on, and a recall was ordered."[155]

Captain Seymour complained, "This want of concert of action on the part of our Generals was the chief cause of the loss of the great battle of Gettysburg. The army was fought by Divisions instead of Corps, which was a great and unfortunate mistake." His was perhaps the most common reason among the Confederate soldiers why their seemingly invincible Army of Northern Virginia had failed in their charges.[156]

Major Tate, who had led part of the 6th North Carolina into Ricketts' lunettes, was enraged at the lack of supports, particularly from his own brigade. Upon finally reaching the Confederate lines before midnight, he sought out Colonel Archibald Godwin and demanded to know why he had not been properly supported. He was "coolly informed that it was not known we were in the works." Tate, with a touch of exaggeration, would write the Governor of North Carolina, Zebulon Vance, just a few days later, "To think of the monstrous injustice done us! I assure you that the fighting was no fantasy or fancy picture; such a fight as the Yankees made inside of their works has never been equaled. Inside the enemy were left lying in great heaps, most all with bayonet wounds, and many with their skulls broken by the stocks of our guns. We left not a living man on the hill."[157]

However, some Confederates were still full of fight, believing they could yet achieve a decisive victory on Union soil. The adjutant of Roy Stone's I Corps brigade, Captain John Parsons of the 149th Pennsylvania, had stayed with his wounded commander in the old stone house that was now Hays' brigade hospital. He remembered, "The desperate charges made by this brigade on the evening of the 2d brought ambulance after ambulance of their wounded to the hospital. I could gather nothing satisfactory from their surgeons or their wounded as to the result of the day; but they were in good spirits and appeared sanguine of success in the end. Some of the officers who were slightly wounded, said to me that they were certain of success, and had marked out on their pocket-maps the line of march to Baltimore, Washington, Philadelphia, and New York."[158]

Captain Seymour remarked in his journal, "The charge was a daring and desperate one, and, although unsuccessful on account of the failure of our supports to come up, we gained great credit for it." Major William H. Manning of the 6th Louisiana would later write that his men "took part in the charge on Cemetary [sic] Heights on the 1 of July (1863) and if the Regiment had been supported, we could have held them." Private Thomas Reed echoed the officers' opinions. "We were hustled around to the heights, which we charged and took, but, our support not coming up in time, we had to fall back."[159]

Despair, grief, shock, and rage intermingled among the enlisted men as they regained their old lines. One of Early's staff officers, future U.S. Senator John W. Daniel, rode along Middle Street and observed Hays' men lying along the sidewalks, many suffering from wounds. There seemed to be no military order. He was stunned at the display: "All was in confusion, distress." However, the major marveled at the courage of the men who had tried so valiantly in the darkness to wrest the artillery-crowned hill from the Yankees: "it is manhood indeed which faces danger & does not shrink."

One Federal prisoner overheard several Louisianans venting their frustration: "A madder set of men I never saw. They cursed their officers in a way and manner that showed experience in the business . . . it was simply fearful . . . they said their officers didn't care how many were killed, and especially old Hays, who received his share of the curses." Professor Michael Jacobs of Pennsylvania College wrote, "There seemed to be an entire absence of that elation and boastfulness which they manifested when they entered this town on the evening of the first of July." One Louisianan moaned, "It was worse than Malvern Hill!" Youthful Gates Fahnestock observed, "What was left of the Louisiana Tigers were not so jubilant—they were tired, exhausted, and discouraged; and what they said of the Germans in Howard's command on Cemetery Hill was not complimentary."[160]

Accolades would eventually pour in for the gallantry of the soldiers on both sides, but Harry Hays would particularly call attention to the efficiency of colonels Leroy Stafford of the 9th Louisiana and Davidson Penn of the 7th Louisiana. Colonel Clement Evans of Gordon's Brigade, who had watched the aerial theatrics and gun flashes from his reserve position, later wrote, "Harry Hays and his brigade exhibited their old-time endurance and valor." Early's "gallant array of fighters" also impressed many of their foes. Private Andrew Diembach of the 73rd Pennsylvania termed the Tigers' struggle to take possession of East Cemetery Hill as "a grand, though gory, example of the heroism of the American soldier."[161]

While Confederates fretted about the lack of support and praised the valor of their officers and men, many campfire discussions among the Union survivors on Cemetery Hill centered on the ferocity of the melees around the guns and the quality of the Teutonic infantry assigned to protect them. Pennsylvania artillery Captain Bruce Ricketts was livid at the Germans who had collapsed in his front and exposed his guns (von Gilsa's 68th and 54th New York). The Pennsylvanian bore a deep hatred for the XI Corps "flying Dutchmen" the rest of his life. He was, however, quite thankful for "Red" Carroll's 14th Indiana, who had rescued his battery and drove off Major Tate's North Carolinians and the handful of 7th Louisiana Tigers. "If I had received no support, my men would have been overpowered."[162]

Captain Ben Fox of the 75th Ohio, one of only two officers left in the shattered regiment, commented, "I began to fear a panic in the 'Running half moons,' but fortunately we whipped them without assistance although reinforcements were at hand." The regiment had been split apart by the attack of the 8th and 9th Louisiana. Dozens of men had run to the rear, but the other remaining officer, Lieutenant Oscar Ladley, was pleased that in his limited front, "we finally drove them back. I never saw such fighting in my life. It was a regular hand to hand fight. Our Brig[ade] had sworn never to turn, so they stood, but it was a dear stand for some of them. I have 6 men left [in Company G]; the Regt. had 60; the Brig. 300 out of 1500."[163]

By contrast to Fox's sarcastic "running half-moons," Professor Michael Jacobs related, "The rebels returned to our street at ten P. M., and prepared their supper; and soon we began to hope that all was not lost. Some of them expressed their most earnest indignation at the foreigners—the Dutchmen—for having shot down so many of their men. This led us to believe that the Eleventh Corps, of whom many were foreign Germans, and whom, on the previous evening, they tauntingly told us they met at Chancellorsville—had done their duty and had nobly redeemed their character." Chambersburg historian Jacob Hoke believed, "The Louisiana Tigers had met their match, and

Howard's Germans redeemed themselves from the reproach of Chancellors-ville. This whole engagement lasted but a short time, but in that short space these noted fighters were sadly worsted."[164]

A young contract military surgeon from Pennsylvania, Dr. Mosser, had remained in Gettysburg after the July 1 retreat to tend the wounded of the I Corps. Now, he had plenty more patients, as Hays' injured men streamed into town seeking medical aid. Mosser later related to Colonel Wainwright that a Rebel had witnessed "one of the [Wiedrich's] battery men snatch a musket out of the hands of one of their men and drive the bayonet right through [a Rebel] captain." To the xenophobic Wainwright, "This would show that the Germans had some fight in them; the fault must be in the officers, most of whom are adventurers, political refugees, and the like." Wiedrich had lost three men killed and ten wounded in the valiant struggle to save his guns.[165]

J. L. Dickelman of the 4th Ohio, the veteran regiment from Carroll's Brigade that had cleared the 7th Louisiana and Major Tate's 6th North Carolina from Bruce Ricketts' guns, perhaps best summed up the twilight attack on East Cemetery Hill, believing it a "never-to-be-forgotten day." Colonel Adin Underwood of the 33rd Massachusetts and his men "thanked God for that narrow escape." One of his men, Private John J. Ryder, wrote to his mother, "By the mercy of God I escaped without a scratch. . . . Carroll's regiment came to our rescue just in time. . . . I did not think I should come out alive, but I do not fear to die, for I'm in a sacred cause and doing my duty. Better men than me have fallen and have lived." Another Federal infantryman, realizing the Confederates had accomplished so little for all their strenuous efforts that night, deemed Hays' assault "another fruitless display of magnificent bravery, in which life and zeal were thrown away."[166]

The question was whether the battered Union lines could withstand another hammering in the morning. Gettysburg physician Dr. J. W. C. O'Neal, assisting the wounded, echoed the sentiment along Cemetery Ridge. At midnight, he noted in his journal, "The day is over and I might as well admit the situation is grave. . . . Our army has not lost heart but it must be confessed that the situation is critical." Long after dark in his headquarters just south of Cemetery Hill, George Meade held a council of war in the tiny Widow Leister house with his senior commanders. After much discussion about the options open to his army, Meade reached a fateful decision—despite his massive casualties, his enemy was in just as bad shape, and he would stay and fight it out. This time, the Army of the Potomac would not retreat.

Robert E. Lee guessed as much, and he was determined to stay and dislodge his stubborn opponent. He later wrote, "The result of this day's operations induced the belief that, with proper concert of action, and with the increased support that the positions gained on the right would enable the artillery to render the assaulting columns, we should ultimately succeed, and it was accordingly determined to continue the attack. The general plan was unchanged."[167]

Gettysburg residents also took stock of the long day, unsure if the armies would slip away in the night, or if tomorrow would bring a resumption of the nerve-rattling musketry and cannonades. An anxious Sarah Broadhead took her pen and wrote, "We expect to be compelled to leave town tomorrow, as the Rebels say it will most likely be shelled. I cannot sleep, and as I sit down to write, to while away the time, my husband sleeps as though nothing was wrong. I wish I could rest so easily, but it is out of the question for me either to eat or sleep under such terrible excitement and such painful suspense. We know not what the morrow will bring forth, and cannot tell the issue of today."[168]

# 6 | The Aftermath

### Still Full of Fight

BEFORE DAYBREAK ON Friday, July 3, Major General Jubal Early ordered Harry Hays to withdraw his brigade from its advanced position and reoccupy the same street he had held the previous afternoon. In the darkness, the Tigers pulled back from the Winebrenner Run ravine and returned to Middle Street in downtown Gettysburg. They occasionally could hear the cries of the wounded in hastily improvised field hospitals established in various churches, houses, outbuildings, and stables.

As the eastern sky brightened, the debris of war and the scars from the afternoon cannonry and Hays' twilight assault became visible on East Cemetery Hill. About 8:00 a.m., Cincinnati *Gazette* correspondent Whitelaw Reid returned to the hill that had been so peaceful the previous morning. Now, the old picnic grounds, the clover fields, the broken down fences, and Evergreen Cemetery itself reflected the unmistakable signs of war. "Yesterday's conflict was more plainly inscribed on the tombstones than the virtues of the buried dead they commemorated. Shells had plowed up the lately sodden graves; round shot had shattered marble columns; dead horses lay about the monuments; and the gore of dead men soaked the soil and moistened the roots of the flowers on the old graves."[1]

One young Federal infantryman related,

The village cemetery was a frightful spot. The batteries on this eminence had been exposed to a devastating artillery fire and had suffered severely, as shown by the numbers of dead horses lying about, the dismounted cannon and broken caissons which cumbered the ground, the defaced monuments and fractured tombstones which showed the effects of the shelling the place had received. Here and there were wounded men who had not yet been taken to the hospital, and hundreds of infantry lying on the graves or stretched out in the paths, while the ground everywhere was covered with the litter and refuse and *débris* of the battlefield—broken rammers from the cannon, cast-off wheels, abandoned knapsacks, torn blankets, ruined muskets, discarded bayonets, saddles, harness, ammunition cases, caps, hats, coats, and an indescribable lot of other rubbish accumulated amid the confusion and havoc of the battle and lying on every side.[2]

A Pennsylvania reporter surveying the carnage wrote, "Next morning after the assault a man might have walked from the muddy stream below, up to the very muzzles of the cannon above, on dead and bleeding bodies. All this occurred just outside the gates of the Cemetery. It seems as if war in cruel mockery of death, had flung a thousand victims at his door."[3]

Several Confederate bodies were bloating as decomposition set in, and many of them had their pockets turned inside out by looters. Lieutenant Albert Peck of the 17th Connecticut noted "a rebel color bearer lying dead near our batteries. . . . I also saw a large dead reb who had a straw hat on; his sleeves were rolled up. He had no coat on, he wore a U.S. belt with the U.S. plate turned upside down. I picked up a couple of stars that had been torn from a rebel flag and a piece of the flag also." That may have been a part of the flag of the 9th Louisiana, which had been torn apart for souvenirs. The captured banner of the 8th Louisiana, which Adjutant Peter Young had seized during his tussle with its bearers, was still intact. It had been entrusted to Sergeant Major John Brinker, who in the morning gave it to Lieutenant Fernando C. Suhrer, who turned it in to the XI Corps headquarters.[4]

Downhill, corpses dotted the brickyard lane and the undulating terrain in the ravine between Cemetery and Wolf's hills. They were too far away from Confederate lines to allow safe passage to collect them, and most Yankees were not venturesome enough to risk enemy sharpshooter fire to probe for bodies among the trampled grasses and battle-damaged woodlots. Patrols collected water from the two springs in the meadows beyond the brickyard lane.

Sergeant Frederick Nussbaum of the 107th Ohio scrambled down to the northernmost spring. The carnage appalled him:

The lane was covered with dead men from both sides, also a number of horses, cows, and mules, so that it was impossible for me to get to the spring without stepping on the dead. In the middle of the lane, I stopped to pick up a rifle and exchange it for mine, when a bullet passed close by my ears; I dropped the gun, and a few steps further on another ball went whizzing above my head, and so on until seven shots were fired at me by a Rebel sharpshooter from one of the windows of the [German] Reformed church. The sixth shot struck a gate post directly in front of my head, while the seventh touched the sole of my right shoe as I alighted on the ground, leaping over a gate to reach the regimental line.

Shaken after this extremely close call, he added, "I succeeded in bringing eleven canteens full of water; these I left near the gate, telling the boys to go after them themselves. I had a very narrow escape."[5]

Hays' and Avery's skirmishers were still ensconced in the buildings on the southern outskirts of Gettysburg, as well as in the thicket-covered fields beyond the brickyard. Watching from the relative safety of the brick-walled German Reformed Church, Private Reuben Ruch of the 153rd Pennsylvania was fascinated by the nearby sharpshooters' cat-and-mouse game. "I saw one get on the roof of a two-story house. He was firing over the chimney, and I thought it a bad position. If he were to get hit and stunned, the fall would kill him. He had fired four rounds and was getting ready for another, and in the act of looking over the chimney was hit and fell off the gable end. After the battle I looked up the fellow to see where he was hit, and found that the ball had pierced his forehead."[6]

Others tried as best as they could to ignore the incoming missiles of death. Huddling behind a stone wall along Cemetery Hill, Private John J. Ryder of the 33rd Massachusetts took time to write a letter to his mother. "At this moment the bullets are whistling over the wall and striking near us. We've got used to them. So long as hear them, we are safe. We cannot dodge them, but trust in God."[7]

On Cemetery Hill, reporter Whitelaw Reid continued, "This morning it was comparably quiet again. Sharpshooters from the houses in town were picking off officers who exposed themselves along the crest. They knew that we did not want to shell the place, and presumed upon the forbearance of our artillery. The annoyance had at last become too annoying, and one of our guns had been directed to dislodge a nest of the most audacious and the surest aimed by battering down the house from which they were firing. It was the only house in Gettysburgh [sic] we harmed throughout the battles." Confederate officers scurried through town to warn residents the Federals intended to shell the town to flush out the sharpshooters. A few residents collected personal items and departed for safer environs. At least one family buried its valuables in the cellar in case their home burned.[8]

Among the Tigers who were deployed as skirmishers this day were the Stafford Guards, Company B of the 9th Louisiana. Ohio-born Lieutenant Henry E. Handerson, a twenty-eight-year-old former private tutor from Alexandria, had just rejoined the regiment that morning after his release from a hospital in Richmond on June 20. With a small group of other recuperated Confederates, he had hiked all the way from Virginia in pursuit of the brigade. Another soldier offered to guide him through downtown to the spot where his men were located. The lieutenant later wrote,

Accordingly, we proceeded towards the southern edge of the town, and scurrying hastily across the main street [Baltimore Street], which was swept by the bullets of the enemy's skirmishers, made our way through the gardens and enclosures to a large, frame house, into the back door we entered.

Here an amusing sight met my view. Around a table at the center of the room were gathered the majority of my company, engaged in discussing a generous meal, apparently procured by ransacking the pantry and cellar of the mansion, while at each of the front windows a couple of men were occasionally exchanging shots with the enemy, being relieved at intervals by their comrades and retiring to join the feast until their turn once more came around. Of course I was met with a hearty welcome. . . .

Learning that an outpost was placed at the foot of the garden, I asked one of the men to lead me to the spot. Passing through a gate leading to a garden, we scampered at full speed across an open space of about one hundred yards to the shelter of another house, still nearer the enemy, behind which I found half-a-dozen comrades skirmishing with a force of the enemy a short distance below.

One of his men was firing from behind a large oak tree, whose scarred bark testified how close the Yankees had come to hitting their antagonist. The man finally screamed in pain when a Federal sharpshooter drilled him in the right arm with a well-placed shot. Handerson directed him to lie down on the ground with his feet extended toward the house. During a brief lull, Handerson and a comrade rushed out, grabbed the man by his feet, and dragged him across the exposed garden to safety behind the house, where they could temporarily dress his wound.[9]

Few Confederates dared expose themselves to the Union sharpshooters without risking their lives. Private Thomas Reed was ordered to take a detail of men and "go and have a lot of rations cooked." He soon attracted the attention of Howard's snipers on Cemetery Hill. "While we were getting ready, and while I was going into a house, whack! went something. Then I heard something drop on the floor on the other side of the house. I went and picked it up, and it was ball shot from one of those globe-sighted guns. The ball had struck the wall of the house some two feet from the door, and about two feet up from the floor. He had come that nigh getting me, and I know he was at least half a mile away. The way those devils did was to climb trees with their guns, and then pop away at us."[10]

For some, the sniping became almost a sport. Private William Warren and his comrades in Company C of the 17th Connecticut were on skirmish duty near East Cemetery Hill. Toward Gettysburg, they could see an old well near a brick house. Several times, thirsty Confederates cautiously approached the well and cranked the old-fashioned windlass to raise the bucket. The Federal soldiers would allow them to get the bucket most of the way up before unleashing a torrent of Minié balls, sending the southerners scattering for safety behind the house. They repeated the process at intervals, at great amusement to the Connecticut boys, but "probably it was not much fun for the thirsty Johnnies."[11]

For others, the results were tragic. Corporal William H. Poole of Company H entered the red brick Samuel McCreary house and climbed the stairs to the second floor. He noticed an old wooden table, which he pushed into a balcony doorway that faced south and offered a view of the Union skirmishers. He knelt behind the table and rested his rifle on it to steady his aim as he tried to pick off distant Yankees. A Federal sharpshooter spotted him and fired a bullet that ripped through the table and struck Poole in the chest. His blood seeped onto the floorboards as he died in the Pennsylvania home. Throughout the long day, the First Louisiana Brigade would lose at least sixty-seven men.[12]

The persistent sniping also claimed the life of twenty-year-old Mary Virginia "Ginnie" Wade, who was busy baking bread in her sister's house on Baltimore Street. The sibling, Georgia McClellan, had given birth three days earlier and Wade was staying with her. The brick McClellan house was located between the Federal and Confederate sharpshooters' nests. A Minié ball, presumably fired from one of the Confederate snipers along Breckinridge Street, slammed through the north-facing wooden door about 8:30 a.m., penetrated a second door, and then ripped into the unsuspecting Wade's back. She slumped to the kitchen floor and died, a pool of blood staining the floorboards.

General Ewell had a narrow escape while riding near Hays' line with Early's chief engineer, Captain Henry B. Richardson. They were warned to beware of the enemy sharpshooters, some of whom had telescopic sights on their long-range rifles. Ewell ignored the danger, commenting that the Federals were at least fifteen hundred yards away. However, within minutes, he was struck in his wooden leg by a Minié ball, and Richardson tumbled off his horse after taking a bullet in his torso.[13]

By midmorning, the firing tapered off somewhat. Whitelaw Reid reported, "To the front, skirmishers were still at work, but in a desultory way." He left General Howard's headquarters about 9:45 a.m. and rode to Meade's headquarters on Taneytown Road, even as the skirmishing in the fields west of Cemetery Hill intensified. However, before he left, Reid observed that the sniping to the north from the Rebels hidden in the town "revived occasionally, and then died away again."[14]

Perhaps an account from Major Eugene Blackford of the 5th Alabama explains why the sharpshooting had slacked off. He commanded the sharpshooters of Rodes' Division, which had positioned themselves east of Baltimore Street, with the Tigers' skirmishers to its west. The twenty-four-year-old Virginia native wrote, "About 10 a.m. an officer reported to me from my left saying that he commanded the skirmishers of Hays' Louisiana Brig[ade] and had been ordered to receive directions from me. I showed him where to connect with me, and left him." He added,

About an hour or more after I went over to see what he was about, and found a truly amusing scene. His quarters were in a very [nice] house, and he had selected the parlor as his own bivouac. Here one was playing the piano, which sounded sadly out of harmony with the roar of musketry. Without, several men were laying around on the sofas, and the room was full of prints & engravings which the rude fellows examined, and then threw down on the floor. On the table there was a doz[en] brands of wines and liquors, of which all partook freely. The commanding officer thought it was very strange that I at once insisted upon his visiting his posts, and making the men fire. I ran rapidly back across the street.[15]

While the day wore on and the sharpshooters occasionally sniped at one another, surgeons and townspeople feverishly tended to the hundreds of wounded from both sides. In Elizabeth Wible's barn on her farm two miles northeast of Gettysburg, the 6th Louisiana's twenty-two-year-old Captain Louis A. Cormier lay in agony from a severe gunshot wound to his stomach. Young and handsome, he attracted the attention of some of Gettysburg's young ladies, who ministered to him in the morning. As they were leaving to visit other injured men, the Cajun officer asked the ladies to stop by later in the day "to see him die." About noon, the women returned and gathered close around the mortally wounded Louisianan. Cormier summoned enough strength to tell them about his mother and two sisters at home, and that he wished he could be with them again. He asked the women to kiss him farewell. One by one, they complied, some with tears in their eyes for the fallen enemy soldier. Soon after, he was dead.[16]

Private Edward McCrahon of the 7th Louisiana was thankful he had survived the charge on East Cemetery Hill unscathed. A native of County Kerry, Ireland, he was raised in the small railroad center of Fishers, New York, and later worked as a fireman on a wood-burning locomotive. By 1861, tired of the railroad, he became a traveling salesman for a Rochester horticultural firm. His business took him to New Orleans, where he signed up for Confederate service following the bombardment of Fort Sumter. Originally hired as a teamster, he had been assigned to brigade headquarters as an orderly. Unknown to him at the time, at Antietam his younger brother Alexander served in the opposing army in the 108th New York. Here at Gettysburg, brother fought against brother once again, for sixteen-year-old Aleck was now a member of Battery C, 4th U.S. Artillery. The younger McCrahon was severely wounded in the lower leg during the battle, an injury that invalided him the rest of the year.[17]

Ed McCrahon and his comrades in the depleted First Louisiana Brigade remained stationary on Middle Street throughout the humid day, prepared to attack again if ordered forward by General Ewell. In the early afternoon, they listened with interest to the massive roar from the prolonged artillery bombardment that preceded what became popularly known as Pickett's Charge.

Lieutenant Handerson, back with his 9th Louisiana less than a day after his exhausting hike, recalled, "Never before or since have I listened to such an uproar, which fairly made the earth tremble and the air vibrate with successive shocks." Lieutenant J. Warren Jackson, no longer on skirmish duty this day, wrote, "The Inhabitants of Gettysburg will never forget the 3rd day of July of the La Brigade—tremendous cannonade & musketry on our right. Longstreet & A. P. Hill were repulsed with heavy loss."[18]

At dusk, Union gunners on the northern face of Cemetery Hill noticed a distant Confederate picket make a break for Federal lines, apparently deserting his comrades. A couple of bullets whizzed from the stunned Rebels, but the man made his escape and ran up the slope. Surprised XI Corps pickets stopped him at the first stone wall and disarmed the solitary Rebel. After some dialogue, they allowed him to proceed. He walked up to the lunettes of Stewart's Battery B, 4th U.S. Artillery, opposite Baltimore Pike from the Evergreen Cemetery gatehouse, where the veteran gunners "received him cordially."

The man stated he was from Pittsburgh, but he had been in working on a steamship out of New Orleans in 1861 when, in a drunken stupor, he and his friends had signed up for the Confederate Navy. With the fall of New Orleans in 1862, he was drafted into the army and found himself in the 5th Louisiana. He claimed to have made the charge up Cemetery Ridge to the Union side of the stone wall, where he lay down and pretended to be wounded. However, when the regiment withdrew toward the town, his comrades grabbed him and dragged him along in the rush.

Intrigued, the cannoneers gave him a meal of pork, hardtack, and coffee, and the hungry Pennsylvania Rebel provided his fascinated hosts with information from the Confederate perspective. He suggesting that morale had dropped with the repeated failures to crack the Union line. The erstwhile Tiger mentioned that after the success of the first day, they expected the Army of the Potomac to retreat to Washington, allowing the Confederates free reign "to forage at will through the rich country they were in." He also repeated the forlorn belief that if Stonewall Jackson had been in command instead of Ewell, they would have stormed the hill on the evening of July 1, instead of a day later.[19]

Well after dark, the skirmishing finally ended, and Tom Reed and his fellow Louisianans could get some rest. Gettysburg residents again were able to emerge from their cellars, and many hoped this was the last night the Confederates would occupy the beleaguered borough. Dr. John O'Neal recorded at 10:00 p.m., "Everything is now quiet and profound silence reigns over the field, except the moans of the wounded and the rattle of the ambulances. The firing has entirely ceased. It is believed that the enemy will at once abandon their present position and march south, but the morning will tell." He summed up what most soldiers and civilians were thinking. "Everyone is worn out and exhausted by the past three days' fatigue and fighting. . . . Whole brigades are lying in line of battle sound asleep, the dead and the living mingled together."[20]

### Federals Retake Gettysburg

In the early hours before Independence Day dawned, Harry Hays received orders to leave his Middle Street position and march westward to Seminary Ridge, along with the rest of Jubal Early's division. Officers roused his weary Confederate soldiers from their slumber and instructed them to fall in. Sometime before 3:00 a.m., the remnant of the First Louisiana Brigade formed into column in the darkness and "withdrew slowly and sullenly" to a new position about two miles away, leaving behind a few deserters who had slipped away during the night to seek refuge, as well as those men too badly injured to be moved. Scores of other widely scattered men were still fast asleep and could not be located or notified. As rain fell, the Tigers filed into battle line on McPherson's Ridge to the rear of Rodes' Division, where they threw up earthworks and awaited a possible Union counterattack. Smith's brigade deployed just to the right, with Gordon next in line.[21]

Among the Federal prisoners in the rear lines was Captain John Parsons of the 149th Pennsylvania, still at Hays' hospital tending to the wounded Colonel Roy Stone. The adjutant witnessed a marked change in the Confederates' attitudes as the battle progressed. From high spirits on the evening of July 1, they had mellowed after the fight at East Cemetery Hill. When news of the failure of the grand assaults of July 3 on Culp's Hill and Cemetery Ridge trickled through the hospital, the prevailing attitude was now markedly different. "On the evening of the 3d, however, they seemed depressed in spirits, which first gave me the intimation of our victory. On the morning of the 4th, they commenced to haul to the rear all of their wounded that could be removed. Then I was satisfied that our army was victorious and that the enemy was getting ready to retreat."[22]

Federal officers on Cemetery Hill discerned the Rebels' westward movement. General Ames sent a courier to Colonel William H. Noble, the newly
arrived commander of the 17th Connecticut who had just rejoined his regiment in the night after recovering from a Chancellorsville wound. Noble sent
out skirmishers to investigate the apparent retreat. They were to enter the
meadows at the foot of East Cemetery Hill and proceed toward the town,
feeling for the enemy. The detail consisted of Lieutenant Milton H. Daniels
of Company C, Sergeant Patrick Wade of Company K, and ten privates.

At 3:45 a.m., the party deployed in the wet fields and began picking cautiously across the trampled grass and partially dismantled fencing toward the
southeastern part of town. Nerves were on edge, as three days of skirmishing with the Louisiana Tigers had taught the Connecticut boys to stay under
cover and not expose themselves in this manner. To complicate the hazardous situation, the men in the dawn patrol "were half starved, thirsty and very
nervous from the constant strain of three days of firing and three nights of
alarm." Sergeant Wade added, "And then to start out on what seemed to be
a mission the result of which could hardly be anything but death, it is no
wonder we proceeded with the greatest caution."

Wade, respecting the Tigers' marksmanship, related that the earlier sniping had been "so severe that a man who showed himself for a minute dropped
back dead or wounded. . . . It was the first time in my army experience that I
felt as though the odds were greatly against us." Silently and only using hand
signals to communicate, the patrol split into two six-man teams, with Daniels leading the rightmost group and Wade the left detachment. They carefully and slowly walked through the low damp meadows in a dense fogbank,
"making it almost impossible to see 300 feet ahead."

After advancing about four hundred yards, they flopped to the ground and
listened carefully for indications of enemy activity. Not hearing anything
suspicious, they slowly rose, proceeded across the quiet fields, and crossed
over the low rise in front of Winebrenner's Run. Wade reasoned, "We knew
well that we were treading on dangerous ground, as the Louisiana Tigers and
Hoke's brigade of Early's division lay between us and the town, a position
which they had occupied for three days. We passed over that portion of the
ground where the rebel line had been stationed. We knew it by the trampled
grass and by the bits of cracker and bread which had been dropped."

Cautiously exploring the deserted line in the small ravine, Wade "felt as if
we were being led into a trap. This was the line which for three days had been

occupied by one of the most celebrated brigades in the rebel army, and yet where was the enemy? There was no sign of him, except the long grass which had been trampled flat, or the pieces of cracker, an empty canteen and all the refuse left by a line which had been sleeping on its arms." The feared Louisiana Tigers were gone.

The patrol merged and slowly worked its way up the slope toward the town, less than a half-mile away. To the Union soldiers' surprise and relief, there were still no signs of the Tigers' current whereabouts. Suddenly, the fog cleared, and the Connecticut skirmishers could see the cupola of the German Reformed Church at the corner of East High and South Stratton streets. They knew this landmark indicated the southeastern edge of Gettysburg, as it had been plainly visible for the past three days and had housed several annoying enemy snipers.

The scouting party

advanced a little further, and discerned objects moving about in the yard. Another advance and we saw that these objects were men, some clad in gray and some in blue. They discovered our advance, and some stooped to look under the fog, while others hastened away. Shortly afterward, an officer appeared in the middle of the street waving his hat. We increased our pace to a double quick and in a few minutes reached the officer, who informed us that General Lee had been retreating since 3 o'clock in the morning.

This officer also informed us that the barns and cow sheds all over the city were full of rebels, asleep, who had crawled into them the night before and had been left behind. We started toward the center of the town, on the way going up to the barn doors and pounding on them with the butts of our muskets, making all the noise possible, and commanding the Johnnies to come out at once, and to leave their guns behind. Each man as he appeared was laughed at for being caught napping. We kept onward, and as soon as the hospital was reached we gave three cheers which were echoed back to our lines. This cheer was heard by General Ames, sitting in his headquarters at the cemetery gate, and it was the first intimation to our boys that the battle had been won.

By the time Lieutenant Daniels' detachment reached the town square, they had captured eighteen Confederates, including some Louisianans. They escorted the prisoners to East Cemetery Hill and turned them over to the provost. For some of the Tigers, this was their second trip to that prominence in less than twelve hours. They were marched to the rear, where they sullenly joined their compatriots captured the night before.[23]

With confirmation that Gettysburg was free of organized Confederates, Adelbert Ames sent Colonel Noble and the rest of the brigade sweeping toward the town. Their battle line stretched across East Cemetery Hill from Baltimore Street downhill to the brickyard lane. The remnant of the 25th Ohio fronted the line as skirmishers in case of any residual Rebel resistance. Finding no opposition, they moved quickly, "yelling like demons," and drove out the remaining Confederates. In the process, they snagged three hundred prisoners, mostly stragglers and wounded, and sent them back under guard to Cemetery Hill. Among the men collected that morning was Private James Mulholland, a drummer in the 6th Louisiana. The Pennsylvania native would take the oath of allegiance to the Union and never fight again. Another prisoner was White Murrell, the odiferous 9th Louisiana private who refused to change his clothes until they wore out, and who offended his comrades with his gluttony and thievery.

Lieutenant Oscar Ladley of the heavily depleted 75th Ohio was amazed at the reception the Federals received in town. "We went like a set of devils and raining as hard as it could pour down, and all of the waveing [sic] of handkerchiefs and smiling faces, you never saw the equal." Perhaps even more important to the hungry young officer, one of the liberated townspeople invited him to stay for a home-cooked breakfast, an offer he eagerly accepted.[24]

When the 17th Connecticut reached the temporary prisons at the brick schoolhouse and the German Reformed Church, they captured a sleeping guard and freed their wounded comrades. Justus Silliman later reported that the Louisianans had evacuated the town so quickly they left behind the thousands of captured Union rifles that had been left stacked in the streets. He did a little souvenir hunting: "I have captured a La tiger belt plate; also a piece of a reb flag."[25]

Word quickly spread among the remaining residents that the Rebels had abandoned the town. With the Louisianans finally gone from the sniper's nests in their house, Samuel McCreary and his family emerged and surveyed the damage done to their red brick, two-story home, pockmarked with bullets fired from both sides. Upstairs, near one of the open doors that opened to their porch, they found the lifeless body of a Confederate with a gaping chest wound. The Rebel had apparently pushed one of their tables in front of the doorway, and a bullet hole through the table marked the path of the fatal missile. McCreary and a neighbor wrapped the body in a blanket and carried it out to Long Lane, where they buried it and marked the location. The remains were of the 9th Louisiana's Corporal William Poole, killed on July 3.[26]

As they surfaced from their cellars, several families were stunned at the destruction wrought to private property by the Rebels. Young Albertus McCreary wrote, "There were some sorry looking homes in our neighborhood." One of his friend's houses was especially hard hit. "Pieces of furniture were burned or broken, a desk had been destroyed, bookcases knocked down and the books torn and scattered. To add more to the disorder and destruction, the soldiers had taken half a barrel of flour, mixed it with water to make a thin paste, put into this the feathers from feather beds and thrown it over everything—walls, furniture, and down the stairways."[27]

As Independence Day progressed, Union soldiers began venturing out into the low-lying fields where the Rebel dead and wounded still lay untended. In many cases, plunder-seeking Yankees took knives, wallets, coins, food, buttons, and other souvenirs from their fallen enemies. Sometimes, the relics were more personal. One soldier picked up a small piece of paper with two locks of hair attached to it. The sheet was addressed in flowing feminine handwriting to a "Mr. Wellerford," from Louisiana, by his wife. Below one lock was written "Fanny Wellerford"; below the other tuft was "Richard Wellerford." At the bottom of the page was the poignant phrase, "Our Darlings!" The owner apparently had carried this memento of home with him to Pennsylvania, where it may have fluttered out of his dying grasp.[28]

A lieutenant of the 7th Louisiana had been slightly wounded in the arm and captured when Hays retired from East Cemetery Hill. Downhearted, he encountered Lieutenant J. Clyde Miller of the 153rd Pennsylvania, who directed him to the regimental surgeon and wrote a note requesting that the prisoner be given "special attention." However, during the night, the Confederate died. In the morning, Miller went through the dead Rebel's pockets to find some identification so he could inform his family. In the officer's blouse pocket, he discovered an envelope containing a photograph of three little girls. Unfortunately, the name and address on the envelope were illegible. Miller sent the letter and the photo home to his mother, who, in turn, forwarded the story to *Harper's Weekly*. However, despite the resulting publicity, no one stepped forward to identify the fallen Confederate.

Years later, Miller's daughter attended graduate school in Alabama, where her roommate coincidentally was the daughter of a former 7th Louisiana soldier who had fought at Gettysburg. While visiting her roommate's Louisiana home, Miss Miller mentioned the long-lost photograph her father had taken from the dead lieutenant. To her surprise, the former Rebel knew the officer. He informed her that the three daughters were living only twenty miles from his sugar plantation.[29]

The scars of war were still very evident around Cemetery Hill in the days after the battle. Harrisburg attorney and amateur historian John B. Linn was among the hundreds of visitors who flocked to the battlefield once the armies left. His traveling party left their conveyances at the cavalry field east of town and walked to Gettysburg along the Hanover Road. They hiked across the Benner farm fields where Johnson's Division had charged Culp's Hill, picking up relics and mementos, including some articles left by the Second Louisiana Brigade.

Wading across Rock Creek, they ascended into the trampled fields over which Avery and Hays had charged, ground where now the 2nd Pennsylvania Cavalry was encamped as the troopers secured the battlefield. They "seemed to be on a hotly contested part of the battle, coats, knapsacks etc. lying about and the stench awful." Awestruck by the devastation and the overpowering odor, Linn and his party made their way over to the area where Hays' sharpshooters had dueled with Ames' skirmishers. "As we passed up the alley behind the [German Reformed] church, I noticed the fences perforated with balls. Here Early's brigade lay before supporting Stonewall Jackson's Brigade in their charge upon the Cemetery on Friday. As we passed up into the town, the smell of putrefying blood was very disagreeable to me."[30]

Another early out-of-town visitor to East Cemetery was Cortland, New York, newspaper editor Charles P. Cole, who traveled to Gettysburg to locate and secure the remains of his close friend Major Andrew Grover, killed on July 1. Cole later reported, "The ground about our guns was literally strewn with shot and shell; tombstones erected over the remains of beloved relations were thrown from their positions and broken into fragments; graves were turned up by plunging shot; tasteful railings and other ornamental works around the lots were badly shattered, and even the beautiful archway over the entrance to the sacred enclosure was splintered and penetrated. One thing remained untouched, which was the placard at the entrance reading: 'All persons are prohibited from disturbing any flower or shrub within these grounds.'"[31]

Townspeople joined in the sightseeing, with perhaps more emotion than the out-of-towners, since most of the residents had been born and raised in the area and knew the hills, ridges, and valleys long before the armies and the American press memorialized them. Teenager Tillie Pierce perhaps best summed up the emotions of the Gettysburg civilians as they surveyed the carnage around their town. Gettysburg would never be the same again.

Fondly do I cherish the scenes of my childhood. Often do I think of the lovely groves on and around Culp's Hill; of the mighty bowlders which there abound, upon which we often spread the picnic feast; of the now famous Spangler's Spring, where we drank the cooling draught on those peaceful summer days. There too, our merry peals of laughter mingled with the sweet warbling of the birds. What pleasant times were ours as we went berrying along the quiet, sodded lane that leads from the town to that now memorable hill.

From my mind can never be effaced those far off mountains to the west, whose distant horizon gave a gorgeousness to sunsets, which, when once seen, can never be forgotten. Beholding those various tinted ephemeral isles, in that sea of occidental glory, one could not help thinking of the possibilities of the grandeur in the beyond. The effect could be none other than transporting.

As I often stood in the quiet Evergreen Cemetery, when we knew naught but the smiles of Peace, gazing to the distant South Mountains, or the nearer Round Tops, or Culp's Hill, little did I dream that from those summits the engines of war would, in a few years, belch forth their missiles of destruction; that through those sylvan aisles would reverberate the clash of arms, the roar of musketry, and the booming of cannon, to be followed by the groans of the wounded and dying.

Little did I think that those lovely valleys teeming with verdure and the rich harvest, would soon be strewn with the distorted and mangled bodies of American brothers; making a rich ingathering for the grim monster Death; that across that peaceful lane would charge the brave and daring 'Louisiana Tigers,' thirsting for their brother's blood, but soon to be hurled back filling the space over which they advanced with their shattered and dead bodies.[32]

On July 6, New York *Herald* reporter Thomas W. Knox examined Evergreen Cemetery and then walked around the battlefield, covering the ground young Tillie Pierce had known so well before the war.

Monuments and head-stones lie here and there overturned. Graves, once carefully tended by some loving hand, have been trampled by horses feet until the vestiges of verdure have disappeared. The neat and well-trained shrubbery has vanished or is but a broken and withered mass of tangled brush-wood. On one grave lies a dead artillery horse, fast decomposing under the July sun. On another lie the torn garments of some wounded soldier, stained and saturated with his blood. Across a small headstone, bearing the words, "To the memory of our beloved child, Mary" lie the fragments of a musket shattered by a cannon shot.

In the centre of a space enclosed by an iron fence, and containing a half dozen graves, a few rails are still standing where they were erected by our soldiers and served to support the shelter tents of a bivouacking squad. A family shaft has been broken in fragment by a shell, and only the base remains, with a portion of the inscription thereon. Stone after stone felt the effects of the *feu d'enfer* that was poured upon the crest of the hill. Cannon thundered, and foot and horse soldiers trampled over the sleeping place of the dead. Other dead were added to those who are resting here, and many a wounded soldier still lives to remember the contest above those silent graves.

The hill on which this cemetery is located was the center of our line of battle and the key to our position. Had the Rebels been able to carry this point, they would have forced us into retreat, and the battle would have been lost. To pierce our line in this locality was Lee's great endeavor, and he threw his best brigades against it. Wave after wave of living valor rolled up that slope, only to roll back again under the deadly fire of our artillery and infantry. It was on this hill, a little to the right of the cemetery, where the 'Louisiana Tigers' made their famous charge. It was their boast that they were never yet foiled in an attempt to take a battery; but on this occasion they suffered a defeat, and were nearly annihilated. Sad and dispirited, they mourn their repulse and their terrible losses in the assault.[33]

News of the stunning fighting at Gettysburg trickled via telegraph to various northern newspapers, and a few southern papers picked up the story, although initially few believed the Yankee reports that Lee had been defeated. In Richmond, a notice appeared for several days in the *Daily Dispatch*, beginning on July 4, offering amnesty to those members of the First Louisiana Brigade who had been left behind to face charges for various infractions. If they appeared at the headquarters of the recruiting services by the end of the month to return to active duty, all charges would be dropped. Anyone not in compliance with the order "will be treated with the utmost rigor." The threatening order was signed by Colonel Henry Forno of the 5th Louisiana, who was performing administrative duty in the Confederate capital while recuperating from a serious wound suffered at Second Manassas.[34]

While townspeople began their slow recovery from the battle and Confederate occupation, Hays' Tigers lounged in their new battle line throughout Independence Day and reorganized their shattered ranks. Lieutenant Harry Handerson and the 9th Louisiana "spent the Fourth of July listening to the music of the bands of the Federal host." A sarcastic Tom Reed recorded, "We are still in line of battle, and we enjoyed a soaking rain and had a delightful time this Fourth of July."[35]

Some Louisiana officers visited the McDonnell home along Seminary Ridge to warn the residents that the house was going to be shelled by Federal artillery to flush out some of the Confederate sharpshooters. Mary Jane McDonnell gathered up her food, clothing, dishes, and bedding, and tied them up in a flowered counterpane and departed with her children to her father's house. The house was not shelled, and the Tiger sharpshooters continued to look for opportune targets.[36]

Harry Hays and his remaining regimental officers reassigned surviving line officers and tried to restore the command infrastructure. Lieutenant J. Warren Jackson recalled, "Preparations were made during the day for falling back—rained during the day & I passed a miserable time of it. I was placed in command of Co. D on the 3rd and command it yet." Colonel Stafford selected Handerson to replace the slain Lieutenant Richard T. Crawford as the adjutant of the 9th Louisiana. He received Crawford's horse and boots, an emblem of the position that "constituted a rare outfit for an officer of inferior rank." Orders came to cook three days' rations, and the men prepared to leave Gettysburg.[37]

### Retreat

Shortly after 2:00 a.m. on Sunday, July 5, the lead elements of Ewell's Corps began to retreat toward Maryland in a driving rainstorm. When Early pulled back from Gettysburg that morning, he had taken most of his wounded with him, moving them to a variety of farms behind the new divisional line. The patients in the field hospitals were under the care of Dr. Lewis Gott. Most soon were taken prisoner by Union forces that swept through the areas abandoned by the Confederates.[38]

In the early morning, the 4th Pennsylvania Cavalry scoured the area east of Gettysburg to collect and process Confederate prisoners, including several Louisianans. Lieutenant Colonel William E. Doster narrated, "The ground is still wet with the night's rain but the air is sultry and the day extremely hot. At 6 a.m. we march over to the York Road and take possession of about five hundred prisoners who are stowed away in every place that has a roof—houses, barns, outhouses, haymows, threshing floors, corncribs. They have nothing to say, and crawl about at our coming with kind of a dazed and stupid stare."[39]

West of town, Harry Hays formed what was left of his First Louisiana Brigade into column about 9:00 a.m. and began the long walk to Hagerstown. "We began our retreat and marched along very leisurely," said Lieutenant Jackson. "Our Division brought up the rear." Irish-born Catholic priest James B. Sheeran captured the attitude of the Second Corps' Louisianans. "They were as cheerful a body of men as I ever saw, and to hear them, you would think they were going to a party of pleasure instead of retreating from a hard fought battle."[40]

General Ewell had ordered Early's Division to guard the rear as the Second Corps column headed southwest toward the South Mountain range and the vital Monterey Pass, the most expeditious route into the Cumberland Valley. Thousands of wounded men were loaded into ambulances, freight and supply wagons, and other conveyances and sent westward across the Chambersburg Pike. Lee ordered Brigadier General John D. Imboden's cavalry to safeguard the lengthy train.

The retreating Army of Northern Virginia abandoned nearly seven thousand badly injured soldiers to the mercy of the townspeople and a handful of civilian doctors and army surgeons and nurses who stayed with their patients, including nurses Michael Coleman of the 5th Louisiana and Dennis Healy of the 6th. Early reluctantly left behind 259 of his most seriously wounded men. He also left "ample provisions for them, for several days," including a large sum of money from the York ransom, which was to be used by the surgeons to purchase medical supplies and other items needed to comfort the wounded.[41]

Several injured Louisiana Tigers received treatment and care at the John Crist farm on Herr's Ridge Road, where they quartered in his barn and stone farmhouse. The site offered a source of water from Willoughby Run and convenient access to the Chambersburg Pike for transporting supplies, medical personnel, and the wounded Tigers. Some men may have also been taken to the William Douglas farm just west of Seminary Ridge. Those too badly injured to be transported to Maryland were left in various houses north and east of Gettysburg, including the Almshouse, Crawford house, and other locales.[42]

Over the next few days, a covey of civilian doctors and other volunteers arrived from across the region to augment the military surgeons left by the withdrawing armies to treat the wounded. One volunteer relief aide at the Second Corps Hospital, Emily Souder, was incensed to discover "R.H. was here, the miserable fellow acting as chaplain of the Louisiana Tigers, but I did not happen to see him." She deplored his disloyalty to the Union: "For a Northern man with Southern principles, I have the most thorough contempt." As the relief efforts became more organized, attempts were made to group the wounded as much as possible by their command structure. By July 14, those Tigers still recuperating in private residences would be transported to the formal divisional hospitals or east of Gettysburg to the George Wolf farm along the York Road. There, the U.S. Army had established a sprawling tent city, known as Camp Letterman after its commander, Dr. Jonathan Letterman, as a more permanent hospital.[43]

Several Tigers left at Gettysburg would soon die from their injuries or complications and infections. Major Henry L. N. Williams, shot during the 9th Louisiana's attack on Wiedrich's guns, was transported to the Crist farm, where he died on July 5 while Hays' Brigade was marching away from Gettysburg. The Mansfield merchant was interred under a gum tree. He left behind a small child and a widow, who would not find out for some time that her husband had expired in Pennsylvania. Private Thomas McCarty of the 8th Louisiana was also among the early fatalities. After he suffered a severe wound in the attack on East Cemetery Hill, Yankees carried him to the XI Corps hospital at the George Spangler farm on Culp's Hill, where the Baton Rouge resident died. He was buried in the corps' graveyard behind Spangler's barn.[44]

Other Tigers lingered for weeks, or even months, before expiring from their wounds or complications. They included twenty-one-year-old T. B. Bate of the 9th Louisiana, who died July 21. Private William Ford of the 7th Louisiana sustained a severe leg wound on July 2 that incapacitated him. The resident of East Baton Rouge Parish had been taken to one of the temporary field hospitals for initial treatment of his injury. Eventually, the Company B rifleman was moved to a bed in Camp Letterman and appeared to be recovering. However, the limb became infected, necessitating amputation. His condition soon worsened and the twenty-four-year-old infantryman died on August 24. He was buried in the hospital's graveyard.[45]

Gettysburg physician Rufus B. Weaver would disinter many of Hays' dead between 1871 and 1873 and transport them to the South for reburial, many to Hollywood Cemetery in Richmond. The doctor carried on the work of his father, Samuel Weaver, who had been instrumental in cataloguing thousands of burial sites (along with Dr. John W. O'Neal) and helping to collect and remove Federal dead to the National Cemetery. Weaver's crews located and boxed the remains of 3,320 Confederates. They did not locate those abandoned and forgotten Confederate graves that were not in the lists and records, so it is conceivable that a few Louisianans might still lie beneath the rich Pennsylvania topsoil.[46]

The majority of Hays' captive wounded Tigers would recover sufficiently to be transported eventually to Union prisons. Among them was twenty-two-year-old Private John L. Johnson of the 9th Louisiana. After regaining enough strength to travel, he arrived at the De Camp General Hospital at Davids' Island, a secure facility in New York Harbor that would quarter more than 2,500 Confederates wounded at Gettysburg. Johnson received his parole on August 24. Taken by ship to the South, he was exchanged at City Point, Virginia, on October 28, but he never returned to the ranks. The Livingston farmer had seen enough of the war. In April 1864, he was declared to have "deserted on wounded furlough."

A similar story was Corporal William A. Abney, an Alabama-born student from Collinsburg, Louisiana, who had enlisted at the age of twenty-two in Company D of the 9th Louisiana. When the Tigers withdrew from town on July 4, he was "left in the hands of the enemy." He arrived at Davids' Island on July 17 but did not stay long. One week later, he was paroled, and, like Johnson, was taken by steamship to City Point, where he was exchanged the day after Johnson, on October 29. He went back to the ranks of the 9th Louisiana but deserted in March 1864 and never returned. He was dropped from the muster rolls in November of that year.

Private Alfred Renaud, a French immigrant in the 6th Louisiana, was incarcerated in Fort Delaware. He took the Oath of Allegiance later that year and, in order to win his release from captivity, enlisted in the Union Army in the 3rd Maryland Cavalry, which had four companies composed of former Rebel prisoners. He was among several Tigers who fought on East Cemetery Hill who later took up arms against the Confederacy. Ironically, the regiment traveled to Louisiana by steamboat to participate in Major General Nathaniel Banks' ill-fated Red River Expedition. As he charged up Cemetery Hill in the twilight on July 2, Renaud could have never dreamed that within six months he would return to the Pelican State wearing the blue uniform of the Federal army.[47]

While most imprisoned Tigers would eventually be released, several died in captivity, including Private George Dwire of the 9th Regiment. A farmer from Mansfield who had enlisted at the age of nineteen in July 1861, he was captured on July 4 after Hays withdrew from Gettysburg. The bachelor was taken to Fort Delaware, where he and dozens of other Tigers were incarcerated. Unused to the cold harsh northern winters, Dwire would die January 11, 1864, of chronic bronchitis.

Hundreds of wounded men had been loaded into wagons and sent off well to the rear toward the Potomac River during Independence Day. Among the suffering patients was Charles Moore Jr. of the 5th Louisiana, who wrote in his diary, "Things quiet today. Left the hospital for Winchester. Traveled all day & nearly all night. We were stopped on the Mountain Road about midnight for fear of being captured by Yankee Cavalry."[48]

As torrential rain fell on Sunday morning the 5th, the remnants of Hays' Tigers accompanied Early's Division westward on the Chambersburg Turnpike, pursued at a distance by Federal cavalry and infantry. The men were "wading to their knees in the mud and mire." During the long, stormy night, Early kept Gordon's Brigade in the rear of his column to protect the supply wagons, ambulances with their groaning human cargo, and Jones' guns. They arrived at the Fairfield Road shortly after sunrise and halted for several hours to allow the passage of the bulk of Ewell's Corps and its trains. The Tigers could hear the boom of long-range Federal artillery in the distance, firing at the rear guard, but Early's Division sustained no damage from this mild annoyance.[49]

Several farmers accused the retreating Confederates of theft and property destruction. Despite the downpour, soldiers occasionally broke ranks to forage for supplies, food, and provender for their horses and mules. Lieutenant Warren Jackson noted the retreat that day was "orderly & well conducted, but we paid no respect for fence or grain." A North Carolinian was more concerned about the enemy pursuit: "The morning of the 5 we left befour day and it a raining as hard as it could poor and marched in the direction of Hagerdstown and didnt get but about 6 miles all day for the Yanks calvry kep a running up on ous all day."[50]

After Ewell finally cleared the road, Early's column reached Fairfield, which the general described as being "situated in a wide and low plain surrounded by hills." His forward progress was again blocked by the lengthy wagon trains, and he ordered a halt until traffic cleared. The Tigers rested on their arms, and many cursed the delay. Soon, a courier galloped in from Lieutenant Colonel Elijah White's cavalry battalion to inform Early that an enemy force was advancing on his rear. An anxious Early sent word ahead to hasten the trains, but they remained stationary, blocking the road. He ordered his artillery commander, Lieutenant Colonel Hilary Jones, to "fire a blank cartridge or two for the purpose of quickening their pace."

As Jones was preparing to stimulate the teamsters into action, a column of Federal troops appeared on a hill beyond Gordon's Georgians. Jones quickly switched to shell and opened fire. Soon, a Union battery unlimbered and replied. The exchange of cannonry got the wagon master's attention, and "the trains soon cleared the road." Early deployed the 26th Georgia Volunteers to delay the Federals, while he gradually moved the rest of his division beyond Fairfield. There, in a "favorable position" on a ridgeline, he formed his division into battle line. Hays deployed the Tigers, many of whom were ready for another scrap, their confidence returning with another chance to whip the Yankees.[51]

With the immediate threat averted, General Ewell ordered Early to camp not far from Fairfield and posted his division to protect the corps supply train, which parked closer to South Mountain. The fields were soggy, after nearly 1.4 inches of rain had soaked the region. Guards watched for signs of enemy activity, but the evening was quiet. During the night, Early's weary skirmishers were relieved by those of Robert Rodes' division, which was designated to be the rear guard the next day. Meanwhile, the division's wounded suffered in the lengthy procession of ambulances, which had crossed the mountain ahead of Ewell's Corps and had now camped two miles into the Cumberland Valley. Charles Moore Jr., nursing a wounded foot that would later require amputation, wrote, "Slept in the ambulance all night. It rained all the time."[52]

At daybreak on Monday, July 6, Early's Division arose, ate what breakfasts could be scrounged from nearly empty haversacks, and formed into march column. After the supply trains headed out, Early broke camp and moved to the front of the Second Corps' line. Within a few miles, his men slowly ascended South Mountain. The well-traveled road was uneven, miry and slippery from the rain and the passage of the other two corps to the front, and it was filled with ruts and holes. Wounded men suffered in agony as springless wagons bounced over the road. The First Louisiana Brigade passed by Monterey Springs on the summit of the mountain and trudged wearily down the mountain road into the Cumberland Valley to Waynesboro.

The Tigers had last seen that town on the morning of June 27 when they marched off to Greenwood. Under much unhappier circumstances, they were now back in the valley and heading home, their numbers smaller and their dreams of a decisive victory on northern soil severely dashed. Lieutenant Jackson wrote, "Crossed the mountains and marched to our old camp near Waynesboro. All this time we had had nothing scarcely to eat and were pretty well starved out. But that night we drew ample rations." Foraging patrols fanned out throughout the region, and the Rebels "seized all they could lay hands on." Early spread his four brigades north and west of town. There, he learned the identity of the Union troops that were passively following them— the VI Corps under Major General John Sedgwick.[53]

According to sixteen-year-old Lida Welsh, daughter of the chief burgess of Waynesboro, "As a number of us watched the planting of a battery on a hill about a half-mile distant, at the eastern entrance to the town, an officer, seeing us through his field glasses, rode down to tell us that they were sorry to have caused us alarm and that they had no intention of shelling the town or injuring anyone, they were merely protecting their troops."

When the foragers reached town, Welsh added,

> We expected the worst, but although the soldiers entered stores and took what they could carry away, as a rule private property was not molested. The only exception to the rule was that they helped themselves to hats from citizens' heads and compelled some to sit on horse-blocks or curbs and take off their shoes or boots. One of our neighbors was a very decided Unionist, while his wife, a Virginian, gave her sympathy to the South. A barefoot soldier asked her for shoes, and he was scarcely out of sight with all she could find when her husband came home bareheaded, barefooted, and in a towering rage. He had to go shoeless, for there were no shoes to be had in town for love or money."[54]

That same evening, several injured Louisianans were involved in a rear guard action four miles from the Potomac River crossing at Williamsport, Maryland. Rising floodwaters made it impossible for Brigadier General John Imboden to escort the long wagon train hauling Lee's wounded across the swollen ford. Commanding a mixed force of infantry, cavalry, and artillery, Imboden dug earthworks in anticipation of a probable attack. Many of the ambulatory wounded, including some Tigers, grabbed muskets and joined in the firing line. Two of Early's regiments that had remained in Winchester, the 54th North Carolina and 58th Virginia, marched northward to help protect the crucial crossing.

Union cavalry divisions under brigadier generals H. Judson Kilpatrick and John Buford soon arrived and prepared to attack. About 5:00 p.m. near St. James College, one of Buford's brigade attacked Imboden, and Kilpatrick joined in the growing fray not long afterward. Early simply wrote of the ensuing two-hour fight, "A body of the enemy's cavalry had previously come upon that part of our trains that had preceded the army in the retreat, but was repulsed by a few guards accompanying the trains without being able to accomplish any damage of consequence."[55]

From Jubal Early's military point of view, there was no "damage of consequence." However, a few more Louisiana families would mourn the loss of loved ones in the Gettysburg Campaign. Among the casualties in the skirmish was Private Allen Gideon Jr. of the 9th Louisiana. Only eighteen years old when he enlisted in 1861, the Pineville farmer had survived several battles, as well stints as a prisoner of war in Washington's Old Capitol Prison and in Fort Delaware west of Philadelphia. He had been exchanged on May 23, less than two weeks before the Tigers left for the summer campaign. He lived through Colonel Stafford's attack on Wiedrich's guns on East Cemetery Hill, but his luck ran out before crossing the Potomac River back into Virginia. He died during the Williamsport firefight with the Federal pursuers.[56]

Most of the long train of ambulances and wagons was not involved in this brief action. Charles Moore Jr. noted in his diary entry for July 6, "Moved a little after daylight. We got as far as Hagerstown with our ambulance train when the Yankee cavalry put a stop to our movements. We then came back 3 miles on the turnpike then we parked until 10 o'clock. Then we moved and passed through Hagerstown as the town clock struck twelve [noon]." Despite the pain from his throbbing foot, Moore was able to function, and he took up pen and paper. "Wrote to Mrs. T. G. Robinson. We halted 3 miles from Williamsport for the night."[57]

Miles behind the wagon train, the First Louisiana Brigade rose very early on Tuesday morning, July 7, and continued its southwesterly trek toward the Potomac, marching through Waynesboro and reentering Maryland. Lee's retreat had left the Cumberland Valley in a sad state. One reporter wrote,

> Of the amount of damage done to the farming interest of this valley, those who have not seen, can form no conception of it. Hundreds of fields of fine wheat and grass are now a mixture of mud, broken wagons, dead horses, &c., while thousands of farmers have not a horse, cow, hog, chicken, wagon, harness, or a pound of meat or flour in the house. . . . The road was strewn with cast-off clothing, blankets, knapsacks, guns and empty haversacks. . . . On the road you can see large quantities of ammunition-powder, shell and shot, which has been abandoned. In less than a half a mile I counted three dismounted guns. Whole wagon loads of small arms were burnt, or rendered useless by bending them over wagon wheels.[58]

Private Thomas Reed of the 9th Louisiana, still mourning his brother-in-law's death on the July 1 skirmish line, wrote of the sarcasm that filled the ranks, "Rain began falling about 10 o'clock, and oh! such a nice time as did we have. Some places the mud was up over our shoe tops and we were as wet as we could be. While marching in this plight, some fellow would holler out, 'Hello! John, how would you like to be a soldier boy?' Then someone else would say: 'Knock that fool in the head.' That would get up a big laugh and we would move on better. The soldier's is the most miserable life that can be thought of."[59]

The Louisianans wearily tramped through Leitersburg, in a region they had visited on their much happier northward march less than two weeks before. On this day, Early's Division was now in the center of Ewell's long column, with Rodes now on the point and Allegheny Johnson's men now the rear guard in the usual daily rotation. About two miles north of Hagerstown, Early halted his division about 2:00 p.m., and his weary brigades encamped along the Hagerstown-Chambersburg turnpike, where they remained for the next two days, "crammed between a raging Potomac River and the hired legions of the North," according to Reed.

With the Union cavalry threat turned aside, many wounded Confederates were unloaded from the wagons and placed in nearby hospitals. Years later, Dr. Charles H. Todd of the 6th Louisiana reflected on his subsequent service at Williamsport's Catholic Church Hospital. "Many grave wounds had received no medical attention for several days since leaving the [Gettysburg] field hospitals, and the treatment consisted in exposing all wounds to the air, cleansing them simply with water, and giving nutritious food and stimulants and enforcing perfect stimulation—using nature's restoratives, pure air, pure water, pure food; preventative medicine—and the success attending this treatment which was wrought out under such adverse conditions by the Confederate Medical Staff, could not be surpassed by the modern hospital of today."[60]

A determined stand at Boonsboro on July 8 by Jeb Stuart's cavalry significantly delayed the Union cavalry pursuit, as did roads turned into quagmires from heavy rainstorms. Diarist Reed recorded, "We lay still today—and such a rainfall; it seemed as if all the elements had turned to water. We were in a close place, but we wool-hat fellows did not know it." For the next two days, the Tigers remained near Hagerstown, resting and collecting several stragglers who occasionally walked into camp to rejoin their regiments. A few soldiers, sick of the prospects of the grind of a continued war, slipped away during the night.

Among those who unexpectedly arrived was George Wren of the 8th Louisiana. In mid-June, he and a group of recuperated wounded and ill soldiers had left Richmond. They had followed the army northward through the Shenandoah Valley trying to return to active duty. Despite pain from a badly sprained ankle that had not fully healed, Wren persisted for two weeks, although he constantly wished he had stayed in Richmond. Just after crossing the Pennsylvania line, he had taken ill. He stayed with a farmer until he felt well enough to resume the trek, and consequently missed the Battle of Gettysburg. After walking to Williamsport, he learned on July 8 that his brigade was in Hagerstown, still waiting for the river to recede, and immediately set out to rejoin them. Arriving in camp, he found his comrades "all in good spirits and willing for another fight which was expected to take place in a few days."[61]

After a day of "great clamor and exciting reports" on July 9, the Tigers broke camp about 6:00 p.m. and tramped through downtown Hagerstown an hour later. They camped on a high ridge a mile southwest of town, along the Cumberland Road. One command change occurred, as "Extra Billy" Smith requested a leave of absence to return to Richmond to fulfill his obligations as the governor-elect of Virginia. Jubal Early granted his request, and Colonel John S. Hoffman of the 31st Virginia assumed Smith's command. The 58th Virginia, which had been left at Winchester, returned to the brigade that same day. In addition, while near Hagerstown, the 54th North Carolina rejoined Hoke's Brigade, which was now under Colonel Godwin. The fresh troops reinforced Early's heavily depleted ranks. The newcomers eagerly sought out their old comrades to hear firsthand accounts of the battle they had missed.[62]

The following day, the Louisiana Tigers moved to the right to take a position near Gordon's Brigade near the Williamsport Road. The Confederates stayed busy with foraging for supplies. Major General William F. "Baldy" Smith, commanding the militia brigades involved in the slow pursuit of Lee, wrote, "Every effort was made to supply the command with rations from the country people, but with little success, the rebels having cleaned out the region." Unknown to Hays' men, among the pursuing Yankee army was the 110th Ohio, Colonel J. Warren Keifer's regiment the Tigers had chased out of the West Fort at Second Winchester the previous month.[63]

On the 11th, Ewell moved Early farther to the right, placing his division in a good defensive position in woods, with the right flank resting near the road from Hagerstown to Williamsport. Early's men began throwing up breastworks in preparation for an attack by the Yankee pursuers. Lieutenant J. Warren Jackson of the 8th Louisiana wrote, "At 10:00 a.m. moved to the right & took position in line of battle, and I tell you what. Mr. Yank would have smelt powder & ball before getting us out of the breastworks we had there."[64]

With no signs of significant enemy activity, Confederate soldiers rested behind their sturdy works until the following evening. Unknown to them, Army of the Potomac commander George G. Meade held a council of war with his subordinates that day, coming to the decision to launch a major attack on Lee's army on July 14. The objective was to cut off Lee before he could cross the still swollen river to safety.[65]

The 12th was marked by yet another fierce thunderstorm, and loud peals of thunder reverberated from the distant mountain slopes. After dark, Ewell ordered Early to move even farther to the right, across the Williamsport Road, where his men aligned behind elements of A. P. Hill's old "Light Division" as support in case of a determined Federal attack. Hays' Louisianans were directly behind Brigadier General Edward Thomas's Georgians. Early's line faces the road leading to Sharpsburg. In Hill's front, a "considerable force of the enemy had been massed," and Confederate high command feared that the long expected Union assault was now imminent. However, all was quiet, and the Tigers "lay in reserve all day."

When the threat of an enemy attack subsided, Early received orders to withdraw his division after dark on Monday, July 13. By 8:00 p.m., the troops were on the road again for a second consecutive night without sleep. Hays left several wounded Tigers behind in hospitals in Hagerstown and Williamsport under the care of the assistant surgeon of the 6th Louisiana, Dr. William B. Watford. Among them were J. P. Barnard, J. J. McQuithy, and Daniel McDonald of the 7th Louisiana and James Cahill of the 9th. Private Richard Kelly of the 6th Louisiana died on July 14 from a gunshot wound to the back of his head; he was "killed in the discharge of his duty by an assassin." He apparently had been bushwhacked on July 8.[66]

Bringing up the rear of the corps, the Tigers marched in a driving rain to Williamsport. Lieutenant Jackson wrote, "Moved along in the rain, slush & mud at a snail's pace—our Brigade (as usual) the rear guard of the whole concern." The next two days, Lee would move the bulk of the Army of Northern Virginia across the receding river at Falling Waters on hastily constructed pontoon bridges, foiling Meade's plan for a decisive July 14 attack.[67]

Just after sunrise that morning, Hays' Brigade and the Second Corps artillery battalions were detached from the column and sent upriver to Falling Waters. There, the guns and wagons crossed a pontoon bridge into the eastern panhandle of West Virginia. General Hays, Adjutant Seymour, and the brigade staff crossed about 4:00 a.m. on a scow. The Tigers lost only "a few disabled wagons & two pieces of cannon which the horses were unable to drag through the deep mud." Private Tom Reed mentioned another loss. "There were two teamsters who became impatient or got scared. Anyway, they broke ranks and drove around to the river. Each man was driving six mules and they just drove right into the river. The mules did pretty well until they got near the middle of the stream, when they became unruly and began to circle, and soon went under. Men, mules, and wagons were lost." Reed and a comrade in the 9th Louisiana forded the river upstream from the pontoon, wading through icy water up to their waists.[68]

Shortly after the Louisianans crossed, Union cavalry attacked the Third Corps' rear guard, killing Brigadier General Johnston Pettigrew and capturing hundreds of men. However, the majority of the Army of Northern Virginia was already safely across before the Federals arrived. Early's other three brigades got their feet wet, wading "up to their armpits" across the broad Potomac at the Williamsport ford. The division reunited on the main road to Martinsburg and camped that night near Hainesville in Berkeley County, about six miles south of the Potomac.[69]

The Tigers were not far from the July 1861 battlefield of Falling Waters, or Hoke's Run, where Stonewall Jackson had fought a successful delaying action. That engagement, and subsequent slow movements by Federal forces, helped allow Brigadier General Joseph E. Johnston's Army of the Shenandoah to march from the Valley to Manassas Junction in time to support Brigadier General P. G. T. Beauregard's army at the First Battle of Manassas.

On Wednesday, July 15, the Tigers moved to "an old field" to rest for five hours before resuming the march. They passed through Martinsburg, where a significant number of Federals had surrendered to Ewell shortly after Second Winchester, a battle that now seemed so long ago. After a short day of marching (about seven miles), the men were allowed to camp. The following day, Early marched down the Winchester Pike to Darkesville, where his division camped for the next three days. The Tigers finally were able to relax a little, drawing refreshingly cool water from the meandering Middle Creek and foraging in the rich Shenandoah Valley for food and supplies. Supply wagons were refilled, food stocks replenished, and haversacks stuffed with provisions. Tom Reed mentioned, "I went out foraging, and when I got back to camp, Jack [Dawkins] and I had a good supper."[70]

Stalled in camp by rainy weather and bad roads, Reed made July 18 his washday to clean the grime from his tattered clothing. He rejoiced over two letters he received that day. "Oh! what a treat it was to get a letter from home!" In response, he penned letters to his wife Elizabeth and his father. Lieutenant Warren Jackson finally had time to write a lengthy letter to his recuperating younger brother, Stark, in Richmond. He believed "the conduct of our troops while in the enemy's country was very good; in fact they behave worse in Va. than they did in Penna. The effect of our retreat is not discouraging to them. Some few grumblers, but that's always the case."

Several Tigers had seen enough of the war, long marches, and seemingly endless campaigning. Slipping away from the brigade, they melted into the countryside. Private John W. Jones deserted the 9th Louisiana at Darkesville on July 20. Four days later, Yankees captured the dark-haired, thirty-year-old Mississippi native and sent him to Wheeling Military Prison in West Virginia. In early August, authorities transferred Jones to Columbus, Ohio, and imprisoned him at Camp Chase. He asked to take the Oath of Allegiance on June 10, 1864. However, the Homerville farmer soon died of an unspecified illness. He was buried in the camp's Confederate Cemetery. Private James McDonough, perhaps tired of the tedium of long infantry marches, abandoned the 6th Louisiana and joined Albert Jenkins' cavalry brigade. The Tiger-turned-trooper perished in action in November.[71]

Within a few days after crossing the Potomac River, many wounded Tigers arrived in Richmond for treatment at the Louisiana Hospital. Private George H. Walker of Company A of the 9th Regiment was suffering from a gunshot wound to his left ilium. The ball had lodged next to his hipbone and caused him excruciating pain. Surgeons at the field hospital in Gettysburg had cleanly removed the bullet, and he had survived the jostling of the long wagon ride during the retreat. He was admitted to the Richmond medical facility on July 18, but within days, the wound became infected with erysipelas, a severe skin rash caused by streptococcal bacteria. Doctors applied an ointment of iron sulphate and lard to the infected area each morning and evening, but the rash spread and Walker suffered from an intense fever. Within a few days, he became delirious, developed diarrhea, and finally slipped into a coma. Doctors frantically worked to save him with their crude understanding of medicine and bacteria. Amazingly, by August 25, he was no longer in grave condition and, although very weak, was on the road to recovery.[72]

On the afternoon of July 20, Ewell ordered Early to break camp and form his division. Reports had come in from the cavalry that enemy troops had advanced to Hedgesville, a West Virginia hamlet well to the Confederates' rear. Early's Division marched to the base of North Mountain and camped for the night at Gerrardstown. After two consecutive nights with good suppers, Private Reed and his comrades in Company A of the 9th Louisiana spent a miserable night on picket duty. The next morning, they struggled up the mountainside, crossed the barrier at Mills Gap, and "marched like fury all day," following Back Creek northward to intercept the Yankees. Lieutenant Jackson added more text to his lengthy letter to his brother, commenting that the Tigers "halted once in a large field, and had you been there, you would have seen about 4,000 hungry devils pitching into Dew berries. . . . I never saw so many before—the ground was covered with them for acres."[73]

However, once the division arrived west of Hedgesville, the Rebels discovered the Yankees were gone. Brigadier General Benjamin F. Kelley and eight thousand men had hastily retreated the previous night. A disappointed Tar Heel wrote, "we expected to bag the Yankees at plais but when we got ther they was all gon." Early marched through the village and camped nearby, after backtracking nearly twenty-five miles since leaving Darkesville. George Wren of the 8th Louisiana deemed it a "desperate hard march which availed us nothing." Captain Thomas Redmond of the 6th Louisiana deemed it a "fruitless attempt." The men went to sleep with no rations. During the night, a courier arrived from General Ewell with orders for Early to resume the march toward Winchester.[74]

Early's footsore men arose at daylight and walked eighteen miles through Martinsburg and Darkesville to Bunker Hill, all on empty stomachs. Dozens of Confederates straggled or deserted during the day. Finally, at three o'clock in the afternoon, the division camped and finally cooked rations. By now, many Tigers were exhausted, both physically and mentally. Captain R. J. Hancock's badly wounded thigh had swelled to twice its normal size during his eighteen-day ride in a rickety wagon. Lieutenant Jackson wrote, "I haven't heard from home since last winter and I am terribly anxious. I would give oceans for a furlough." He was not alone in his sentiments.[75]

At sunrise, they were on the road again. Within hours, they marched through Winchester, where a few Tigers were still convalescing from wounds received during the June 13–14 battle. There, the 13th Virginia rejoined what was now Hoffman's Brigade. Early's column moved on the Front Royal Road past Parkins' Mill and crossed Opequon Creek. They turned at Cedarville toward the Valley Pike and camped six miles southwest of Winchester.[76]

On July 23, Army of the Potomac commander George Meade ordered Major General William French's III Corps to cut off Lee's retreat by forcing passage through Manassas Gap. In the subsequent Battle of Manassas Gap or Wapping Heights, Lee's rear guard (elements of Richard Anderson's and Robert Rodes' divisions) defeated French's poorly coordinated attacks. The daylong delaying action allowed the Confederates to slip away into the Luray Valley, finally out of Meade's reach.[77]

Despite the realization that the Federal pursuit had finally abated, the Louisiana Tigers still faced days of marching in steaming July weather before they reached their final destination across the broad mountains into northern Virginia. The trip would take them through a litany of small towns—Strasburg, Mount Jackson, New Market, Fisher's Gap, Madison Court House, and Locust Dale—before arriving at Rapidan Station, halfway between Richmond and Washington D.C.

On July 30, a relieved J. Warren Jackson wrote, "Stopped at last. . . . We arrived here last evening after marching 153 miles in 9 days." The next day, the Louisiana Tigers reached their Orange County destination, marching through Rapidan Station and establishing a base four miles beyond the railroad near Pisgah Church. In the shadow of Clark's Mountain, they could rest. Over the next few weeks, several sick and wounded comrades rejoined the ranks once they were well enough to resume field duty.

The Tigers settled back into the monotony of camp life, while a religious revival swept through the Army of Northern Virginia. Private Thomas Reed wrote, "So time rolled on without much change. We had a lot of preaching, some drilling and inspection, a few extra dinners, and so on." The preaching affected the once rowdy Louisiana Tigers. On August 25, Early's divisional chaplain reported, "In Hayes's [sic] Brigade, particularly in the Ninth Louisiana . . . congregations were very large and many interested in the salvation of their souls. Christians seemed alive, and had interested themselves in obtaining a chaplain. . . . The revival in Hays' Brigade was one of very great power and happiest results."[78]

For Tom Reed and his fellow Tigers of the First Louisiana Brigade, the long and unfruitful Gettysburg Campaign was now a part of history, as were their dreams of a decisive victory on northern soil. The majority of the Pelican State men would never again set foot north of the Mason-Dixon Line. Although not a Louisianan, Captain G. Campbell Brown of Ewell's staff perhaps best summed up the prevailing attitude of the Confederates as they reflected on the summer campaign: "It would be ridiculous to say that I did not feel whipped—or that there wasn't a man in that Army who didn't appreciate the position just as plainly. But the 'fight' wasn't out of the troops by any means—they felt that the position & not the enemy had out done us."[79]

Safely away from the Federal pursuit, on August 22, Jubal Early belatedly wrote his official report of the Gettysburg Campaign. Several pages long, the report detailed his men's movements and battle actions. Early closed with some words of praise for selected officers ("Extra Billy" Smith being conspicuously absent in his commendation):

In all the operations in the neighborhood of Gettysburg, I am happy to state that both officers and men, while animated with a spirit of daring that disdained to concede any obstacle to their progress unsurmountable, were yet amenable to all the orders of their leaders, and accepted readily any position assigned them. . . . The conduct of my troops during the entire campaign, on the march as well as in action, was deserving of the highest commendation. To Brigadier-Generals Hays and Gordon I was greatly indebted for their cheerful, active, and intelligent co-operation on all occasions, and their gallantry in action was eminently conspicuous.[80]

Richard Ewell reported that Hays' attack on East Cemetery Hill "was worthy of the highest praise. In this and at Winchester, the Louisiana brigade and their gallant commander gave new honor to the name already acquired on the old fields of Winchester and Port Republic, and wherever engaged." From the Tigers' campsite on August 25, John F. Gruber, who had not been a fan of Harry Hays prior to the Gettysburg Campaign, wrote, "He is growing more popular in the army and disappointment is manifested,

that he has not been ere this made a Major General. He has wonderfully im-
proved, he handled his Brigade at Winchester & Gettysburg very skillfully,
while the great requisite to keep cool, is more with him a matter of course;
add to this his gallantry and the magical influence it has over his men, it is
not to be wondered at, that [the Tigers] look for some appreciation of them
and their leader's service." Another admirer would later write of Hays, "no
braver, knightlier soldier ever drew sword."[81]

## Requiem

Many of the Louisiana Tigers captured at Gettysburg were paroled and exchanged over the next year, although a significant number took the oath of
allegiance or deserted rather than return to the ranks. For months, reports
circulated that the famed Louisiana Tigers had been wiped out as a formal organization on East Cemetery Hill, suffering 80 percent casualties. This false-
hood was perpetuated long after the war in various Union regimental histories and in other historical accounts of the battle. Among the dozens of
accounts scattered in postbellum literature was that of noted New York historian Rossiter Johnson: "Of the seventeen hundred Tigers, twelve hundred had
been struck down, and that famous organization was never heard of again."

Even the veterans who should have known better participated in the rumor mill. Lieutenant Milton Daniels of the 17th Connecticut, who had helped
defend the brickyard stone wall, later wrote, "It was the brigade of which
our regiment was a part that destroyed the Tigers, for after their charge they
ceased to exist or to be recognized as a body in the Southern army." Colonel
Adin Underwood of the 33rd Massachusetts of von Gilsa's Brigade repeated
the myth: "in ten short minutes, the Tigers' career is finished. Half of them
are dead, the other half prisoners." One wounded Louisianan, whose leg was
amputated above the knee, was sitting in a railroad car in Gettysburg awaiting
transport to prison. A little boy asked him what regiment he was from. Tears
welled in the eyes of the "big officer" as he sadly replied, "I don't know now.
I did belong to the Louisiana Tigers, but they were wiped out of existence."[82]

While Hays had lost a little more than a quarter of his men, the First Louisiana Brigade was still a potent and dangerous fighting force. With Ewell ill,
Early temporarily assumed command of the Second Corps in the early autumn and Hays took over Early's Division. Colonel William Monaghan of the
6th Louisiana, recovered from his Winchester illness, was assigned to lead the
remnants of both the First Louisiana Brigade and Hoke's Brigade. In October,

Leroy Stafford of the 9th Louisiana was promoted to brigadier general and assigned command of the Second Louisiana, or "Pelican," Brigade. In turn, the massive William R. Peck replaced Stafford as colonel of the regiment.

Harry Hays and three-quarters of his nine hundred remaining men were captured in November in a disastrous fight at Rappahannock Station, but the general was able to escape and return to the shattered remnants of the brigade. Desertion and illness continued to thin the ranks. Few replacements were available, and a significant number of exchanged prisoners never returned to the ranks, taking extended medical furloughs or simply not reporting for duty as expected. Similar attrition affected many of Robert E. Lee's other brigades, several of which by late winter were smaller than a regulation regiment in strength.[83]

In mid-March 1864, a large number of paroled Tigers were loaded onto boats in New York Harbor and shipped south to City Point, Virginia, to be exchanged. After the paperwork was processed, they returned to the boats for the passage across to Confederate-controlled territory. On Wednesday, March 16, newspapers reported an emotional and symbolic gesture that had the Tigers again roaring. "When the boats moved off, Ensign Godfrey Gaisser of Company K, 6th Louisiana regiment, hoisted, on a rough sycamore sapling, the battle flag he had concealed about his person ever since his capture . . . , and flaunted it defiantly in the face of Yankees on board the other boats; there arose from the six hundred of Hays' brigade such a shout as has seldom been heard on this earth."[84]

The replenished First Louisiana Brigade fought at the Battle of the Wilderness, where on May 5, 1864, Hays lost one-third of his remaining men, and longtime Tiger Leroy Stafford fell mortally wounded while leading his Second Brigade. Five days later at Spotsylvania, a Yankee artillery shell fragment severely wounded Hays, and Colonel William Monaghan assumed command. Harry Hays never again served in the Army of Northern Virginia. After recovering, he transferred to the Trans-Mississippi Theater and later commanded troops in his beloved Louisiana. Promoted to major general at the end of the war, his appointment came too late for the Confederate Congress to ratify it prior to the collapse of the Confederacy.

Not long after Spotsylvania, Robert E. Lee ordered a sweeping reorganization of his army in the late spring, and, among the many changes, the heavily depleted First Louisiana Brigade merged with the Second Louisiana Brigade.

Colonel Zebulon York of the 14th Louisiana received a promotion to briga-dier general and was assigned command of the amalgamated brigade. He sub-sequently led it into the Shenandoah Valley that summer as a part of Jubal Early's independent force. The remnants of the Louisiana Tigers once again crossed the Potomac River and invaded Maryland for a third time, partici-pating in the Battle of Monocacy and Early's Raid on Washington. Returning to the valley, the Louisianans were involved in several engagements in the autumn, with General York incapacitated and knocked out of the war at the Third Battle of Winchester, or Opequon.

With York down, Colonel Peck assumed command. Following the debacle at Cedar Creek where most of Early's force was crushed, what was left of the combined Louisiana Brigade returned to the Army of Northern Virginia, where they again manned the trenches. "Big Peck" would finish the war as the only Louisiana Tiger to rise from private to brigadier general when he was promoted in February 1865 and reassigned to the Western Theater.

Colonel Eugene Waggaman of the 10th Louisiana became the final com-mander of the Louisiana Brigade, which numbered about four hundred men as the Appomattox Campaign began. When the Army of Northern Virginia surrendered in early April 1865, the five regiments that had comprised Hays' Brigade at Gettysburg were a mere skeleton of their former size, strength, and braggadocio. The 5th Louisiana was down to one officer and eighteen en-listed men. The few dozen remaining Tigers from the night charge on East Cemetery Hill headed home to the Pelican State, their military service fi-nally over.[85]

As Reconstruction began, Harry Hays became a sheriff in New Orleans. He played a prominent role in the July 1866 New Orleans Race Riot, at one time deputizing nearly two hundred of his former soldiers who were now members of the "Hays' Brigade Relief Society." It was the final time the Loui-siana Tigers took up arms as a formal organization. They dispersed when cooler heads prevailed, and went home to swap war stories about their days as Tigers.[86]

In the decades after the war, the families and friends of scores of fallen Confederates visited Gettysburg in the hope of locating their loved ones' graves. In some cases, they were successful. Corporal William H. Poole of the 9th Louisiana had been killed while skirmishing from the Samuel McCreary house on July 3. McCreary and a neighbor had buried him in a field near Long

Lane. In the late 1860s, Poole's grieving parents traveled to Pennsylvania to recover his body. They were directed to their son's weathered grave. After a period of mourning, they had the bones disinterred and removed to Louisiana for reburial. The Mississippi-born Poole had been a farmer in Brush Valley, Louisiana, prior to the war, and had enlisted in July 1861 at the young age of nineteen.[87]

Not all of the bones of the Louisiana Tigers who gave their last measure of devotion on East Cemetery Hill were recovered and sent to the South after the war. In July 1890, workers digging sand along the brickyard lane found the skeletal remains of a man, and buttons recovered from the grave indicated he was a Confederate. Although the location of the grave makes it likely he was one of Ike Avery's North Carolinians, he could have been from the 7th Louisiana, which was also in the general vicinity.[88]

There may have been other Louisianans missed in the mass disinterment and collection of bones from known gravesites. In early April 1910, the superintendent of the Gettysburg Water Company, Robert Caldwell, discovered several bones while cleaning up the premises on the northern part of East Cemetery Hill. The location of the badly decomposed remains was consistent with the known path of the right flank of the Tigers, the 5th and 6th Louisiana, during the attack on Harris's Buckeyes. The man most likely had been buried hastily near where he fell. In addition to the bones and bone fragments, Caldwell found a table knife and a spoon, as well as the frame of a disintegrated pocket purse containing an old Indian arrowhead. Any other personal possessions, including any money that might have been in the purse, had either disintegrated or been stolen from the body before burial. He discovered nothing else that would give a clue about the man's identity or specific regiment. Caldwell reburied the bones and marked the spot where he had discovered them while he waited for instructions from the battlefield commissioners.[89]

One by one, most of Hays' old veterans died in the six decades after the war. Many succumbed to the lingering effects or complications of old war wounds. Several former Tigers came to the 25th Anniversary Commemoration of the Battle of Gettysburg in 1888. By the turn of the century, the numbers of men left to carry on the reunions and meetings had noticeably dwindled. For the 50th Anniversary in 1913, only a handful of men who had fought on East Cemetery Hill in either army were again present in Gettysburg to relive that nightmarish evening on July 2, 1863, when the Louisianans had made "another fruitless display of magnificent bravery, in which life and zeal were thrown away."[90]

Yet, their opponents took special delight in claiming they had grappled with the famed Louisiana Tigers, even if in reality they had not. One former Rebel, with tongue in cheek, noted, "Nearly every account of the war which I have read by Northern writers gives great prominence in every battle to the 'Tigers,' and I am of the opinion that every soldier in the Union Army actually thought he fought the 'Tigers.' I cannot estimate the number they must originally have mustered, according to the amount of fighting they are represented by the boys in blue to have done, but there was certainly more than a million of them, or they wouldn't 'go around.'"[91]

Hawaiian-born Captain Samuel C. Armstrong was among the many Federals who claimed an encounter with the famed Louisianans. On the second day at Gettysburg, the 125th New York charged into a valley full of Rebels sheltered by a dense growth of underbrush. The hidden Confederates called out, "Do not fire on your own men!" Armstrong and his comrades immediately ceased fire, and then were stunned when a sharp volley rang out from the trees. Years later the captain wrote, "These fellows were the famous Louisiana Tigers, but we rushed at them with fixed bayonets, drove them out of the bush, and plunged our fire into them as they ran." The problem was his regiment was charging from Cemetery Ridge westward into Longstreet's First Corps positions in the Trostle thicket, far from the positions occupied by the two Louisiana brigades.[92]

The actual Tigers, both Hays' men and the Second Louisiana Brigade that also carried the sobriquet, certainly did not need their exploits embellished or credited to others. James Longstreet commented at a speech years later in Gettysburg, "Comrades, there never lived men who were any braver than the Louisiana Tigers."[93]

The 1,200 men of the First Louisiana Brigade who fought at Gettysburg are now long gone, but their legacy lives on in Harry Hays' timeless summation of their service in the summer campaign of 1863. "In all the operations in the neighborhood of Gettysburg, I am happy to state that both officers and men, while animated with *a spirit of daring* that disdained to concede any obstacle to their progress unsurmountable, were yet amenable to all the orders of their leaders, and accepted readily any position assigned them." They truly were Tigers.

# APPENDIX A

## Order of Battle
## East Cemetery Hill

All troop strengths listed below are from Busey & Martin, and reflect the approximate strength at the start of the day on July 1. By the afternoon of July 2, perhaps as many as 40–60 percent of the Union soldiers were missing from the ranks in many regiments (more in some). Where available, the actual strength on July 2 is listed. Hays and Avery had likewise suffered casualties on the first day, but to a far lesser extent. Hays reported only sixty-three casualties on Day 1, and Avery's losses were likely even less.

There were other troops at times involved in the defense of East Cemetery Hill that played minor roles. These are not listed, nor are all the artillery batteries involved in the afternoon gun duel.

**CONFEDERATE**

**Elements of the Army of Northern Virginia, Ewell's Second Corps**

*Elements of Early's Division—Major General Jubal Anderson Early*

HAYS' BRIGADE (1,295 MEN)—BRIGADIER GENERAL HARRY
THOMPSON HAYS
  5th Louisiana—Major Alexander Hart, Captain Thomas H. Briscoe
    (196 men)
  6th Louisiana—Lieutenant Colonel Joseph Hanlon (218 men)
  7th Louisiana—Colonel Davidson Bradfute Penn (235 men)
  8th Louisiana—Colonel Trevanion Dudley Lewis, Lieutenant Colonel
    Alcibiades De Blanc, Major German A. Lester (296 men)
  9th Louisiana—Colonel Leroy Augustus Stafford (347 men)

HOKE'S BRIGADE (1,254 MEN)—COLONEL ISAAC E. AVERY, COLONEL
ARCHIBALD CAMPBELL GODWIN
  6th North Carolina—Major Samuel McDowell Tate (509 men)
  21st North Carolina—Colonel William Whedbee Kirkland (436 men)
  57th North Carolina—Colonel Archibald Campbell Godwin (297 men)


## UNION

### Elements of Eleventh Corps, Army of the Potomac—Major General Oliver Otis Howard

*First Division—Brigadier General Adelbert Ames*

FIRST BRIGADE—COLONEL LEOPOLD VON GILSA
  41st New York (nine companies)—Lieutenant Colonel Detleo von
    Einsiedel (218 men)
  54th New York—Lieutenant Ernst Both (183 men)
  68th New York—Colonel Gotthilf Bourry (226 men)
  153rd Pennsylvania—Major John F. Frueauff (487 men)

SECOND BRIGADE—COLONEL ANDREW L. HARRIS
  17th Connecticut—Major Allen G. Brady (386 men / 225 on the
    morning of July 1)
  25th Ohio—Lieutenant William Maloney, Lieutenant Israel White
    (220 men/ 60 on the morning of July 1)
  75th Ohio—Captain George B. Fox (269 men / 91 on the morning of July 2)
  107th Ohio—Adjutant Peter F. Young, Captain John M. Lutz
    (458 men / 179 on the morning of July 2)

*Elements of Second Division*

  27th Pennsylvania—Lieutenant Colonel Lorenz Cantador (277 men)
  73rd Pennsylvania—Captain D. F. Kelly (284 men)
  33rd Massachusetts—Colonel Adin B. Underwood (481 men)

*Elements of Third Division—Major General Carl Schurz*

SECOND BRIGADE—COLONEL WLADIMIR KRZYZANOWSKI
  58th New York—Captain Emil Koenig (193 men)
  119th New York—Lieutenant Colonel Edward F. Lloyd (257 men)

*Artillery—Colonel Charles S. Wainwright (I Corps artillery, commanded guns east of Baltimore Pike)*

1st New York Light, Battery I—Captain Michael Wiedrich (six 3-inch rifles, 141 men)

1st Pennsylvania Light, Batteries F and G, Captain R. Bruce Ricketts (six 3-inch rifles / 144 men)

Maine Light, 5th Battery (E), Captain Greenleaf T. Stevens, Lieutenant Edward N. Whittier (six 12-pounder Napoleons, 119 men)

4th United States, Battery B, Lieutenant James Stewart (six 12-pounder Napoleons, 124 men)

1st New York Light, Battery L (Battery E attached), Lieutenant George Breck (five 3-inch rifles, 124 men)

*Element of the Third Division, Second Corps, Army of the Potomac*

ELEMENTS OF FIRST BRIGADE—COLONEL SAMUEL S. CARROLL

14th Indiana—Colonel John Coons (191 men)

4th Ohio—Lieutenant Colonel Leonard W. Carpenter (299 men)

7th West Virginia—Lieutenant Colonel Jonathan H. Lockwood (269 men)

# APPENDIX B

## Harry Hays' Official Reports
## for the Gettysburg Campaign

### SECOND WINCHESTER

HEADQUARTERS HAYS' BRIGADE, *August 4, 1863.*

Maj. JOHN W. DANIEL,
*Asst Adjt. Gen., Early's Division.*

MAJOR: I have the honor of submitting the following report of the operations of my brigade on June 13 and 14, in the vicinity of Winchester, Va.:

On the morning of June 13, being encamped on the south side of the Shenandoah River, I crossed that stream at daylight, and, joining the division, was marched in the direction of Winchester, taking the Newtown road.

Reaching Newtown, we took the Valley turnpike, and proceeded to within a short distance of Kernstown, where we met with Colonel Herbert's command of the Maryland Line, engaged in skirmishing with the enemy. Having halted here for a short time, I was conducted by Major-General Early to another road, to the left and west of the Valley turnpike. I then advanced my brigade about half a mile on this road, halted, and sent out the Ninth Regiment, Colonel [L. A.] Stafford commanding, to deploy as skirmishers, and drive the enemy from a wooded eminence between my position and the Valley turnpike. This having been effected, I advanced my brigade, and formed it in line of battle on the above-mentioned hill, throwing out six companies as skirmishers, to advance to another piece of woods in my front.

At this juncture. I was ordered by General Early to remain in my position until Gordon's brigade should have swept around and entered the woods to my left. Gordon, having met the enemy, drove him steadily before him, my six companies of skirmishers advancing with his brigade. My brigade was then put in motion, and continued to advance until both brigades were halted, by command of General Early, when we were formed in line on the crest of a hill in front of the Cedar Creek road, and in rear of Barton's Mills, on the Valley turnpike, Gordon's right resting on the pike and my brigade on his left. In this position we remained during that evening and night.

At daylight on the morning of June 14, brisk skirmishing took place, and at sunrise, in obedience to orders from General Early, I sent the Seventh Regiment, Colonel Penn commanding, with directions to advance with a regiment of Gordon's brigade, to take possession of a hill in front of the old mill, the same taken by the Louisiana brigade in May, 1862. This was accomplished after a short engagement with the enemy's skirmishers.

Sharp skirmishing continued during the morning, and at 11 o'clock I received orders from General Early to withdraw the Seventh Regiment and my skirmishers so soon as they should be relieved by General Gordon, and to form my brigade on the Cedar Creek Grade. From this place we were marched around to the left and weal of Winchester, until we reached, at about 3.30 p.m., a position to the north of the Romney road, and between that road and the Pughtown road, in the rear of a fortified hill, to the north of and commanding the main fort. There we halted.

The artillery having been put in position, I was ordered by General Early at about 5 p.m. to form my brigade, and be in readiness to charge and take the fortified position of the enemy in our front, which was the key to all the other fortifications in and around Winchester. Having, in company with General Early, made a careful reconnaissance. I proceeded to form my line on the slope of a wooded hill, in advance of and between the two positions selected for our artillery, placing the Sixth, Seventh, and Ninth Regiments (commanded, respectively by Colonels Monaghan, Penn, and Stafford) in the front line, and the Fifth and Eighth Regiments (commanded by Colonels Forno and Lewis) at a convenient distance in the rear, to be used on the flanks or in support, as occasion might require.

Having informed General Early that my arrangements were completed, and my brigade in readiness to advance, the artillery at once opened a heavy fire upon the enemy's position. So well directed was this fire, that in a few minutes the enemy were forced to seek shelter behind their works, and scarcely a head was discovered above the ramparts.

At this time, a favorable opportunity presenting itself for me to advance from the woods and cross the open field in my front (at about 6 or 6:30 o'clock).

I gave the order to forward. I continued to advance slowly and steadily, and succeeded in clearing the woods, crossing the field, and had begun to ascend the hill upon which were the enemy's fortifications, when, coming in view of our own artillery, it ceased firing. The enemy immediately arose from their hiding-places behind their works, and discovered us just as we had reached the edge of an abatis of felled timber, about 150 yards from the fortifications. The order to charge was given, and so rapidly did this brigade push forward that the enemy had time to give us but a few volleys of musketry and only four or five rounds of canister from their field pieces before the position was reached and carried.

About 150 yards above and to the left of the main fortifications was a small redoubt, manned by infantry and mounted with two pieces of artillery. This work was abandoned by the enemy immediately upon the fall of the other; but as they attempted to carry off their artillery, the Seventh Regiment was at once faced to the left, and, by shooting a few of the horses, saved both guns and caissons.

Owing to the difficulty experienced by my men in getting over the ditches and embankments after the works had been reached, and the precipitate flight of the enemy, the loss of the enemy in killed, wounded, and prisoners was very small. We captured one battery of the Fifth U.S. Artillery (regulars), of six guns, with caissons and trappings complete, and all the horses belonging thereto, save a few which we found it necessary to shoot in order to secure some of the guns.

Shortly after the fortifications had been carried, the enemy made a demonstration to retake it, and with that view had formed three columns. Two of the captured guns were immediately turned upon them, being served by some of my men who had previously been for a short time in the artillery service, and after a few well-directed rounds they were compelled to retire. Smith's brigade and Colonel Jones' battalion of artillery came up to my support shortly afterward. With the exception of quite a brisk cannonading, there was no further fighting that night.

The next morning, June 15, it was discovered that the enemy, seeing the key to all his other works in our possession, had evacuated Winchester, whereupon my brigade, with the remainder of the division, took up the line of march in the direction of Martinsburg.

The loss of my brigade in this engagement was 2 officers and 10 men killed, 8 officers and 59 men wounded, making a total of 12 killed and 67 wounded.

My loss on June 13 was as follows: 2 men killed, 3 officers and 8 men wounded, and 3 men missing. Total of the two days' operations: 14 killed, 78 wounded, 3 missing.

I desire here to mention that my officers and men won my highest admiration by the cool, steady, unflinching bravery they exhibited in this action, and particularly would I call attention to the conspicuous gallantry of Lieutenant [John] Orr, adjutant of the Sixth Regiment, who was the first to mount the parapet of the enemy's redoubt, receiving while doing so a severe bayonet wound in the side.

To my staff—Capt. W. J. Seymour, assistant adjutant-general, and Lieut. John Freeland, aide-de-camp—I am again indebted for valuable services. Also to Capt. John G. Campbell, acting brigade quartermaster and commissary, who rendered me important assistance during this engagement. Captain [J. H.] New, assistant adjutant-general and inspector, was absent, sick. I have the honor to be, very respectfully, your obedient servant,

HARRY T. HAYS,
*Brigadier-General, Commanding.*

## GETTYSBURG

HEADQUARTERS HAYS' BRIGADE,
*August 3, 1863.*

Maj. JOHN W. DANIEL,
*Assistant Adjutant-General, Early's Division.*

MAJOR: I respectfully submit the following report of the operations of the troops under my command near the city of Gettysburg, Pa.:

On Wednesday, July 1, after a march of 12 or 14 miles, returning from the city of York, I arrived with my brigade on the Heidlersburg road, within a mile and a half of Gettysburg. At this point I discovered that a space in the division line of battle had been left for my command, which had been marching in the rear of the column.

Brigadier-General Gordon having deployed to the right, Brigadier-General Hoke's brigade (commanded by Colonel Avery) and Smith's brigade to the left, I formed my line of battle, extending across the road, placing the Fifth, Sixth, and right wing of the Ninth Regiments on the right of the road, the left wing of the Ninth, Seventh, and Eighth Regiments on the left.

This arrangement being completed, Brigadier-General Gordon, a little after 2 o'clock, was ordered to advance. In a short time, Brigadier-General Gordon having encountered the enemy in force, I received an order to advance in support, Hoke's brigade moving forward at the same time on my left. Pressing steadily on, I met with no other opposition than that presented by the enemy's skirmishers and the firing of his artillery until I came up to the line of Gordon's brigade. Here I found the enemy in considerable strength. I still continued to move on, however, succeeding in driving before me all the force opposed until I arrived at the railroad, which here runs from east to west, just striking the edge of the city of Gettysburg. In my progress to this position, the fire to which my command was subjected from the enemy's batteries, posted upon well-selected rises of the ground, was unusually galling. But so rapid and impetuous was the movement of my troops in this advance, that my skirmishers, keeping well to the front, captured two pieces of artillery.

I had barely time to pause at the railroad referred to when I discovered a heavy column of the enemy's troops, which had been engaged with Gordon's brigade and the division of Major-General Rodes, advancing rapidly, threatening my right. Perceiving that a forward movement on my part would expose my flank to an attack from this force, exceeding in numbers that under my command, I immediately changed front forward on the first company, First Battalion, of a portion of my brigade—the Fifth, Sixth, and the right wing of the Ninth Regiments. With this line, after several well-directed volleys, I succeeded in breaking this column on my right, dispersing its men in full flight through the streets of the city. But for this movement on my flank, I should have captured several pieces of artillery opposite the left of my line, upon which the Seventh Regiment was advancing in front and the Eighth by a side street at the time I halted.

After reforming my line of battle, I advanced through the city of Gettysburg, clearing it of the enemy and taking prisoners at every turn. During this time, as well as in my progress to the city, a great number of prisoners were captured by my command, but unwilling to decrease my force by detailing a guard, I simply ordered them to the rear as they were taken. Many of these following the road to the left, fell into the possession of Major-General Rodes' troops. I am satisfied that the prisoners taken in the above-mentioned movements by my brigade exceeded in numbers the force under my command.

My loss this day was small—1 officer and 6 men killed, 4 officers and 37 men wounded, and 15 men missing. The loss of the enemy cannot be known with exactness, but it was apparent from an inspection of the field that his loss exceeded ours by at least six to one.

Having driven the enemy entirely out of the city, I rested my line on one of the upper southern streets, Hoke's brigade, on my left, extending beyond the eastern suburbs. In this position I remained until 12 o'clock that night. At that hour I received an order from Major-General Early to make a reconnaissance of the ground between my situation and that of the enemy, who, after abandoning the city, had intrenched himself on Cemetery Hill, a commanding height, one of a series or chain of hills belting Gettysburg on the south.

After a careful examination of the locality indicated, about 2 o'clock in the morning (July 2) I moved my troops into an open field between the city and the base of a hill intervening between us and Cemetery Hill, throwing out skirmishers to the front. In this field we remained the entire day of July 2, prominently exposed to the fire of the enemy's skirmishers and sharpshooters. During the afternoon of this day, I was directed by Major-General Early to hold my brigade in readiness at a given signal to charge the enemy in the works on the summit of the hill before me, with the information that a general advance of our entire line would be made at the same time.

A little before 8 p.m. I was ordered to advance with my own and Hoke's brigade on my left, which had been placed for the time under my command. I immediately moved forward, and had gone but a short distance when my whole line became exposed to a most terrific fire from the enemy's batteries from the entire range of hills in front, and to the right and left; still, both brigades advanced steadily up and over the first hill, and into a bottom at the foot of Cemetery Hill.

Here we came upon a considerable body of the enemy, and a brisk musketry fire ensued; at the same time his artillery, of which we were now within canister range, opened upon us, but owing to the darkness of the evening, now verging into night, and the deep obscurity afforded by the smoke of the firing, our exact locality could not be discovered by the enemy's gunners, and we thus escaped what in the full light of day could have been nothing else than horrible slaughter.

Taking advantage of this, we continued to move forward until we reached the second line, behind a Stone wall at the foot of a fortified hill. We passed such of the enemy who had not fled, and who were still clinging for shelter to the wall, to the rear, as prisoners. Still advancing, we came upon an abatis of fallen timber and the third line, disposed in rifle pits. This line we broke, and, as before, found many of the enemy who had not fled hiding in the pits for protection. These I ordered to the rear as prisoners, and continued my progress to the crest of the hill.

Arriving at the summit, by a simultaneous rush from my whole line, I captured several pieces of artillery, four stands of colors, and a number of prisoners. At that time every piece of artillery which had been firing upon us was silenced.

A quiet of several minutes now ensued. Their heavy masses of infantry were heard and perfectly discerned through the increasing darkness, advancing in the direction of my position. Approaching within 100 yards, a line was discovered before us, from the whole length of which a simultaneous fire was delivered. I reserved my fire, from the uncertainty of this being a force of the enemy or of our men, as I had been cautioned to expect friends both in front, to the right, and to the left, Lieutenant-General Longstreet, Major-General Rodes, and Major-General Johnson, respectively, having been assigned to these relative positions; but after the delivery of a second and third volley, the flashing of the musketry disclosed the still-advancing line to be one of the enemy.

I then gave the order to fire; the enemy was checked for a time, but discovering another line moving up in rear of this one, and still another force in rear of that, and being beyond the reach of support, I gave the order to retire to the stone wall at the foot of the hill, which was quietly and orderly effected. From this position I subsequently fell back to a fence some 75 yards distant from the wall, and awaited the further movements of the enemy.

Only contemplating, however, to effect an orderly and controlled retreat before a force which I was convinced I could not hope to withstand—at all events, where I then was—I was on the point of retiring to a better position when Captain Campbell, the brigade quartermaster, informed me that Brigadier-General Gordon was coming to my support.

I immediately dispatched an officer to hasten General Gordon with all possible speed, but this officer returning without seeing General Gordon, I went back myself, and finding General Gordon occupying the precise position in the field occupied by me when I received the order to charge the enemy on Cemetery Hill, and not advancing, I concluded that any assistance from him would be too late, and my only course was to withdraw my command. I therefore moved my brigade by the right flank, leading it around the hill, so as to escape the observation of the enemy, and conducted it to the right of my original position, then occupied, as above stated, by Gordon's brigade. This was about 10 o'clock. I remained in this position for the night.

About daybreak in the morning, I received an order from Major-General Early to withdraw my command from its position, and to occupy that street in the city which I had held during July 1. I continued to remain here that day (the 3d), and until early in the morning of July 4, when I was ordered by Major-General Early out of the city to a range of hills on the west. Here I put my brigade in line of battle, the division line being on the left of Major-General Rodes.

In this position I remained with my command until 2 o'clock on the morning of July 5, when the line of march was taken toward Hagerstown, Md.

My loss was:

| Officers and Men | Killed | Wounded | Missing | Total |
|---|---|---|---|---|
| July 2 | | | | |
| Officers | 5 | 15 | 3 | 23 |
| Enlisted Men | 16 | 104 | 38 | 158 |
| July 3 | | | | |
| Officers | 1 | 3 | 1 | 5 |
| Enlisted Men | 7 | 37 | 18 | 62 |
| July 4 | | | | |
| Officers | — | — | — | — |
| Enlisted Men | — | — | 20 | 20 |
| Total | 29 | 159 | 80 | 268 |

Total loss: 7 officers and 29 men killed, 22 officers and 178 men wounded, and 4 officers and 91 men missing. The missing, I fear, were either killed or wounded.

The artillery captured on the heights of Cemetery Hill I was compelled to abandon. The prisoners sent to the rear, being under charge of no guard, escaped in the darkness; 75 were brought back by my men in retreating from the hill. The colors taken I have now in my possession.

In all the operations in the neighborhood of Gettysburg, I am happy to state that both officers and men, while animated with a spirit of daring that disdained to concede any obstacle to their progress unsurmountable, were yet amenable to all the orders of their leaders, and accepted readily any position assigned them.

While rendering this tribute to the merit of all my command, I would call attention particularly to the efficiency of Cols. L. A. Stafford, Ninth Louisiana Regiment, and D. B. Penn, Seventh Louisiana Regiment. In the engagements of July 1 and 2, each of these officers distinguished himself by an exhibition of gallant bearing in leading his respective regiment into action, and of soldierly skill in its management and control.

My thanks are due to the several members of my staff, each of whom in his respective department was attentive to the discharge of his duties; Captain New, assistant adjutant-general and acting inspector; Captain Seymour, assistant adjutant-general, and Lieutenant Freeland, aide-de-camp.

I have the honor to be, very respectfully, your obedient servant,

HARRY T. HAYS,

*Brigadier-General, Commanding*

# APPENDIX C

## Casualties of Hays' Brigade

Regimental Strengths and Losses of Hays' Brigade at Gettysburg

| Regiment | Engaged | Killed | Wounded | Captured or missing | Percentage |
|---|---|---|---|---|---|
| 5th Louisiana | 196 | 7 | 30 | 30 | 34.2 |
| 6th Louisiana | 218 | 8 | 32 | 21 | 28 |
| 7th Louisiana | 235 | 13 | 40 | 5 | 24.7 |
| 8th Louisiana | 296 | 14 | 50 | 11 | 25.3 |
| 9th Louisiana | 347 | 19 | 35 | 19 | 21 |
| Brigade totals[a] | 1295 | 61 | 187 | 86 | 26 |
| Harry T. Hays' official report | — | 36 | 200 | 95 | — |

[a]Includes brigade staff.
Sources: John W. Busey and David G. Martin, *Regimental Strengths and Losses at Gettysburg* (Hightstown, N.J.: Longstreet House, 1982), 160, 287; *O.R.*, vol. 27, part 2, 482.


**MEMORIAL ROLL**
Following is a partial list of Hays' Louisiana Tigers who were killed in action or died from wounds or disease during the Gettysburg Campaign. The list is derived primarily from Booth's *Records of Louisiana Confederate Soldiers*, as well as other sources, but does not represent all fatalities in the brigade. See also Jubal Early's casualty lists in *Confederate States Army Casualties: Lists and Narrative Reports, 1861–1865*, file M836, roll 7, National Archives.

**5TH LOUISIANA**
Pvt. James Davine, Co. K, July 3
Pvt. Martin Heenahan, Co. K, July 2 or 3

Pvt. Simon Long, Co. K, mortally wounded July 2

Pvt. Adolph Piterit, Co. D, July 2

Capt. Frederick Richardson, Co. F, July 1

Sgt. Robert F. Wilson, Co. F, color bearer, July 2

## 6TH LOUISIANA

Sgt. William Burke, Co. H, June 14 at Winchester

Corp. Robert Cahill, Co. F, mortally wounded June 14 at Winchester, died June 20

Pvt. John Carroll, Co. F, July 2

Sgt. Thomas Casey, Co. B, July 2

Capt. Louis A. Cormier, Co. C, July 3

Pvt. John Good, Co. B, July 2

Pvt. Michael Gleason, Co. E, June 14 at Winchester

Corp. Ulysses W. Fisher, Co. C, mortally wounded July 2, died early September at Davids' Island, NY

Pvt. James D. Haines, Co. C, July 2

Pvt. James Keegan, Co. B, June 14 at Winchester

Pvt. Richard Kelly, Co. I, wounded July 8, died July 14 at Hagerstown, "killed in the discharge of his duty by an assassin"

Pvt. Michael Kirwin, Co. K, June 13 at Winchester

Pvt. John McClung, Co. B, June 14 at Winchester

Sgt. Patrick McGuinn, Co. B, July 2

Pvt. William Murray, Co. F, mortally wounded July 2, died July 29 at Gettysburg

Corp. Frederick Roose, Co. H. mortally wounded June 14 at Winchester, died July 9 at Jordan Springs Hospital

Pvt. B. O. Scarborough, mortally wounded June 14 at Winchester, died June 18 at Jordan Springs Hospital

Pvt. Isaac R. Scott, Co. C, mortally wounded June 14 at Winchester, died in August as a POW

Pvt. Ozemus Smith, Co. C, mortally wounded June 14 at Winchester

## 7TH LOUISIANA

Pvt. William F. Campbell, Co. H, June 14 at Winchester

Sgt. Joachim Gibson, Co. I, July 2

Pvt. William Ford, Co. B, mortally wounded July 2, died August 24

Pvt. James Flynn, Co. H, June 13 at Winchester

Pvt. Jerry Lynch, Co. I, July 2
Pvt. William Powers, Co. K, undated
Pvt. Henry Rathbert, Co. K, July 2
Pvt. Frank Rhorer, Co. D, June 14 at Winchester
Pvt. B. H. Saunders, Co. G, mortally wounded June 14 at Winchester, died July 9
Lt. Wallace P. Talbot, Co. E, July 2
Lt. Vitrivius V. Terry, Co. K, June 14 at Winchester
Capt. William R. Thompson, Co. A, mortally wounded July 2, died July 21
Sgt. Thomas Thorpe, Co. G, color bearer, July 2
Lt. Louis Worchester, Co. B, July 2

**8TH LOUISIANA**

Sgt. Justinien F. Braud, Co. K, July 2
Pvt. Stanislas Broussard, Co. C, mortally wounded July 2, "died same month"
Corp. Charles Brown, Co. I, June 28, supposedly "killed by the citizens of Penn."
Pvt. Charles L. Comes, Co. K, July 1
Capt. Albert Dejean, Jr., Co. F, July 13 at Winchester
Pvt. Horthere Fontenot, Co. F, mortally wounded July 3, subsequently died
Pvt. Patrick Gaffney, Co. B, June 14 at Winchester
Corp. Leon P. Gusman, Co. A, color bearer, July 2
Pvt. William Henry Harris, Co. F, July 2
Corp. George H. Jemison, Co. B, July 1
Pvt. Aristide Lague, Co. F, undated
Col. Trevanion D. Lewis, July 2
Capt. Victor J. St. Martin, Co. K, July 2
Pvt. Thomas McCarty, Co. I, mortally wounded July 2
Pvt. Perry J. Murrell, Co. G, mortally wounded July 2
Capt. Auguste D. Randolph, Co. D, July 2
Pvt. John Lowery Simmons, Co. G, July 1
Sgt. Jefferson B. Smith, Co. K, July 1, Pennsylvania native
Corp. James S. Vay, Co. A, July 2

**9TH LOUISIANA**

Pvt. J. J. Anderson, Co. H, ill, died at Winchester, undated
Pvt. L. B. Barnard, Co. K, July 4
Pvt. T. B. Bate, Co. C, mortally wounded July 2, died July 21 at Gettysburg

Pvt. John C. Calhoun, Co. I, July 2

Pvt. Elias Carlton, Co. C, July 2, missing, "supposed to be dead"

Lt. Richard T. Crawford, Adjutant, July 2

Pvt. John M. Davis, Co. I, July 2

Pvt. Allen Gideon, Jr., Co. D, July 6 at Williamsport skirmish

Pvt. John F. Hodges, Co. D, July 2

Pvt. John H. McClannahan, Co. D, July 2

Corp. Milledge Magee, Co. D, mortally wounded July 2, died July 21 at Gettysburg

Pvt. David T. Moore, Co. A, July 1

Pvt. Charles Palmore, Co. C, July 2

Pvt. Thomas B. Pate, Co. A, undated

Pvt. William H. Poole, Co. H, July 3

Pvt. Willis H. Rabon, Co. C, July 2

Pvt. John C. Rogers, Co. I, undated

Pvt. John D. Rogers, Co. F, July 4

Pvt. John W. Shackleford, Co. D, died of exhaustion June 30 near Gettysburg

Pvt. Stephen Smith, Co. E, July 3

Pvt. Julius D. Stall, Co. C, June 14 at Winchester

Pvt. James A. Stewart, Co. A, June 14 at Winchester

Sgt. E. Blake Tooke, Co. C, June 14 at Winchester

Maj. Henry L. N. Williams, mortally wounded July 2, died July 5 at Gettysburg

Pvt. Simon A. Williams, mortally wounded July 2, died August 13 at Mount Jackson, Virginia

# APPENDIX D

## The Weather During Hays' March through Pennsylvania

The Reverend Dr. Michael Jacobs was professor of mathematics and science at Pennsylvania College during the Confederate invasion. He enjoyed meteorology and kept meticulous notes on the weather at Gettysburg beginning in 1839. These provide an unusually detailed record of the atmospheric conditions encountered by the Louisiana Tigers during the last week of June 1863.

"The entire period of the invasion is remarkable for being one of clouds, and, for that season of the year, of low temperature," wrote Jacobs. "From June 15th until July 22nd, 1863, there was not an entirely clear day. On the evening of June 25th at 8 p.m. a rain began. . . . This rain continued at intervals until Saturday June 27th, at 7 a.m., the precipitation being in inches 1.280. At all the observations made on Saturday and Sunday, and until the nine o'clock observation of Monday night, the entire sky was covered with clouds" (Michael Jacobs papers, Musselman Library, Gettysburg College).

The following table shows temperatures at Gettysburg in the days preceding the battle, as reported by Jacobs' son Henry in the Gettysburg *Star and Sentinel*, July 30, 1885, based on information from his father's notes.

Temperatures at Gettysburg, 1863 (°F)

|  | 7:00 a.m. | 2 p.m. | 9 p.m. |
|---|---|---|---|
| Thursday, June 25 | 59 | 51 | 63 |
| Friday, June 26 | 60 | 63 | 62 |
| Saturday, June 27 | 61 | 63 | 67 |
| Sunday, June 28 | 63 | 67 | 68 |
| Monday, June 29 | 66 | 72 | 69 |
| Tuesday, June 30 | 68 | 79 | 71 |

During the Battle of Gettysburg, Professor Jacobs recorded the weather as follows:

*July 1:* The entire sky was covered with clouds all day, cumulo-stratus at 7 a.m. and 2 p.m., cirrostratus at 9 p.m. A very gentle warm southern breeze (2 mph). Thermometer: 7 am—72; 2 pm—76; 9 pm—74

*July 2:* At 8 a.m., sky still covered (cumulostratus). At 2 p.m., 3/10 clear. At 9 p.m. cirrus clouds. Wind same as preceding day. Thermometer: 7 a.m.—74; 2 p.m.—81; 9 p.m.—76

*July 3:* At 8 a.m., sky again completely covered with cumulo-stratus clouds, at 2 p.m., sky only 4/10 covered, but with cumulus or the thunderclouds of summer; at 9 p.m., 7/10 cumulus. Wind SSW, very gentle. Thunderstorm in neighborhood at 6 p.m. The thunder seemed tame, after the artillery firing of the afternoon. Thermometer: 7 a.m.—73; 2 p.m.—87; 9 p.m.—76

*July 4:* Rain showers at 6 a.m., from 2:15 until 4 p.m., and at 4 a.m. on July 5, totaling 1.39 inches. Thermometer: 7 a.m.—69; 2 p.m.—72; 9 p.m.—70

As Henry Jacobs reported, Lee's Army of Northern Virginia broke camp and marched toward the Shenandoah Valley under a full moon. There was virtually no moon when Early's division reached Winchester, Virginia. As Harry Hays began his march through Adams and York counties, the moon began to wax, reaching full on July 1.

# APPENDIX E

## Chronology of Hays' Louisiana Tigers in the Gettysburg Campaign

June 3—McLaws' Division of the Confederate Army of Northern Virginia departs Fredericksburg, Virginia, heading northwest toward Culpeper Court House. Hays' Brigade of Louisiana Tigers rests in camp at Hamilton's Crossing.

June 4—Rodes' Division moves out. Hays packs supply wagons and breaks camp, marching to Spotsylvania Court House toward Ewell's Corps' rendezvous point at Culpeper.

June 5—The remainder of Ewell's Corps leaves camp. Hays halts after crossing Catharpin Creek, while division commander Jubal Early awaits orders concerning developments along the Rappahannock line.

June 6—Union forces demonstrate at Fredericksburg. Hays stays in camp in a driving rain, ready to countermarch in case of a strong Yankee attack. It does not come. In the afternoon, Hays resumes the march toward Culpeper.

June 7—Hooker sets his Union cavalry in motion. Hays passes through Verdiersville and crosses the Rapidan River at Somerville Ford.

June 8—Lee reviews Stuart's cavalry near Culpeper. Hays marches through Culpeper and camps three miles to the west.

June 9—Federal cavalry surprises Stuart at Brandy Station; bitter fighting ends in a tactical draw. Hays marches toward Brandy Station, but the fighting is over before his brigade arrives.

June 10—Concerned about a possible invasion of Pennsylvania, the U.S. War Department creates the Department of the Susquehanna and assigns Major General Darius Couch as commander. Elements of Ewell's Corps leave Culpeper, marching toward the Shenandoah Valley.

June 11—Hooker gets some of his infantry in motion, chasing Lee, who has a significant head start. Most of the Army of the Potomac sits in camp awaiting orders to move.

June 12—Hays crosses the Blue Ridge Mountains at Chester Gap, enters the Shenandoah Valley, and marches to Front Royal.

June 13—Hays approaches Winchester, guarded by Robert Milroy's Yankees. Hays and Gordon drive defenders from Pritchard's Hill, and Federals retreat to Bower's Hill. Milroy concentrates his forces at night.

June 14—Hays attacks and seizes the West Fort, a key Union defense. Milroy retires at night toward Harper's Ferry.

June 15—Johnson cuts off Milroy near Stephenson's Depot, capturing thousands of Yankees. Jenkins occupies Chambersburg. Lincoln calls for 100,000 men from Pennsylvania, Ohio, Maryland, and West Virginia to serve for up to six months to meet the Confederate threat. Governor Curtin calls for 50,000 Pennsylvanians.

June 16—Chambersburg is still in Jenkins' hands. Hays rests near Stephenson's Depot.

June 17—Cavalry battles are fought at Aldie and Middleburg.

June 18—Hays marches through West Virginia toward Shepherdstown and the Potomac River crossing.

June 19—Longstreet's corps enters the Shenandoah Valley and heads north. Hooker's Army of the Potomac halts for six days, allowing Lee to further increase the gap between his army and the Yankees. Hays is delayed at Shepherdstown by a flooded Potomac River.

June 20—Imboden's Southern cavalrymen approach Bedford, Pennsylvania, and threaten the Baltimore & Ohio Railroad. Workers begin to remove rolling stock across the Susquehanna River toward Philadelphia. Hays rests at Shepherdstown waiting for the Potomac to recede.

June 21—Cavalry battle fought at Upperville. Federal cavalry cannot penetrate Stuart's screen, and Lee's recent movements are uncertain to Union intelligence. Lee continues northward in the Shenandoah Valley. Hays rests at Shepherdstown.

June 22—Jenkins retakes Chambersburg as Union militia withdraws to Harrisburg. Hays fords the Potomac at Boteler's Ford and marches to Boonsboro, Maryland.

June 23—Stuart starts his ride around Hooker's army. Hays enters Pennsylvania, camping near Waynesboro.

June 24—Rumors reach Harrisburg that Ewell is approaching with 30,000 soldiers. Rodes enters Chambersburg. Hays marches through Quincy and Altodale, camping at Greenwood near South Mountain.

June 25—Early meets Ewell at Chambersburg and receives orders to advance to Gettysburg the following day. More Confederate divisions cross the Potomac into Maryland. After a six-day halt, the Army of the Potomac finally heads north. Hays' men "laid in camp all day cooking rations."

June 26—Ewell heads northeasterly from Chambersburg toward Carlisle. Early marches eastward, burns the Caledonia Iron works, and enters Adams County. Early chases off state militia near Gettysburg. Hays camps west of town.

June 27—Hays camps at Big Mount. Robert E. Lee enters Pennsylvania. Longstreet and Hill occupy Chambersburg. Ewell reaches Carlisle's outskirts. Jenkins camps at Mechanicsburg, less than ten miles from Harrisburg. The War Department dispatches an officer to relieve Hooker.

June 28—At 3:00 a.m., Meade takes over the Army of the Potomac. Early occupies York. Copeland's 5th and 6th Michigan Cavalry occupy Gettysburg. Hays marches to York.

June 29—Hays stays in York. Early plans to assist Ewell if needed with an assault on Harrisburg. Ewell reaches Oyster's Point, two miles from the Susquehanna River. Lee recalls Ewell and orders his army to concentrate near Cashtown.

June 30—Ewell leaves the Harrisburg area, intending to return after whipping the Yankees. Ewell orders Early to march toward Cashtown and Gettysburg. Buford enters Gettysburg after skirmishing near Fairfield. Hill sends Pettigrew's brigade to Gettysburg, but it withdraws when officers spot Federals, assuming them to be militia. Hays camps near Round Hill.

July 1—Ewell orders Early to turn south to Gettysburg, where a battle has begun. Hays arrives about 3:00 p.m. and forms into battle line, supported by Avery on the left flank and Gordon on the right. They sweep through Yankee lines, and Hays seizes Gettysburg.

July 2—Hays and Avery fail to take a fortified East Cemetery Hill in a determined twilight assault.

July 3—Lee's last attempts to crack the Union "fish hook" line are thwarted. Hays, other than skirmishing, is relatively idle. Hays has suffered 268 casualties in the Battle of Gettysburg.

July 4—Before daylight, Early pulls back from Gettysburg. Hays takes a new position west of Gettysburg supporting Rodes. After dark, in a driving rainstorm, Lee begins withdrawing toward Virginia.

July 5—At 2:00 a.m., Hays' Brigade starts the long walk to Virginia, leaving dozens of wounded in the care of Gettysburg citizens and military doctors.

July 6—Hays crosses South Mountain at Monterey Pass and camps near Waynesboro.

July 7—Hays marches through Leitersburg, Maryland, arrives at Hagerstown, and camps a mile north of town.

July 8—Hays rests in camp near Hagerstown and collects stragglers.

July 9—Hays rests in camp near Hagerstown.

July 10—Hays marches through Hagerstown and camps on a ridge by the Cumberland Road.

July 11—Hays forms a battle line near the Williamsport Road, expecting an assault by pursuing Federals. The Yankees do not attack.

July 12—Hays remains in a defensive posture behind temporary works. Nearby Yankees are also stationary.

July 13—At twilight, Hays retires toward Williamsport.

July 14—Hays crosses the Potomac at Falling Waters, enters West Virginia, and camps 6 miles from the river.

July 15—Hays marches up the Shenandoah Valley to Martinsburg.

July 16—Hays marches to Darkesville, West Virginia.

July 17—Hays is stationary in camp at Darkesville.

July 18—Hays is stationary in camp at Darkesville.

July 19—Hays is stationary in camp at Darkesville.

July 20—Concerned about reports of Union movement near Hedgesville, Early's Division is sent back to block any threat from the rear. Hays marches to the foot of the North Mountain range and camps at Gerrardstown.

July 21—Hays marches to Hedgesville, where there are no Yankees, despite the reports. The brigade camps nearby.

July 22—Hays marches 18 miles south to Bunker Hill.

July 23—Hays returns to Winchester, Virginia, scene of the June 13–14 triumph over Milroy. The Battle of Manassas Gap (or Wapping Heights) enables much of Lee's army to slip into the Luray Valley and relative safety.

July 24—Hays marches along the Shenandoah River toward the mountains, but the pass on the Blue Ridge is in the Yankees' hands. Hays marches 23 miles through Middletown to Strasburg.

July 25—Hays marches south through Woodstock, traveling 18 miles on the turnpike toward distant Staunton and stopping at Edinburg.

July 26—Hays marches through Hawkinstown and Mount Jackson to New Market.

July 27—Hays leaves the Stanton turnpike and moves on a side road to Gordonsville in Orange County. His Tigers traverse Massanutten Mountain and cross the Shenandoah River on pontoon bridges. They stop for the night at the base of the Blue Ridge Mountains, 18 miles from New Market.

July 28—Hays crosses over the Blue Ridge on a 14-mile march and camps near Criglersville.

July 29—After a short 6-mile march, Hays stops at Madison Court House.

July 30—Hays' Brigade rests in camp at Madison.

July 31—In the early afternoon, Hays marches toward Culpeper, camping at 5:00 p.m. along the Robinson River.

August 1—Hays crosses the Robinson and Rapidan rivers, marches through Culpeper, and camps four miles past Rapidan Station. Hays stays until September 14, when the Louisiana Tigers participate in the Bristoe and Mine Run campaigns.

# NOTES

## ABBREVIATIONS

ACHS    Adams County Historical Society
GNMP    Library of the Gettysburg National Military Park
LHAC    Louisiana Historical Association Collection
OR      Official Records of the War of the Rebellion
SHSP    Southern Historical Society Papers
YCHT    York County Heritage Trust

## CHAPTER 1

1. *Harper's Weekly,* June 7, 1862. Dahomey was a country in western Africa noted for its ferocity and inhumanity. A series of cruel kings accentuated this reputation by selling captive
enemy African soldiers and, at times, even their own people, to European slave traders. The
proceeds often were used to purchase British guns and large quantities of alcohol. Patagonia
is the southernmost part of South America, a remote region legendary for its tales of giant
warriors who reached the height of twelve feet. The myth persisted through the nineteenth
century and was retold in a series of books popular before the Civil War.

2. *Louisiana History,* Journal of the Louisiana Historical Association, vol. 25, Winter 1984,
393. A pre-war New Orleans militia battery, the Washington Artillery, used a tiger in its sym-
bol. Eight years after being established in 1838, James B. Walton created its characteristic emblem, an irate tiger over crossed cannon barrels, with the motto "Try Us." The unit survives
to this day as a part of the Louisiana National Guard.

3. Terry L. Jones, *Lee's Tigers: The Louisiana Infantry in the Army of Northern Virginia*
(Baton Rouge: Louisiana State University Press, 1987), 35; Gary J. Schreckengost, "1st Louisiana Special Battalion at the First Battle of Manassas," *America's Civil War,* May 1999.

4. David E. Johnston, *The Story of a Confederate Boy in the Civil War* (Portland, Ore.: Glass
and Prudhomme Co., 1914), 80–81; Clement A. Evans, *A Confederate Military History,* vol. 10
(Atlanta, Ga.: Confederate Publishing Co., 1899), 208. During the Gettysburg Campaign,
Evans was colonel of the 31st Georgia in Gordon's Brigade of Early's Division. Later in the
war, he became a brigadier general and took command of the brigade when Gordon replaced
Early in division command.

5. Richmond *Daily Dispatch,* September 26, 1861.

6. Richmond *Daily Dispatch*, November 13, 1861; Johnston, *A Confederate Boy*, 81.

7. John S. Robson, *How a One-Legged Rebel Lives: Reminiscences of the Civil War: The Story of the Campaigns of Stonewall Jackson, as Told by a High Private in the "Foot Cavalry"* (Durham, N.C.: The Educator Co., 1898), 84.

8. Ezra J. Warner, *Generals in Gray: Lives of the Confederate Commanders* (Baton Rouge: Louisiana State University Press, 1959), 130.

9. Jack B. Welsh, *Medical Histories of Confederate Generals* (Kent, Ohio: Kent State University Press, 1995), 96; *The War of the Rebellion: A Compilation of the Official Records of the Union and Confederate Armies*, 70 volumes in 4 series (Washington D.C.: Government Printing Office, 1880-1901), series 1, vol. 19, part 1 (Serial 27), 918. Cited as *O.R.* from here on; all subsequent citations are from series 1 unless otherwise noted.

10. Robert Stiles, *Four Years Under Marse Robert* (New York and Washington: The Neale Publishing Co., 1904), 186.

11. John Herbert Roper, ed., *Repairing the "March of Mars": The Civil War Diaries of John Samuel Apperson* (Macon, Ga.: Mercer University Press, 2001), 312; David French Boyd, *Reminiscences of the War in Virginia*, ed. T. Michael Parrish (Austin, Texas: Jenkins Publishing Co., 1989), 34. Major Boyd's reminiscences were initially published in the New Orleans *Times-Democrat* on January 31 and February 7, 1897.

12. Arthur W. Bergeron Jr., *Guide to Louisiana Confederate Military Units 1861–1865* (Baton Rouge and London: Louisiana State University Press, 1989), 82–84. Camp Moore was located on 450 acres of land near Tangipahoa, a small town northeast of Baton Rouge. The training camp was named for Louisiana Governor Thomas Overton Moore.

13. Simon Wolf, *The American Jew as Patriot, Soldier and Citizen* (Philadelphia: The Levy-type Co., 1895), 192; Robert N. Rosen, *The Jewish Confederates* (Chapel Hill: University of North Carolina Press, 2002), 101.

14. James P. Gannon, "The 6th Louisiana Infantry at Gettysburg," *The Gettysburg Magazine*, no. 21, 88, July 1999; Bergeron, *Guide to Louisiana Confederate Military Units*, 84–87.

15. Files of the Archives and Manuscripts Collection, Austin History Center, Austin Public Library, Austin, Texas.

16. Edmund Gunderson obituary, January 27, 1924, Mason City *Globe-Gazette*, Mason City, Iowa.

17. Bergeron, *Guide to Louisiana Confederate Military Units*, 84–87.

18. Muster rolls, 7th Louisiana Infantry, Louisiana State Archives; Bergeron, *Guide to Louisiana Confederate Military Units*, 90–92.

19. *The News-Virginian*, Waynesboro, Virginia, July 20, 1961. Roden survived the Gettysburg Campaign but was captured along the Rappahannock River in November 1863. After being exchanged, he returned to duty in Hays' brigade sharpshooters during the Overland Campaign of 1864. At the Battle of Spotsylvania Court House on May 12, he suffered a severe wound to his left arm that necessitated an operation to resection his elbow, crippling him and causing him great pain for the rest of his life. He settled in Waynesboro after the Civil War and became a store clerk, eventually saving enough money to buy the establishment. He married, joined the Methodist Church, and abstained from alcohol, something that must have

required substantial willpower for the hard-drinking Irishman and former Louisiana Tiger. He was killed in a runaway carriage accident in August 1913.

20. Mrs. D. W. Leahy, "Colonel Davidson Bradfute Penn," *Louisiana Genealogical Register,* vol. 24, 1977, 247–52. In 1872, Penn was a candidate for lieutenant governor of Louisiana but lost a hotly disputed election. Claiming a legitimate right to the office, he urged the state militia to take power by force and throw out the Republican "usurpers." Penn's followers briefly revolted and seized the statehouse, and Louisiana's governor appealed to President Ulysses S. Grant for assistance. The militia dispersed after five days, but many in the former Confederacy supported Penn's position.

21. Bergeron, *Guide to Louisiana Confederate Military Units,* 87–90.

22. Terry L. Jones, "Going Back in the Union at Last: A Louisiana Tiger's account of the Gettysburg Campaign," *Civil War Times Illustrated,* vol. 29, no. 6, January/February 1991, 12.

23. Arthur W. Bergeron Jr., "Free Men of Color in Grey," *Civil War History,* vol. 32, no. 3, September 1986.

24. Bergeron, *Guide to Louisiana Confederate Military Units,* 92–95.

25. Thomas Benton Reed, *A Private in Gray* (Camden, Ark.: self-published, 1902), 5–7, 27, 32. Patrick Reed died at Second Manassas in August 1862 and Green Reed at Second Fredericksburg in May 1863.

26. Warner, *Generals in Gray,* 287–88; Bergeron, *Guide to Louisiana Confederate Military Units,* 93–95.

27. Warner, *Generals in Gray,* 231.

28. William L. Clements Library, University of Michigan, owners of the William and Isaac Seymour Papers in the Schoff Civil War Papers collection.

29. James B. Sheeran, *Confederate Chaplain: A War Journal of Rev. James B. Sheeran, c.ss.r., 14th Louisiana, C.S.A,* ed. Joseph T. Durkin (Milwaukee: Bruce Publications, 1960).

30. James Gannon, *Irish Rebels, Confederate Tigers: A History of the 6th Louisiana Volunteers, 1861–1865* (Campbell, Calif.: Savas Publishing Co., 1998), 95–96; Rev. John William Jones, *Christ in the Camp: Or Religion in Lee's Army* (Richmond: B. F. Johnson and Co., 1887), 516. Dr. J. William Jones, the chaplain for "Extra Billy" Smith's Brigade, spearheaded efforts to coordinate the activities of the various brigade and regimental chaplains within Early's Division, including Dr. Strickler. Jubal Early had previously commanded Smith's Brigade, and Reverend Jones was a familiar personage around divisional headquarters.

31. *O.R.,* vol. 12, part 3, 978–79; Warner, *Generals in Gray,* 130.

## CHAPTER 2

1. Randolph H. McKim, *A Soldier's Recollections: Leaves from the Diary of a Young Confederate* (New York: Longmans, Green, and Co., 1910), 134.

2. Richmond *Daily Dispatch,* June 1, 1863. According to the National Park Service, Hamilton's Crossing was named for Captain George Hamilton, whose home "Forest Hill" was located not far from the intersection of Mine Road and the Richmond, Fredericksburg, and Potomac Railroad. Hamilton's Crossing marked the right flank of Stonewall Jackson's defensive line during the Battle of Fredericksburg in December 1862. It had since become a major sup-

ply depot for the Army of Northern Virginia. Early's Division was camped on the low foothills along the Military Road, with advance pickets toward the Richmond Stage Road (River Road).

3. Richmond *Daily Dispatch,* June 6, 1863. The reporter added, "Senator Semmes was a citizen of New Orleans. His house is now occupied by the officials under Lincoln's brutal Military Governor of the Department [Major General Benjamin Butler, nicknamed "Beast Butler" by the southern media]. For the present he resides in Richmond."

4. G. W. Nichols, *A Soldier's Story of His Regiment (61st Georgia)* (Jesup, Ga.: self-published, 1898), 112.

5. Gannon, *Irish Rebels,* 170, quoting the George P. Ring diary, Louisiana Historical Association Collection (LHAC), Howard-Tilton Memorial Library, Tulane University; Reed, *A Private in Gray,* 34.

6. *O.R.,* vol. 27, part 3, 5–7, 70; Pharris Deloach Johnson, ed., *Under the Southern Cross: Soldier Life with Gordon Bradwell and the Army of Northern Virginia* (Macon, Ga.: Mercer University Press, 1999), 115; Ring diary, LHAC.

7. William J. Seymour, "A Louisiana Tiger: The Civil War Memoirs of Captain William J. Seymour," typescript manuscript, copy in the Library of the Gettysburg National Military Park (GNMP). Original (ed. Terry Jones) from the William J. Seymour Papers, Schoff Collection, Clements Library, University of Michigan; Jubal A. Early, *Lieutenant General Jubal Anderson Early, C.S.A.: Autobiographical Sketch and Narrative of the War Between the States* (Philadelphia: J. B. Lippincott Co., 1912), 238.

8. *The Diary of Bartlett Y. Malone* (Chapel Hill, N.C.: The University of North Carolina, The James Sprunt Historical Publications, vol. 16, no. 2, 1919), 36. Also, Diary of Sgt. B. Y. Yancy, 6th North Carolina State Troops, Brake Collection, U.S. Army Military History Institute, Carlisle, Pa.; William Seymour account, GNMP; Gannon, *Irish Rebels,* 170.

9. Reed, *A Private in Gray,* 47–48.

10. Jubal A. Early, "A Review by General Early," *Southern Historical Society Papers,* vol. 4, July 1887, Richmond, Virginia, 243.

11. *O. R.,* vol. 27, part 3, 55. Couch had requested another assignment after he became disillusioned with the command capabilities and indecisiveness of Army of the Potomac commander Joseph Hooker. He had returned to Washington to await further orders when the Confederates began moving from Culpeper toward the Shenandoah Valley. On June 10, the War Department created the Department of the Susquehanna and soon assigned Couch to organize and staff the new department and, more importantly, to defend Harrisburg until the Army of the Potomac could arrive. (For more on General Couch, see Al Gambone's book *Enigmatic Valor: Major General Darius N. Couch,* published by Butternut and Blue.)

12. Nichols, *61st Georgia,* 113.

13. Jedediah Hotchkiss, *Make Me a Map of the Valley: The Civil War Journal of Stonewall Jackson's Topographer,* ed. Archie McDonald (Dallas: Southern Methodist University Press, 1973), 150. Gaines' Crossroads is now known as Ben Venue, named for a nearby estate owned in 1863 by William Fletcher. The red brick mansion was General Ewell's headquarters.

14. *O.R.,* vol. 27, part 2, 43. General Milroy listed his strength as 6,900 effectives, not counting Colonel Andrew T. McReynolds' brigade at Berryville.

15. Winchester had 4,403 residents according to the 1860 U.S. Census. It is likely with the periodic exodus of refugees from the various military campaigns, as well as the hundreds of local men serving in the opposing armies, that less than 2,000 remained by the time of the Second Battle of Winchester.

16. Hotchkiss, *Make Me a Map*, 150.

17. Edward A. Moore, *The Story of a Cannoneer Under Stonewall Jackson* (New York and Washington: The Neale Co., 1907), 186. Moore was a member of the Rockbridge Artillery in Ewell's corps reserve artillery.

18. Reed, *A Private in Gray*, 68.

19. Lucy Rebecca Buck Diary, entry for June 12, 1863, in Elizabeth R. Baer, ed., *Shadows on My Heart: The Civil War Diary of Lucy Rebecca Buck of Virginia* (Athens, Ga.: University of Georgia Press, 1997), 212. Front Royal had been incorporated in 1788 and had grown steadily in the intervening seven decades before the Civil War. According to the 1860 U.S. Census, nearly a quarter of the population of 6,000 was slaves. Lucy Buck (1842–1918) was a member of one of the town's leading families. An ardent secessionist, she joined in the enthusiastic crowd as the troops passed near her family's farm, "Bel Air."

20. Thomas A. Ashby, *The Valley Campaigns: Being the Reminiscences of a Non-Combatant While Between the Lines in the Shenandoah Valley During the War of the States* (New York: Neale Publishing Co., 1914), 240.

21. James Gannon, *Irish Rebels*, 171; Early, *Autobiographical Sketch*, 238–39. Cedarville is about twelve miles south of Winchester.

22. George R. Prowell, *History of the Eighty-seventh Regiment, Pennsylvania Volunteers* (York, Pa.: The Press of the York Daily, 1903), 66; *O.R.*, vol. 27, part 2, 42; Michael G. Mahon, ed., *Winchester Divided: The Civil War Diaries of Julia Chase and Laura Lee* (Mechanicsburg, Pa.: Stackpole Books, 2002), 91. A small Confederate force under Captain W. L. Rasin, with the 14th Virginia Cavalry and a battalion of Maryland cavalry, was driven back by elements of the 87th Pennsylvania Infantry, 13th Pennsylvania Cavalry, and Randolph's Battery L, 5th U.S. Artillery. While the Federals reported no casualties, Milroy claimed the Rebels lost 87 men, 37 of whom were taken prisoner.

23. The stone Fahnestock house still stands near the old Pughtown Road (now known as the North Frederick Pike or U.S. Route 522). The village of Pughtown, about nine miles northwest of Winchester, was renamed Gainesboro well after the Civil War. An early settler named Job Pugh had laid out the hamlet in 1798.

24. During the Second Battle of Winchester, Milroy had a total of twenty-four guns—the six heavy guns in the Main Fort, the six guns of Battery L, 5th U.S. Artillery in the West Fort area, the six guns of Alexander's Baltimore Battery that moved into the Star Fort, and Carlin's six West Virginia pieces. (See Charles S. Grunder and Brandon H. Beck, *The Second Battle of Winchester* [Lynchburg, Va.: H. E. Howard, 1989] for more details.)

25. New York *Herald*, June 22, 1863. According to Milroy's report in the *Official Records*, these troops were the 18th Connecticut, 110th and 123rd Ohio, 87th Pennsylvania, and the 12th West Virginia, supported by Pennsylvania cavalry and Battery L, 5th U.S. Artillery.

26. Herbert's seven-company battalion, a part of Brigadier General George Steuart's brigade of Johnson's Division, had been raised primarily from remnants of an earlier battalion of

the same name that had been disbanded in August 1862, coupled with fresh recruits who had slipped into the South from eastern Maryland. Herbert would be severely wounded and captured at Gettysburg in the assault on Culp's Hill. (For more information, see W. W. Goldsborough's *The Maryland Line in the Confederate Army, 1861–1865*, from Butternut and Blue, 1983.)

27. Early, *Autobiographical Sketch*, 240. According to his service records, the New York–born Davis died May 25, 1862. A clerk in a New Orleans store before the war, he became the second lieutenant of Company A of the 7th Louisiana shortly after enlisting. He was twenty-seven at the time of his death at Front Royal. After the war, his remains were reinterred in the Stonewall Confederate Cemetery.

28. Hotchkiss, *Make Me a Map*, 151. The profitable Nathan Parkins mill was burned down by Union Major General David Hunter in 1864 as he destroyed the industrial and agricultural capabilities of Shenandoah Valley residents. It was not rebuilt until 1872, but the replacement turbine wheel-powered mill was unable to survive financially and soon closed (Winchester–Frederick County Historical Society).

29. *O.R.*, vol. 27, part 2, 476; Early, *Autobiographical Sketch*, 241–42. Bartonsville, a small community along the Opequon Creek in Frederick County, was also known as Barton's Mills or Bartonville.

30. Pritchard House marker, Kernstown Battlefield. Shenandoah Valley Battlefields National Historic District. The home was constructed in 1854. It was abandoned in the 1940s and fell into disrepair prior to its acquisition by the Kernstown Battlefield Association, which has restored and preserved it. Sixteen Union guns had occupied the hill during the First Battle of Kernstown; six were present during Second Winchester. The hill would again be an important position in the 1864 Second Battle of Kernstown.

31. Early, *Autobiographical Sketch*, 242.

32. *The Reminiscences of Private Lorenzo D. Barnhart, 110th Ohio Volunteer Infantry, Company B*. Transcribed by Roger Barnhart, 1998.

33. *O.R.*, vol. 27, part 2, 477; Early, *Autobiographical Sketch*, 242; David Lowe, *Study of Civil War Sites in the Shenandoah Valley of Virginia* (Washington D.C.: U.S. Department of the Interior, National Park Service, 1992). Gordon reported the loss of seventy-five men at Winchester, including several officers. The 123rd Ohio of Elliott's Brigade lost nearly one hundred men during the fight with Early's Division on the 13th.

34. Abram's Creek was also called Abrahams' Creek. It flows southeasterly through the Winchester region before turning east and flowing into Opequon Creek. The creek was named for prominent early Quaker businessman Abraham Hollingsworth, who constructed a grist mill along its banks in the mideighteenth century (Winchester–Frederick County Historical Society).

35. Early, *Autobiographical Sketch*, 243.

36. Johnson, *Under the Southern Cross*, 117, quoting Isaac G. Bradwell's article on Second Winchester from *Confederate Veteran*, September 1922.

37. Reed, *A Private in Gray*, 35–36; Johnson, *Under the Southern Cross*, 117.

38. *O.R.*, vol. 27, part 2, 54.

39. Charles H. Lynch, *The Civil War Diary, 1862–1865, of Charles H. Lynch, 18th Conn. Vol's* (Hartford, Conn.:, The Case, Lockwood and Brainard Co., 1915), 19.

40. Prowell, *History of the Eighty-seventh Regiment, Pennsylvania*, 70; *O.R.*, vol. 27, part 1, 42. The old spelling, *Harper's Ferry*, is used throughout this book in preference to the modern *Harpers Ferry*. Among the few Confederates taken prisoner on June 13 was Private Joseph E. Freeman of the 8th Louisiana. He had been captured at Second Fredericksburg in May, released and paroled, and then captured again at Second Winchester. He died from scurvy in 1864 in prison at Fort Delaware.

41. *O.R.*, vol. 27, part 2, 45.

42. Lowe, *Study of Civil War Sites.*

43. Reed, *A Private in Gray*, 36.

44. J. Warren Jackson to R. Stark Jackson, July 20, 1863, as quoted in Jones, "Going Back in the Union at Last," 12; Early, *Autobiographical Sketch*, 243.

45. *O.R.*, vol. 27, part 2, 440.

46. Early, *Autobiographical Sketch*, 244; *O.R.*, vol. 51, 1055.

47. *O.R.*, vol. 27, part 2, 440; Early, *Autobiographical Sketch*, 244.

48. Grunder and Beck, *Second Battle of Winchester*, 41; Early, *Autobiographical Sketch*, 244. Dr. Lupton is believed to have planted the first commercial apple orchard in the Shenandoah Valley in the 1850s, and within twenty years, he was one of the most successful and well known apple growers in Virginia, despite early skepticism from neighboring farmers. The sprawling farm, which eventually encompassed four thousand acres, was used at various times by Confederates as a campsite, including the Rockbridge Artillery for several days in late January 1862. During Milroy's 1863 occupation of the Winchester area, Lupton had hidden supplies of dried corn in his attic, awaiting a possible return by the Confederate army. However, squirrels darting in and out of the building revealed the corn's presence to Union officers. The old country lane used by Early to get into position behind Apple Pie Ridge is approximated by today's Echo Lane (Winchester–Frederick County Historical Society).

49. Early, *Autobiographical Sketch*, 245.

50. *O.R.*, vol. 27, part 2, 45, 55, 96.

51. Early, *Autobiographical Sketch*, 246; *O.R.*, vol. 27, part 2, 153. Captain Walter A. Powell, Milroy's chief engineer, had dispatched work crews cutting trees up to Saturday morning when General Milroy recalled all of them to man the defenses. Powell later testified that, in his opinion, the West Fort would not have fallen had the tree line been clearcut back 1,500 yards from the earthworks as intended. Time did not allow him the luxury of finishing the job before the Rebels arrived. He also planned to construct two traverses and add another flanking entrenchment to one of the lunettes.

52. Smith's Brigade formed into battle line in Mrs. Brierly's cornfield and then rested in the nearby woods, while Avery split his troops, sending the 57th North Carolina farther north. They would eventually cross the Pughtown Road and occupy some abandoned Federal works west of the Star Fort.

53. Thomas F. Wildes, *Record of the One Hundred and Sixteenth Regiment Ohio Infantry Volunteers in the War of the Rebellion* (Sandusky, Ohio: I. F. Mack and Bro., 1884), 57; J. Warren

Keifer, *Slavery and Four Years of War* (New York: G. P. Putnam's Sons, 1900), 10. Barnhart, *Reminiscences; O.R.*, vol. 27, part 2, 58. Company C of the 116th OVI, sporting brand new Springfield Model 1863 Rifles, was under the command of Captain Frederick H. Arckenoe.

54. Early, *Autobiographical Sketch*, 246–47.

55. Stiles, *Four Years Under Marse Robert*, 192; Jennings Cropper Wise, *The Long Arm of Lee, of the History of the Artillery of the Army of Northern Virginia*, vol. 2 (Lynchburg, Va.: J. P. Bell Co., 1915), 602–3.

56. Early, *Autobiographical Sketch*, 247. Carrington commanded his own Charlottesville Artillery, as well as Garber's Staunton (Virginia) Artillery, during the cannonade.

57. Keifer, *Slavery and Four Years of War*, 11.

58. Samuel H. Chisholm, "Forward the Louisiana Brigade," *Confederate Veteran*, vol. 27, November 1919, 449.

59. *O.R.*, vol. 27, part 2, 477; Seymour account, GNMP.

60. Napier Bartlett, *A Soldier's Story of the War* (New Orleans: Clark and Hofeline, 1884), 181.

61. *O.R.*, vol. 27, part 2, 77; Jackson letter, July 20, 1863, as quoted in Jones, "Going Back in the Union at Last," 12; Wise, *The Long Arm of Lee*, 603; Tom Reed of the 9th Louisiana mentioned in his diary hearing the report of a pistol as the signal just before Jones opened up. Carpenter's Battery, deployed east of the Valley Pike, was under the temporary command of Lieutenant William T. Lambie. Milroy had deployed the Baltimore Battery in the Star Fort, Carlin's West Virginians in the entrenchments south of Fort Milroy, and the Heavy Artillery inside the fort.

62. Barnhart, *Reminiscences; O.R.*, vol. 27, part 2, 477.

63. Lucy Buck, *Sad Earth, Sweet Heaven: The Diary of Lucy Rebecca Buck*, ed. William P. Buck (Birmingham, Ala.: Cornerstone, 1973), 197; Harry Gilmor, *Four Years in the Saddle* (New York: Harper and Brothers, 1866), 89; Cornelia Peake McDonald, *A Woman's Civil War: A Diary with Reminiscences of the War, from March 1862*, ed. Minrose C. Gwin (Madison, Wis.: University of Wisconsin Press, 1992), 156–57. Colonel James A. Mulligan of the 23rd Illinois commanded a garrison of Federal troops in Cumberland, Maryland. His men were not en route to relieve Milroy's beleaguered troops, despite the wishful thinking of the Union soldiers near Cornelia McDonald's house. Ironically, Mulligan would be mortally wounded south of Winchester on July 24, 1864, at the Second Battle of Kernstown. The antebellum Irish-American attorney from Chicago died two days later in the Samuel Pritchard house. His pregnant wife Marian hastened from their temporary Cumberland home to Winchester but arrived after Mulligan had expired (historical marker for Mulligan on the Kernstown Battlefield).

64. McKim, *A Soldier's Recollections*, 146.

65. William H. Beach, *The First New York (Lincoln) Cavalry: From April 19, 1861 to July 7, 1865* (New York: Lincoln Cavalry Association, 1902), 236.

66. Keifer, *Slavery and Four Years of War*, 11–12.

67. Seymour account, GNMP; Wise, *The Long Arm of Lee*, 603; Early, *Autobiographical Sketch*, 247; *O.R.*, vol. 27, part 2, 494. James C. Zimmerman of Avery's 57th North Carolina

wrote his wife on June 19 that "a shell would go over us at almost every second," but no one in the rear ranks was injured by the wild overshots.

68. Stiles, *Four Years Under Marse Robert*, 196–97.

69. J. Warren Keifer, *Official Reports of J. Warren Keifer, Major General of Volunteers* (Springfield, Ohio: Daily Republic Steam Job Office, 1866), 6; *O.R.*, vol. 27, part 2, 146; Beach, *The First New York (Lincoln) Cavalry*, 236.

70. Reed, *A Private in Gray*, 37.

71. S. D. Buck, *With the Old Confeds. Actual Experiences of a Captain in the Line* (Baltimore: H. E. Houck and Co., 1925).

72. Jones, *Lee's Tigers*, 159–60; *O.R.*, vol. 27, part 2, 63; John J. Rivera, "Two Heroines of the Shenandoah Valley," *Confederate Veteran* (8), November 1900, 495. Elizabeth A. "Lizzie" Yonley became known as "the Maid of Winchester" for her humanitarian efforts. She was sixteen and Alma eighteen according to the 1860 census of Hampshire County, [West] Virginia, where they lived at the time. The family was forced to move to Winchester when their large farmhouse was destroyed by Union troops.

73. Gilmor, *Four Years in the Saddle*, 89; McKim, *A Soldier's Recollections*, 146.

74. *O.R.*, vol. 27, part 2, 477; Keifer, *Official Reports*, 6.

75. Reed, *A Private in Gray*, 37.

76. Barnhart, *Reminiscences*.

77. Keifer, *Slavery and Four Years of War*, 11.

78. Andrew B. Booth, *Records of Louisiana Confederate Soldiers and Louisiana Confederate Commands*, 3 vols. (Spartanburg, S.C.: Reprint Co., 1984). On July 26, the one-legged Barnett would be captured by Federal troops at Jordan Springs, not far from Winchester. He was paroled in early August but never fought again. He returned to Livingston Parish, where he lived for more than five decades, dying in October 1918. Jordan Springs, known for its therapeutic sulfur water, was a logical choice for the Confederate field hospital.

79. Gilmor, *Four Years in the Saddle*, 89–90; Keifer, *Slavery and Four Years of War*, 12; *O.R.*, vol. 27, part 2, 46, 63.

80. Belle Boyd, *Belle Boyd, In Camp and Prison*, vol. 1 (London: Saunders, Otley, and Co., 1865), 250–51. The nineteen-year-old Boyd, a celebrity for her assistance in helping Stonewall Jackson capture Front Royal in the 1862 Valley Campaign, was returning to her parents' home in Martinsburg following an extended tour of the South. She had ridden within four miles of Winchester when she heard the artillery. Anxious to see the outcome, she rode onto the heights, joined by the unidentified crippled officer, and sat for some time "absorbed in the struggle that was going on beneath us." Mounted on a white horse on the hilltop and accompanied by other riders, she made a conspicuous target for Union gunners three-quarters of a mile away. Pleased with Milroy's defeat, Miss Boyd later wrote, "The battle was not of long duration. The terms were too [un]equal to leave the issue long in doubt."

81. *O.R.*, vol. 27, part 2, 74; Barnhart, *Reminiscences*; Reed, *A Private in Gray*, 37.

82. *O.R.*, vol. 27, part 2, 478; Janet B. Hewitt, Noah Andre Trudeau, and Bryce A. Suderow, eds., *Supplement to the Official Records of the Union and Confederate Armies* (hereafter cited as *O.R. Supplement*), part 2, Record of Events, vol. 24, Serial 36 (Wilmington, N.C.: Broadfoot

Publishing, 1994), 80. Orr survived his wound and returned to duty. He was captured later in the war and spent months in the Johnson's Island prison camp near Sandusky, Ohio. After the war, he moved to Austin, Texas.

83. Barnhart, *Reminiscences.*

84. John R. Rhoades Papers, Rutherford B. Hayes Presidential Center, Fremont, Ohio; Thomas E. Pope, *The Weary Boys: Colonel J. Warren Keifer and the 110th Ohio Volunteer Infantry* (Kent, Ohio: Kent State University Press, 2002), 41.

85. Lt. James C. Bush, "The Fifth Regiment of Artillery," *The Army of the United States: Historical Sketches of Staff and Line with Portraits of Generals-in-Chief,* ed. Theo. F. Rodenbaugh (New York: Maynard, Merrill, and Co., 1896), 383; *O.R.,* vol. 27, part 2, 74; Stiles, *Four Years Under Marse Robert,* 192. Stiles, a Yale-educated Kentucky native who was raised in New York City and Connecticut, had moved to Richmond before the war to practice law. He joined the Richmond Howitzers and later served on a volunteer basis in the Gettysburg Campaign with the Charlottesville, Virginia, Artillery. Lieutenant Randolph would be left behind in Winchester to recuperate and would be captured by the Confederates. Randolph and the Cincinnati resident Spooner had been promoted to lieutenant on May 16, 1861, and assigned to the 5th Artillery. Later in 1863, Spooner would be assigned permanent command of Battery H, 5th U.S. Artillery at Chattanooga following the death of Lieutenant Howard M. Burnham in the Battle of Chickamauga.

86. Keifer, *Official Reports,* 6; Keifer, *Slavery and Four Years of War,* 11.

87. Reed, *A Private in Gray,* 37; Chisholm, "Forward the Louisiana Brigade," 449; Larry B. Maier, *Gateway to Gettysburg: The Second Battle of Winchester* (Shippensburg, Pa.: Burd Street Press, 2002), 122.

88. Barnhart, *Reminiscences.*

89. Wildes, *116th Ohio Infantry,* 57, 305–6, 331. In 1864, Lieutenant Horney would die in captivity in a prison camp in Columbia, South Carolina. Levi Lupton was not related to Dr. John Lupton, the owner of Walnut Grove where Early had stopped earlier in the day. The lieutenant would spend much of the rest of the year locked up in Libby Prison in Richmond. Frederick Arckenoe had been educated at some of Germany's finest military schools and had traveled to the United States after the failed Revolution of 1848. He had enlisted in the 116th in September 1862 with the rank of captain. The majority of his Company C was also Germans, who deeply mourned his loss.

90. Bush, "The Fifth Regiment of Artillery," 383; *O.R.,* vol. 27, part 2, 74, 112, 146.

91. Wise, *The Long Arm of Lee,* 604.

92. Gilmor, *Four Years in the Saddle,* 90.

93. *O.R.,* vol. 27, part 2, 478.

94. Jackson letter, July 20, 1863, as quoted in Jones, "Going Back in the Union at Last," 55; Seymour account, GNMP.

95. Reed, *A Private in Gray,* 37.

96. *O.R.,* vol. 27, part 2, 478.

97. Lynch, *Civil War Diary,* 20. The 18th Connecticut had been organized in August 1862 but had spent most of its service time in various posts around Baltimore, including Fort McHenry. Second Winchester was their first battle.

98. Wise, *The Long Arm of Lee*, 604; Beach, *The First New York (Lincoln) Cavalry*, 238.

99. Stiles, *Four Years Under Marse Robert*, 192–94, 197. In other contemporary accounts of Captain Thompson's death, he suffered a wound to his left wrist and bled to death before he could be treated.

100. Beach, *The First New York (Lincoln) Cavalry*, 238.

101. Early, *Autobiographical Sketch*, 248.

102. Gannon, *Irish Rebels*, 179. Lt. M. McNamara, "Lieutenant Charlie Pierce's Daring Attempts to Escape from Johnson's Island," *Southern Historical Society Papers*, vol. 8, 1880, 61. Charles H. Pierce would reluctantly break the prized sword over his knee rather than surrender it when much of his brigade was captured at Rappahannock Station in November 1863. He handed the hilt to his captor. He would try in vain to escape from Johnson's Island in Lake Erie but would not be paroled until the end of the war.

103. Reed, *A Private in Gray*, 38.

104. McKim, *A Soldier's Recollections*, 147; Buck, *Sad Earth, Sweet Heaven*, 197; McDonald, *A Woman's Civil War*, 160. The historian of the 87th Pennsylvania, George R. Prowell, believed the "terrible artillery duel" stopped about 8:00 p.m., but most other accounts place its cessation later in the evening. He mentioned that General Milroy ascended the flagpole in his basket during the height of the cannonade to observe the enemy. Milroy remained there with "remarkable coolness and bravery" as solid shots whizzed by and large shells exploded around him.

105. John B. Gordon, *Reminiscences of the Civil War* (New York: Charles Scribner's Sons, 1904), 68.

106. Richmond *Daily Dispatch*, June 25, 1863; Jackson letter, July 20, 1863, as quoted in Jones, "Going Back in the Union at Last," 55.

107. Stuart Sifakis, *Compendium of the Confederate Armies: Louisiana* (New York: Facts on File, 1992), 78–80. Colonel Keifer reported fifty-five casualties from his 110th Ohio Volunteer Infantry in the three days of fighting. He claimed the Confederates lost one hundred men killed and four hundred wounded. He based this inaccurate assessment on secondhand information from Winchester citizens, Confederate prisoners taken in the weeks after the battle, and Rebel accounts (*O.R.*, vol. 27, part 2, 64).

108. James Perrin, "The Thomas M. Terry Family, Tangipahoa Parish, Louisiana," self-published. Vitrivius Terry is buried in the Louisiana section of the Confederate cemetery in Winchester, along with scores of other victims of the various battles in the region.

109. Booth, *Records of Louisiana Confederate Soldiers*, vol. 3, 677; vol. 1, 216.

110. Wildes, *116th Ohio Infantry*, 57, 83.

111. Rivera, "The Heroines of the Shenandoah Valley," 496. After the war, both sisters married and moved to Little Rock, Arkansas. Alma V. Chapman died in 1891. Captain Rivera was a New-York born former New Orleans newspaper printer. He would move to New York City, work in the newspaper business, and outlive all the other field officers of the 6th Louisiana. In 1900, he, John Orr, and another surviving Tiger presented Lizzie Heironimus with a commemorative medal to thank her for her gracious care for the wounded at Second Winchester.

112. After the war, Charlestown became known as Charles Town to avoid confusion with

Charleston, West Virginia. The Blue Ridge foothill town was named for George Washington's brother Charles, who plotted the streets and laid out the plan for the original village.

113. Beach, *The First New York (Lincoln) Cavalry*, 241; Lowe, *Study of Civil War Sites*; O.R., vol. 27, part 2, 56.

114. O.R., vol. 27, part 2, 53, 88, 464.

115. Seymour account, GNMP. General Gordon later wrote that the planned attack on Fort Milroy was the only time in the war he had a strong presentiment of dying, and he wrote a farewell letter to his wife to be delivered after his death. He "expected the storm of shell and ball that would end many a life, my own among them." He was relieved to learn the fort had been evacuated during the night (Gordon, *Reminiscences of the Civil War*, 68–69).

116. Laura Lee diary, entry for June 15, 1863. Handley Regional Library, Winchester–Frederick County Historical Society, Winchester, Va.; original in the collection of the College of William and Mary; McDonald, *A Woman's Civil War*, 160.

117. Mahon, *Winchester Divided*, 93; Johnson, *Under the Southern Cross*, 119. Following the war, Bradwell wrote a series of illustrative articles that were published in various issues of *Confederate Veteran*, including one entitled "Capture of Winchester, Va., and Milroy's Army in June, 1863." He reported that General Gordon rode out of Fort Milroy triumphantly dragging the garrison's huge flag, which "floated out thirty feet behind on the morning air." Seventeen women were captured in Winchester following the Confederate occupation on the fifteenth. The historian of the 87th Pennsylvania mentioned that the "loyal ladies" were kept in the Castle Thunder prison in Richmond for ten days before being released and sent to Washington D.C. under a flag of truce.

118. Richmond *Daily Dispatch*, June 17, 1863; Stiles, *Four Years Under Marse Robert*, 192. Although the field over which the Louisiana Brigade attacked West Fort has been divided in modern times by the Route 37 bypass, the basic terrain is still intact as pastures and apple orchards, and this adds to the interpretation of the battle.

119. Richmond *Daily Dispatch*, June 20, 1863; Michael Jacobs, *Notes on the Rebel Invasion of Maryland and Pennsylvania and the Battle of Gettysburg* (Philadelphia: J. B. Lippincott and Co., 1864), 9. Miss Cassandra Small of York, Pennsylvania, later wrote a descriptive account of Jubal Early's men during their occupation of York on June 28–30. Of particular interest were those Confederates who wore knapsacks emblazoned 87 PA Regt., for much of that regiment hailed from the York County region. It was widely scattered following Milroy's debacle at Stephenson's Depot on June 15.

120. Edmond Stephens to parents, June 20, 1863, Stephens Collection, Northwestern State University, as quoted in Jones, *Lee's Tigers*, 163.

121. Booth, *Records of Louisiana Confederate Soldiers*, vol. 1, 59.

122. Bergeron, *Guide to Louisiana Confederate Military Units*, 84–86; Ella Lonn, *Foreigners in the Confederacy* (Chapel Hill: University of North Carolina Press, 2002), 108; New Orleans *Commercial Bulletin*, February 24, 1862; Gannon, "The 6th Louisiana at Gettysburg," 89.

123. Early, *Autobiographical Sketch*, 250–51; *Pennsylvania at Salisbury, North Carolina: Ceremonies at the Dedication of the Memorial . . .* (Harrisburg, Pa.: C. E. Auginbaugh, State Printer, 1912), 49; Reed, *A Private in Gray*, 38. Major White would be sent to Libby Prison in Richmond and then to a prison camp in Salisbury, North Carolina. He would escape in 1864 and rejoin the Union army.

124. Seymour account, GNMP.

125. McKim, *A Soldier's Recollections*, 155; Jackson letter, July 20, 1863, as quoted in Jones, "Going Back in the Union at Last," 55; Seymour account, GNMP; *O.R. Supplement*, part 2, Record of Events, vol. 24, serial 36, 68.

126. Nichols, *61st Georgia*, 114. Boteler's Ford, about a mile downstream from Shepherdstown, is also known as Pack Horse Ford, Shepherdstown Ford, and Blackford's Ford. It had been used by travelers since the Native Americans lived in the region. Because the highway bridge across the Potomac River at Shepherdstown had been destroyed earlier in the war, most of Lee's army had waded across this ford during the Maryland Campaign. The Louisiana Tigers would cross it again during Early's 1864 raid on Washington D.C.

127. Early, *Autobiographical Sketch*, 252; Early, "Review," *Southern Historical Society Papers*, 244.

128. Seymour account, GNMP; Johnson, *Under the Southern Cross*, 120.

129. *Evergreen City Times*, Sheboygan, Wisconsin, vol. 10, no. 19, quoting the correspondent of the New York *World*; *O.R.*, vol. 27, part 3, 297. Couch had requested another assignment after he became disillusioned with the command capabilities and indecisiveness of Army of the Potomac commander Joseph Hooker. He had returned to Washington to await further orders when the Confederates began moving from Culpeper toward the Shenandoah Valley. On June 10, the Department of the Susquehanna had been created, with Couch assigned to organize and staff the new department and, more importantly, to defend Harrisburg if it was threatened until the Army of the Potomac could arrive.

130. Terry L. Jones, *Cemetery Hill: The Struggle for the High Ground, July 1–3, 1863* (New York: Da Capo Press, 2003), 18; James B. Sheeran, *Confederate Chaplain: A War Journal of Rev. James B. Sheeran, c.ss.r., 14th Louisiana, C.S.A.*, ed. Joseph T. Durkin (Milwaukee: Bruce Publications, 1960), 47.

## CHAPTER 3

1. *O.R.*, vol. 27, part 3, 914.

2. *Staunton Vindicator*, July 3, 1863. General Orders no. 49.

3. Early, *Autobiographical Sketch*, 254. Colonel William Henderson French was an antebellum friend of Jubal Early but would draw the general's ire on the march through Pennsylvania when he headed to the rear, citing exhaustion.

4. Seymour account, GNMP; Jackson letter, July 20, 1863, as quoted in Jones, "Going Back in the Union at Last," 55.

5. Richmond *Daily Dispatch*, June 27, 1863.

6. Early, *Autobiographical Sketch*, 254; *O.R.*, vol. 27, part 2, 25–27. Beeves is a colloquial term for cattle. Union scouts erroneously reported to Brigadier General Daniel Tyler, commander of the Eighth Army Corps' cavalry, that Early's Division had 34 guns and 15,000 infantrymen. In reality, Early had Jones' 16 guns and less than 6,000 men as he crossed the Potomac.

7. Malone diary, 36: *O.R.*, vol. 27, part 3, 289. The 6th North Carolina of Avery's Brigade found a "good meney Secesh" among the 475 residents in Smithsburg, a rarity as most of the Marylanders encountered by Early's Division were clearly northern sympathizers. Smithsburg was only four miles from decidedly Yankee-leaning Waynesboro, Pa., and residents of the two villages often quarreled over secession (Jacob H. Stoner, *Historical Papers: Franklin*

*County and the Cumberland Valley, Pennsylvania* [Chambersburg, Pa.: The Craft Press, 1947], 368). The two residents, John P. Shank and Adam C. Hildebrandt, relayed information to Professor Winchester that Early had twelve infantry regiments. He actually had eleven, although his divisional pioneers are known to have marched into York on June 28 as a separate body. If they did the same at Smithsburg, it would explain the minor discrepancy in number of units. The duo exaggerated the number of troops Early had with him (estimating 8,000), which in reality was less than 4,500 (Gordon's six regiments were on the parallel Leitersburg Road).

8. Jackson letter, July 20, 1863, as quoted in Jones, "Going Back in the Union at Last," 56; Booth, *Records of Louisiana Confederate Soldiers,* vol. 2, 140.

9. U.S. Census of 1880 (National Archives, Washington D.C., microfilm T9-1132, page 591C).

10. Stoner, *Historical Papers,* 368. Waynesboro was originally named "Waynesburg" in honor of Revolutionary War General "Mad" Anthony Wayne. John Wallace, one of Wayne's former soldiers, plotted the new town in 1797. The name was changed to Waynesboro in 1831 to avoid confusion with other Pennsylvania settlements also named Waynesburg. The area had witnessed several battles with Native Americans during the French and Indian War, including a widely reported massacre of two sisters named Rinfrew.

11. Stoner, *Historical Papers,* 370.

12. Lida Welsh Bender, "Civil War Memories," *The Outlook,* June 24, 1925, Franklin County Historical Society, Chambersburg, Pa., reprinted January 12, l961, by the *Record Herald.*

13. Stoner, *Historical Papers,* 369–70; Seymour account, GNMP. Fairfield was also known as Millerstown.

14. Bender, "Civil War Memories."

15. Jackson letter, July 20, 1863, as quoted in Jones, "Going Back in the Union at Last," 56; Bender, "Civil War Memories; Stoner, *Historical Papers,* 369.

16. Stiles, *Four Years Under Marse Robert,* 201. Major Stiles does not precisely locate where this anecdote occurred, simply stating it was "a bright day toward the end of June" and that "two or three of my Yale classmates were from the very region we were traversing." Stiles graduated in 1859 with ten Pennsylvanians, one of whom was from Lancaster County and another from Huntingdon County, according to Yale records. None of his classmates were from the Cumberland Valley or York County, the "very region" Stiles was traversing, so exactly which town he referred to remains unidentified. I have chosen to locate it near Waynesboro since the Tigers camped in woods within walking distance of a small town on a bright day—guesswork indeed, but within reason.

17. Bender, "Civil War Memories."

18. Stoner, *Historical Papers,* 369–70.

19. Bender, "Civil War Memories"; Stoner, *Historical Papers,* 369–70.

20. Bender, "Civil War Memories."

21. Stoner, *Historical Papers,* 370–71.

22. *Mobile Advertiser and Register,* August 9, 1863. Written by "an Alabamian in Lee's army" (ascribed to Lieutenant William D. Lyon of Gordon's Brigade).

23. Jackson letter, July 20, 1863, as quoted in Jones, "Going Back in the Union at Last," 56.

24. J. Arthur Taylor to his father, W. S. Taylor, July 9, 1863; Richmond *Daily Whig,* July 23, 1863. Vertical Files of the Gettysburg National Military Park; Stoner, *Historical Papers,* 371.

25. Bender, "Civil War Memories."

26. Bender, "Civil War Memories"; *Valley Spirit,* June 5, 1863.

27. John Lockwood, *Our Campaign Around Gettysburg* (Brooklyn: A. H. Rome, 1864), 120. While Lockwood does not identify the Confederate unit involved in this incident, it is consistent with other accounts from Early's Division. Altodale is today known as Mount Alto. During the Civil War era, it was also known as Funkstown, after its founder, John Funk.

28. Nichols, *61st Georgia,* 115. Nichols, who at times exaggerated or twisted the facts, later reported that, during the retreat of Lee's army following Gettysburg, he saw an immense crowd of sheep and cattle near Mount Jackson, Virginia. Within a two-mile stretch of clover fields at Horseshoe Bend in the Shenandoah River bottom were 26,000 head of cattle and 22,000 sheep. The bend was "almost full" of confiscated livestock, mostly from Pennsylvania's Cumberland Valley.

29. Seymour account, GNMP.

30. Reed, *A Private in Gray,* 39.

31. *O.R.,* vol. 27, part 3, 297.

32. Early, *Autobiographical Sketch,* 254–55.

33. Jackson letter, July 20, 1863, as quoted in Jones, "Going Back in the Union at Last," 56; Seymour account, GNMP.

34. Clement Evans' diary entry for June 25, 1863, as quoted in Robert Grier Stephens Jr., ed., *Intrepid Warrior: Clement Anselm Evans* (Dayton, Ohio: Morningside Press, 1992), 218.

35. Early, "Review," *Southern Historical Society Papers,* vol. 4, 241–81; *O.R.,* vol. 27, part 2, 316.

36. Early, *Autobiographical Sketch,* 255–56. Among these guides were the Latimer brothers from York, who were privates serving in the 1st Maryland of Steuart's Brigade in Johnson's Division. Another was one of Rodes' staff officers, known to history through his pen name of Colonel W. H. Swallow. He had been detached while Ewell was at Hagerstown and ordered to report to Early. Swallow was acquainted with many of the leading residents of York.

37. Malone diary, 37; Seymour account, GNMP.

38. Early, *Autobiographical Sketch,* 256; *O.R.,* vol. 27, part 2, 465.

39. Early, *Autobiographical Sketch,* 257; Malone, 36. Avery and Smith's brigades camped in the southwestern corner of the village, accompanied by Jones' artillery battalion. In the early evening, Jones dispatched Captain William Tanner's battery to Gettysburg per Jubal Early's orders.

40. Seymour account, GNMP. The Tigers marched that day fifteen miles, with twelve additional miles for the two regiments sent off on the fruitless chase of the 26th PVM.

41. Sue King Black to Belle Miller Willard, files of the Adams County Historical Society (ACHS).

42. Isaac G. Bradwell, "The Burning of Wrightsville, Pennsylvania," *Confederate Veteran,* vol. 27 (1919), 300.

43. Fannie Buehler account, GNMP and ACHS.

44. Samuel Bushman account, ACHS; Reed, *A Private in Gray,* 39.

45. *Philadelphia Press,* July 2, 1863.

46. Jacobs, *Notes on the Rebel Invasion,* 17; Jackson letter, July 20, 1863, as quoted in Jones, "Going Back in the Union at Last," 56.

47. Vertical files, Library of the York County Heritage Trust (YCHT).

48. Early, *Autobiographical Sketch*, 258; Jackson letter, July 20, 1863, as quoted in Jones, "Going Back in the Union at Last," 56; Henry E. Jacobs, Adams County *Star and Sentinel*, Gettysburg, July 30, 1885. Professor Michael Jacobs of Pennsylvania College kept detailed notes on the weather in Gettysburg, including June and July of 1863. He wrote, "The entire period of the invasion is remarkable for being one of clouds, and, for that season of the year, of low temperature. From June 15th until July 22nd, 1863, there was not an entirely clear day. . . . On the evening of June 25th at 8 p.m. a rain began. . . . This rain continued at intervals until Saturday June 27th, at 7:00 a.m., the precipitation being in inches 1.280." Years after the battle, Jacobs' son Henry published the Gettysburg-related entries in a local newspaper.

49. Seymour account, GNMP; Reed, *A Private in Gray*, 40.

50. Reed, *A Private in Gray*, 40–41.

51. Charles Moore Jr. account, Robert F. Brake Collection, Army Education and Heritage Center, U.S. Army Military History Institute (USAMHI), Carlisle, Pennsylvania; Compiled Service Records.

52. Booth, *Records of Louisiana Confederate Soldiers*, vol. 1, 141–42. According to researcher Dr. Mark Snell, York County lore is that a Confederate deserter was killed by a citizen while trying to steal a horse. The dead southerner was buried near the intersection of Canal Road and East Berlin Road.

53. Seymour account, GNMP.

54. Adams County Damage Claims, ACHS; Files of the York County Heritage Trust.

55. Charles Moore account, USAMHI. Now the paper mill town of Spring Grove, Spring Forge was originally called Lichey's Church (YCHT).

56. John A. Gibson, *History of York County, Pennsylvania, with Illustrations* (Chicago: F. A. Battey Publishing Co., 1886), 686.

57. Cassandra Morris (Small) Blair to Lissie Latimer, June 30, 1863, York County Heritage Trust, York, Pennsylvania (Reprinted as *Letters of '63* [Detroit: Stair-Jordan-Baker, 1988]). The thirty-four-year-old daughter of prominent merchant Philip Albright Small, Cassandra wrote three letters to her cousin that were discovered sixty-five years later in a wooden box in the attic of her relative's home.

58. Thomas W. Cutrer and T. Michael Parrish, *Brothers in Gray: The Civil War Letters of the Pierson Family* (Baton Rouge: Louisiana State University Press, 1997), 213. Captain Pierson went into the Battle of Gettysburg carrying a musket in the ranks; he would not be formally restored to command of Company C until mid-November, after petitioning for a formal hearing on the charges. The Georgia-born graduate of Mount Lebanon University was the oldest of four brothers in the Confederate service. He died July 28, 1864, in a minor skirmish at Snicker's Gap during Early's Valley Campaign.

59. McClure, *East of Gettysburg*, 57.

60. George R. Prowell, *History of York County, Pennsylvania* (Chicago: J. H. Beers and Co., 1907), 1072. The Loucks Mill would be destroyed by fire in 1864 and rebuilt as a five-story wooden building. Neither the Loucks Mill nor the Codorus Mill stands today, and the Tigers' campsite has been essentially swallowed up by modern construction.

61. Pennsylvania Adjutant General's office, Records Referring to Civil War Border Claims:

Damage Claim Applicants, RG-2, York County Damage Claims, reel 25, Samuel Hively claim. Pennsylvania State Archives, Harrisburg.

62. Seymour account, GNMP.

63. *O.R.*, vol. 27, part 2, 467; Civil War files of the York County Heritage Trust.

64. Prowell, *History of York County*, 411.

65. Charles Moore account, USAMHI.

66. Seymour account, GNMP. Mrs. Codwise may have been Louise C. Beatrice Codwise. She and her husband George attended the St. John's Episcopal Church in downtown York. Seymour claims the fee for the tickets was five dollars; most other contemporary accounts state it was one dollar.

67. Early, *Autobiographical Sketch*, 265.

68. James W. Latimer to Bartow Latimer, letter dated July 8, 1863. Latimer Family Files, YCHT.

69. Gibson, *History of York County*, 208.

70. Gibson, *History of York County*, 208; James W. Latimer to Bartow Latimer, July 8, 1863, YCHT.

71. Cassandra Small to Lissie Latimer, July 20, 1863, YCHT.

72. Prowell, *History of York County*, 412; Gettysburg *Compiler*, June 28, 1911.

73. Cassandra Small to Lissie Latimer, July 8, 1863, YCHT.

74. James W. Latimer to Bartow Latimer, July 8, 1863, YCHT; McClure, *East of Gettysburg*, 63.

75. Early, *Autobiographical Sketch*, 261–62; *O.R.*, vol. 27, part 2, 443.

76. McClure, *East of Gettysburg*, 72; Prowell, *History of York County*, 411.

77. *Documents of the U.S. Sanitary Commission*, vol. 2, nos. 61 to 95 (New York, 1865), Report no. 71, 5–8.

78. Samuel P. Bates, *Martial Deeds of Pennsylvania* (Philadelphia: T. H. Davis and Co., 1876), 180–81.

79. Prowell, *History of York County*, 413.

80. Cassandra Small to Lissie Latimer, July 8, 1863, YCHT; E. A. Patterson, "Story of the War," Files of the National Park Service, Fredericksburg and Spotsylvania National Military Park, Fredericksburg, Va.

81. Richmond *Times-Dispatch*, February 19, 1905.

82. Seymour account, GNMP.

83. Pennsylvania Adjutant General's office, Records Referring to Civil War Border Claims: Damage Claim Applicants, RG-2, York County Damage Claims, reels 28, 30, and 31. Pennsylvania State Archives, Harrisburg. Several merchants who received worthless Confederate money or drafts later filed claims to the government for recompense. None was forthcoming.

84. Gibson, *History of York County*, 209.

85. Reed, *A Private in Gray*, 41.

86. Philadelphia *Press*, July 11, 1863.

87. Seymour account, GNMP; Cassandra Small letters, YCHT.

88. Civil War vertical files, YCHT.

89. Seymour account, GNMP.

90. York County Damage Claims, rolls 29–30, Pennsylvania State Archives. Eyewitness Adam Hake watched Rebels under General "Hayes" take the Rutters' property. He later presented sworn testimony on their behalf during legal dispositions to determine if they were entitled to any recompense. The Rutters asked for $705; they received nothing. Few Pennsylvanians were awarded any significant cash for their claims.

91. York County Damage Claims, Reel 25, John C. Hake claim.

92. Fernando G. Cartland, *Southern Heroes, or, The Friends in War Time* (Cambridge, Mass.: The Riverside Press, 1895), 241.

93. *Biographical and Historical Memoirs of Northwest Louisiana* (Chicago and Nashville: The Southern Publishing Co., 1890), 279.

94. *O.R.*, vol. 27, part 2, 467. A copy of Early's handbill is in the files of the Library of the York County Heritage Trust.

95. Jackson letter, July 20, 1863, as quoted in Jones, "Going Back in the Union at Last," 56.

96. Charles Moore account, USAMHI.

97. Prowell, *History of York County*, 414; Jackson letter, July 20, 1863, as quoted in Jones, "Going Back in the Union at Last," 56.

98. Early, *Autobiographical Sketch*, 263.

99. *O.R. Supplement*, part 2, Record of Events, vol. 24, Serial 36, 87.

100. Bates, *Martial Deeds of Pennsylvania*, 180–81; Booth, *Records of Louisiana Confederate Soldiers*, vol. 1, 570. Derie's entry reads "deserted to the enemy, June 30th, 1863." The former New Orleans store clerk was paroled at Fort McHenry on July 6.

101. James W. Latimer to Bartow Latimer, June 30, 1863, YCHT; Early, "Review," *Southern Historical Society Papers*, 267.

102. Gettysburg *Compiler*, July 5, 1905, as quoted in Gregory A. Coco, *Wasted Valor: The Confederate Dead at Gettysburg* (Gettysburg: Thomas Publications, 1990), 110; National Archives, Compiled Service Records. Microcopy M320. Regimental service records indicate he was "absent, left sick about June 28 near Gettysburg, supposed to be a prisoner ... left sick on march through Penn., supposed to be dead." At least twenty-two other Confederates, nearly all of them unknown from Rodes' Division, were buried on the Schriver farm after the Battle of Gettysburg. By 1873, all trace of their graves was gone, and there are no records that the remains of the unfortunate Shackleford were ever recovered or removed to the South for reburial.

103. Prowell, *History of York County*, 414. One of these CSA bills was preserved and presented to the Historical Society of York County by George W. Gross, of Admire, Dover Township, in 1904.

104. *Commemorative Biographical Record of Washington County, Pennsylvania* (Chicago: J. H. Beers and Co., 1893), 389. While a prisoner of the 5th Louisiana, Sergeant Bell witnessed the three-day fight at Gettysburg, spending his time during the first day in helping to dress the wounds of his fellow prisoners and directing them to hospitals. He was paroled on July 4 and sent to Carlisle with roughly 1,400 other prisoners of war whom Lee chose not to take back to Virginia during his retreat. Bell eventually returned to his regiment to be remounted and re-equipped for active duty. After the war, he became a prosperous banker.

105. Jackson letter, July 20, 1863, as quoted in Jones, "Going Back in the Union at Last," 56.

106. Seymour manuscript, GNMP.

107. Early, *Autobiographical Sketch*, 264.

## CHAPTER 4

1. *O.R.*, vol. 27, part 2, 468, 479; Charles Moore account, USAMHI; Richmond *Daily Dispatch*, February 22, 1864.

2. Henry E. Jacobs, Adams County *Star and Sentinel*, Gettysburg, July 30, 1885.

3. Early, *Autobiographical Sketch*, 265.

4. William H. Swallow, "The First Day at Gettysburg," *Southern Bivouac*, December 1885, 439; Jacob Hoke, *The Great Invasion of 1863; or General Lee in Pennsylvania* (Dayton, Ohio: W. J. Shuey, 1887). "W. H. Swallow" was a prolific postbellum writer who served as the adjutant general of Rodes' Division according to Jacob Hoke and other nineteenth-century sources. Some contemporary scholars believe this may have been a pseudonym because Confederate service records do not show a commissioned officer by that name, nor does Swallow appear in the *Official Records* of the Gettysburg Campaign. While at Hagerstown, the Marylander had been dispatched by Ewell to join Early's column because of his familiarity with the Gettysburg and York regions, particularly the latter.

5. Seymour account, GNMP; Augustus Buell, *The Cannoneer: Recollections of Service in the Army of the Potomac* (Washington D.C.: The National Tribune, 1890), 98.

6. *O.R.*, vol. 27, part 2, 444; Early, *Autobiographical Sketch*, 266; vertical files of the Library of the GNMP. The third section (Merkel's) was deployed separately.

7. Early, *Autobiographical Sketch*, 267.

8. Early, *Autobiographical Sketch*, 267.

9. *O.R.*, vol. 27, part 2, 495–97. Captain Charles A. Green had replaced Captain Charles Thompson, the previous battery commander who had been killed at Second Winchester. A Union gun captured from Captain Louis Heckman's Ohio battery was later added to Jones' battalion to replace the permanently damaged gun.

10. *Pennsylvania History*, January 1962, 188; Richmond *Times-Dispatch*, February 15, 1905. Lieutenant Jackson of the 7th Louisiana reported that the regiment arrived at 3:00 p.m. and immediately went into battle line. Other accounts suggest that the Confederates did not attack until 4:00 p.m.

11. Harry W. Pfanz, *Gettysburg: The First Day* (Chapel Hill: University of North Carolina Press, 2001), 229.

12. Jackson letter, July 20, 1863, as quoted in Jones, "Going Back in the Union at Last," 56.

13. Reed, *A Private in Gray*, 42. "Lib" Barnard, Thomas Reed's brother-in-law, had helped him bury his brother Green just seven weeks beforehand following the Second Battle of Fredericksburg.

14. *O.R.*, vol. 27, part 2, 495.

15. James McDowell Carrington, "First Day on the Left at Gettysburg," *Southern Historical Society Papers*, vol. 35, 1907, 332; Richmond *Times-Dispatch*, February 19, 1905; Stiles, *Four Years Under Marse Robert*, 210.

16. *O.R.*, vol. 27, part 1, 748.

17. *O.R.*, vol. 27, part 1, 712–13; Early, "Review," *Southern Historical Society Papers*, 254.

18. Andrew L. Harris, letter dated July 11, 1863, printed in the Eaton (Ohio) *Weekly Register,* July 23, 1863; William B. Southerton reminiscences, as quoted in Richard A. Baumgartner, *Buckeye Blood: Ohio at Gettysburg* (Huntington, W.Va.: Blue Acorn Press, 2003), 63–64.

19. *O.R.*, vol. 27, part 1, 717.

20. *O.R.*, vol. 27, part 2, 480; Campbell Brown, "Reminiscences of the Civil War," vol. 2, 57; as quoted in Jones, *Lee's Tigers*, 167; Charles Moore account, USAMHI.

21. *National Tribune*, December 12, 1869.

22. Gettysburg *Compiler*, July 5, 1892; *O.R.*, vol. 27, part 1, 729, 748, 755; Cecil C. Reed, July 13, 1863, in the Cleveland *Morning Leader*; as quoted in Baumgartner, *Buckeye Blood*, 61. The old Harrisburg Road, which was relocated after the war, and Heckman's probable gun position have been swallowed up in what is now a residential neighborhood. The battery's monument was placed on the grounds of Pennsylvania College where it was most visible.

23. Jackson letter, July 20, 1863, as quoted in Jones, "Going Back in the Union at Last," 56; Seymour account, GNMP. Broussard survived his wound and eventually returned to St. Martinsville on an extended medical furlough. He died in 1905 and is buried in the local Catholic Cemetery. It is not known when during the attack Comes and Smith were killed, although it is likely they were among the canister victims.

24. *O.R.*, vol. 27, part 1, 755; part 2, 480.

25. *O.R.*, vol. 27, part 1, 735.

26. Frederick C. Winkler, *The Letters of Frederick C. Winkler, 1862–1865* (Milwaukee, Wis.: William K. Winkler, 1963), 70.

27. *O.R.*, vol. 27, part 1, 721–22: Charles W. McKay, "Three Years or During the War, with the Crescent and Star," *National Tribune Scrap Book* (New York: National Tribune, no date). McKay would win the Medal of Honor for his actions at the May 8, 1864, Battle of Dug Gap in Georgia, where he risked his life to save a wounded comrade lying between the opposing lines.

28. Samuel P. Bates, *History of the Pennsylvania Volunteers, 1861–65,* vol. 1 (Harrisburg, Pa.: B. Singerly, 1868), 391.

29. Pfanz, *Gettysburg: The First Day*, 264; Taylor account, GNMP; Reed, *A Private in Gray*, 42.

30. Seymour account, GNMP.

31. Winkler, *Letters*, 71.

32. Seymour account, GNMP; *O.R.*, vol. 27, part 1, 751: Baumgartner, *Buckeye Blood*, 62. Lieutenant Schiely returned to Cleveland with a gunshot wound to his right shoulder. Unfit for further duty, he was medically discharged three months after the Battle of Gettysburg.

33. Gettysburg *Compiler*, July 5, 1892.

34. Carrington, "First Day on Left at Gettysburg," 332; Stiles, *Four Years Under Marse Robert*, 212–14. Stiles claimed Burgoyne was a member of the 9th Louisiana, which would have been advancing on the Harrisburg Road in the right position for such an event. However, no one by that surname appears on the muster rolls of any company in the 9th. It may have been a nickname, or Stiles didn't recall it correctly, or the fistfight was anecdotal. There was a Burgoyne in the 6th Louisiana, but service records do not match.

35. *O.R.*, vol. 27, part 2, 479; Coco, *Wasted Valor*, 48.

36. *O.R.*, vol. 27, part 2, 479. This was normally Major General Carl Schurz's division, but the German had tactical control of all XI Corps north of Gettysburg, while nominal corps commander Oliver Howard acted as overall Union commander following the death of the I Corps' John Reynolds in the morning. Schimmelfennig assumed command of Schurz's Division in the progression of officers, with Colonel George von Amsberg of the 45th New York taking over Schimmelfennig's Brigade. In turn, Lieutenant Colonel Aldolpus Dobke now commanded the 45th.

37. *O.R.*, vol. 27, part 1, 742.

38. John D. Vautier, *History of the Eighty-eighth Pennsylvania Volunteers in the War for the Union, 1861–1865* (Philadelphia: J. B. Lippincott, 1894), 141; Swallow, "The First Day at Gettysburg," 441. Robinson was among the few field officers killed as the Federals entered Gettysburg, although the unknown leader may have been a line officer, several of whom were gunned down as the Confederates entered the borough.

39. *O.R.*, vol. 27, part 1, 729–30; Gannon, "The 6th Louisiana at Gettysburg," 90.

40. *O.R.*, vol. 27, part 1, 756–57.

41. *O.R.*, vol. 27, part 1, 735.

42. Jackson letter, July 20, 1863, as quoted in Jones, "Going Back in the Union at Last," 56.

43. Reed, *A Private in Gray*, 42.

44. *O.R.*, vol. 27, part 1, 939.

45. *O.R.*, vol. 27, part 1, 717–18.

46. Jackson letter, July 20, 1863, as quoted in Jones, "Going Back in the Union at Last," 56.

47. *O.R.*, vol. 27, part 2, 479.

48. William R. Kiefer, *History of the One Hundred and Fifty-third Regiment Pennsylvania Volunteers Which Was Recruited in Northampton County, Pa. 1862–1863* (New York: The Chemical Publishing Co., 1909), 131.

49. Early, "Review," *Southern Historical Society Papers*, 254.

50. *O.R.*, vol. 27, part 2, 480; Compiled Service Records of Louisiana. Microcopy M320. Contrary to some Confederate accounts of as many as 6–7,000 prisoners taken during Ewell's advance, the XI Corps only officially reported 1,510 captured during the entire Battle of Gettysburg. It is conceivable that several Union prisoners slipped away unnoticed because they were lightly guarded and eventually returned to their units before being officially counted as missing. It is more likely the Confederate accounts are biased to the high side.

51. Elizabeth Thorn account, GNMP. The eastern part of Cemetery Hill was owned by Edward Menchey and Peter Raffensberger.

52. *O.R.*, vol. 27, part 1, 720.

53. Bates, *Martial Deeds of Pennsylvania*, 229–30.

54. *O.R.*, vol. 27, part 1, 721.

55. *O.R.*, vol. 27, part 1, 368.

56. *O.R.*, vol. 27, part 1, 748.

57. *O.R.*, vol. 27, part 1, 751; Early, "Review," *Southern Historical Society Papers*, 254.

58. Jackson letter, July 20, 1863, as quoted in Jones, "Going Back in the Union at Last," 56–57.

59. Eric Campbell, "'A Field Made Glorious.' Cemetery Hill: From Battleground to Sacred Ground," *Gettysburg Magazine*, no. 15, January 1996; Reed, *A Private in Gray*, 42; Seymour account, GNMP.

60. *O.R.*, vol. 27, part 2, 469; Early, "Review," *Southern Historical Society Papers*, 255–56; J. William Jones, *Army of Northern Virginia Memorial Volume* (Richmond, Va.: J. W. Randolph and English, 1880), 104. Jones quoted an address made in October 1875 at the fifth annual reunion of the Army of Northern Virginia Association by Major John W. Daniel, Early's assistant adjutant general during the Gettysburg Campaign. Daniel was an eyewitness to most of the general's movements and statements on July 1.

61. *O.R.*, vol. 27, part 1, 230.

62. Swallow, "The First Day at Gettysburg," 441; Hoke, *Great Invasion*, 286–88; Bartlett, *A Soldier's Story*, 186. According to Hoke, ten years after the war General Longstreet discussed the battle with Hays, who emphatically told Longstreet that he could have taken Culp' Hill at that critical juncture "without the loss of ten men." He blamed Jubal Early's technical adherence to Ewell's orders, despite Early's personal belief that the hill should have been assaulted.

63. Gates D. Fahnestock speech, February 14, 1934, National Arts Club, New York City, collection of ACHS. Transcribed by David Reichley; Gettysburg *Compiler*, April 27, 1907. The Fahnestock house was at the intersection of Baltimore and Middle streets, a block south of the town square.

64. William McLean account, ACHS.

65. Jones, *Cemetery Hill*, 42–43.

66. Amelia Harmon Miller account, *Gettysburg Compiler*, Vertical Files of the Gettysburg National Military Park; Pfanz, *Gettysburg: The First Day*, 279.

67. Jackson letter, July 20, 1863, as quoted in Jones, "Going Back in the Union at Last," 55–56.

68. Matilda "Tillie" Pierce Alleman, *At Gettysburg, or, What a Girl Saw and Heard of the Battle. A True Narrative* (New York: W. Lake Borland, 1889).

69. Gettysburg *Compiler*, July 1, 1903.

70. Early, "Review," *Southern Historical Society Papers*, 272–73; *Autobiographical Sketch*, 271.

71. Reed, *A Private in Gray*, 42; Bartlett, *A Soldier's Story*, 186; New York Monuments Commission for the Battlefields of Gettysburg and Chattanooga, *Final Report on the Battlefield of Gettysburg (New York at Gettysburg)* (Albany, N.Y.: J. B. Lyon Co., 1902), 1247.

72. Bates, *Martial Deeds of Pennsylvania*, 225.

73. Seymour account, GNMP; William H. Warren, *History of the Seventeenth Connecticut: The Record of a Yankee Regiment in the War for the Union* (Bridgeport, Conn.: The Danbury Times, 1886), 591. Typescript in the Bridgeport Historical Society.

74. *O.R.*, vol. 27, part 1, 740.

75. Charles Moore account, USAMHI; Record of Confederate Burials, ACHS.

76. Gettysburg *Compiler*, July 1, 1903.

77. *O.R.*, vol. 27, part 2, 480; U.S. Naval Observatory, Washington D.C. A full moon occurred at 1:46 a.m. (Eastern Standard Time), as Hays was preparing his line to move forward.

78. Jackson letter, July 20, 1863, as quoted in Jones, "Going Back in the Union at Last," 57.

79. Frank Moore, ed., *The Rebellion Record: A Diary of American Events . . .*, vol. 7 (New York: G. P. Putnam, 1861–68), 96.

## CHAPTER 5

1. U.S. Naval Observatory, Washington D.C.; Professor Jacobs' weather observations, Henry E. Jacobs (Rev. Dr. Jacobs' son), Adams County *Star and Sentinel,* Gettysburg, July 30, 1885. Ewell, Rodes, Johnson, Early, Hays, and other Confederate generals met with Robert E. Lee early in the morning. Harry Hays believed Lee to be "full of fight," and the commander "appeared to be deeply impressed with the importance of an immediate attack" by Ewell on the left of the line. That plan was shelved in favor of an *en echelon* attack from the right led by two divisions of Longstreet's Corps. See Hoke, *Great Invasion,* 311, and other sources.

2. Jacob D. Smith, *Camps and Campaigns of the 107th Ohio Volunteer Infantry, Based on a Wartime Diary,* 1910 edition (Navarre, Ohio: Indian River Graphics, 2000), 93.

3. Catherine M. W. Foster, "Battle of Gettysburg: A Citizen's Eyewitness Account," ACHS. The Fosters reported the behavior of the two thieves, and General Rodes placed a guard at their home, on the corner of South Washington and High streets. The brick two-story house was used as a Union I Corps hospital for several days. It was struck at least three times by artillery shells on July 3, one of which broke forks on the kitchen table and drove the counterweights from a clock through a wall.

4. Jackson letter, July 20, 1863, as quoted in Jones, "Going Back in the Union at Last," 57; *O.R.,* vol. 27, part 2, 470; Gettysburg *Compiler* July 5, 1892.

5. Chambersburg, Pa., *Franklin Repository,* July 22, 1863.

6. Warren, *History of the Seventeenth Connecticut,* 592; *O.R. Supplement,* part 2, Record of Events, vol. 24, serial 36, 109.

7. Seymour account, GNMP.

8. *O.R.,* vol. 27, part 1, 715.

9. Campbell, *Gettysburg Magazine,* no. 15.

10. Carl Schurz, *The Reminiscences of Carl Schurz,* vol. 3 (New York: The McClure Co., 1908), 20.

11. Campbell, "A Field Made Glorious," *Gettysburg Magazine,* no. 15.

12. Warren, *History of the Seventeenth Connecticut,* 625–26.

13. Seymour account, GNMP.

14. *O.R.,* vol. 27, part 1, 752; *New York at Gettysburg,* 1247.

15. David and Audrey Ladd, eds., *The Bachelder Papers,* vol. 2 (Dayton, Ohio: Morningside Press, 1994), 1212. McCreary co-owned the brickyard with his brother-in-law John Houck, who also owned the land around Devil's Den and what is now called Houck's Ridge.

16. Charles S. Wainwright, *A Diary of Battle: The Personal Journals of Charles S. Wainwright, 1861–1865,* ed. Allen Nevins (New York: Da Capo Press, 1998), 243; *O.R.,* vol. 27, part 1, 716, 751. One of these batteries was the 1st Rockbridge Artillery, posted on Benner's Hill. That battery had participated in the shelling of Fort Milroy at Second Winchester.

17. Broadhead account, GNMP.

18. In January 1892, Edward Whittier (1840–1902) would be awarded the Medal of Honor for his actions in the September 1864 Battle of Fisher's Hill in the Shenandoah Valley. "While

acting as assistant adjutant general, Artillery brigade, 6th Army Corps, went over the enemy's works, mounted, with the assaulting column, to gain quicker possession of the guns and to turn them upon the enemy." Captain Stevens survived his leg wounds and lived until 1918.

19. Broadhead account, GNMP.

20. William J. K. Beaudot and Lance J. Herdegen, *An Irishman in the Iron Brigade: The Civil War Memoirs of James P. Sullivan* (New York: Fordham University Press, 1993), 99.

21. Philadelphia *Press,* July 20, 1863. Rev. E. W. Rutter of Philadelphia visited Gettysburg in the weeks after the battle to minister to the wounded and distribute supplies. He spent time conversing with the residents, who informed him of General Early's braggadocio. Rutter also claimed residents heard Early threaten to burn down Philadelphia if it didn't pay its share of Confederate war expenses.

22. Gettysburg *Compiler,* September 22, 1896, reprinted from the Bridgeport *Standard.* This was undoubtedly Elizabeth Thorn's well beside the Evergreen Cemetery Gatehouse.

23. O.R., vol. 27, part 2, 480; Kiefer, *153rd Pennsylvania,* 219.

24. Edward Marcus, ed., *A New Canaan Private in the Civil War: The Letters of Justus M. Silliman* (New Canaan, Conn.: New Canaan Historical Society, 1984), letter dated July 3, 1863; Warren, *History of the Seventeenth Connecticut Volunteers,* 690.

25. Bates, *Martial Deeds of Pennsylvania,* 314.

26. Moore, *Rebellion Record,* vol. 7, 94.

27. Warren, *History of the Seventeenth Connecticut,* 593.

28. Broadhead account, GNMP.

29. Philadelphia *Press,* July 6, 1863; Adin B. Underwood, *The Three-Years' Service of the Thirty-third Mass. Infantry Regiment, 1862–1865* (Boston: A. Williams and Co., 1881), 123; Moore, *Rebellion Record,* vol. 7, 94.

30. William B. Southerton reminiscences, as quoted in Baumgartner, *Buckeye Blood,* 92.

31. Jesse Bowman Young, *What a Boy Saw in the Army* (New York: Hunt and Eaton, 1894), 328. See also Jesse Bowman Young, *The Battle of Gettysburg: A Comprehensive Narrative* (New York: Harper and Brothers, 1863), 275–76.

32. O.R., vol. 27, part 1, 753; Confederate Major Joseph H. Latimer was not related to attorney James W. Latimer, who commented on the Confederate occupation of his native York, Pennsylvania.

33. *Evergreen City Times,* Sheboygan, Wisconsin, vol. 10, no. 19, quoting the correspondent of the New York *World.*

34. Sarah M. Broadhead account, GNMP.

35. *Pennsylvania at Gettysburg,* vol. 2 (Harrisburg, Pa.: Wm. Stanley Ray, State Printer, 1914), 930–31; Ezra D. Simons, *A Regimental History: The One Hundred and Twenty-fifth New York State Volunteers* (New York: self-published, 1888), 114. Ricketts' Battery was mostly recruited from Montour, Northumberland, Columbia, and Schuylkill counties, a coal mining and farming region northeast of Harrisburg. The diminutive Ricketts, a native of Orangeville in Columbia County, had attracted attention for his coolness in battle. He was assigned command of Battery F in mid-April 1863 following the promotion of its previous commander, Ezra

Matthews. On May 2, Ricketts was promoted from lieutenant to captain. The depleted Battery G was amalgamated with Battery F after Chancellorsville.

36. *Evergreen City Times,* Sheboygan, Wis., vol. 10, no. 19, quoting a correspondent from the New York *World.*

37. Broadhead account, GNMP.

38. *O.R.,* vol. 27, part 1, 715, 718.

39. Andrew Harris to John Bachelder, March 14, 1881, Ladd, *The Bachelder Papers,* vol. 2, 746.

40. *O.R.,* vol. 27, part 2, 470; "Hon. Thomas J. Semmes," *Southern Historical Society Papers,* vol. 22, 1894, 317–18. Dr. Semmes (born in 1826 in Georgetown, D.C.) was the younger brother of Confederate Senator Thomas J. Semmes, the politician who had made the speech to the Tigers at their camp in Hamilton's Crossing a few days prior to the commencement of the Gettysburg Campaign. The French-educated physician was married to the daughter of another prominent lawmaker, Senator John M. Berrien of Georgia.

41. Hoke, *Great Invasion,* 347.

42. Seymour account, GNMP.

43. As with most Civil War battles, accounts vary widely in regard to times quoted for specific events. Standardized time zones did not exist at the time of the war, and soldiers often set their watches to one locale but did not adjust them with any uniformity from location to location. Most descriptions of the beginning of Early's two-brigade assault range from 7:15 to 7:45 p.m. Note that no contemporary sources reveal Hays' exact disposition. The most common placement of his regiments along the battle line assumes they stayed relatively in the same order as on July 1, when their formation was documented. In addition, accounts of the fighting can be used to reconstruct which Confederates encountered which Union regiments, whose alignment is more certain. Several Union accounts suggest the Rebels advanced in lines two ranks deep.

44. R. J. Hancock to John W. Daniel, J. W. Daniel Papers, Duke University, as quoted in Bradley M. Gottfried, *Brigades of Gettysburg: The Union and Confederate Brigades at the Battle of Gettysburg* (New York: Da Capo Press, 2002), 504.

45. Marcus, *A New Canaan Private,* 42.

46. Kiefer, *153rd Pennsylvania,* 219.

47. Edward N. Whittier, "The Left Attack (Ewell's), Gettysburg," Civil War Papers Read before the Commandery of the State of Massachusetts, Military Order of the Loyal Legion of the United States (MOLLUS). Printed by the Commandery, Boston, Mass., vol. 1, 1900.

48. Whittier, "The Left Attack (Ewell's), Gettysburg."

49. *Maine at Gettysburg: Report of Maine Commissioners* (Portland, Maine: The Lakeside Press, 1898), 95.

50. *O.R.,* vol. 27, part 2, 480; Jackson letter, July 20, 1863, as quoted in Jones, "Going Back in the Union at Last," 57; Seymour account, GNMP.

51. Seymour account, GNMP; Marcus, *A New Canaan Private,* 42; Schenectady *Republican,* July 5, 1863.

52. Andrew Harris to John Bachelder, March 14, 1881, Ladd, *The Bachelder Papers,* vol. 2,

746. The open farmland traversed by the Tigers has been dramatically altered since 1863. A schoolhouse now sits on the low ridge where the Louisianans were first exposed to the Union artillery, and a football field is placed where the center of Hays' line approached the brickyard lane. Winebrenner Run now is essentially underground, having been covered over for most of its natural course.

53. Kiefer, *153rd Pennsylvania*, 219–20.

54. Jackson letter, July 20, 1863, as quoted in Jones, "Going Back in the Union at Last," 57; Seymour account, GNMP; R. J. Hancock to John W. Daniel, J. W. Daniel Papers, Duke University, as quoted in Gottfried, *Brigades of Gettysburg*, 505.

55. Underwood, *The Thirty-third Mass. Infantry*, 129.

56. Van R. Willard, *With the 3rd Wisconsin Badgers: The Journal of Van R. Willard*, ed. Steven S. Raab (Mechanicsburg, Pa.: Stackpole Books, 1999), 194.

57. William Hamilton Bayly account, GNMP and the Adams County Historical Society.

58. *O.R.*, vol. 27, part 2, 480.

59. Ladd, *The Bachelder Papers*, vol. 2, 212.

60. Whittier, "The Left Attack (Ewell's), Gettysburg."

61. Campbell, *Gettysburg Magazine*, no. 15.

62. Andrew Harris to John Bachelder, March 14, 1881, Ladd, *The Bachelder Papers*, vol. 2, 746.

63. *Maine at Gettysburg*, 95–96; Whittier, "The Left Attack (Ewell's), Gettysburg." Whittier places the time of the wheel movement as 8:30. Most other accounts are consistent with this timing. He estimated his guns fired a total of 46–49 rounds, almost the entire content of his ammunition chests.

64. Walter Frederick Beyer and Oscar Frederick Keydel, *Deeds of Valor: From Records of the Archives of the United States: How American Heroes Won the Medal of Honor*, vol. 1 (Detroit, Mich.: The Perrien-Keydel Co., 1907), 159. Young Private Chase woke up in a wagonload of dead soldiers being taken to a trench for burial. He would spend months recovering in various hospitals in Gettysburg and Philadelphia before returning home to Augusta, Maine. He would receive the Medal of Honor for his bravery at the 1862 Battle of Malvern Hill.

65. Wainwright, *A Diary of Battle*, 245; *O.R.*, vol. 27, part 2, 480.

66. Charles P. Hamblen, *Connecticut Yankees at Gettysburg* (Kent, Ohio: Kent State University Press, 1993), 58.

67. Warren, *History of the Seventeenth Connecticut*, 632.

68. *O.R.*, vol. 27, part 2, 480; Seymour account, GNMP.

69. *O.R.*, vol. 27, part 1, 718. Brady stayed with the regiment until July 8, when he was sent home to Wolcottville to recuperate under a doctor's care for the rest of the summer and fall. He was medically discharged from the 17th Connecticut on October 21. A few weeks later, Brady received a commission as the major of the 20th Regiment, Veteran Reserve Corps, and was sent to Baltimore. After brief duty in the rear lines in Virginia, he was the provost marshal of the Point Lookout prisoner-of-war camp in Maryland for the rest of the war.

70. Kiefer, *153rd Pennsylvania*, 141; Frederick O. von Fritsch, *A Gallant Captain of the Civil War* (New York: Joseph Tyler Butts, 1902), 84.

71. von Fritsch, *A Gallant Captain*, 85–86; Whittier, "The Left Attack (Ewell's), Gettys-

burg." When he later came to his senses, von Fritsch tried to find the scoundrel who had clubbed him but never did.

72. O.R., vol. 27, part 1, 894.

73. *Pennsylvania at Gettysburg*, vol. 2, 931; Luther W. Minnigh, *Gettysburg: "What They Did Here"* (Gettysburg, Pa.: self-published, 1920), 127. Minnigh was one of the most prominent Gettysburg battlefield tour guides, authors, and lecturers in the early twentieth century. He frequently escorted old veterans around the battlefield and often later recited their anecdotes and stories in his books and expositions.

74. Wainwright, *A Diary of Battle*, 245.

75. William B. Southerton reminiscences, as quoted by Baumgartner, *Buckeye Blood*, 113.

76. Ladd, *The Bachelder Papers*, vol. 2, 746; Southerton account, as quoted in Baumgartner, *Buckeye Blood*, 113.

77. Ladd, *The Bachelder Papers*, vol. 2, 746. Lieutenant Ladley's mother would write to him after the battle to scold him for not having a good revolver at his side.

78. Booth, *Records of Louisiana Confederate Soldiers*; Bergeron, *Guide to Louisiana Military Units*. In the spring of 1861, Williams had enrolled in Company F (the DeSoto Blues), a unit recruited primarily from residents of DeSoto Parish. He received a promotion to major dating from April 24, 1862.

79. Baumgartner, *Buckeye Blood*, 113.

80. George B. Fox to his father, written July 4, 1863, on East Cemetery Hill, as quoted in Baumgartner, *Buckeye Blood*, 113.

81. 75th Ohio folder, Vertical Files, GNMP; Edward N. Whittier, "The Left Attack (Ewell's), Gettysburg"; Ladd, *The Bachelder Papers*, vol. 2, 746.

82. Southerton reminiscences, paraphrased in Baumgartner, *Buckeye Blood*, 114–15.

83. O.R., vol. 27, part 2, 715; Pfanz, *Gettysburg: The Second Day*, 249.

84. Gilmor, *Four Years in the Saddle*; O.R., vol. 27, part 2, 480.

85. National Archives, Washington D.C., Compiled Service Records of Confederate Soldiers Who Served in Organizations from the State of Louisiana, War Record Group 109, Microcopy 320. Lieutenant Hancock survived his wound and eventually returned to action, only to be wounded again in the Third Battle of Winchester in 1864. Hodges would replace the fallen Henry Williams as major of the regiment.

86. Gilmor, *Four Years in the Saddle*.

87. Early, "Review," *Southern Historical Society Papers*, 280.

88. Albertus McCreary, "Gettysburg: A Boy's Experience of the Battle," *McClure's Magazine*, vol. 33, May to October 1909, 246–47; Gettysburg *Compiler*, July 14, 1909.

89. Edward C. Culp, July 5, 1863, in the Norwalk *Reflector*, July 21, 1863, as quoted in Baumgartner, *Buckeye Blood*, 109–10.

90. Andrew Harris to John Bachelder, March 14, 1881, Ladd, *The Bachelder Papers*, vol. 2, 746; Edward C. Culp, *The 25th Ohio Vet. Vol. Infantry in the War for the Union* (Topeka, Kans.: Geo. W. Crane and Co., 1885), 29.

91. O.R., vol. 27, part 1, 719–20.

92. Booth, *Records of Louisiana Confederate Soldiers*; Gannon, "The 6th Louisiana at Gettysburg," 94–95. Jefferson Davis Van Benthuysen was a relative of Confederate President

Jefferson Davis and accompanied Davis for most of his flight through the South after the fall of Richmond in April 1865. Color Phillip Bolger would survive his wound and live well into the twentieth century. He was among the final members of the regiment to die; his name appears in a 1911 article in *Confederate Veteran* listing the last sixteen survivors of the regiment. Lieutenant John Orr, who was bayoneted at Winchester, was also among the names, as was Major John J. Rivera.

93. George S. Clements, "The 25th Ohio at Gettysburg," *The National Tribune*, August 6, 1891.

94. Jones, *Cemetery Hill*, 78; Booth, *Records of Louisiana Confederate Soldiers*, vol. 3, 390. Briscoe would be killed in action on May 5, 1864, during the Battle of the Wilderness.

95. Charles Moore account, USAMHI. St. Clair Johns was an 1857 graduate of Mount St. Mary's College in Emmitsburg, Maryland, less than twenty miles south of Gettysburg. He was captured after being wounded in the Battle of Gettysburg but was paroled later in the summer. The Concordia Parish native was taken captive a second time at Rappahannock Station in November 1863 and briefly sent to the Old Capitol Prison in Washington D.C. before being transferred to Johnson's Island in Ohio. He stayed there until the war was over and he took the Oath of Allegiance. After the war, be became a bookkeeper (Booth, *Records of Louisiana Confederate Soldiers*).

96. Buell, *The Cannoneer*, 83.

97. *O.R.*, vol. 27, part 1, 706.

98. George B. Fox to his father, written July 4, 1863, on East Cemetery Hill, as quoted in Baumgartner, *Buckeye Blood*, 113.

99. Noah Andre Trudeau, *Gettysburg: A Testing of Courage* (New York: Harper Collins, 2002), 405; Simons, *One Hundred and Twenty-fifth New York State Volunteers*, 116. The severely wounded Taifel would be taken later to a Philadelphia hospital, where he died on July 18.

100. Jackson letter, July 20, 1863, as quoted in Jones, "Going Back in the Union at Last," 57–58. The flag eventually made its way to the Grand Army of the Republic's post in Auburn, New York, where it was kept until 1941. When the post closed, an attempt was made to return the flag to Louisiana, but that effort failed and the flag disappeared. Arthur Duchamp, wounded in the wrist at Gettysburg, was killed at Spotsylvania on May 11, 1864, while carrying the regiment's replacement colors.

101. Gilmor, *Four Years in the Saddle*.

102. Jones, *Cemetery Hill*, 78; Smith, *Camps and Campaigns of the 107th Ohio Volunteer Infantry*, 93.

103. Simons, *One Hundred and Twenty-fifth New York State Volunteers*, 116; Ladd, *The Bachelder Papers*, vol. 1, 311–12.

104. Smith, *Camps and Campaigns of the 107th Ohio Volunteer Infantry*, 101.

105. Warren, *History of the Seventeenth Connecticut*, 562–63, 717.

106. Warren, *History of the Seventeenth Connecticut*, 562; *O.R.*, vol. 27, part 2, 484.

107. Ladley, 143, 147.

108. Kiefer, *153rd Pennsylvania*, 142.

109. *Pennsylvania at Gettysburg*, vol. 2, 932. Louis Worcester, an antebellum Baton Rouge

attorney, was the second lieutenant of Company B. Married with a family, he had enlisted at the age of thirty-four in 1861.

110. Young, *What a Boy Saw*, 326–27; Young, *The Battle of Gettysburg*, 275.

111. Major Samuel Tate's report of July 8, 1863, to Governor Andrew Vance of North Carolina. Quoted by Alexander Hunter, *Billy Yank and Johnny Reb* (New York and Washington: The Neale Publishing Co., 1904), 407.

112. *Pennsylvania at Gettysburg*, vol. 2, 932; Whittier, "The Left Attack (Ewell's), Gettysburg." One of the Pennsylvania gunners, John M. Given, was badly wounded and died in Confederate hands. The other two, Oscar G. Lannabe and Francis Nied, were exchanged.

113. Malone diary, 37.

114. Frederick Smith, "Battery I, 1st New York Light Artillery," in *New York at Gettysburg*, vol. 3, 1247.

115. Southerton reminiscences, paraphrased in Baumgartner, *Buckeye Blood*, 115.

116. Kiefer, *153rd Pennsylvania*, 141.

117. Schurz, *Reminiscences*, 25.

118. Edwin A. Davis, ed., "A Louisiana Volunteer, Letters of William J. Walter, 1861–62," *Southwest Review*, 19 (Dallas, Texas: Southern Methodist University Press, 1933), 87. Earlier in the war, the Irish-born McGinsey was described as "good looking," a man who could inflame the hearts of women. Major Lester had less than a year to live. He would be killed in action at Cold Harbor. St. Martin, the father of seven, was buried in Baltimore. His blood-stained sash is in the collection of the Confederate Memorial Hall in New Orleans.

119. Bergeron, "Free Men of Color in Grey." Lutz was taken to the Davids' Island Prison on Long Island, where he recuperated until he was well enough for steamship travel. He was paroled on September 16, 1863, and exchanged for the second time in the war. He traveled from his release place at City Point, Virginia, home to Opelousas, Louisiana, and was off duty for the rest of the war on medical furlough. In some unknown altercation in his hometown in May or June of 1864, he was shot in the right arm, which necessitated its amputation. He then moved to Polk County, Texas, to live with his brother. At the close of the Civil War, Lutz was formally discharged from the Confederate army in Houston in May 1865. He later married twice and returned to Louisiana, where he owned an eighty-one-acre farm. He filed three times to collect a pension, succeeding in 1900. With his light skin, he was listed in the U.S. Censuses of 1880 and 1900 as a white man. He died April 9, 1910, and was buried in Magnolia Cemetery in Westlake, Louisiana.

120. Jackson letter, July 20, 1863, as quoted in Jones, "Going Back in the Union at Last," 58; Taylor account, GNMP; Richmond *Daily Whig*, July 24, 1863; Record Rolls of 8th Louisiana Infantry—LHA Collection, Howard-Tilton Memorial Library, Tulane University, New Orleans, Louisiana.

121. Charles D. Page, *History of the Fourteenth Regiment, Connecticut Vol. Infantry* (Meriden, Conn.: Horton Printing Co., 1906), 142.

122. Schurz, *Reminiscences*, 24.

123. Schurz, *Reminiscences*, 23–24.

124. *O.R.*, vol. 27, part 2, 480–81.

125. Seymour account, GNMP.

126. Bates, *History of the Pennsylvania Volunteers*, 391.

127. Schurz, *Reminiscences*, 25.

128. Jackson letter, July 20, 1863, as quoted in Jones, "Going Back in the Union at Last," 58.

129. Oliver O. Howard, *Autobiography of Oliver Otis Howard, Major General United States Army*, vol. 1 (New York: Baker and Taylor, 1907), 430.

130. Joseph L. Dickelman, "Gen. Carroll's Gibraltar Brigade at Gettysburg," *National Tribune*, December 10, 1908.

131. Luther Baker Mesnard Diary, privately owned, courtesy of Ronald Mesnard. Used by permission.

132. Evans, *Confederate Military History*, 260.

133. Buell, *The Cannoneer*, 83.

134. Seymour account, GNMP.

135. *O.R.*, vol. 27, part 2, 481.

136. Southerton reminiscences, paraphrased in Baumgartner, *Buckeye Blood*, 118–19.

137. Wainwright, *A Diary of Battle*, 246.

138. Dickelman, "Gen. Carroll's Gibraltar Brigade at Gettysburg"; *O.R.*, vol. 27, part 1, 460.

139. Gettysburg *Compiler*, July 5, 1892.

140. Seymour account, GNMP, *O.R.*, vol. 27, part 2, 481; Thomas E. Causby, "Storming the Stone Fence at Gettysburg," *Southern Historical Society Papers*, vol. 29, 340–41.

141. Wainwright, *A Diary of Battle*, 247.

142. Bayly account, ACHS and GNMP; *Pennsylvania at Gettysburg*, vol. 2, 932.

143. Marcus, *A New Canaan Private*, 42.

144. Buell, *The Cannoneer*, 83.

145. *O.R.*, vol. 27, part 1, 720; Buell, *The Cannoneer*, 83.

146. George B. Fox to his father, written July 4, 1863, on East Cemetery Hill, as quoted in Baumgartner, *Buckeye Blood*, 120.

147. Baungartner, *Buckeye Blood*, 109; *O.R.*, vol. 27, part 1, 740.

148. Howard, *Autobiography*, 431; Trudeau, *Gettysburg: A Testing of Courage*, 409.

149. George M. Vickers, *Under Both Flags: A Panorama of the Great Civil War* (New York: Veterans Publishing Co., 1896), 72. The 73rd Pennsylvania was part of Coster's Brigade. Diembach, who would be severely wounded in November at Missionary Ridge and would suffer through the death of his father in the same battle, wrote, "Our brigade, charging through the cemetery, met a sight of awful sublimity—our artillerymen defending their guns with rammers and stones, and the 'Tigers' struggling like their fierce namesakes for possession."

150. Booth, *Records of Louisiana Confederate Soldiers; Maine at Gettysburg*, 98. The showers were apparently scattered, as few soldiers mentioned any rainfall. Artillery Lieutenant Whittier stated, "Some rain during the night refreshed while it wetted us thoroughly, though many men slept through it all, so great was their fatigue."

151. Booth, *Records of Louisiana Confederate Soldiers*, vol. 2, 853; John F. Walter, "The Confederate Dead in Brooklyn," Juniper Park Civic Association, 2007. Corporal Fisher, a single farmer from Big Cane, Louisiana, died on September 6. He had been wounded and captured at Antietam previous to having the same misfortune at Gettysburg.

152. Smith, *Camps and Campaigns of the 107th Ohio Volunteer Infantry,* 226–27. The dead color bearer was Corporal Leon Gusman, a Baton Rouge student who had enlisted in 1861 at the age of nineteen. He had been wounded at First Winchester and taken prisoner, then exchanged in August 1862 after spending time in the prison camp at Fort Monroe.

153. James Stewart, "Battery B Fourth United States Artillery at Gettysburg," *Ohio MOLLUS,* vol. 4, 180–93. Note that Cooper's Battery had been withdrawn before to the reserve artillery park, so perhaps Stewart meant Ricketts, whose battery had replaced Cooper's, not far from Stewart's lunettes.

154. Colonel Evans' postbellum history places Hays' losses on July 2 as 26 killed, 151 wounded, and 55 missing (Evans, *Confederate Military History,* vol. 10, 260). Other accounts have slightly different figures for the Tigers' losses. Gottfried puts it at 334, with 51 killed, 187 wounded, and 86 missing or captured.

155. Jones, *Campbell Brown's Civil War,* 322; *O.R.,* vol. 27, part 2, 470, 556.

156. Seymour account, GNMP.

157. Hunter, *Billy Yank and Johnny Reb,* 407.

158. Bates, *Martial Deeds of Pennsylvania,* 314–15.

159. Seymour account, GNMP; Gannon, "The 6th Louisiana at Gettysburg," 98, citing the files of the 6th Louisiana at Tulane University; Reed, *A Private in Gray,* 42; Manning was writing from the trenches in front of Petersburg, Virginia, in late 1864 as he reflected on the Battle of Gettysburg. He incorrectly remembered the date as July 1, not July 2.

160. Gottfried, *Brigades of Gettysburg,* 505–6; Henry Jacobs account, ACHS; Fahnestock account, ACHS; Bates, *Martial Deeds of Pennsylvania,* 294. The Confederates attacked Union troops on Malvern Hill, well protected by artillery, during the Peninsula Campaign. The attack on Cemetery Hill was reminiscent of this earlier failed assault.

161. *O. R.,* vol. 27, part 2, 481; Evans, *Confederate Military History,* vol. 10, 305; *Pennsylvania at Gettysburg,* 929 (remarks by Brevet Brigadier General J. P. S. Gobin at the dedication ceremonies for the monument on Cemetery Hill to Ricketts' Battery); Vickers, *Under Both Flags,* 72.

162. Ladd, *The Bachelder Papers,* vol. 1, 236.

163. George B. Fox to his father, written July 4, 1863, on East Cemetery Hill, as quoted in Baumgartner, *Buckeye Blood,* 113; Ladd, *The Bachelder Papers,* vol. 2, 746. Four of the 75th Ohio's officers were taken prisoner; the rest were all gunned down over the first two days of the battle. The half-moons comment was an allusion to the XI Corps' distinctive crescent-shaped emblem.

164. Bates, *Martial Deeds of Pennsylvania,* 293–94; Hoke, *Great Invasion,* 339. Jacobs' home was near the lines of Rodes' Division.

165. Wainwright, *A Diary of Battle,* 247; Inscription on the monument for Battery I, 1st New York Light Artillery on Cemetery Hill in the Gettysburg National Military Park.

166. Dickelman, "Gen. Carroll's Gibraltar Brigade at Gettysburg"; Underwood, *The Thirty-third Mass. Infantry,* 131; *Gettysburg Compiler,* July 23, 1913; Young, *The Battle of Gettysburg,* 272.

167. *Gettysburg Compiler,* July 5, 1892; *O.R.,* vol. 27, part 2, 320.

168. Broadhead account, GNMP.

## CHAPTER 6

1. Moore, *The Rebellion Record*, vol. 7, 96.

2. Young, *What a Boy Saw in the Army*, 319.

3. Chambersburg, Pa., *Franklin Repository*, July 29, 1863.

4. Kiefer, *153rd Pennsylvania*, 256; Ladd, *The Bachelder Papers*, vol. 1, 311–13.

5. Smith, *107th Ohio*, 226–27.

6. Kiefer, *153rd Pennsylvania*, 221.

7. Gettysburg *Compiler*, July 23, 1913.

8. Moore, *The Rebellion Record*, vol. 7, 96.

9. Henry E. Handerson, *Yankee in Gray* (Cleveland, Ohio: The Press of Western Reserve University, 1962), 62–64.

10. Reed, *A Private in Gray*, 42–43.

11. Warren typescript in the Bridgeport Historical Society.

12. Coco, *Wasted Valor*, 136–37; Gottfried, *Brigades of Gettysburg*, 506. The wooden table is in the collection of the Visitors Center of the Gettysburg National Military Park, where it is viewed by thousands of battlefield visitors each year. A small card in the display case informs visitors of Poole's story.

13. Richardson, suffering from a severely bruised lung, would be left behind when the Confederates retreated and he was captured by the Federals. He was sent to Johnson's Island. The Louisianan was paroled in February 1865.

14. Moore, *The Rebellion Record*, vol. 7, 96.

15. Eugene Blackford account, Civil War Miscellaneous Collection, United States Military History Institute, Carlisle, Pa.

16. Gannon, "The 6th Louisiana at Gettysburg," 99, citing an unidentified newspaper clipping in the Seymour family scrapbook, Seymour Papers, SWCW, University of Michigan. Cormier was buried in back of the barn, off of Shealer Road east of the Old Harrisburg Road. At least one other Tiger was also laid to rest on Mrs. Wible's farm, Private John L. Simmons of Company G of the 8th Louisiana. The remains of both men were taken up in September 1872 and sent to Richmond's Hollywood Cemetery.

17. Gettysburg *Times*, April 2, 1964. In Confederate muster records, his surname is spelled McCrane, the same spelling used by his American-born brother. After being captured at Rappahannock Station in November, he took the Oath of Allegiance. He returned to New York, went to work for the New York Central Railroad, married, and raised ten children in Syracuse. Unreconstructed, "Stonewall" remained a staunch advocate of the Lost Cause and even named one of his sons Francis Robert E. Lee McCrahon. He died in 1918, one of the last Louisiana Tigers living in the North. His brother Aleck died in 1925 at the Soldier's Home in Washington D.C.

18. Handerson, *Yankee in Gray*, 64; Jackson letter, July 20, 1863, as quoted in Jones, "Going Back in the Union at Last," 58.

19. Buell, *The Cannoneer*, 98. Augustus Buell, not always regarded as being an authentic eyewitness to the myriad events he described in his book, added that the Rebel mentioned a rumor that was going around the Tigers camp that Ewell had ordered Gordon to attack Cemetery Hill on the morning of July 3, but the Georgians "would not try it."

20. Gettysburg *Compiler,* July 5, 1892.

21. Handerson, *Yankee in Gray,* 64; B. Y. Malone of the 6th North Carolina mentioned in his diary (page 37) that "The nex morning about a hour befour day we went back about a mile from town and staid ther all day." Times vary as to when Early began to pull back, but most agree that it was still dark when the movement started, and within two to three hours, the entire division had withdrawn.

22. Bates, *Martial Deeds of Pennsylvania,* 315.

23. Gettysburg *Compiler,* September 22, 1896, reprinted from the Bridgeport (Conn.) *Standard;* Gannon, "The 6th Louisiana at Gettysburg," 99; Compiled Service Records of Louisiana Troops. Murrell, who lost two family members in his company to measles in May 1862 at Swift Gap, Virginia, spent the rest of the war in Federal prison camps in Delaware and Maryland.

24. Jones, *Cemetery Hill,* 99.

25. Marcus, *A New Canaan Private,* 42.

26. Coco, *Wasted Valor,* 137.

27. Gettysburg *Compiler,* July 14, 1909.

28. Adams *Sentinel,* July 28, 1863; Philadelphia *Press,* August 6, 1863. "Wellerford," also spelled Willeford in some accounts, was never identified and probably was buried in one of the trenches along Culp's Hill or along Cemetery Hill, where the Louisianans suffered most of their casualties. However, no one by that name appears in records of Gettysburg casualties for the First or Second Louisiana Brigades.

29. Kiefer, *153rd Pennsylvania,* 141–42. Lieutenants Wallace P. Talbot, a bachelor, and Louis Worchester were both fatalities at Gettysburg on July 2. Worcester was married, so it is likely he who encountered Clyde Miller. Worcester, a Baton Rouge attorney, was "supposed to have been taken prisoner" according to his service record, which later states, "Killed July 2, 1863, at Gettysburg." However, the only specific reference to his injury is Captain Bruce Ricketts' account that Worcester was "brained by a blow with a handspike." However, Ricketts knew his name, so it is conceivable Worcester initially survived his head wound and had spoken with Ricketts prior to wandering into Miller. Perhaps he perished later that night from his head injury and not his "slightly wounded" arm.

30. John B. Linn, "A Tourist at Gettysburg," *Civil War Times Illustrated,* vol. 29, September/ October 1990, 56–57. Linn later wrote several historical books, including documenting the history of a few Pennsylvania counties. His description of Cemetery Hill dates from July 7.

31. Cortland (N.Y.) *Gazette and Banner,* July 16, 1863.

32. Tillie Pierce account, GNMP.

33. Thomas W. Knox, New York *Herald,* July 8, 1863, reprinted in Chambersburg (Pa.) *Franklin Repository,* July 22, 1863.

34. Richmond *Daily Dispatch,* July 4 and July 7, 1863. The sixty-six-year-old Forno had been an officer in the antebellum Louisiana Militia. During the Mexican-American War, he was lieutenant colonel of the 1st Louisiana Regiment in the U.S. Army. In May 1861, he helped establish Camp Moore, near Tangipahoa, Louisiana, the state's recruit training and mustering site. He then joined the 5th Louisiana Infantry as its first lieutenant colonel. Not long afterward, he was promoted to colonel. He was wounded on August 29, 1862, at Second

Manassas while temporarily commanding Hays' Brigade, as the senior officer present. (*The Army and Navy of the United States 1776–1891* [Philadelphia: George Barrie Publisher, 1890]; Camp Moore Historical Society website, accessed January 30, 2008).

35. Handerson, *Yankee in Gray,* 64; Reed, *A Private in Gray,* 43.

36. Mary McDonnell account, ACHS. The McDonnell farm was located on the eastern slope of Seminary Ridge a little more than halfway between West Middle Street and the McMillan farmhouse.

37. Jackson letter, July 20, 1863, as quoted in Jones, "Going Back in the Union at Last," 58.

38. Louis C. Caspar, *The Medical Department of the United States Army in the Civil War* (Washington D.C.: U.S. Army, 191?; reprinted by Butternut Books, Gaithersburg, Md., 1985), 17.

39. William E. Doster, *Lincoln and Episodes of the Civil War* (New York and London: G. P. Putnam's Sons, 1915), 220.

40. *O.R.,* vol. 27, part 2, 481; Handerson, *Yankee in Gray;* 64; Jackson letter; Gannon, *Irish Rebels,* 203.

41. Jubal A. Early, "The Invasion of Pennsylvania, by the Confederate States Army, in June 1863," *The Historical Magazine,* vol. 1, third series, no. 4, April, 1873 (Morrisania, N.Y.: Henry B. Dawson, 1873), 240; but see: George R. Prowell, "The Invasion of Pennsylvania by the Confederates Under Robert E. Lee and Its Effect Upon Lancaster and York Counties," *Historical Papers and Addresses of the Lancaster County Historical Society,* vol. 29, no. 4, 1925.

42. Gregory A. Coco, *A Strange and Blighted Land: Gettysburg: The Aftermath of a Battle* (Gettysburg: Thomas Publications, 1995), 219. The John Crist house and barn are no longer standing. They were some 500 yards northwest of the Michael Crist farm, which was used as a hospital from early on July 1 for Heth's Division. The latter farm is still extant and is marked as a Gettysburg field hospital site.

43. Mrs. Edmund A. Souder (Emily Bliss Thacher Souder), *Leaves from the Battlefield: A Series of Letters from a Field Hospital* (Philadelphia: Caxton Press of C. Sherman, Son and Co., 1864), 58. Mrs. Souder was a Philadelphian, the wife of a prominent attorney. She and a group of friends traveled through Baltimore to Hanover Junction and on to Gettysburg to minister to the wounded. The identity of "R.H." is uncertain.

44. Gettysburg burial records, ACHS.

45. Coco, *Wasted Valor,* 48.

46. Coco, *Wasted Valor,* 48; Coco, *A Strange and Blighted Land,* 135–42.

47. Gannon, "The 6th Louisiana at Gettysburg," 99.

48. Charles Moore account, USAMHI.

49. Gannon, *Irish Rebels,* 203; Early, *Autobiographical Sketch,* 280.

50. Jackson letter, July 20, 1863, as quoted in Jones, "Going Back in the Union at Last," 58; Malone diary, 38.

51. Early, *Autobiographical Sketch,* 280.

52. Charles Moore account, USAMHI. Moore's wound festered and his leg was amputated in Richmond. The New Orleans antebellum salesman returned to Louisiana after his recovery.

53. Jackson letter, July 20, 1863, as quoted in Jones, "Going Back in the Union at Last," 58; Lockwood, *Our Campaign Around Gettysburg,* 123.

54. Bender, "Civil War Memories."

55. Early, *Autobiographical Sketch*, 281.

56. Compiled Service Records of Louisiana Troops, Microcopy M320.

57. Charles Moore account, USAMHI.

58. Lancaster, Pa., *Daily Express,* July 11, 1863.

59. Reed, *A Private in Gray*, 43.

60. Deering J. Roberts, ed., *The Southern Practitioner,* vol. 28 (Nashville, Tenn.: Southern Publishing Association, 1906), 294–95. Dr. Todd served at Williamsport from July 7 until July 13, when Jubal Early ordered him to rejoin his regiment. Assistant surgeon Dr. William Watford was left with the troops. Todd, a native of Owensboro, Kentucky, had studied medicine at Tulane University in New Orleans and had served at Camp Moore before joining the 6th Louisiana in the field. At Second Fredericksburg, his assistant surgeon, Dr. F. M. Traylor, had been killed beside him by a stray shell fragment while reading a religious tract given to him by a missionary.

61. George Lovick Pierce Wren diaries, Manuscript, Archives, and Rare Book Library, Emory University.

62. Reed, *A Private in Gray,* 44; Early, *Autobiographical Sketch,* 281.

63. *O. R.,* vol. 27, part 2, 220–27. The 110th OVI had escaped the debacle at Stephenson's Depot and reassembled in Harper's Ferry before making a circuitous route to Washington D.C. at the end of June. The regiment had been sent to Frederick, Maryland, and reassigned on July 1 to the 2nd Brigade, 3rd Division of the III Corps in the Army of the Potomac. Keifer's "weary boys" pursued Lee through Williamsport, Loudoun, and Upperville to Manassas Gap, where it fought in the Battle of Wapping Heights on July 23. It eventually reached the Rappahannock River at Fox's Ford, where the men finally rested for two weeks after their long and eventful campaign. On August 15, the 110th was shipped to New York Harbor, where it garrisoned Governor's Island and then South Brooklyn. In September, Keifer's Buckeyes rejoined the Army of the Potomac for the autumn campaigns. They would be reassigned to the VI Corps in early 1864 and would fight in the Overland Campaign. Ironically, they would be on the same battlefield as the Tigers again at the Battle of Monocacy in July of that year, where 130 men would be lost.

64. Jackson letter, July 20, 1863, as quoted in Jones, "Going Back in the Union at Last," 58.

65. Malone diary, 38.

66. "Sick and Wounded Confederate Soldiers at Hagerstown and Williamsport," *Southern Historical Society Papers,* vol. 26, 1898, 241–50; Booth, *Records of Louisiana Confederate Soldiers,* vol. 3, 1004. Dr. S. B. Morrison, the Chief Surgeon of Early's Division, ordered several of his regimental surgeons to leave with the army, including Dr. Charles H. Todd of the 6th Louisiana. Dr. Watford was ordered to remain behind. Dr. J. M. Gaines of the 18th Virginia was in overall charge of the hospitals in Hagerstown and Williamsport. He, his assistants, and his patients became Union prisoners of war. Gaines was sent to various prison camps over the next few months to care for the wounded. He was released and exchanged in mid-December 1863.

67. Jackson letter, July 20, 1863, as quoted in Jones, "Going Back in the Union at Last," 59; Reed, *A Private in Gray,* 44.

68. Reed, *A Private in Gray,* 45.

69. Malone diary, 38; Jackson letter, July 20, 1863, as quoted in Jones, "Going Back in the Union at Last," 59; Seymour account, GNMP.

70. Early, *Autobiographical Sketch*, 283; Reed, *A Private in Gray*, 45.

71. Booth, *Records of Louisiana Confederate Soldiers*, vol. 2, 474, 1180.

72. United States Surgeon General's Office, *The Medical and Surgical History of the War of the Rebellion (1861–1865)*, part 3, vol. 2, *Surgical History* (Washington D.C.: Government Printing Office, 1883), 852. The Louisiana Hospital was located at the west end of Broad Street in Richmond. Other injured Louisiana troops were treated in the 4th Division of the Jackson Hospital, situated near the Hollywood Cemetery.

73. Jackson letter, July 20, 1863, as quoted in Jones, "Going Back in the Union at Last," 59. The Tigers' route was along today's Back Creek Valley Road, which skirts Little North Mountain.

74. Malone diary, 38; Wren diary, Emory University; *O.R. Supplement*, part 2, Record of Events, vol. 24, serial 36, 60.

75. Jackson letter, July 20, 1863, as quoted in Jones, "Going Back in the Union at Last," 59; Jones, *Lee's Tigers*, 176. Bunker Hill, some ten miles north of Winchester on the Valley Pike, featured a good water supply, making it a popular campsite for troops from the opposing sides in several campaigns.

76. Early, *Autobiographical Sketch*, 284.

77. French had assumed command of the III Corps following the Battle of Gettysburg. Previous commander Daniel Sickles had been taken to a hospital after his leg was wounded and subsequently amputated.

78. Reed, *A Private in Gray*, 49; Jones, *Christ in the Camp*, 525, 350, 260. The Protestant chaplains in the Second and Third Corps had been meeting regularly prior to the Gettysburg Campaign to orchestrate and coordinate the ministerial aspects of their roles, and to plan special events, as well as to report on religious efforts within their regiments. These efforts were suspended in late May 1863, and the Chaplains' Association formally resumed their meetings in August at a Baptist Church in Orange Court House. They would again be postponed during the autumn Mine Run and Bristoe campaigns. The converts of the 9th Louisiana would get their wish, as Rev. F. McCarthy was assigned as their first regimental chaplain.

79. Jones, *Cemetery Hill*, 100.

80. *O.R.*, vol. 27, part 2, 477.

81. *O.R.*, vol. 27, part 2, 450; John F. Gruber to David F. Boyd, August 25, 1863, in Boyd Civil War Papers, Louisiana State University, as quoted by Jones, *Lee's Tigers*, 177; James A. Walker, "The Bloody Angle," *Southern Historical Society Papers*, vol. 19, 1891, 232. Walker was a fellow brigadier general who commanded the famed Stonewall Brigade in many of the same battles as Hays' Tigers.

82. Rossiter Johnson, *A Short History of the War of Succession, 1861–1865* (Boston and New York: Houghton, Mifflin and Co., 1889), 263; *Gettysburg Compiler*, September 22, 1896, reprinted from the Bridgeport (Conn.) *Standard*; Underwood, *The Thirty-third Mass. Infantry*, 131; *Gettysburg Compiler*, July 1, 1884.

83. Evans, *Confederate Military History*, vol. 10, 268.

84. Charleston (South Carolina) *Mercury*, March 22, 1864.

85. Bergeron, *Guide to Louisiana Confederate Military Units,* 84. The other regiments in Hays' old brigade mustered the following non-commissioned officers and enlisted men at Appomattox—6th Louisiana 48 men, 7th Louisiana 42, 8th Louisiana 54, and 9th Louisiana 64.

86. Following the New Orleans Race Riot, Harry Hays was removed from office by the order of General Sheridan. He returned to his law practice and died in the Crescent City on August 21, 1876, as a result of Bright's Disease. He is buried in Lafayette Cemetery number 1.

87. Coco, *Wasted Valor,* 137; Compiled Service Records of Louisiana Troops, Microcopy M320. Poole's older brother John also was in Company H of the 9th Louisiana at Gettysburg; he would desert the regiment in June 1864.

88. Gettysburg *Star and Sentinel,* July 22, 1890, as quoted in Coco, *Wasted Valor,* 167.

89. *Adams County News,* April 2, 1910; Gettysburg *Compiler,* April 6, 1910.

90. Young, *The Battle of Gettysburg,* 272.

91. Robson, *One-Legged Rebel,* 82.

92. Edith Armstrong Talbot, *Samuel Chapman Armstrong: A Biographical Study* (New York: Doubleday, Page and Co., 1904), 25. Armstrong was the son of missionaries. He was born in Maui and educated at Oahu College, making him one of the few combatants at Gettysburg from Hawaii. He and most of his comrades in the 125th New York had been captured by Stonewall Jackson in September 1862 with the surrender of the garrison at Harper's Ferry. Armstrong would finish the war as a brigadier general. He was later instrumental in the founding and development of Hampton Institute, an early school for black students. The Confederates encountered by Armstrong were likely some of William Barksdale's Mississippians.

93. Gettysburg *Times,* July 5, 1938.

# BIBLIOGRAPHY

PRIMARY SOURCES

**Newspapers and Periodicals**
Adams County *News*
Adams County *Sentinel*
Atlanta *Constitution*
Boston *Morning Journal*
Chambersburg *Valley Spirit*
Charleston (S.C.) *Mercury*
Cleveland *Morning Leader*
Cortland (N.Y.) *Gazette & Banner*
Eaton (Ohio) *Weekly Register*
*Forney's War Press*
Franklin *Repository*
Gettysburg *Compiler*
Gettysburg *Star and Sentinel*
*Harper's Weekly*
Harrisburg *Daily Telegraph*
Harrisburg *Patriot and Union*
Mason City (Iowa) *Globe-Gazette*
New Orleans *Commercial Bulletin*
New York *Times*
New York *Tribune*
Norwalk (Ohio) *Reflector*
Philadelphia *Inquirer*
Philadelphia *Press*
Philadelphia *Weekly Times*
Richmond *Daily Dispatch*
Richmond *Daily Whig*
Richmond *Times-Dispatch*

Schenectady (N.Y.) *Republican*
Sheboygan (Wis.) *Evergreen City Times*
York (Pa.) *Gazette*
York *Republican*

**Archival Sources**

ADAMS COUNTY HISTORICAL SOCIETY, GETTYSBURG, PA.
Nellie Auginbaugh account
Sue King Black account
Samuel Bushman account
Gates Fahnestock account
Catherine Foster account
John B. Linn account

EMORY UNIVERSITY, ATLANTA, GA.
George L. P. Wren diary

GETTYSBURG COLLEGE, GETTYSBURG, PA.
Michael Jacobs papers, Musselman Library

GETTYSBURG NATIONAL MILITARY PARK, GETTYSBURG, PA.
Sarah M. Broadhead account
Fannie Buehler account
J. Warren Jackson account
Amelia Harmon Miller account
William Seymour account
J. Arthur Taylor account

LIBRARY OF CONGRESS, WASHINGTON D.C.
Jubal A. Early letters

LOUISIANA HISTORICAL ASSOCIATION COLLECTION, HOWARD-TILTON
MEMORIAL LIBRARY, TULANE UNIVERSITY, NEW ORLEANS
George Ring diary

NATIONAL ARCHIVES, WASHINGTON D.C.
Compiled Service Records of Confederate Soldiers Who Served in Organizations
from the State of Louisiana. War Record Group 109. Microcopy 320. 414 reels.

RUTHERFORD B. HAYES PRESIDENTIAL CENTER, FREMONT, OHIO
John R. Rhoades Papers

PENNSYLVANIA STATE ARCHIVES, HARRISBURG
Civil War Border Claims (Pennsylvania Adjutant General's Office, Records Referring to Civil War Border Claims: Damage Claim Applicants, RG-2, York County Damage Claims)
Peter Rothermel papers

TULANE UNIVERSITY, NEW ORLEANS, LA.
Record Rolls of 8th Louisiana Infantry, LHA Collection, Howard-Tilton Memorial Library
Father James B. Sheeran diary

UNITED STATES ARMY MILITARY HISTORY INSTITUTE, CARLISLE, PA.
Civil War Miscellaneous Collection
Eugene Blackford account
Henry Handerson account
Charles Moore Jr. account
B. Y. Yancy account

WINCHESTER–FREDERICK COUNTY HISTORICAL SOCIETY, HANDLEY REGIONAL LIBRARY, WINCHESTER, VA.
Laura Lee diary

WRIGHT STATE UNIVERSITY, DAYTON, OHIO
Oscar D. Ladley letters

YALE UNIVERSITY, NEW HAVEN, CONN.
William H. Warren journal

YORK COUNTY HERITAGE TRUST, YORK, PA.
James W. Latimer letters
Cassandra Small letters

## Maps

*Atlas of the War of the Rebellion.* Washington D.C.: United States Government Printing Office, 1880–1901.

*Shearer's Map of York County, Pennsylvania.* Philadelphia: W. O. Shearer and D. J. Lake, 1860.

**ARTICLES**

Bender, Lida Welsh. "Civil War Memories." *The Outlook,* June 24, 1925.

Bradwell, Isaac G. "The Burning of Wrightsville, Pennsylvania." *Confederate Veteran,* vol. 27, 1919.

Bush, Lt. James C. "The Fifth Regiment of Artillery." *The Army of the United States: Historical Sketches of Staff and Line with Portraits of Generals-in-Chief.* Ed. Theo. F. Rodenbaugh. New York: Maynard, Merrill, and Co., 1896.

Carrington, James McDowell. "First Day on the Left at Gettysburg." *Southern Historical Society Papers,* vol. 35, 1907.

Causby, Thomas E. "Storming the Stone Fence at Gettysburg." *Southern Historical Society Papers,* vol. 29. 1901.

Chisholm, Samuel H. "Forward the Louisiana Brigade." *Confederate Veteran,* vol. 27, November 1919.

Clements, George S. "The 25th Ohio at Gettysburg." *The National Tribune,* August 6, 1891.

Davis, Edwin A., ed. "A Louisiana Volunteer, Letters of William J. Walter, 1861–62." *Southwest Review,* 19. Dallas, Texas: Southern Methodist University Press, 1933.

Dickelman, Joseph L. "Carroll's Brigade at Gettysburg." *National Tribune.* June 10, 1909.

———. "Gen. Carroll's Gibraltar Brigade at Gettysburg." *National Tribune.* December 10, 1908.

Early, Jubal A. "The Invasion of Pennsylvania, by the Confederate States Army, in June 1863." *The Historical Magazine.,* vol. 1, third series, no. 4, April, 1873. Morrisania, N.Y.: Henry B. Dawson, 1873.

———. "A Review by General Early." *Southern Historical Society Papers,* vol. 4, July 1887, Richmond, Va.

"Hon. Thomas J. Semmes." *Southern Historical Society Papers,* vol. 22, 1894, Richmond, Va.

Jackson, J. Warren. "Diary of J. Warren Jackson." *Pennsylvania Magazine of History and Biography.* Harrisburg: Pennsylvania Historical Association, April 1963. Also cited in Terry L. Jones, "Going Back in the Union at Last: A Louisiana Tiger's Account of the Gettysburg Campaign." *Civil War Times Illustrated,* vol. 29, no. 6, January/February 1991.

Linn, John B. "A Tourist at Gettysburg." *Civil War Times Illustrated,* vol. 29, September/October 1990.

McCreary, Albertus. "Gettysburg: A Boy's Experience of the Battle." *McClure's Magazine*, vol. 33, May to October 1909.

McKay, Charles W. "Three Years or During the War, with the Crescent and Star." *National Tribune Scrap Book*. New York: National Tribune, no date.

McNamara, Lt. M. "Lieutenant Charlie Pierce's Daring Attempts to Escape from Johnson's Island." *Southern Historical Society Papers*, vol. 8, 1880.

Rivera, John J. "Two Heroines of the Shenandoah Valley." *Confederate Veteran*, 8, November 1900.

"Sick and Wounded Confederate Soldiers at Hagerstown and Williamsport." *Southern Historical Society Papers*, vol. 26, 1898.

Swallow, W. H. "The First Day at Gettysburg." *Southern Bivouac*, December 1885.

Walker, James A. "The Bloody Angle." *Southern Historical Society Papers*, vol. 19, 1891.

Whittier, Edward N. "The Left Attack (Ewell's), Gettysburg." Civil War Papers Read before the Commandery of the State of Massachusetts, Military Order of the Loyal Legion of the United States (MOLLUS). Printed by the Commandery, Boston, Mass. Vol. 1, 1900.

**Books**

Alleman, Matilda "Tillie" Pierce. *At Gettysburg, or, What a Girl Saw and Heard of the Battle. A True Narrative*. New York: W. Lake Borland, 1889.

*The Army and Navy of the United States 1776–1891*. Philadelphia: George Barrie Publisher, 1890.

Ashby, Thomas A. *The Valley Campaigns: Being the Reminiscences of a Non-Combatant While Between the Lines in the Shenandoah Valley During the War of the States*. New York: Neale Publishing Co., 1914.

Baer, Elizabeth R., ed. *Shadows on My Heart: The Civil War Diary of Lucy Rebecca Buck of Virginia*. Athens, Ga.: University of Georgia Press, 1997.

Barnhart, Lorenzo D. *The Reminiscences of Private Lorenzo D. Barnhart, 110th Ohio Volunteer Infantry, Company B*. Transcribed by Roger Barnhart, 1998.

Bartlett, Napier. *A Soldier's Story of the War*. New Orleans: Clark and Hofeline, 1884.

Bauer, Keith G. *A Soldier's Journey, The Civil War Diary of Henry C. Caldwell, Co. E, 7th Louisiana Infantry, CSA*. New Orleans: Le Comite' des Archives de la Louisiane, 2002.

Beach, William H. *The First New York (Lincoln) Cavalry: From April 19, 1861 to July 7, 1865*. New York: Lincoln Cavalry Association, 1902.

Blair, Cassandra Morris (Small). *Letters of '63*. Detroit: Stair-Jordan-Baker, 1988.

Boyd, Belle. *Belle Boyd, In Camp and Prison,* vol. 1. London: Saunders, Otley, and Co., 1865.

Boyd, David French. *Reminiscences of the War in Virginia.* Ed. T. Michael Parrish. Austin, Texas: Jenkins Publishing Co., 1989.

Buck, S. D. *With the Old Confeds. Actual Experiences of a Captain in the Line.* Baltimore: H. E. Houck and Co., 1925.

Buck, William P., ed. *Sad Earth, Sweet Heaven: The Diary of Lucy Rebecca Buck.* Birmingham, Ala.: Cornerstone, 1973.

Buell, Augustus. *The Cannoneer: Recollections of Service in the Army of the Potomac.* Washington D.C.: The National Tribune, 1890.

Caspar, Louis C. *The Medical Department of the United States Army in the Civil War.* Washington D.C.: U.S. Army, 191?; reprinted by Butternut Books, Gaithersburg, Md., 1985.

Culp, Edward C. *The 25th Ohio Vet. Vol. Infantry in the War for the Union.* Topeka, Kan.: Geo. W. Crane and Co., 1885.

Cutrer, Thomas W., and T. Michael Parrish. *Brothers in Gray: The Civil War Letters of the Pierson Family.* Baton Rouge: Louisiana State University Press, 1997.

*Documents of the U.S. Sanitary Commission, Volume II, Numbers 61 to 95.* New York: 1865.

Early, Jubal A. *Lieutenant General Jubal Anderson Early, C.S.A.: Autobiographical Sketch and Narrative of the War Between the States.* Philadelphia: J. B. Lippincott Co., 1912.

Evans, Clement A. *Confederate Military History,* vol. 10. Atlanta, Ga.: Confederate Publishing Co., 1899.

Gilmor, Harry. *Four Years in the Saddle.* New York: Harper and Brothers, 1866.

Gordon, John B. *Reminiscences of the Civil War.* New York: Charles Scribner's Sons, 1904.

Handerson, Henry E. *Yankee in Gray.* Cleveland, Ohio: The Press of Case Western Reserve University, 1962.

Hewitt, Janet B., Noah Andre Trudeau, and Bryce A. Suderow, eds. *Supplement to the Official Records of the Union and Confederate Armies,* part 2, Record of Events, vol. 24, serial 36. Wilmington, N.C.: Broadfoot Publishing, 1994.

Hoke, Jacob. *The Great Invasion of 1863; or General Lee in Pennsylvania.* Dayton, Ohio: W. J. Shuey, 1887.

Hotchkiss, Jedediah. *Make Me a Map of the Valley: The Civil War Journal of Stonewall Jackson's Topographer.* Ed. Archie McDonald. Dallas: Southern Methodist University Press, 1973.

Howard, Oliver O. *Autobiography of Oliver Otis Howard, Major General United States Army,* vol. 1. New York: Baker and Taylor, 1907.

Hunter, Alexander. *Billy Yank and Johnny Reb.* New York and Washington: The Neale Publishing Co., 1904.

Jacobs, Michael. *Notes on the Rebel Invasion of Maryland and Pennsylvania and the Battle of Gettysburg.* Philadelphia: J. B. Lippincott and Co., 1864.

Johnson, Pharris Deloach, ed. *Under the Southern Cross: Soldier Life with Gordon Bradwell and the Army of Northern Virginia.* Macon, Ga.: Mercer University Press, 1999.

Johnston, David E. *The Story of a Confederate Boy in the Civil War.* Portland, Ore.: Glass and Prudhomme Co., 1914.

Jones, J. William. *Army of Northern Virginia Memorial Volume.* Richmond, Va.: J. W. Randolph and English, 1880.

———. *Christ in the Camp: Or Religion in Lee's Army.* Richmond, Va.: B. F. Johnson and Co., 1887.

Keifer, J. Warren. *Official Reports of J. Warren Keifer, Major General of Volunteers.* Springfield, Ohio: Daily Republic Steam Job Office, 1866.

———. *Slavery and Four Years of War.* New York: G. P. Putnam's Sons, 1900.

Kiefer, William R. *History of the One Hundred and Fifty-third Regiment Pennsylvania Volunteers Which Was Recruited in Northampton County, Pa. 1862–1863.* New York: The Chemical Publishing Co., 1909.

Ladd, David and Audrey, eds. *The Bachelder Papers.* Dayton, Ohio: Morningside Press, 1994.

Lockwood, John. *Our Campaign Around Gettysburg.* Brooklyn: A. H. Rome, 1864.

Lynch, Charles H. *The Civil War Diary, 1862–1865, of Charles H. Lynch, 18th Conn. Vol's.* Hartford, Conn.: The Case, Lockwood and Brainard Co., 1915.

Mahon, Michael G., ed. *Winchester Divided: The Civil War Diaries of Julia Chase and Laura Lee.* Mechanicsburg, Pa.: Stackpole Books, 2002.

*Maine at Gettysburg: Report of Maine Commissioners.* Portland, Maine: The Lakeside Press, 1898.

Malone, Bartlett Y. *The Diary of Bartlett Y. Malone.* The James Sprunt Historical Publications, vol. 16, no. 2. Chapel Hill: The University of North Carolina Press, 1919.

Marcus, Edward, ed. *A New Canaan Private in the Civil War: The Letters of Justus M. Silliman.* New Canaan, Conn.: New Canaan Historical Society, 1984.

McDonald, Cornelia Peake. *A Woman's Civil War: A Diary with Reminiscences of the War, from March 1862.* Ed. Minrose C. Gwin. Madison: University of Wisconsin Press, 1992.

McKim, Randolph H. *A Soldier's Recollections: Leaves from the Diary of a Young Confederate.* New York: Longmans, Green, and Co., 1910.

Moore, Edward A. *The Story of a Cannoneer under Stonewall Jackson.* New York and Washington: The Neale Co., 1907.

Moore, Frank, ed. *The Rebellion Record: A Diary of American Events . . . ,* 7 vols. New York: G. P. Putnam, 1861–68.

New York Monuments Commission for the Battlefields of Gettysburg and Chattanooga. *Final Report on the Battlefield of Gettysburg (New York at Gettysburg).* Albany, N.Y.: J. B. Lyon Co., 1902.

Nichols, G. W. *A Soldier's Story of His Regiment (61st Georgia).* Jesup, Ga.: self-published, 1898.

Page, Charles D. *History of the Fourteenth Regiment, Connecticut Vol. Infantry.* Meriden, Conn.: Horton Printing Co., 1906.

*Pennsylvania at Gettysburg,* Harrisburg, Pa.: Wm. Stanley Ray, State Printer, 1914.

*Pennsylvania at Salisbury, North Carolina: Ceremonies at the Dedication of the Memorial . . .* Harrisburg, Pa.: C. E. Auginbaugh, State Printer, 1912.

Prowell, George R. *History of the Eighty-seventh Regiment, Pennsylvania Volunteers.* York, Pa.: The Press of the York Daily, 1903.

———. *History of York County, Pennsylvania.* Chicago: J. H. Beers and Co., 1907.

Reed, Thomas Benton. *A Private in Gray.* Camden, Ark.: self-published, 1902.

Robson, John S. *How a One-Legged Rebel Lives: Reminiscences of the Civil War: The Story of the Campaigns of Stonewall Jackson, as Told by a High Private in the "Foot Cavalry".* Durham, N.C.: The Educator Co., 1898.

Roper, John Herbert. *Repairing the "March of Mars": The Civil War Diaries of John Samuel Apperson.* Macon, Ga.: Mercer University Press, 2001.

Schurz, Carl. *The Reminiscences of Carl Schurz,* vol. 3. New York: The McClure Co., 1908.

Sheeran, James B. *Confederate Chaplain: A War Journal of Rev. James B. Sheeran, c.ss.r. 14th Louisiana, C.S.A.* Ed. Joseph T. Durkin. Milwaukee: Bruce Publications, 1960.

Simons, Ezra D. *A Regimental History: The One Hundred and Twenty-fifth New York State Volunteers.* New York: self-published, 1888.

Smith, Jacob D. *Camps and Campaigns of the 107th Ohio Volunteer Infantry, Based on a Wartime Diary,* 1910 edition. Navarre, Ohio: Indian River Graphics, 2000.

Souder, Mrs. Edmund A. (Emily Bliss Thacher Souder). *Leaves from the Battlefield: A Series of Letters from a Field Hospital.* Philadelphia: Caxton Press of C. Sherman, Son and Co., 1864.

Stiles, Robert. *Four Years Under Marse Robert.* New York and Washington: The Neale Publishing Co., 1904.

Underwood, Adin B. *The Three-Years' Service of the Thirty-third Mass. Infantry Regiment, 1862–1865.* Boston: A. Williams and Co., 1881.

United States Surgeon General's Office. *The Medical and Surgical History of the*

*War of the Rebellion (1861–1865),* part 3, vol. 2, *Surgical History.* Washington
D.C.: Government Printing Office, 1883.

Vautier, John D. *History of the Eighty-eighth Pennsylvania Volunteers in the War for
the Union, 1861–1865.* Philadelphia: J. B. Lippincott, 1894.

Vickers, George M. *Under Both Flags: A Panorama of the Great Civil War.* New
York: Veterans Publishing Co., 1896.

von Fritsch, Frederick O. *A Gallant Captain of the Civil War.* New York: Joseph
Tyler Butts, 1902.

Wainwright, Charles S. *A Diary of Battle: The Personal Journals of Charles S. Wainwright, 1861–1865.* Ed. Allen Nevins. New York: Da Capo Press, 1998.

*The War of the Rebellion: A Compilation of the Official Records of the Union and Con-
federate Armies,* 70 vols. in 4 series. Washington D.C.: United States Government Printing Office, 1880–1901.

Warren, William H. *History of the Seventeenth Connecticut: The Record of a Yankee
Regiment in the War for the Union* Bridgeport, Conn.: The Danbury Times, 1886.

Wildes, Thomas F. *Record of the One Hundred and Sixteenth Regiment Ohio Infantry
Volunteers in the War of the Rebellion.* Sandusky, Ohio: I. F. Mack and Bro., 1884.

Winkler, Frederick C. *The Letters of Frederick C. Winkler, 1862–1865.* Milwaukee,
Wis.: William K. Winkler, 1963.

Young, Jesse Bowman. *The Battle of Gettysburg: A Comprehensive Narrative.* New
York: Harper and Brothers, 1863.

———. *What a Boy Saw in the Army.* New York: Hunt and Eaton, 1894.

SECONDARY SOURCES

**Articles**

Bergeron, Arthur W. Jr. "Free Men of Color in Grey." *Civil War History,* vol. 32,
no. 3, September 1986.

Bloom, Robert L. "We Never Expected a Battle: The Civilians of Gettysburg,
1863." *Pennsylvania History,* vol. 55 (reprinted 1988, Adams County Historical
Society).

Campbell, Eric. "'A Field Made Glorious.' Cemetery Hill: From Battleground to
Sacred Ground." *Gettysburg Magazine,* no. 15, July 1996.

Chance, Mark. "Prelude to Invasion: Lee's Preparations and the Second Battle of
Winchester." *Gettysburg Magazine,* no. 19, July 1998.

Ent, Uzal. "Rebels in Pennsylvania." *Civil War Times Illustrated,* vol. 37, no. 4, 1998.

Gannon, James P. "The 6th Louisiana Infantry at Gettysburg." *Gettysburg Magazine,* no. 21, July 1999.

Jones, Terry L. "Going Back in the Union at Last: A Louisiana Tiger's Account of the Gettysburg Campaign." *Civil War Times Illustrated,* vol. 29, no. 6, January/February 1991.

———. "Twice Lost: The 8th Louisiana Volunteers' Battle Flag at Gettysburg." *Civil War Regiments: A Journal of the American Civil War,* vol. 6, no. 3, 1999.

Leahy, Mrs. D. W. "Colonel Davidson Bradfute Penn." *Louisiana Genealogical Register,* vol. 24, 1977.

Longacre, Edward G. "Target Winchester, Virginia." *Civil War Times Illustrated,* June 1976.

*Louisiana History,* Journal of the Louisiana Historical Association, vol. 25, Winter 1984, 393.

*Pennsylvania History,* January 1962, 188.

Prowell, George R. "The Invasion of Pennsylvania by the Confederates Under Robert E. Lee and Its Effect Upon Lancaster and York Counties." *Historical Papers and Addresses of the Lancaster County Historical Society,* vol. 29, no. 4, 1925.

Roland, Charles P. "Lee's Invasion Strategy." *North & South,* vol. 1, no. 6, 1998.

Schreckengost, Gary J., "1st Louisiana Special Battalion at the First Battle of Manassas." *America's Civil War,* May 1999.

Sword, Wiley. "Confederate Maj. John W. Daniel Describes the 2nd Battle of Winchester at the Beginning of the Gettysburg Campaign." *Gettysburg Magazine,* no. 35, July 2006.

Tomasak, Peter. "An Encounter with Battery Hell." *Gettysburg Magazine,* no. 12, January 1994.

Wells, Dean M. "Second Battle of Winchester: Ewell Takes Command." *America's Civil War,* March 1997.

## Books

Archer, John M. *"The Hour Was One of Horror": East Cemetery Hill at Gettysburg.* Gettysburg, Pa.: Thomas Publications, 1997.

Bartlett, Napier. *Military Record of Louisiana.* Baton Rouge: Louisiana State University Press, 1964.

Bates, Samuel P. *History of the Pennsylvania Volunteers, 1861–65.* Harrisburg: B. Singerly, State Printer, 1869–1871.

———. *Martial Deeds of Pennsylvania.* Philadelphia: T. H. Davis and Co., 1876.

Bauer, Keith A. *The Destiny of Men: The Road to Gettysburg.* Bloomington, Ind.: AuthorHouse, 2003.

Baumgartner, Richard A. *Buckeye Blood: Ohio at Gettysburg.* Huntington, W.Va.: Blue Acorn Press, 2003.

Beaudot, William J. K. and Lance J. Herdegen. *An Irishman in the Iron Brigade: The*

*Civil War Memoirs of James P. Sullivan*. New York: Fordham University Press, 1993.

Bergeron, Arthur W. Jr. *Guide to Louisiana Confederate Military Units 1861–1865*. Baton Rouge and London: Louisiana State University Press, 1989.

Beyer, Walter Frederick, and Oscar Frederick Keydel. *Deeds of Valor: From Records of the Archives of the United States: How American Heroes Won the Medal of Honor.*, vol. 1. Detroit, Mich.: The Perrien-Keydel Co., 1907.

*Biographical and Historical Memoirs of Northwest Louisiana*. Chicago and Nashville: The Southern Publishing Co., 1890.

Booth, Andrew B. *Records of Louisiana Confederate Soldiers and Louisiana Confederate Commands*. 3 vols. Spartanburg, S.C.: Reprint Co., 1984.

Busey, John W., and David G. Martin. *Regimental Strengths and Losses at Gettysburg*. Hightstown, N.J.: Longstreet House, 1982.

Cartland, Fernando G. *Southern Heroes, or, The Friends in War Time*. Cambridge, Mass.: The Riverside Press, 1895.

Casdorph, Paul D. *Confederate General Richard S. Ewell, Lee's Hesitant Commander.* Lexington: University Press of Kentucky, 2004.

Coco, Gregory A. *A Strange and Blighted Land: Gettysburg: The Aftermath of a Battle*. Gettysburg, Pa.: Thomas Publications, 1995.

———. *Wasted Valor: The Confederate Dead at Gettysburg*. Gettysburg: Thomas Publications, 1990.

Coddington, Edwin B. *The Gettysburg Campaign: A Study in Command*. New York: Charles Scribner's Sons, 1968.

Cole, Philip. *Civil War Artillery at Gettysburg: Organization, Equipment, Ammunition, and Tactics*. New York: Da Capo Press, 2002.

*Commemorative Biographical Record of Washington County, Pennsylvania*. Chicago: J. H. Beers and Co., 1893.

Davis, William J. *Fifteen Days Under the Confederate Flag: Waynesboro, Penna. June 27–July 7, 1863*. Self-published. 1963.

Doster, William E. *Lincoln and Episodes of the Civil War*. New York and London: G. P. Putnam's Sons, 1915.

Dufour, Charles L. *Gentle Tiger: The Gallant Life of Roberdeau Wheat*. Baton Rouge: Louisiana State University Press, 1999.

Duncan, Richard R. *Beleaguered Winchester: A Virginia Community at War 1861–1865*. Baton Rouge: Louisiana State University Press, 2007.

Dunkelman, Mark H., and Michael J. Winey. *The Hardtack Regiment, An Illustrated History of the 154th Regiment, New York Infantry Volunteers*. Rutherford, N.J.: Fairleigh Dickinson University Press, 1981.

Early, Gerald L. *I Belonged to the 116th: A Narrative of the 116th Ohio Volunteer Infantry During the Civil War*. Bowie, Md.: Heritage Books, 2004.

Field, Ron, *The Confederate Army 1861–65 (3): Louisiana & Texas.* London: Osprey Press, 2006.

Gambone, Al. *Enigmatic Valor: Major General Darius N. Couch.* Baltimore: Butternut and Blue, 2000.

Gannon, James. *Irish Rebels, Confederate Tigers: A History of the 6th Louisiana Volunteers, 1861–1865.* Campbell, Calif.: Savas Publishing Co., 1998.

Gibson, John. *History of York County, Pennsylvania: A Biographical History.* Chicago: F. A. Battey Publishing Co., 1886.

Goldsborough, W. W. *The Maryland Line in the Confederate Army, 1861–1865.* Baltimore: Butternut and Blue, 1983.

Gottfried, Bradley M. *Brigades of Gettysburg: The Union and Confederate Brigades at the Battle of Gettysburg.* New York: Da Capo Press, 2002.

Grunder, Charles S., and Brandon H. Beck. *The Second Battle of Winchester, June 12–15, 1863.* Lynchburg, Va.: H. E. Howard, 1989.

Hamblen, Charles P. *Connecticut Yankees at Gettysburg.* Kent, Ohio: Kent State University Press, 1993.

Hess, Earl J. *Field Armies and Fortifications in the Civil War: The Eastern Campaigns.* Chapel Hill: The University of North Carolina Press, 2005.

*History of Franklin County, Pennsylvania.* Chicago: Warner, Beers and Co., 1887.

Johnson, Rossiter. *A Short History of the War of Succession, 1861–1865.* Boston and New York: Houghton, Mifflin and Co., 1889.

Jones, Terry L. *Cemetery Hill: The Struggle for the High Ground, July 1–3, 1863.* New York: Da Capo Press, 2003.

———. *The Civil War Memoirs of Captain William J. Seymour: Reminiscences of a Louisiana Tiger.* Baton Rouge: Louisiana State University Press, 1997.

———. *Lee's Tigers: The Louisiana Infantry in the Army of Northern Virginia.* Baton Rouge: Louisiana State University Press, 1987.

Lash, Gary. *The Gibraltar Brigade on East Cemetery Hill: Twenty-five Minutes of Fighting—Fifty Years of Controversy.* Baltimore: Butternut and Blue, 1996.

Lonn, Ella. *Foreigners in the Confederacy.* Chapel Hill: University of North Carolina Press, 2002.

Lowe, David. *Study of Civil War Sites in the Shenandoah Valley of Virginia.* Washington D.C.: U.S. Department of the Interior, National Park Service, 1992.

Maier, Larry B. *Gateway to Gettysburg: The Second Battle of Winchester.* Shippensburg, Pa.: Burd Street Press, 2002.

McClure, James E. *East of Gettysburg: A Gray Shadow Crosses York County, Pa.* York, Pa.: York County Heritage Trust, York Daily Record, 2003.

Mingus, Scott L. Sr. *Flames Beyond Gettysburg: The Gordon Expedition, June 1863.* Columbus, Ohio: Ironclad Publishing, 2008.

Minnigh, Luther W. *Gettysburg: "What They Did Here."* Gettysburg, Pa.: self-published, 1920.

Moore, Alison. *The Louisiana Tigers: or, The Two Louisiana Brigades of the Army of Northern Virginia, 1861–1865.* Baton Rouge: Ortlieb Press, 1961.

Nofi, Albert A. *The Gettysburg Campaign, June and July 1863.* New York: Gallery, 1986.

Nye, Wilbur S. *Here Come the Rebels!* Baton Rouge: Louisiana State University Press, 1965.

Osborne, Charles C. *The Life and Times of General Jubal A. Early, CSA: Defender of the Lost Cause.* Chapel Hill, N.C.: Algonquin, 1992.

Perrin, James. "The Thomas M. Terry Family, Tangipahoa Parish, Louisiana," Self-published, 2000.

Pfanz, Harry W. *Gettysburg: Culp's Hill and Cemetery Hill.* Chapel Hill: University of North Carolina Press, 1993.

———. *Gettysburg: The First Day.* Chapel Hill: University of North Carolina Press, 2001.

———. *Gettysburg: The Second Day.* Chapel Hill: University of North Carolina Press, 1987.

Pope, Thomas E. *The Weary Boys: Colonel J. Warren Keifer and the 110th Ohio Volunteer Infantry.* Kent, Ohio: Kent State University Press, 2002.

Rigdon, John C. *Historical Sketch & Roster of the Louisiana Fifth Infantry Regiment.* Clearwater, S.C.: Eastern Digital Resources, 1999.

Roberts, Deering J. ed., *The Southern Practitioner,* vol. 28. Nashville, Tenn.: Southern Publishing Association, 1906.

Rosen, Robert N. *The Jewish Confederates.* Chapel Hill: University of North Carolina Press, 2002.

Sauers, Richard, and Peter Tomasak. *Ricketts' Battery: A History of Battery F, 1st Pennsylvania Light Artillery.* Luzerne, Pa.: Luzerne National Bank, 2001.

Schreckengost, Gary. *Wheat's Tigers: The 1st Louisiana Special Battalion in the Civil War.* Shippensburg, Pa.: Burd Street Press, 2006.

Sears, Stephen W. *Gettysburg.* Boston and New York: Houghton Mifflin, 2003.

Sifakis, Stewart. *Compendium of the Confederate Armies: Louisiana.* New York: Facts on File, 1992.

Stafford, Dr. G. M. G. *General Leroy Augustus Stafford: A Genealogy.* Baton Rouge: Claitor's Publishing, 1969.

Stephens, Robert Grier Jr., ed. *Intrepid Warrior: Clement Anselm Evans.* Dayton, Ohio: Morningside Press, 1992.

Stoner, Jacob H. *Historical Papers: Franklin County and the Cumberland Valley, Pennsylvania.* Chambersburg, Pa.: The Craft Press, 1947.

Talbot, Edith Armstrong. *Samuel Chapman Armstrong: A Biographical Study*. New York.: Doubleday, Page and Co., 1904.

Trudeau, Noah Andre. *Gettysburg: A Testing of Courage*. New York: Harper Collins, 2002.

Tucker, Glenn. *High Tide at Gettysburg, The Campaign in Pennsylvania*. New York: Bobbs-Merrill Co., 1958.

Warner, Ezra J. *Generals in Gray: Lives of the Confederate Commanders*. Baton Rouge: Louisiana State University Press, 1959.

Welsh, Jack B. *Medical Histories of Confederate Generals*. Kent, Ohio: Kent State University Press, 1995.

Winters, John D. *The Civil War in Louisiana*. Baton Rouge: Louisiana State University Press, 1991.

Wise, Jennings Cropper. *The Long Arm of Lee, of the History of the Artillery of the Army of Northern Virginia*. 2 vols. Lynchburg, Va.: J. P. Bell Co., 1915.

Wolf, Simon. *The American Jew as Patriot, Soldier and Citizen*. Philadelphia: The Levytype Co., 1895.

# INDEX

Corley, James L., 88
Cormier, Louis A., 163, 182, 194, 240, 282n16
Cortland, N.Y., 201
Coster's Brigade, 112–14, 116, 121, 137, 173, 280n149
Couch, Darius N., 18, 58, 64, 71, 245, 254n11, 263n129
Crawford, John, 109, 116, 126, 128, 133, 206
Crawford, Richard T., 182, 204–5, 242
Crist, John, 206, 284n42
Culp, Edward, 162
Culp, Henry, 131, 147, 153
Culpeper, Va., 16–18, 245, 250
Culp's Hill, 121–22, 124, 136, 140, 145–46, 151, 153, 172, 180, 196, 201–2, 207, 255–56n26, 283n28
Cumberland Valley, 62, 69, 71, 77, 205, 210, 212
Curtin, Andrew G., 18, 58, 246
Curtis, William, 155

Dance, Willis J. (Dance's Battery), 33, 37, 40, 47, 50
Daniel, John W., 184, 230, 233, 272n60
Daniels, Milton H., 155, 166–67, 197–98, 221
Darkesville, W.Va., 216–18, 249
Davids' Island, N.Y., 182, 207–8, 240, 279n119
Davidsburg, Pa., 83, 100
Davis, Aaron, Jr., 25, 256n27
Dawkins, Jackson, 30–31, 51, 77, 217
De Blanc, Alcibiades, 10, 170, 227
De Camp General Hospital, 207
Dearie, George, 99
Dejean, Albert, Jr., 32, 52, 241
Department of the Susquehanna, 18, 58, 64, 245, 254n11, 263n129
Devin, Thomas C., 105, 118
Dickelman, Joseph L., 175, 178, 186
Diembach, Andrew, 181, 185, 280n149
Dilger's Battery, 111, 117
Dobke, Aldolphus, 111–12, 117, 271n36
Doles, George P., 105

Doles' Brigade, 105, 107, 109, 111, 114, 116
Donaldsonville, La., 8
Doster, William E., 205
Doubleday, Abner, 132
Douglas, William, 206
Doussan, Honoré, 9
Duchamp, Arthur E., 165, 278n100
Duncan, Johnson K., 12, 93
Dwire, George, 208

Early, Jubal A.: description, 5–6, 13; troops of, 16, 227–28; in Shenandoah Valley, 17–18, 20, 24; at Second Winchester, 25–30, 32–34, 36–42, 47–53; march to the Potomac, 55–57; enters Pennsylvania, 60–62, 64–69, 71; at Gettysburg on June 26, 72–78; at York, 77–80, 82–97, 98–99; march to Gettysburg, 97, 100–101, 103–5; July 1 at Gettysburg, 105–9, 113, 115, 119, 122–26, 128–32; July 2 at Gettysburg, 133–34, 141–42, 147–48, 150–53, 161, 182–85; July 3 and 4 at Gettysburg, 188, 205–6, 209; retreat to Virginia, 210–11, 213–21; postbattle, 223
Early, Robert D., 125
Early's Division, organization, 227–28; in Shenandoah Valley, 13, 15, 17–20, 24–5; at Second Winchester 27; march into Pennsylvania, 60–62, 70, 73, 76, 79, 82; to Gettysburg, 97, 100–101, at Cemetery Hill, 147–70; retreat to Virginia, 205, 208–10, 213, 218–19, 249
East Baton Rouge Parish, La., 207
East Berlin, Pa., 79–80, 97, 99–101
Ehrlich, Franz, 130
Elliott's Brigade, 26–27, 29, 48
Ely's Brigade, 29
Evans, Clement A., 72, 184, 251n4
Evergreen Cemetery, 120, 144, 166, 172, 175, 188, 195, 202–3
Ewell, Richard S.: rejoins army, 5–6, 13–16; at Second Winchester, 19–20, 22, 24, 29–30,

CPSIA information can be obtained
at www.ICGtesting.com
Printed in the USA
LVHW090932120821
694993LV00013B/105